Latin American Modernization Problems

Latin American Modernization Problems

CASE STUDIES IN THE CRISES OF CHANGE

Edited by Robert E. Scott

UNIVERSITY OF ILLINOIS PRESS
Urbana   Chicago   London

© 1973 by The Board of Trustees of the University of Illinois. Manufactured in the United States of America. Library of Congress Catalog Card No. 72-81263.

ISBN 0-252-00293-8

Foreword

The studies in this volume are individual field investigations carried out over the past several years by staff members of the Center for Latin American Studies at the University of Illinois as part of a collaborative program of research on "Modernization-Urbanization Problems in Latin America." Longer, monograph presentations will appear in due time, but it seems useful to gather some of their findings here because they did grow out of a collective enterprise. A short review of the modernization program should demonstrate just how much collaboration was involved.

During a period of several months beginning in February, 1969, thirteen of the Latin American Center's staff members representing eight disciplines,[1] together with four outside Latin Americanists[2] and five graduate students from various fields,[3] offered a ten-session campus series on Latin American modernization problems, alternating between substantive matters and theoretical concerns. Research designs for eleven distinct field projects were discussed and modified to encourage common approaches and shared under-

[1] Douglas Butterworth, Joseph Casagrande, Tom Zuidema (Anthropology); René Vandendries (Economics); John Thompson (Geography); Joseph Love (History); Roger Findley (Law); Robert Byars, Robert E. Scott (Political Science); Frederick Fliegel, J. C. van Es (Rural Sociology); Sidney Kronus, Mauricio Solaún (Sociology).

[2] Warner Baer (Vanderbilt); Paul Doughty (Indiana); Joseph Kahl (Washington of St. Louis, now at Cornell); Domingo Rivarola (Paraguayan Center for Social Research).

[3] Greg Driver (Comparative Education); Jerome Gagerman (Sociology); Michael Quinn (Political Science); Arthur Piper (Anthropology); Guido Soenens (Economics).

standings about the general research goals of the modernization program. An average of twenty-five other staff members and graduate students interested in Latin America participated in each of the ten sessions, one of which was conducted entirely in Spanish.

Over the summer of 1969 and into the following academic year, nine research projects were carried out in various countries of Latin America, especially those where center staff concentrate their greatest field interest—Mexico, Brazil, and the Andean states of Ecuador, Peru, and Colombia. In March, 1971, following a period for analysis of findings and write-up, the Center for Latin American Studies organized a four-session colloquium on "Latin American Modernization Problems," during which nine field research reports were presented for discussion, again with active audience participation by staff members and graduate students. The present volume contains revised versions of most of those papers, together with an introductory section to place them in context.

In short, although each of the essays included in this collection represents a distinct field-research project within the theoretical framework of a particular discipline, they all involve a great deal of collaboration and cooperation among their authors. Significantly, although the findings presented here are not perfectly integrated they are at least mutually reinforcing. In the present rather anarchical relationship among the social sciences the fact that a number of disciplinary specialists working together closely on a single general topic in a relatively similar culture region can reach reasonably complementary conclusions offers some hope for a unified social science in the future.

Before closing, let me acknowledge the financial and intellectual support for the center's modernization program provided by the University of Illinois' Center for International Comparative Studies and Office of International Programs and Studies. Without their generous cooperation the program could not have succeeded.

CARL W. DEAL, Associate Director
Center for Latin American Studies
University of Illinois

Contents

INTRODUCTION

ROBERT E. SCOTT, "Latin America and Modernization"   1

PART I   THE HUMAN ELEMENT   23

ROBERT BYARS, "Culture, Politics, and the Urban Factory Worker in Brazil: The Case of Zé Maria"   26

SIDNEY KRONUS and MAURICIO SOLAÚN, "Racial Adaptation in the Modernization of Cartagena, Colombia"   87

PART II   THE PHYSICAL SETTING   119

ROGER W. FINDLEY, "Problems Faced by Colombia's Agrarian Reform Institute in Acquiring and Distributing Land"   122

RENÉ VANDENDRIES, "Internal Migration and Economic Development in Peru"   193

DOUGLAS BUTTERWORTH, "Squatters or Suburbanites? The Growth of Shantytowns in Oaxaca, Mexico"   209

PART III HANDLING TRANSITIONAL PROBLEMS 233

Joseph Love, "External Financing and Domestic Politics: The Case of São Paulo, Brazil, 1889–1937" 236

René Vandendries, "An Appraisal of the Reformist Development Strategy of Peru" 260

Robert E. Scott, "National Integration Problems and Military Regimes in Latin America" 285

Contributors 357

Index 361

INTRODUCTION

LATIN AMERICA AND MODERNIZATION

Robert E. Scott

The eight field studies included in this volume are products of a two-year collaborative research program in which University of Illinois Latin Americanists explored modernization problems in the region, focusing primarily on Mexico, Brazil, and several Andean countries. Although as case studies the investigations are separate and independent of each other, their findings are complementary and reinforce the concept of an integrated development process, at least for a single culture area like Latin America. No attempt is made here, however, to move beyond empirical description to elaborate a general theory of the development process, for several reasons. The principal purpose of the modernization program was to illuminate conditions in Latin American states intensively involved in transition from a traditional era toward modernity, and to point up institutional impediments to constructive change and evolutionary development by using depth probes which show the complexity of the problems involved. Moving past this rather pragmatic goal to general theory building would shift attention from the realities of the transitional situation to the abstractions of an idealized conceptualization called "modernity."

Clearly, the attempt to develop a universally applicable model of the growth process is a valid task for social science but, considering the state of our theoretical sophistication, such a goal seems a trifle premature. For all their scientific trappings, the more generalizing discussions of development have not produced any all-purpose definition of modernization that can be applied with any degree of analytical rigor. Their working hypothesis seems to be that man has the capacity to resolve his problems, to end social disorganization, and to achieve economic justice, usually within a democratic framework, but they offer few directions on how to test this optimistic viewpoint. On a more applied level, the general theorists neatly list the analytical concepts associated with modernity—universality of norms, rationalization and secularization, bureaucratization, structural differentiation, industrialization, urbanization, democracy (or at least greater popular participation) —but the various formulations show little agreement on which of these factors, or what combination of them, constitute the defining characteristics of development.

Because our primary interest lies in the problems of the transition period through which most Latin American countries are passing, this tendency of general theorists to define not the process of change but the idealized end product—modernity—makes their work less useful to us. For them a given country is "modernizing" or has become "modern" to the extent that it achieves universal norms, is structurally differentiated, urbanized, or industrialized. But this kind of theory offers little advice on how to achieve a comprehensive, balanced development program or to avoid such traps as stressing economic growth without encouraging complementary evolution of social and political institutions to structure constructively the resulting change. To date, social scientists have not been able to offer either domestic policymakers or international aid officials any operational model of the development process that takes into account the entire range of human and technical problems confronting a given country experiencing basic change.

How could they? Disciplinary interests and a need for parsimony of effort lead most observers to emphasize those peculiar aspects of modernization which relate more directly to their own specialty, as though certain social, economic, or political factors were self-contained and independent variables rather than integral parts of a complex whole operating simultaneously to affect the life of every citizen and to upset the ongoing socioeconomic structures of which he is a part.

Again, in seeking to build general theory that explains the development process much of the literature of social science speaks in such fully inclusive and self-consciously "objective" terms that the unwary reader carries away little sense of the confusion, uproar, and personal insecurity which accompany the transition toward modern life. At this high level of abstraction, the raw materials of survival in a speedily shifting environment take on a kind of sterility; the attempt to set up all-embracing terminology and culture-free approaches so pasteurizes and so homogenizes day-to-day existence that it more nearly resembles artificial life synthesized in a test tube than it does reality. One loses the feeling of dealing with real people, facing real problems in an all too real world.

For the inhabitant of a transitional community, caught up in the daily problems of speedy change, abstract and isolated analytical concepts offer little useful explanation of what is happening to him. Case studies, though limited of scope and focusing on a single problem, compensate in the depth and detail of their explanations and the sense of reality they impart. They can at least make the individual aware of just how technology and its unintended side effects overburden the social, economic, and political structures. This kind of knowledge does not of itself resolve problems, but it can assist the affected citizen and his leaders, who cannot hope to find solutions until they recognize the nature of the difficulties they face. Equally important, as several of the research reports included in this collection illustrate, case studies may demonstrate that certain kinds of problems can be solved. Or that the conventional way of viewing a difficulty may be the principal barrier to its solution. The experience of other persons in another country may suggest an answer that lay hidden but available all the time.

This is not to suggest that these eight reports encompass the complexity and magnitude of the transition problems confronting four or more Latin American countries at very different levels of development. Quite the contrary. Taken collectively, however, they do show how interrelated both the benefits and the problems of modernization can be.

Technology results in easier communications and transport, engendering greater awareness of the nation as a single unit, but also setting off mass migration within the country. Improved social and health services produce population pressures which together with industrialization lead to urbanization. New conditions spark personal adjustment problems within individuals and among groups of people. All these changes underline previously unfelt socio-economic needs—for expanded educational services, more hospitals, increased job opportunities, to suggest just a few. The physical problems of housing and feeding densely congregated groups of people multiply, not simply because more persons move to the city but because those who settle in urban areas acquire new expectations much more quickly than they learn new skills to produce the goods to satisfy their wants.

Paradoxically, land reform adopted to ease rural pressures may result in falling food production, just as the demand for supplies to feed the city grows. Social and economic planners may be so engrossed in grand strategy, considering questions of basic "structural" reform, that they fail to recognize a need for organizing effective large-scale marketing mechanisms to transform harvest and livestock into food and to transport it to the urban consumer. Finally, it is instructive to consider development from another perspective, not from the viewpoint of the individual citizen but from that of the governmental agencies which seek to rationalize the multiple, diffuse, and uncoordinated activities of a people and society involved in mercurial change. We can learn much from the history of a struggle to integrate a semiautonomous region into the national economic and political system, or from the achievements and failures of a less than successful national planning mechanism.

The case studies included in this volume discuss some of these questions and suggest the relevancy of others. They also bring to mind the convergence hypothesis, which posits that modern industrial technology is so pervasive that peoples and countries experiencing development become more alike than their earlier psychological, social, and material differences might indicate. Certainly the degree to which a series of distinct disciplinary approaches investigating diverse subjects relating to modernization do produce findings which complement each other encourages the view that for a relatively similar culture area like Latin America at least development may come in time to be defined as an integral process. For the present, however, such observations are at too high a level of generality to provide theoretical proof, particularly when so many of the countries from which the data are gathered have moved so short a distance down the road to modernity. Indeed, several of the present case studies suggest that varying human and physical factors still tend to differentiate one social group or region from another, even in those states which are most developed. Only after enough additional careful case studies accumulate in the literature, including additional countries which are more industrialized, can we determine whether national differences "wipe out" as world technology expands its influence.

The Modernization Process

Whether the process occurring throughout the emerging world is termed progress, development, westernization, or modernization, it involves basic change, the kinds of disquieting shifts which are particularly hard on the persons experiencing them because so much is happening so quickly to so many people. Not only are traditional life styles and psyches of numerous individuals upset but also the flexibility of national and local institutions—which might combine constructive new patterns of social, economic, or political action with a degree of integrated continuity—is seriously impaired.

Change as such is not all bad, by any means. Witness the eager acceptance of the material goods provided by mass production and the improvements in social conditions, political involvement, and general well-being identified with the technological era. But the costs too are great, for in a transitional situation the individual struggles constantly to evolve some new set of constructive relations with his fellows and to build the complex and interdependent structures required to feed, house, educate, and service a rapidly multiplying mass of citizens whose expectations increase apace. Often the price is paid in blood as well as in money, in human dignity, and in political freedom, as well as in overloaded social and economic mechanisms.

It is difficult to communicate the high costs of overfast modernization to the citizen of the developed world, for he lives in an environment that has harnessed change over centuries, evolving operating structures which maximize the payoffs of industrialization and technology and soften the most harmful effects of major dislocations with a cushion of material resources. This does not mean that in the western world the earlier stages of development caused no disruptions, but that mitigating circumstances reduced their impact by spreading out the consequences in ways which are not available to most inhabitants of today's emerging countries. In Europe and later in North America individuals were ruined and entire ways of life dispoiled in the name of progress, but relatively smaller portions of the populace were affected at any one time, often over centuries rather than years or decades. Physical isolation in rural districts and mental isolation of the uneducated city masses further dispersed popular reaction to change, limiting the communication among the vast majority of citizens that might have produced a united and effective reaction to the distress they suffered. Nor were they exposed to demonstration effect in the form of examples supplied by wealthier and more advanced states whose citizens were known to fare far better.

The western development process did, nonetheless, occasion riots, near civil wars, migrations of starving farm workers to the cities where hungry hoards could be exploited by incipient industrialists in order to accumulate capital. Inevitably, this was followed by appearance of lower-class social and economic defense movements which turned to the political realm. Consider Britain as an example. Starting with the land enclosures of the mid-eighteenth century, followed some seventy years later by the Luddite agricultural revolt against the threshing machine and the Chartist social protests in the industrial areas, Englishmen suffering the consequences of the Industrial Revolution slowly developed social consciousness and gradually joined together in reformist intellectual movements which allied themselves with incipient labor organizations. In 1906 this alliance converted itself into the British Labor party, which in turn helped usher in the welfare state of the post-technological era. Today, the terrible and bloody events of that long process are discreetly blurred by the mists of time, remembered mainly as fictional settings for some of Charles Dickens's grimmer novels or translated into carping complaints by the angry young men who wrote in the 1950s and 1960s.

Only during the past few years have appreciable numbers of persons in the advanced nations begun to consider the full price of uncontrolled development in their own countries—burgeoning populations, spreading pollution, imminent destruction of remaining natural resources, social confrontation, and all the rest—and to question whether all change really equates with progress. Significantly, most members of this aware group in the developed nations do not seem to realize that the inhabitants of the emerging states face all these same problems and many more besides.

Precisely because the developing countries are involved in fundamental and fast-moving change the concerted stresses of modernization crises press in on them. The system of traditional values, with essentially parochial perspectives, often was based upon export-oriented agriculture and extractive raw material production. Currently, the emerging peoples are moving toward a pattern of more nearly general norms reflecting an urbanized environment and industrial technology in a national society, with a central government trying frantically to establish efficient specialized agencies to cope with an ever more complex environment. The resulting development crises—of foreign relations, legitimacy, national integration, popular social and political participation, and distribution of material benefits—seem to generate similar problems in every country as it experiences the process of modernization.

Those states which developed earlier were less affected by the crises of change, perhaps because for most of them the major adjustments were made singly and over longer periods of time, so that in any one period they dealt with a manageable number of issues. Problems of foreign relations took place between countries at more or less equal levels of technical competence, so smaller or weaker states had a reasonable possibility of protecting themselves militarily. National integration could take place at a slower pace, with less danger of disruptive outside pressures. Indeed, war with neighboring countries often acted as a unifying element. Even in states where racial and cultural differences existed, interaction among distinct peoples frequently was so slight that diverse factions could identify with a single central concept, like the nation, until time cemented them together with a sense of national identity. Similarly, crises of governmental legitimacy were minimized where traditionally accepted authority gradually adapted its norms to the needs of a modern nation. Further, the distribution crisis under which society is pressed to allocate a larger portion of material goods to the masses occurred in the earlier modernizing countries only after the interdependent spread of technology and increased productivity of the general work force made possible a higher standard of living for the entire population without ruining the established elites. Finally, the same common experiences which produced national integration and a sense of governmental legitimacy supplied a core of shared understandings about political values around which the debates arising from claims of the emerging popular sectors for a participatory voice in the decisionmaking process could be conducted safely.

Few of these conditions obtain in contemporary emerging countries. If today the specter of foreign military conquest is less frightening for some weaker states it is because the super powers have shifted their expansionist tactics to economic colonialism, though the cases of Hungary, Czechoslovakia, Tibet, Guyana, or the Dominican Republic suggest that pressure through use of military force still exists. The remaining development crises all are exacerbated by unintended by-products of technology; the transportation and communications revolutions have so speeded up the rate and intensity of contact among peoples that time, the one precious commodity that permitted evolutionary solutions to the crises of change, has all but disappeared. Where ethnic groups or regional interests come into social and economic conflict long before any sense of national identity has developed, where traditional ruling elites cannot bring themselves to attune their attitudes to the emerging expectations of a more aware general populace, where political structures and formal governmental agencies cannot adjust their operations to include larger portions of the citizenry, where the productive capacity of the economy lags far behind the needs (much less the desires) of a multiplying population, where both the lower and the middle sectors feel more and more alienated from society and government, where all these crises occur at once, a country is swamped by the crises of modernization.

The fact is that the developing states must survive in a world where every already advanced nation offers a model of national integration, high material standards, and effective social, economic, and political structures. The emerging peoples are exposed constantly to these models—by films, television, radio, and the printed page. This produces a sense of frustration that grows with the knowledge that their country faces superior competition by nations which not only are more efficient industrially but also control the world's markets and, equally important, its marketing systems. Every day a larger number of citizens experience difficulties which prove that their country lives in a dependency relationship with the established powers.

Worse still, their leaders know that this dependency relationship cannot be ended simply by duplicating the development process as it took place in the west. For one thing, the advanced countries already exist and hold the advantage. For another, within their own society the innocent isolation of the past no longer exists so it is not possible to sweat labor in order to amass capital for an independent industrial takeoff. In the west the political participation crisis took place only after a self-sustaining nucleus of productive capacity existed and the workers themselves had acquired the sophistication and factory discipline needed to operate a technical economy. In the emerging states, demonstration effect has brought on the political participation crisis prior to or simultaneously with the material distribution crisis, usually long before economic growth is adequate to satisfy mass demands. Using its political power the general populace forces government to provide desired goods, services, and acceptable social benefits, vetoing the possibility of investing any large portion of either private or public sector resources in expansion of primary industry. The failure of the original concept of the Alliance for Progress—matching foreign, public-sector development capital with domestic investment to expand basic productive capacity—is a case in point. Irresistible popular insistence upon immediate gratification of material and social claims resulted in the Latin American governments substituting short-range nonperpetuating distribution programs for the projected pattern of developing self-renewing, primary production mechanisms.

In sum, both the rank-and-file citizens and the leadership in most developing countries know only too well that the exportation of techniques and knowledge from their advanced neighbors is a mixed blessing. All the crises of change seem to descend upon them simultaneously, so that every expansion of material production is absorbed by a combined population explosion and revolution of rising expectations, and every potential social improvement is hampered by contending human interests in competition with each other. But the emerging peoples have no choice other than to try to modernize, both because they do want the material benefits and because change intrudes itself with or without formal invitation. Unfortunately, in facing all these problems most persons in the emerging areas view the development process in a rather simplistic manner, based on a misunderstanding of the western models.

The problem arises because they take the relatively integrated operation of advanced countries' social and economic systems for granted. Under this interpretation solving the problem of growth and modernization is little more than a matter of accepting and adapting the more efficient economic activities of those states which already have made the transition. They see no need to build a constructive interrelationship between all of the social and economic factors which go to make up an integrated environment, or they underrate the complexity of these relationships. One might add that until very recently, most international technical assistance advisers (many of whom are economists) held the same opinion, or at least acted as though they did.

Here again, the root of the difficulty lies in the time factor, exacerbated by the stress on economic growth without development of ancillary social and political institutions to channel economically induced change into constructive patterns. In the resulting breakdown of social and political controls many persons caught in the disintegrating environment look instinctively for some sort of imposed ordered relationship. Hence the strong attraction in rapidly changing situations to central planning, to some commonly shared, "official" ideology, to a vaguely defined state socialism. This tendency goes far beyond the need for a mechanism to rationalize use of scarce economic and human resources to a kind of dictated "instant integration."

For some members of the political ruling group—paternally inclined *políticos*, technocratic specialists, even many intellectual elitists—who view government as a control device over the general citizenry, this sort of centralized economic solution to integration problems is logical. It permits a dominant minority to impose delayed gratification of popular desires so that scarce resources can be directed to industrial development, much in the style of the Soviet Union. But an economically oriented, socialistic approach may ignore the existence of the very psychological norms and habit patterns, the very ongoing social and economic structures, which produced the centrifugal forces leading to a need for stronger central controls in the first place. It may also fail to take into account constitutional practices which permit opposing members of the elite and the increasingly aware popular masses to apply political pressure against such policies. As long as the economy is unable to accommodate the minimum needs of its citizens and the national community has not evolved a common set of social norms to complement some one economic approach, no set of informal sanctions will operate to encourage conformity and disruptive activities will be "pragmatic" and supportive of the interests of the individuals and groups involved, if not of a general welfare.

If enough time could elapse to permit gradual growth of social norms to order the relationships of newly aware citizens with each other, while economic justice for all was assured, informal political control devices might evolve. And the various social, political, and economic norms might complement each other. Unfortunately, no time buffer exists in most emerging states, so the tendency is to look to government to enforce common social and political patterns through political sanctions. Almost inevitably, in attempting to impose such limits, the political leaders and technocratic planners go too far, so that government becomes rigid and unresponsive to the desires of its citizens.

On the other hand, the experience of the modernizing countries suggests that the disruptions identified with rapid change do call for some sort of coordination to assure comprehensive and balanced development, logically through government action. But to be effective, such coordinating activity must be balanced by large-scale inputs of popular participation or the entire process will become so formalized and technical that the real needs of the rank-and-file citizen are ignored and his potential contribution in resolving popular difficulties is lost forever. Under the forced draft, speedup conditions most developing countries experience, this kind of trial-and-error, evolutionary expansion of complementary relationships among individuals and between socioeconomic structures cannot occur, and the means of involving individuals and groups of citizens in the decisionmaking process are strictly limited.

Examples of many such development problems are illustrated by the Latin American case studies offered in this volume. Before turning to the specific studies, however, let us place them in their broader setting by offering a few observations on modernization problems in the region.

Latin America's Transition Problems

Fifty years ago (and in some cases scarcely ten years ago) life for the great majority of Latin Americans, who lived outside the larger cities and towns, was closer to that of the colonial period than to our present era. Their activities were largely agricultural, with little or no machinery, modern technology, or commercial marketing arrangements, and they clustered in villages or around the big house of an *hacendado*. The farm worker owned or controlled little of his own lands, and counted on collective cooperation for harvesting or other major tasks. Where the common lands still prevailed, each family shared in the overall yield. Elsewhere, the large landholder exercised many of the prerogatives of the pre-independence *grandee.* If for many people life was not plentiful it was adequate, and all sectors of the rural population remained close to each other, with the exception of a few local notables—smaller landowners, priests, perhaps a storekeeper or lawyer, sometimes a schoolteacher, and where he existed, an absentee landlord. The great mass of people were not rich, but neither were they poor.

All that has changed in many areas. New conditions exist, conditions whose consequences are irrevocable. Population growth is so fast that neither mechanization and commercialization of agriculture nor expansion of urban industry has been able to absorb the new multitudes of citizens, or even to sustain them properly. Half of the urban growth is by natural increment of the city's population. Other urban inhabitants come from the countryside because the land no longer can support expanding families, much less satisfy their aspirations, so large-scale migration has occurred, overwhelming the capacity of the cities to provide essential services. With improved communications the growing urban masses are more aware and more demanding, so that their claims on government for physical amenities and social services are harder and harder to satisfy. The gap between rich and poor, between urban and rural, between elites and masses is greater, or at least more acutely felt, and the disadvantaged know it. Their expectations are increasing while their patience is disappearing. The traditional social and political structures no longer can accommodate the demands upon them.

Until quite recently some Latin Americanists maintained that because true revolution had occurred only in Mexico, Bolivia, and Cuba, basic change in the remaining republics was minimal. This view would be hard to sustain today, because the first stirrings of modernization, which began in some countries around the turn of the century and in others only a few years ago, have been drastically speeded up by the technological revolution, encouraged during the 1960s by the United Nations Decade of Development, which was strongly reinforced by the Alliance for Progress. Social and economic indicators such as literacy rates, urbanization, and per-capita income point to a relatively high level of modernization in ten states, with some 80 percent of the region's total population (see

Table 1). Most of the other countries also show a respectable if slower growth rate, though some skeptics suggest that in certain cases official data may be overoptimistic. They claim, for instance, that Brazil, Chile, and perhaps several other countries, have lower literacy rates than a few decades ago.

The real problem in many Latin American countries is not lack of change but too much piecemeal and uneven change without revolution, if we may use that term in its symbolic sense. Because no single major upheaval has occurred in these countries which are experiencing the crises of change en masse, the traditional social, economic, and political structures continue in operation. These traditional structures are not well suited to handling change and, as several of the case studies in this collection demonstrate, they provide institutional impediments to constructive and evolutionary development which compound the difficulties of modernization.

This is not to suggest that the mere occurrence of a revolution assures an integrated and democratic society. Three Latin American countries have experienced this sort of fundamental change. Of these, Bolivia has been unable to achieve continuity or stability in reform government; Cuba has a strong and probably institutionalized revolutionary regime but at high cost in freedom and socioeconomic spontaneity. Only Mexico, which began its revolutionary experiment sixty years ago, long before the technologically induced speedup of change, has managed to evolve a reasonably open, responsible, and legitimate society and political system. Here again we find evidence that the most effective means of transforming a traditional environment into a workable modern system is to evade the institutional barriers to constructive change with the slow but sure flowing waters of time.

Unfortunately, most Latin American republics do not have the luxury of time to evolve smoothly operating control structures, and the very successes of the development process have resulted in disruptive change that swamps existing institutions. The gains of increasing production are canceled out by exploding population and ever more aware citizens whose expectations far surpass the physical possibilities of an expanding economy. This leads to popular frustration and a search for scapegoats. Even many Latins, who

TABLE 1. LATIN AMERICAN POPULATION DATA, CIRCA 1970

Country	Population Rank	Population (000)	% Annual Population Growth	Growth Rank	Urban Rank	Number of Urban Population	% Urban, with Date	Percentage Literate	Literacy Rank	Years of Life Expectancy	Life Rank
Argentina	3	24,352	1.6	17	2	10,211,500	78.9 (70)	91.5	2	66.3	4
Bolivia	12	4,931	2.6	15	19	1,443,783	29.3 (67)	39.8	18	53.0	14
Brazil	1	92,238	2.8	12	10	48,887,200	47.6 (70)	71.0	11	65.4	5
Chile	8	8,836	1.3	18	4	6,556,312	74.2 (69)	89.6	4	62.0	8
Colombia	4	21,116	3.2	8	7	12,183,992	57.7 (70)	72.9	10	60.9	9
Costa Rica	19	1,766	3.5	4	9	865,340	49 (69)	84.4	5	66.8	3
Cuba	7	9,000			6	5,400,000	57.7 (65)	96.1	1		
Dominican Rep.	10	4,012	2.8	13	13	1,604,800	40 (70)	53.1	14	52.0	15
Ecuador	9	6,093	3.4	5	12	2,784,501	45.7 (70)	69.7	12	55.0	13
El Salvador	14	3,515	3.7	1	15	1,613,820	38.8 (68)	49.0	16	56.3	11
Guatemala	11	5,170	3.1	10	18	1,592,360	30.8 (70)	37.9	19	48.8	19
Haiti	13	4,867	2.0	16	20	841,991	17.3 (70)	22.0	20	50.0	17
Honduras	16	2,582	3.4	6	17	831,404	32.2 (69)	47.3	17	48.9	18
Mexico	2	48,313	3.3	7	5	28,359,731	58.7 (69)	83.7	6	63.0	7
Nicaragua	18	1,982	3.5	3	14	786,854	39.7 (69)	49.8	15	50.2	16
Panama	20	1,415	2.8	14	11	666,065	47.1 (69)	76.7	7	67.3	2
Paraguay	17	2,374	3.1	11	16	854,640	36 (70)	74.4	8	59.5	10
Peru	5	13,586	3.1	9	8	7,041,134	51.9 (69)	61.1	13	55.0	12
Uruguay	15	2,886	1.3	19	1	2,305,914	79.9 (70)	90.5	3	68.4	1
Venezuela	6	10,399	3.5	2	3	7,788,851	74.9 (69)	73.9	9	65.3	6
Totals or Averages		269,433	2.9			146,619,132	53.58				

SOURCES: Inter-American Development Bank data, and *The Statesman's Yearbook, 1970–1971*.

should know better, subscribe to the myth of the beggar on a golden stool, which characterizes most countries in the region as possessing vast untapped wealth that could be exploited if only the domestic oligarchs and the foreign imperialists would permit it. The sad fact is that in most cases this is not so, for many of the republics have little premium agricultural land in accessible areas of hospitable climate and their mineral or other natural resources are few or unbalanced, with overconcentration in copper, tin, or petroleum. Moreover, the physical barriers to easy transportation have perpetuated a regionalism within many countries which discourages development of a national internal economy. Finally, despite the beginnings of industrialization and of mechanized agriculture, limited supplies of technically oriented and educated manpower continue to slow down economic growth.

Consider some of the problems associated with modernization in the region. For many Latin American countries an annual growth in gross domestic product of 5 percent is accompanied by population increase of 3 or more percent, a net plus of only 2 percent to satisfy rapidly mounting popular material demands. This leaves little or nothing for capital development investment. Latin America's excessive population growth wipes out potential relative improvement in its domestic standard of living and in its international competitive position. During 1966 to 1969, for example, the region's average per-capita product growth was 2.7 percent a year, slightly higher than the 1.9 percent of the previous five years. But compared with other world regions Latin America's development was less favorable because of its high population increase. According to the Inter-American Development Bank, in the industrialized countries the total of inhabitants grew only about 1 percent; in Southern Europe, 1.4 percent; in Africa, 2.4 percent; in Southern Asia, 2.5 percent; in the Middle East and in Eastern Asia, 2.7 percent. In Latin America as a whole, annual population growth was 2.9 percent.

The negative consequences of excessive population on Latin America's economy can be seen in Table 2, which compares percentages of total growth rates with per capita growth rates in various regions. Moreover, as development occurs elsewhere in the world and as technology develops new products in the laboratory, or as new regional marketing associations appear (the European Common Market, for example), Latin America's established trade relations are disrupted. Synthetic fabrics have weakened the world market for wool and cotton, and new producers in Africa and Asia are making serious inroads into sales of sugar and coffee, contributing to a troublesome surplus of Latin American agricultural labor. The high sulphur content of some Latin American petroleum also produces growing competition from other sources in pollution-conscious markets.

TABLE 2. 1969 GROWTH RATES OF GROSS DOMESTIC AND PER CAPITA PRODUCT

Region	Total	Per Capita
Developing Countries	6.7	4.1
Eastern Asia	10.0	7.1
Middle East	8.7	5.9
Southern Europe	7.3	5.7
Latin America	6.5	2.4
South Asia	6.3	2.7
Africa	4.1	1.7
Industrialized Countries	4.9	4.0

SOURCE: Adapted from a table in *Socio-Economic Progress in Latin America* (Washington, D.C.: Inter-American Development Bank, 1971), p. 2.

Domestically, neither land reform nor the highly touted Green Revolution has done much to improve conditions in the countryside or to slow the exodus of rural people to the city. Despite emotional promises made by seventeen countries at the Punta del Este conference of 1961, during the past decade there has been very little progress in meaningful land reform which would benefit the half of the region's population that still lives in rural areas. Only Mexico, which began a half-century ago, and Bolivia, which began in 1953, have registered any appreciable gains, and they still are far from developing adequately such auxiliary functions as rural credit or extension services. Much more recently, Peru's military regime in 1968 and Chile's Christian Democratic and, since late 1970, Marxist governments have emphasized land reform, and in both cases agricultural production has fallen. Only Mexico, Venezuela, and Colombia have made even mildly effective efforts to combine land distribution with increased agricultural production. The remainder of the Latin American states have enacted reform legislation, issued "emergency decrees," and published hundreds of pages of agricultural planning documents, but the implementation of land distribution and related service facilities have bogged down in red tape and budgetary limitations, or simply have not taken place. In several countries the land reform program clearly is symbolic, consisting of a few much publicized actions followed by long periods of silence and inactivity.

For various reasons the Green Revolution has not had much impact on Latin America. Where it has occurred, the consequences have not been very beneficial to an increasingly restive rural population. The main advantages have gone to large landowners who could apply new techniques to sizable plots and who had financial resources for new seeds and mechanization. Under such circumstances, the share of rural income becomes more rather than less disproportionate, and with technification unemployment among rural workers increases. By the end of the 1960s, for ten important Latin American countries rural income continued to show marked disparities. Subsistence workers representing 65 percent of an 18.6 million person work group earned an average of US $287 a year. An intermediate work group (9.5 million persons) averaged US $1,050, and 517,000 larger proprietors (1.8 percent of the group) averaged US $7,195, or about twenty-five times as much as the bottom group.

Put in other terms, modernization in the form of mechanization and technification, coupled with runaway population growth, means that in rural areas millions of underemployed workers, many of them volatile youth, hold down wage levels, so the per-capita income of some 70 million persons (two-thirds of the region's 1970 agricultural population) averages less than US $90 a year. Many such persons are driven off the farm into the city.

Given lack of capital and weak potential markets, urban industry has not developed quickly enough to absorb these new migrants to the city. Even if it could, their rural backgrounds provide few of the skills necessary for factory work or other urban employment for which they compete with a rapidly expanding second generation of established urban dwellers. Therefore an increasing proportion of the city's residents, many of them young and impatient, are marginal to its economic life. Though data on unemployment are extremely hard to verify, reports indicate that in many republics the rate is over 25 percent and in few less than 10 percent. Speaking broadly, at the beginning of the 1970s with Latin America's population at nearly 275 million and with a labor force between fifteen and sixty-five years of about 83 million, unemployment had risen from 18 million in 1960 to 23 million, or some 27.7 percent of the working age population.

As Table 3 suggests, those who did hold full-time jobs were not necessarily comfortable. Recall that in Latin America food is relatively inexpensive but many other items which in industrialized nations are considered essential cost the same or more than in the United States or Europe for comparable quality. This includes shoes, clothing, and to a lesser degree housing; appliances and automobiles are much more expensive.

TABLE 3. 1968 HOURLY WAGE RATE IN MANUFACTURING
(U.S. Dollars)

Argentina	$ .57	Peru	$ .52
Brazil	.31 (1965)	Venezuela	.79
Chile	.40	Uruguay	.63 (1965)
Colombia	.34	Puerto Rico	1.55
Mexico	.62	U.S.A.	3.01
Paraguay	.32		

SOURCE: *New York Times*, January 25, 1971.

These pressures are felt not only by the working class urbanite, but by the middle sectors as well. Most such persons work as public or private sector bureaucrats on fixed salaries, or struggle to support a small professional office. This requires that they maintain a certain amount of dignity, which means purchasing proper clothing, meeting certain social obligations, and the like. Most of this group are not entrepreneurial small businessmen who can raise the cost of their goods or services to meet rising living costs, so they are hard hit by inflation. If at one time their parents might have identified with upper-class mores and ways of life, today they find more in common with upper-lower-class organized workers who challenge the establishment. Uncontrolled inflation has eroded their stake in the status quo, which helps explain why certain Latin American political systems have begun to come under strong attack recently. In fact, one might almost argue that the inflation index also is an index of political instability. Note the following figures for inflation in several more advanced countries and think of their recent political history.

TABLE 4. INFLATION IN LATIN AMERICA, 1963 TO 1970

Uruguay	Well over 2000 percent
Brazil	Over 1000 percent
Chile	Over 600 percent
Argentina	About 400 percent
Mexico	Less than 100 percent
Venezuela	Less than 100 percent

SOURCE: *New York Times,* January 25, 1971.

A quick review of the situation in one country shows that such problems can have consequences. During 1970, just before President Allende's Marxist government was voted in, Chile's per capita income was about US $600. The wealthiest 5 percent of the population enjoyed 27 percent of the national income, while the poorest 20 percent received only 4 percent. The average real pay of the poorest group was only half the legal minimum wage. The lower half of the populace received only 17 percent of the national income. Inflation during 1970 alone totaled about 35 percent, and 21 percent of the work force in Santiago, the national capital, was unemployed. A glance at Table 1 will demonstrate that according to social indicators Chile is one of the more modern of the region's countries. Is it surprising that a sense of disillusionment with the progress of development under the traditional structures should have led a large portion of the electorate to opt for a new approach?

Without going further into change-induced problems of personal adjustment, social confrontation, or political disintegration, examples of which are included in the following case studies, let me suggest that successful modernization requires cultural and social as well as economic adaptation among the peoples affected, adaptions on an institutional as well as an individual basis. This series of research reports offers some insights into some but by no means all the modernization problems Latin America faces. In one or another study we can see how a given country handled a particular problem or, conversely, how and why it failed to do so. Although every country has its own problems, based on its peculiar set of historical and environmental conditions, we can learn from the experience of others. Again, though there is no unilinear line of development or identical set of "stages" of development, in a relatively unified culture area like Latin America our case studies suggest that enough similarity of conditions exists to produce complementary observations on a variety of modernization problems. It is now time to let the specific studies speak for themselves.

PART I

THE HUMAN ELEMENT

The two research reports in this section deal with human attributes and relationships affected by Latin America's modernization process. They do not purport to range over the entire spectrum of personal and social problems resulting from rapid change in the region. Instead, each report describes in depth a specific and very real case, one in Brazil and the other in Colombia.

Robert Byars's study of Zé Maria, a Brazilian urban factory worker, offers us penetrating insights into one man's perception of his political role in a fluctuating environment, as conditioned by daily experiences with the people who share his world. Using tape-recording techniques similar to those employed by Oscar Lewis in Mexico and Cuba, Byars tests research approaches and findings of Robert Lane and Alex Inkeles, who in earlier projects considered the effects of factory work experience on the political values and "modernity" of laborers in the United States and in selected developing countries.

One might argue with justification that the study of a single individual cannot represent the attitudes of Latin Americans or Brazilians in general, of Brazilian laborers, or even of most factory workers in Belo Horizonte. In an immense country split into disparate regions further broken up into rural and urban areas, a country with a system of widely divergent classes, some of whose members are shifting values dramatically because of industrialization, no one model—real or synthesized—possibly could represent the whole gamut of conflicting types. On the other hand, this comprehensive and well-rounded portrait of Zé Maria spreads before us the mosaic of dreams, desires, insecurities, and internal contradictions experienced by a real person caught up in the currents of change, with emphasis on his political views and his adjustments to the political structures which influence his life and livelihood. Sensitive and probing studies of the thought patterns and travails of Latin Americans undergoing change are extremely rare; even those produced by Lewis included proportionately less on political outlooks and reactions.

Zé Maria does not personify some nonexistent "average Latin American," but he may well portend the prototype citizen of the more industrialized future toward which the region seems to be moving. Born in a city, relatively better educated than many of his counterparts, working in a larger industrial plant, more secular in outlook, more aware and active politically, Zé Maria seems to be a generation ahead of his compatriots. Always recognizing that continuing shifts in the environment and in the mix of problems faced could alter the effect of personal experiences on other persons, we at least can see in Zé Maria shadowy glimpses of the kind of citizen the modernization process may produce over time in Latin America.

The Kronus-Solaún report on race relations in Cartegena offers a potentially significant hypothesis about collective human relationships in a situation of speedy change. Widespread violence has been endemic throughout Colombia for several decades, but the study suggests that in this fast-growing, middle-sized city at least class conflict may be more disruptive than racial differences. Here miscegenation is general, with some degree of penetration into all classes by individuals of mixed blood, so that only the phenotypical European, Indian, or Negro types are identified on racial rather than social or economic bases. Under such conditions, the authors hypothesize, the sort of racially exclusionary patterns found in northwest Europe or North America are less likely to occur, and established social structures exist to absorb all but the most obviously "colored" into higher social strata as their economic, political, or cultural influence grows.

Some social scientists might argue that the authors' evaluational techniques or their use of reputational interpretations of race tend to produce a self-fulfilling prophecy of minimal racial disharmony. Others might claim that Cartegena's situation is rather special. Because of its location on Colombia's Caribbean black littoral, the racial mixture of Europeans, *mestizos*, and Indians is complicated by an unusually large infusion of blacks, but in this particular case blacks who only recently have moved to an urban environment. When this group begins to make stronger demands on the established middle and elite sectors, the nature of their relationship to each other may alter. Only time can prove or disprove the validity of the Kronus-Solaún hypothesis; meanwhile, it affords interesting possibilities for encouraging constructive race relations which ought to be tested in other communities in and outside of Latin America.

Culture, Politics, and the Urban Factory Worker in Brazil: The Case of Zé Maria

Robert S. Byars

> In short, politics may frequently appear to have served labor poorly, but this is because commitment to politics for the mass of workers has been half-hearted, poorly directed, and limited to alternatives not of their own making. The city emancipates and modernizes slowly and selectively.... The city opens the way for the worker to certain limited forms and degrees of economic, political, and intellectual liberation; at the same time the city accommodates, sustains, and feeds on a subculture of poverty that is not far removed from the rural or small-town models. That subculture of poverty is not a mere encumbrance that will be readily dislodged, ejected, or remolded, but an integral part of the social landscape of the city as now constituted.
> —Frank Bonilla, "The Urban Worker," *Continuity and Change*

> I feel sort of happy because I never expected to have the opportunity of giving an interview.... I never expected—in my wildest imagination that my—that my life could serve as a—could serve my

I am grateful to Mike Quinn for his work in this research project. Mr. Quinn, a graduate student in political science at the University of Illinois, was my North American assistant in the field. I would like also to express my special gratitude to Zé Maria for his cooperation and patience during extensive sessions. Without his help, of course, there would be no essay. I have used a pseudonym to protect his anonymity. Where the data might reveal his identity, I have altered or modified it slightly.

country or the world, perhaps. Perhaps it could serve as a lesson for the world! I am very happy about this—and I am only sorry I don't know more details—to respond better to the questions you ask me—sorry for not having sufficient or adequate education for responding in the best possible way.

—Seu Mundo [pseudonym], a marginally employed urban worker in Brazil

Introduction

Not long ago, Professor Robert Lane probed the minds and political worlds of fifteen "common men" in the United States.[1] The respondents were lower-middle and upper-working-class men. Among a myriad of findings is one especially important for the present study. It involves the relationship between a man's occupation and his political outlook and behavior. As Lane writes, "What men learn as they work for a living reaches far beyond their occupational interests; they learn a style of life, a manner of dealing with others, a habit of subordination or assertion."[2] This learning process has obvious consequences for the role of the individual in the polity.

In his study, Lane found a relatively happy marriage between industrial work and citizen support for democratic political processes:

> Work life in industrial society permits and even encourages social relations of a reciprocal team-oriented kind, although this is least noticeable among the machine tenders. The work situation . . . offers men the ground for joint extracurricular action, such as the organization of bowling teams and credit unions. It brings men together to talk and they often talk about the events in the news, thereby rehearsing attitudes and exposing them to comment, including them in the process whereby men merge their experiences and bring them to bear on distant, complex, and unfamiliar situations.[3]

[1] Robert E. Lane, *Political Ideology* (N.Y., 1962).
[2] *Ibid.*, pp. 228–229.
[3] *Ibid.*, pp. 247–248.

And, in a recent study of six developing countries, Professor Alex Inkeles highlights the important possibilities that the factory offers as a "school for politics."[4] Controlling for such factors as education, urbanism, and so forth, Inkeles finds that the "factory experience has a substantial residual effect," and he goes on to state that "there can be no doubt that in itself the factory is, in significant degree, a school in citizenship, inculcating values of interest and active participation in the political process."[5] Inkeles suggests that although "an investment in keeping people in school longer will apparently bring greater returns than an investment in keeping them employed in factories . . . the factory is evidently a school for citizenship. It may work less efficiently, or more slowly, than does education, but it is effective in transforming attitudes, values, and behavior so as to make them more participant citizens."[6] Inkeles considers this finding to be the most "distinctive contribution" of his six-nation study.[7]

One purpose of the present essay, its theoretical goal, is to explore in depth the political world of Zé Maria, an urban factory worker in Brazil, in order to refine and reformulate the findings of Lane and Inkeles. Zé Maria is forty-seven years old, married, and has three children. His wife is a Protestant and Zé Maria himself has entertained thoughts of converting from Catholicism. Zé Maria is a city man, born and raised in Belo Horizonte. His father, a sergeant in the army, died when Zé Maria was just a small boy. Having only four years of formal schooling, Zé Maria has worked at various kinds of jobs during his life. He has made wooden crates, worked in a milk-processing plant, and presently he is a metal worker in a large foreign-owned factory. He has worked in the factory some ten years. Zé Maria's present income is about US $175.00 per month.

Zé Maria lives in a rather attractive stucco house, freshly painted in pastel hues. The most "luxurious" house in the immediate vicinity, it presents to the passerby an enclosed veranda proudly planted

---

[4] Alex Inkeles, "Participant Citizenship in Six Developing Countries," *American Political Science Review*, 63:4 (December, 1969), pp. 1120–41.
[5] *Ibid.*, p. 1136.
[6] *Ibid.*, p. 1137.
[7] *Ibid.*, p. 1139.

with a small tree and a few flowers, surrounded by a protective wall and topped off with a wrought-iron railing. A colorfully tiled floor lies beneath Zé Maria's favorite "easy chair" in which he relaxes on Sundays, listening to the soccer match on his transistor radio—always held about one inch from his ear. He has worked hard to acquire a house he can call his own, plus a few worldly possessions. His present style of life is jealously envied, not so much by those a notch or two below him who appear genuinely to respect his well-deserved accomplishments, as by those scarcely a step above him who seem to fear that Zé Maria will pass them up shortly in the ongoing struggle for the "good life."

Zé Maria's appearance is foreboding. Few would dare tangle with a man whose physical strength, forged from many years of arduous labor at a blast furnace, is clearly visible. The distorted wrought-iron trim on his front door stands as a lasting testament to his potential brute strength. He bent open the frame with his bare hands one night during one of his frequent dream-walking episodes. He described the event to me like this:

> Even today I still dream a lot. Bad dreams. I—I—whenever I work to excess, I might even rip apart the metal framework on the door. There is a broken window in the house where I burst through the front door. I was walking in my sleep I guess. And I crawled through—through the hole in the glass in the door and cut up my shoulders—and bent open the metal framework. I don't remember what I was dreaming about—and—well, it is from working too hard.

A handsome man, Zé Maria has high cheek bones, bronze-colored skin, dark and alert eyes, well-groomed black hair, moustache, and a ready smile which disappears as quickly as it forms—changing into a look of worried melancholy. Zé Maria is punctual, undoubtedly a result of a number of years of punching a time clock in the factory. He arrived for the interview sessions precisely at the appointed hour, which was always in the evening at the completion of his working day. After washing up and eating, he strolled down the dirt road to my place, arriving neatly but casually dressed in a brightly patterned short-sleeve sport shirt open at the neck. His dark sport slacks were neatly pressed. Zé Maria always wore his gold-colored wrist watch face down on his left arm. His comfortable-looking leather sandals provided a means for releasing the tremendous amount of nervous energy that builds up and seeks an acceptable outlet in the constant and repeated shuffling of his feet as he first kicks the sandals off, then quickly slips them on again. Zé Maria had trouble containing himself. He found it difficult to sit still—continually shifting positions, sometimes leaning forward to make a point, other times fidgeting with a rolled up newsletter from the factory which he always carried with him to the discussions. With eyes wide and flashing, fleeting half-smiles, and rapid-fire speech, Zé Maria talked with me about his life experiences and political outlook in order to help me understand where he and workers like him fit into the Brazilian mosaic.

Like all countries, especially those experiencing rapid change, Brazil faces the problem of meshing political culture and political structure. In order to win popular support, the political mechanisms and governmental structures must somehow reflect the underlying political beliefs, values, and attitudes of the citizenry. The problem is magnified several times over in states undergoing social, economic, and political changes where the bonds of traditional legitimacy seem everywhere to be breaking down. Brazil represents such a system and is currently experimenting with different kinds of political structures designed to manage and control the changes. The problem orientation of the study, therefore, relates to the task of harmoniously relating political culture and structure in Brazil. It should be emphasized here, however, that mere congruence of structure and culture is not sufficient to enable a regime to enjoy maximum legitimacy and support. What government policy does for and to the citizenry must reflect and respond to the emotional and material needs of the people as well.

In the pages that follow we examine the political outlook and behavior of a Brazilian urban factory worker in order to see if his views and actions support or conflict with contemporary political structures. We also consider whether or not, from the standpoint of Zé Maria, the regime is meeting the needs of the urban worker. In this connection, Zé Maria presents a case that warrants close inspection. If the factory is the "school for politics" or the "school for modernization" that Inkeles claims it is, then a factory worker's views offer us an opportunity for examining the kind of political structures that the "most schooled" worker in Brazil is likely to support.

In sum, this study seeks a greater understanding of the psychological and cultural dimensions that influence the political behavior of urban labor in Brazil. It attempts to evaluate the impact of one societal mechanism (the factory) on the basic value orientations of the individual, especially as they relate to politics; it considers the implications of political outlooks of individuals for macrolevel political structures and processes. *The thrust of the essay is to demonstrate the rather specialized impact that "modern" institutions, such as the factory, can have on the political outlooks of Brazilian workers, given the environmental and cultural context within which political learning is taking place.* Presently, political learning in Brazil is taking place in a situation involving diverse, but equally legitimate, routes of political access[8] and where basic values emanating from an authoritarian Iberian cultural heritage abound, nourished by economic scarcity and widespread impoverishment. The overwhelming and orchestrated forces act in concert to restrain whatever divergent influences the factory may offer.[9] Before moving to the analysis of the political world of Zé Maria, a brief description of the research setting and the methods used in gathering the data that provide the basis for our examination is necessary in order to orient the reader.

Research Setting and Research Methods

Research Setting

Professor Lane writes in *Political Ideology* that "a man's economic life modifies his ideology, and of the ingredients of that life the opportunity to earn what he considers to be a decent living is

[8] Charles W. Anderson, "The Latin American Political System," *Politics and Economic Change in Latin America* (Princeton, N.J., 1967), pp. 87–114.
[9] Of course, we cannot establish in this study that the political world of Zé Maria has been influenced one way or another, if at all, as a consequence of his job in the

probably the most important. Beyond that, the opportunity to increase his earnings (and status) from time to time counts substantially in framing a social outlook."[10] My extended interview with Zé Maria, along with five other urban workers,[11] took place one summer in the late 1960s in Belo Horizonte, the capital of the state of Minas Gerais in the Eastern Highland region of Brazil. Belo Horizonte is an appropriate city for a study such as ours because it possesses few of the more exotic influences one might encounter in a cosmopolitan and international city like Rio de Janeiro. It is a more manageable city to get a feel for, lacking the extraordinary complexity of a great metropolis like Sao Paulo. And as Professor Wagley writes, "the Eastern Highlands . . . is the region par excellence in which to seek the traditional ideal patterns of Brazilian national character."[12]

What are the opportunities "for earning a decent living" in Belo Horizonte? What are the possibilities for social and economic improvement of the "average" urban worker? Belo Horizonte is the third largest city in Brazil, with a population approximating 1.3 million people, as of 1970. It is not easy, nor often wise, to generalize about a city of even *this* size and complexity, especially in view of the generally unreliable statistics existing (and often not existing) where demographic data is concerned. But some attempt to do this is necessary in order to acquaint the reader with the "existential

---

factory. A longitudinal study would be most appropriate for establishing this kind of causality. Nevertheless, in a case study of a single worker and all his individual complexities we can explore and offer suggestive evidence that might be pursued on a broader scale through the use of survey techniques.

[10] Lane, *Political Ideology*, pp. 215–216.

[11] A book-length study that analyzes the lives and political worlds of all six of the urban workers interviewed is currently under preparation. Each of the six workers selected for intensive interviews represents a theoretically interesting type. Zé Maria represents the "elite" industrial worker. The other five include a janitor who lives in a *favela* and works in a "middle-class" social club, a rural migrant who is marginally employed, a white-collar bank clerk who has descended the status hierarchy to the middle levels, a white-collar stock clerk who has ascended the status hierarchy to the middle levels, and a bookkeeper of the "middle sector" who has migrated to Belo Horizonte from a smaller city in the interior of Minas Gerais. Each worker was selected because he represented a case with potential theoretical interest. The larger work is tentatively entitled: *Six Political Worlds in Brazil: The Political Outlooks and Behavior of Urban Workers*.

[12] Charles Wagley, *An Introduction to Brazil* (N.Y. and London, 1963), p. 58.

base"[13] of the city, an essential if one is to assess the relative impact of a worker's experience upon his social and political outlook.

Turning first to class structure, Pereira estimates that for all of Brazil about 70 percent of the population may be found in the "lower class," 18 percent in the "lower-middle," 6 percent in the "middle-middle," 2 percent in the "upper-middle," and 1 percent in the "upper class" (3 percent are not accounted for).[14] But we are most directly concerned with the city of Belo Horizonte. Data for the city is somewhat scarce, but since Belo Horizonte is one of the three major industrial-commercial urban centers in Brazil, we can expect the "middle sector" to be somewhat larger and the lower class to be smaller than they are for Brazil as a whole. Assis José Leão estimates that 50 percent of the population of Belo Horizonte received less than the minimum salary in 1962.[15] So, we know that *at least* half the population is in the lowest class. If we add to this group those who receive only the minimum salary (which is not sufficient in and of itself to place one in the middle class), the percentage of lower-class members might run as high as 65 percent, as of 1962. Assuming an expansion of the middle sectors since that date, we can *estimate* the present lower-class population of Belo Horizonte as about 60 percent of the total population. Continuing these estimates, perhaps 23 percent of the city's population is in the lower-middle class, 10 percent in the middle-middle, 5 percent in the upper-middle, and some 2 percent in the upper class.

While the opportunity structure is slightly better for the lower-class member who lives in Belo Horizonte than it is for the lower-class Brazilian in general, the odds for upward mobility are heavily weighted against him. It should be pointed out that the possibility

[13] The term "existential base" is from Lane's paradigm for the study of ideological change. It signifies "not only Marx's modes of production but also the technological foundations of a society, the property arrangements, the industrialization, urbanism, gross national product, the shape and content of social stratification, the pattern of community life, the educational arrangements, the geographic and demographic conditions of society—in short, the social and physical patterns of life." In the present essay we touch only on a few of these factors. Lane, *Political Ideology*, p. 416.

[14] L. C. Breeser Pereira, "The Rise of the Middle Class and Middle-Management in Brazil," *Journal of Inter-American Studies*, 4:3 (July, 1962).

[15] Assis José Leão, "Comportamento do Eleitorado de Belo Horizonte Nas Eleições de 1962," *Revista Brasileira de Estudos Políticos*, 16 (January, 1964).

of sliding down the status ladder is always present—both in Belo Horizonte and Brazil in general. An upper-working-class member in Belo Horizonte, like Zé Maria, must fight a constant battle against the prospect of falling to the lower reaches of the lower class. After all, plenty of spaces are "reserved" at the bottom.

There is little abundance for most people in Belo Horizonte; a lot for a few; none for most workers. Life in Center City and the more exclusive *bairros* (Cidade Jardim, Serra, Barroca, and others) is quite different from life in the more impoverished *bairros* (Santa Cruz, Morro de Pedras, Vera Cruz, São Cristóvão, and others).[16] Within the same neighborhood one often encounters a juxtaposition of the affluent and the poverty stricken. Such is the case in *bairros* like Carlos Prates, Santa Efigênia, Nova Suíça, Barro Prêto, and Paraizo. Mike Quinn, my North American research assistant, made a study of various *bairros* in Belo Horizonte, providing me with "thumbnail sketches" of five different neighborhoods. His description of the *bairro* that most closely approximately the one in which Zé Maria resides says that:

> Residents are middle-middle class on down. The average resident is probably either lower-middle or "respectable" working class. This *bairro* has a fixed population of *favelados* or slumdwellers. There are no hospitals here and only one *colégio*. The level of services available here depends on how much money one has—the better homes have electricity, phones, and water; the *favelados* have little or none and live amidst assorted odors of garbage, urine, feces, and worse. Streets off the main thoroughfares are either cobbled or simply made of dirt.

One might compare a *bairro* such as this with a more exclusive one like Cidade Jardim, where one encounters truly magnificent homes that compare favorably with the finest in the United States. Of course, only the very wealthy can afford to live in Cidade Jardim, other than as household servants of one kind or another. Its princi-

---

[16] For a listing of the "better" and "poorer" *bairros* in Belo Horizonte, see Hélio Ponte, *et al.*, "O Pleito de 66 em Belo Horizonte," *Revista Brasileira de Estudos Políticos*, 23/24 (July, 1967–January, 1968), pp. 311–312.

pal residents have late model automobiles—chauffeur driven—and the most modern of appliances. Not uncommonly, a *favela* is located a stone's throw from the most exclusive residential areas. And it is not rare to see the residents of the wealthiest *bairros* accommodating *favelados* by allowing them to come for buckets of water from the hoses that service the lawns and gardens. To be sure, there are no Zé Marias living in neighborhoods such as Cidade Jardim.

Most of the "better" residential *bairros* are in the city's southeast quadrant, but the poorest people are not concentrated in any single section. Some can be found in the *favelas* on the outskirts of Belo Horizonte, some within reasonably "nice" *bairros*, and some live face-to-face with the city's most affluent citizens.

The minimum salary at the time the field research was conducted was a scant US $37.00 per month. But, as noted above, José Leão estimates that in 1962 about one-half of the population of Belo Horizonte received less than the minimum! A monthly income of the equivalent of US $37.00 does not go very far in a city where unfurnished apartments of reasonable, but by no means luxurious, quality rent for from US $75.00 to $150.00 per month; where a *small*, standard model refrigerator sells for about US $250.00; where a family of four would have to spend between US $80.00 and $90.00 a month for food in order to have three meals a day with meat at most servings; and so on. And this does not consider medical expenses, clothing, transportation, and the other of life's necessities. Obviously, it is a life of frightening scarcity for most, if not all, urban workers. Most simply must do without even the most basic of necessities.

Frank Bonilla's observations on the urban worker in Latin America in general certainly apply to the urban laborer in Belo Horizonte: "The typical urban worker is but a step above his rural counterpart—poorly schooled, ill-housed, granted a survival wage by government fiat, cozened by politicians, weakly organized when not regimented."[17] Bonilla categorizes the Latin American work force in this way:

[17] Frank Bonilla, "The Urban Worker," in John J. Johnson, ed., *Continuity and Change in Latin America* (Stanford, Calif., 1964), p. 187.

Only a small fraction of the work force is in industry, and of those in industry only a small proportion have industrial skills or work in plants that can be regarded as "modern" in size, technology, or management. The small proprietary enterprise, family firm, and partnership remain dominant, not only in numbers, but in the proportion of the work force they absorb and the total value of their production. The average wage earner is unskilled, and only marginally or insecurely employed in menial services or unspecialized tasks in construction and manufacturing.[18]

Although most urban workers have migrated from even worse conditions of life, the average city worker has not improved his lot substantially by coming to the city. For the great majority of urban laborers the struggle for survival is a "ferocious and often degrading competition."[19] For most of the urban poor "legally fixed low wage scales, the abundant labor supply, and inflation that is chronic when not acute create a treadmill on which the worker must constantly struggle for no more than a subsistence wage."[20]

So, with surplus labor continually pouring in from outlying regions, with prices constantly outdistancing salaries as a result of government attempts to contain inflation through a heavy emphasis on a wage freeze, with workers' wages at or under a subsistence level to begin with, and with very low opportunity for upward mobility, the average worker in Belo Horizonte has little to look forward to in terms of advancing his standard of living—at least for the immediate future. It is against such an existential base that we examine the life and political world of Zé Maria. While most urban workers have migrated to the city from smaller towns and villages in the interior of the state of Minas Gerais, Zé Maria has lived in Belo Horizonte all his life. Perhaps for this reason, unlike the great mass of urban poor in Brazil, Zé Maria's situation presents a somewhat brighter picture. We have selected him for close inspection precisely because of his "atypicality."

Zé Maria works for a large industrial plant in a semiskilled capacity. As one of a relatively select group of wage earners in Brazil

[18] *Ibid.*, p. 196.
[19] *Ibid.*
[20] *Ibid.*

—in 1960 only 9.1 percent of the total labor force was employed in manufacturing in Brazil[21]—Zé Maria can serve as a guide and provide a glimpse into the future.

Research Methods

During the three months I was in the field I lived with and among different kinds of urban workers in Belo Horizonte. With one foot in a *favela* and the other in a working- to lower-middle-class neighborhood, I came to know the workers well. My children played with theirs, our wives exchanged visits, and I spent countless hours chatting informally with the working men of the neighborhood. We talked informally over patio walls; we shared a hot *cafezinho*, a glass of beer, or a *Guaraná*—sometimes in their home, sometimes in mine.

With six of the workers there were also formally structured interviews, recorded on tape. Zé Maria is one of the men interviewed at length. Our discussions ranged over a wide variety of topics.[22] We talked, for example, about such very practical matters as the acute shortage of water in Belo Horizonte and the problems associated with choked traffic in a city that has already "outgrown its first pair of shoes."[23] We discussed the difficulties involved in trying to provide an education for the children under circumstances where the value of a son's contribution to the family income may be crucial to the economic survival of the family unit.[24] We considered more philosophical or idealistic matters as well, addressing ourselves to a variety of questions. Why are we here? What is our purpose on earth? What would life be like in a perfect society?

[21] Glaucio Ary Dillon Soares, "The New Industrialization and the Brazilian Political System," in James Petras and Maurice Zeitlin, eds., *Latin America: Reform or Revolution?* (N.Y., 1968), p. 191.

[22] Professor Robert E. Lane graciously sent me the complete interview guide which he used in *Political Ideology*. His interview schedule, modified and adapted to the Brazilian political context, was used to gather the data for the present study. Thanks are due to Sérgio for his assistance in translating the interview questions into Portuguese.

[23] Belo Horizonte was a "planned city." Although fewer than half a million lived in the city in the early 1960s, the population swelled to well over a million by the late 1960s. The city was founded in 1896.

[24] For a discussion of the education problems facing Brazil, see Charles Wagley, *Introduction to Brazil*, pp. 204–231.

What constitutes an ideal government, a model citizen, the most desirable kind of politician?

No attempt was made to gather a probability sample. I simply interviewed, after careful consideration, what I deemed to be six different and important types of urban workers. Zé Maria was selected because he was urban born and bred and because he worked in a large industrial plant. I returned with a set of taped interviews with three "white-collar" and three "blue-collar" workers. Ranging in length from six to seventeen hours and averaging approximately ten hours each, the six interviews produced a total of some 1,100 pages of verbatim transcript.[25]

The interviews were conducted in my living room at the convenience of the worker. The discussions varied from one to three hours per session, until we exhausted all the questions in the interview guide. The atmosphere for the "formal" exchanges was relaxed. We talked over *cafezinhos* or a glass of cold beer. My Brazilian research assistant sat in on most of the interview sessions to help clarify my oftentimes clumsily phrased questions to the workers.[26] But his presence did not appear to inhibit the respondents. In fact, the discussions were often enhanced since it was my Brazilian assistant who had made the formal contacts and arranged the interview sessions. The workers knew him and trusted him, or they would not have been there.

Each respondent was given an "honorarium" for completing the interview, the equivalent of US $35.00 in Brazilian *Cruzeiros*. Since this amount was about the same as the minimum monthly salary in Brazil at the time, I would be less than candid if I were to claim that the financial inducement was not at all important. The financial reward was not, however, the only factor motivating the respondents. We lived among them; we became their friends. They were curious, pleased, amazed, and indeed flattered that someone wanted to listen to what *they* might have to say.[27] Before moving

---

[25] I would like to thank Sylvia for the patience and accuracy she brought to the task of transcribing the taped interviews.

[26] Among countless other things, my Brazilian research assistant helped to arrange the interviews. I am grateful for his help and friendship.

[27] In view of the rather tense political climate existing in Brazil, a word or two should be said about the openness of the discussions with the workers. While, under-

directly to our examination of the life and political world of Zé Maria, let us consider more generally the potential role of the factory in the development of individual political modernity.

The Factory as a School for Individual Political Modernity

In his study of six developing nations, Inkeles provides persuasive evidence for the existence of a "syndrome" peculiar to modern political individuals.[28] According to Inkeles, regardless of the nature of the political regime under which he lives, modern political man tends to exhibit the following five traits or characteristics: (1) "identification and allegiance,"[29] (2) "interest in politics,"[30] (3) "participation in civic affairs,"[31] (4) "political information,"[32] and (5) "political rationality."[33]

Inkeles "discovers" the syndrome through an analysis of his data from Argentina, Chile, Israel, East Pakistan, India, and Nigeria. He argues that the five traits are those "any modern man might be expected to manifest"; moreover, "any modern polity is likely to desire, perhaps even require" that the citizen possess them.[34] The modern political individual is an active citizen. Active citizenship

---

standably, there was some hesitation to refer to contemporary political *personalities*, the men were open and frank for the most part. They spoke about intimate family problems, often with considerable psychological pain; they viewed the discussions from the perspective of good citizens anxious to be of service to their country.

[28] Inkeles, "Participant Citizenship."

[29] "The individual's identification of himself as a political personage, as a citizen rather than someone limited to primordial ties, and . . . following national or modern rather than purely local or parochial, leadership in case he receives competing advice," Inkeles, "Participant Citizenship," p. 1125.

[30] "A man's interest in political rather than purely personal, familial, or parochial matters as judged by what he most follows in the news, is able to say about the problems facing his nation, and talks about with his wife," *ibid.*

[31] "Whether a man actually joins civic organizations, contacts government officials or politicians, and is prepared to take active measures to oppose a government regulation he considers unfair," *ibid.*

[32] "A man's knowledge of international and national political figures and his ability to identify major world capitals," *ibid.*

[33] "The belief that a government should sooner grant a petition to the man with the *right* to it by law rather than to a man more needy or influential; that education more qualifies a man to hold public office than do illustrious origins or charismatic personality; and that the country would benefit more from a good government plan or hard work by people than from prayer or good luck," *ibid.*

[34] *Ibid.*, p. 1123.

is closely related to an individual's level of economic status. This is especially the case in the so-called developing nations. Active citizens cannot be created out of a condition of general impoverishment. As Inkeles writes, "to leave men in a condition of poverty so extreme that they are outside politics, in effect noncitizens, is to create an apathetic mass which is not integrated in society and cannot be mobilized for the purpose of national growth and development."[35]

Inkeles suggests that the modernity syndrome he has uncovered is prerequisite to either democratic or nondemocratic development. He writes: "Those familiar with *The Civic Culture* will recognize these traits as very similar to those delineated by Almond and Verba as defining the model of a democratic citizen. . . . I quite agree that these are the qualities appropriate to, and expected in the citizen of a democracy. *But I hold that exactly the same qualities are appropriate to, and expected of, the citizen of a one-party dictatorship.* . . ."[36] It matters not whether the individual "participates" on the policymaking side of the political process or whether he is "mobilized" in support of policy outputs, he still manifests the same basic traits. If the five traits of Inkeles are the defining characteristics of *modern political individuals in general,* can we list sets of traits or different syndromes to describe different species of modern political men? Is there, for example, a set of characteristics descriptive of modern *democratic* political man on the one hand, and modern *authoritarian* political man on the other?

According to Inkeles, the following items provide the core characteristics of *authoritarian* political man: (1) an "exaggerated faith in powerful leaders and absolute obedience to them," (2) a "hatred of outsiders and deviates," (3) "excessive projection of guilt and hostility," (4) "suspicion and distrust of others," and (5) "dogmatism and rigidity."[37] These items overlap to some extent the five criteria that Lane employs to describe the "undemocrat": (1) "a scorn for the mass electorate," (2) "distaste for the confusion and

---

[35] *Ibid.,* p. 1134.
[36] *Ibid.,* p. 1123 [emphasis added].
[37] *Ibid.;* see also Inkeles's work on "National Character and Modern Political Systems," in Francis L. K. Hsu, ed., *Psychological Anthropology: Approaches to Culture and Personality* (Homewood, Ill., 1961).

delay of parliamentary procedures," (3) "a preference for temporary dictatorship in time of threat," (4) "unrelieved cynicism about democratic procedures in the organization they know," and (5) "doubt about the future of democracy."[38] An "exaggerated faith in powerful leaders and absolute obedience to them" implies "a scorn for the mass electorate," as well as a "distaste for the confusion and delay of parliamentary procedures"; similarly, "suspicion and distrust of others" indicates "unrelieved cynicism about democratic procedures" as well as "doubt about the future of democracy" in general; and so on.

Summarizing the literature on the "authoritarian personality," Greenstein offers the following traits as descriptive of individual authoritarianism: (1) domination of subordinates, (2) deference toward superiors, (3) a sensitivity to relationships involving power, (4) the need to perceive a structured and orderly world, (5) excessive stereotyping, (6) adherence to convention, (7) superstitiousness, (8) undue concern for virility, (9) a hardboiled and rugged outlook, (10) a pessimistic view of human nature, (11) cynicism as to the motives of other individuals, (12) a jungle view of the world, (13) a preoccupation with sex that is puritanical in nature, (14) an inclination to severely punish sex violators, (15) an impatience with tendermindedness, and (16) an inability to introspect.[39] Many of these basic traits have obvious implications for more specifically political beliefs and attitudes, as well as for political behavior. Once again, there is some obvious overlapping here with the criteria of both Inkeles and Lane.

Unfortunately, there has been little systematic research on a corresponding trait list for the *democratic* personality. Certainly, to some extent the qualities directly opposing those of the authoritarian personality are suggestive of a cluster of items that might coalesce in a democratic personality syndrome. For instance, democratic man would tend to be more optimistic in his view of human nature; he would tend to treat subordinates and superiors alike, facing them on an equal footing; he might have a greater respect for the masses of voters; and so forth. But an independently gen-

[38] Lane, *Political Ideology*, p. 98.
[39] Fred Greenstein, *Personality and Politics* (Chicago, 1969), pp. 104–106.

erated syndrome for the democratic personality is yet to be discovered, although perhaps the most insightful work in the area has been done by Harold Lasswell in his discussions of the "democratic character."[40]

At any rate, it is with respect to the development of the five traits of *general* individual political modernity that Inkeles finds the factory to be an important factor. His study tells us nothing about what *kind* of modern political man the factory helps to produce—democratic or undemocratic. Nor does it tell us anything about the impact of the situational context (that is, cultural heritage, economic situation, and regime nature) of the factory job upon the individual modernization process. It is with such concerns that the remainder of this essay deals.

The Life and Political World of Zé Maria

The Factory as a "School for Politics"

If, as Inkeles argues, the factory is a "school for politics" in the developing nations, we can reasonably expect Zé Maria to be among the most politically aware and active of Brazil's urban workers. As such, we want to look closely at his views for clues to the kind of political structures that would be most compatible with the political mind set of the most "modern" type of Brazilian worker.

We recall here Inkeles's syndrome of the "active citizen"—the traits of modern political man. The modern political individual is "informed about politics"; he is "likely to identify with the national state in competition with local leaders." He takes an "active interest in political affairs." He is most likely to "participate actively in civic matters"; and he tends "to support the use of more rational rules impersonally applied as a basis for running governmental affairs."[41] In this section we examine the "goodness of fit" between

---

[40] Harold Lasswell, "Democratic Character," in the *Political Writings of Harold D. Lasswell* (Glencoe, Ill., 1951); Professor Greenstein elaborates on Lasswell's themes in "Personality and Political Socialization: The Theories of Authoritarian and Democratic Character," *The Annals of the American Academy of Political and Social Science*, 361 (1965), pp. 81–95, and in "Harold D. Lasswell's Concept of Democratic Character," *Journal of Politics*, 30 (1968), pp. 696–709.

[41] Inkeles, "Participant Citizenship," p. 1129.

Inkeles's criteria for individual political modernity and the political outlook and behavior of Zé Maria. The following part of the essay explores the political world of Zé Maria in greater depth, considering in particular the specialized impact of the factory job on the basic value of orientations of our urban worker.

At the outset we might state that on balance Zé Maria does qualify as a modern political man, according to the five criteria established by Inkeles. We cannot "prove" that this directly relates to his factory work experiences, of course, but on each of the five items Zé Maria unquestionably approximates *general* individual political modernity. He is, however, by no means completely modern in orientation, for he often displays traits that reflect distinctly traditional qualities, so that in the face of modernity Zé Maria is able to carry over substantial traditional attitudes which lend a note of "Latin American uniqueness" to his political outlook and behavior.[42]

First, let us look at "identification and allegiance." Zé Maria considers himself to be a citizen of a nation-state—to be a Brazilian. Zé Maria is very much interested in national political life, in spite of persistent local ties and allegiances. That interest oftentimes may be expressed in personalistic terms that combine fortuitously the local with the national. After all, Zé Maria is first and foremost a *mineiro* (from Minas Gerais). The interplay of dual interests and loyalties shines through in his references to Brazil's former president—Juscelino Kubitschek, also a *mineiro*: "Juscelino . . . I was a real 'fan' of his, y'know?—at least of his government. A real 'fan' of his. Here was a man who moved Brazil forward with giant steps. He did so many things! Juscelino was very dynamic. . . . A very dynamic man—and a *mineiro*, too! A fellow-*mineiro*! . . . from Diamantina, y'know?"

It is easy to see here an authentic awareness of nation. But the fact that Mr. Kubitschek was, like Zé Maria, a native of Minas Gerais makes him even more appealing as a national political figure. Such dual loyalties may be found in an urban-industrial nation like the United States as well, but Zé Maria's comments about the form-

[42] Almond and Powell conceptualize with respect to the "mixed" nature of changing political cultures in *Comparative Politics* (Boston and Toronto, 1966), p. 33.

er president do illustrate the mixed traditional-modern nature of political culture patterns—a mix not uncommon even in the most "modern" of political systems.

With respect to Inkeles's second item, "interest in politics," we find that Zé Maria's interest centers on the problems of the city. What are the main problems facing Brazil today? In his characteristic "shotgun" style, here is Zé Maria's response:

> There are many problems in Brazil. Too many! Many problems. Want me to cite a few? Here—the main problem here is—a shortage of water. Very little water, y'know? And people who need help—who live in the gutters, y'know? And they are spreading disease all over the city.... People who—who don't have anyone to look after them—just cast out in the streets hereabouts—sleeping in the damp outdoors. And if this person happens to be ill, he transmits it to others. Even—even where the worker is employed—he isn't on a satisfactory diet. And, well, he takes sick and spreads disease throughout the plant, y'know? And the shower facilities aren't adequate either—at the same time you are taking a hot shower you find cold water falling down on your shoulders. And one gets sick. You have all these problems—right here in this city, y'know?

Zé Maria pauses a second or two and continues:

> And the city is—well, it's very dirty, y'know? The sewer system is inadequate. Here on this very street, for example, there is this pipeline that passes over my lot carrying wastes from the houses up there on the hill. On occasion it gives off a bad smell that comes right into the house. You can't even open the kitchen door. It could bring problems to my family—a sickness or a contagious disease. My lot amounts to a drainage ditch for about five other houses—because of that pipe, y'know? ... Let me see.

After reflecting a bit, he bursts forth again:

> Oh, my God! There are so many problems here! So many problems! I think—I think another big problem here is the narrow streets. Cars climbing up over the curb, picking people off. One goes out of the house nowadays and never knows if he will ever return.... Why, just the other day, for example, *I waited almost ten minutes* trying to cross Avenida Amazonas, y'know? It's a problem trying to cross the streets. The government ought to look into

this because, if it doesn't, people will keep on getting killed without ever knowing what hit them—a car coming down a one-way street the wrong way; another leaping up over the curb onto the sidewalk.

Any other problems, I asked? Zé Maria was quick to come up with a few more:

> The government ought to help the working class a little more. Workers have so little now. The majority of them are going hungry at the job. I have proof—people who work right alongside me: four days after payday they don't have even a crumb left in their pockets! . . . The majority of them do not eat properly, y'know?—and they take sick and—there are an infinity of problems I could cite, y'know? Problems of educating the kids. . . . There is a shortage of schools—*ginásio* is very expensive. The worker doesn't earn enough to pay the monthly costs—and, well, his son grows up to be illiterate because his father could not—did not earn enough to pay for his *ginásio*, y'know?

The indictment is a long and exhaustive one. Zé Maria readily perceives the problems of a rapidly expanding, crowded urban center where the scarcities of underdevelopment complicate and compound matters. There are problems of educating one's children, unemployment and underemployment, water shortages, traffic-choked streets, low wages, inadequate sanitary facilities, disease, and so on. And Zé Maria's horizons are not limited to the city in which he lives and works—they even cross national boundaries and encompass the international political arena:

> I think Brazil ought to dip into its own pockets and buy what is needed, y'know? Buy and sell; import and export. And—well, I think Brazil should exploit its own riches better—the riches that we already have here but which are exploited by foreigners. All the heavy industry that we have here in Brazil is foreign-owned. And the Brazilian himself could do the exploiting, y'know?—because he is intelligent enough to do so and—there are many capable people here. But, no—it isn't done. The Brazilian is very lazy this way and sometimes—it's something that—that makes one even a little sad to be a Brazilian. Because everywhere you look the entire heavy industry sector here in Brazil is foreign-owned—even the very gold mines of Minas here are run by foreigners! And, well, I

think that the government ought to look into this more carefully—allow foreign industry to be here too, but why not exploit some of our own resources ourselves?—because we have everything of value right here in Brazil? manganese, gold—everything, y'know? But it seems that the Brazilian doesn't know how to exploit them. He leaves them for the others to exploit, y'know?

Turning to the third trait for individual political modernity, "political information," we find Zé Maria to be a reasonably well-informed and articulate citizen. According to Inkeles, modern political man is more concerned with news and events of national and international magnitude than he is with local matters. Modern political man is a "cosmopolitan"; traditional political man is a "local."[43] The thoughts expressed by Zé Maria in the last quotation certainly qualify him as a cosmopolitan in terms of "political information."

For purposes of brevity, we can combine the remaining two characteristics of Inkeles's modernity syndrome: "participation in civic affairs" and "political rationality." Before the 1964 "civilian/military movement" deposed President João Goulart and interrupted "constitutional government" of "liberal-democratic" form in Brazil, Zé Maria was a genuinely "active" and "rational" participant in the political process. Not only aware of many of the multitude of problems facing his country, his city, and his neighborhood, Zé Maria acted to improve the situation—at least with respect to the problems impinging most directly upon him and his family. Take, for example, the problem of inadequate sewer facilities in Belo Horizonte, which he alluded to when citing some of the problems facing the city. He has persistently attempted, though to date without success, to alleviate the situation, as it concerns him most directly. "I already have—for the past ten years or so—I have been waging a battle with the proper city agency—to get them to install sewers in the neighborhood. But they simply won't do it! I have already tried in several different agencies."

[43] The terms, "cosmopolitan" and "local" were used by Lane, *Political Ideology*, p. 303. They stem from the work of Robert K. Merton, "Patterns of Influence," in Paul F. Lazarsfeld and Frank N. Stanton, eds., *Communications Research, 1948–49* (N.Y., 1949), pp. 108–209.

I asked Zé Maria how he might "go about getting the streets paved in his neighborhood." He retorted: "First, I would go to City Hall—become informed, y'know? Then, well,—I would make an appointment with the head of the—of the proper department, y'know?—the one responsible for paving the streets. Then, later, I would go to see the Mayor—and, well, that would be it—either he says 'yes' or he says 'no.' " Zé Maria has traveled this path before, though unsuccessfully, with respect to having street lights installed in his neighborhood: "I made an appointment with Dr. ———. I spoke with him—explained what I wanted—and asked if he could illuminate the streets hereabouts." When asked during the interview if he knew anyone with political influence who might be able to intercede in his behalf, he paused, then said: "Now?—now I don't have anyone, no. I used to [before 1964] and I spoke with him about the street lighting problem—many times. I had arranged other things I wanted with the help of this politician, y'know?"

To be sure, Zé Maria has employed personalistic means in his capacity as an active citizen. But in an environment where personalistic political solutions are the norm, one could hardly expect any other pattern. Yet, his job in the factory and his experiences with labor unions have provided him with the knowledge that there is strength in numbers and organized political action. I inquired if labor unions should be actively involved in politics. With amazement, he responded sharply: "Geez! Why not, huh? Geez!" After a moment's thought he added:

> I think the government ought to treat labor unions with greater responsibility. The labor union—let the workers resolve matters as they think they ought to be resolved. Because, today, the unions are totally worthless—they are controlled by the government. The worker can't even raise his voice. If he does, he is punished, y'know? ... And strikes—you can't strike anymore. This business of striking —I guess it's all over now. ... You used to be able to strike—and I think it is something the government ought to permit. Because if the boss doesn't want to increase the workers' salaries—and they are not satisfied—well, the workers must have some means, y'know? But, today, you can't go on strike because the leaders are in prison. And well, with the leaders in prison—being punished—who is going

to try anything? The worker can die of hunger, but he can no longer go on strike. . . .

It is unfortunate that Zé Maria's experiences with labor-union activity took the turn they did as a result of tightened governmental controls. In effect, the growth of Zé Maria as an active participant has been stunted, "nipped in the bud." Out of fear of economic and political reprisals, Zé Maria has shied away from all union activity since the 1964 "revolution": "Ah! I—with respect to this—what can I do? Because, nowadays, you know that if a person wants to join in some union activity on behalf of the workers, or something like this it is—it can even be dangerous, y'know? So,—I was even asked to do this—but I refused. Because I have seen my coworkers suffer from such activity and, well,—I prefer to stay away, y'know?—to stay neutral." Zé Maria is not simply imagining the potential dangers that might befall such activity. His fears are grounded in reality. One of his friends has already suffered:

> I have this friend who used to work with me—a very intelligent guy—and a real fighter for his fellow-workers. He was fired because of his activity in a union that went on strike. And, today his family is just about starving because no one will hire him—anywhere. He is—I think he is a very special kind of person. And all he did was do what he thought was right! Well, he was punished . . . and today he is suffering the consequences. He's just a young fellow—a hard worker and an honest man—and he has a family—four children.

Other evidence speaks to the "rational" and "active participation" of Zé Maria in Brazilian politics—at least before 1964. He was actively involved in electoral politics, supporting a number of PTB (Brazilian Labor party) candidates. During Juscelino Kubitschek's campaign for the presidency in the mid-1950s, Zé Maria worked in behalf of a local politician who was running for office on the PTB ticket. "I worked hard in that political campaign, y'know? I worked hard." What kinds of things did you do, I asked? "I—I informed all my friends about the candidate. And I helped in the street campaign hereabouts—putting up posters and signs, y'know? Because he deserved to be elected—he really deserved it, y'know?" When I pressed Zé Maria as to why the candidate was so deserving of election, he said:

> Because he was a very special kind of guy—straightforward, honest, and a real hard worker. He worked hard for his people— for his people. He did everything he could for them, y'know? He had already served one term. I went to help him during his second campaign. The first time he was in office he worked very hard—he did many things, so—the second time he ran, I worked for him. I already knew what he was like. . . . If there were a thousand candidates of his stature, I would be most happy to work for all of them.

And his participation in the campaign was not without personal expense. When I asked if he had ever contributed money for the election of a candidate, he answered: "Let me see—no. But I have contributed in a way—by spending money out of my own pocket to—to help in the campaign of that candidate. So, I guess I have contributed, right?"

Zé Maria attended several gatherings of the PTB, before the old, multiparty system was formally abolished during the Castelo Branco regime. Although partially lured by the festive atmosphere of the gatherings, he did not minimize the "business" of the meetings: "I went because all the meetings had—well, afterwards there would always be a celebration of sorts. And, well—one gets an invitation: 'Guest of Honor,' y'know?—to take part. And, well—one goes. But not just for the festivities! One goes first of all for the business part of the meeting—and simply takes advantage of the festivities."

Zé Maria not only is *aware* of many of the problems that face his nation and his locality, he has *acted* in various capacities to cope with them through a variety of political channels. He has sought audiences with high political figures, he has participated in union activity, and he has engaged in electioneering and party politics. Because of the prevailing political climate in Brazil at present, however, Zé Maria has turned away from all such activity. Like all "modern" political men—even the most "modern"—Zé Maria is not entirely without personalistic, paternalistic, and other "traditional" tendencies. Most decidedly, Zé Maria is a modern political man, as far as "civic participation" and "political rationality" are concerned.

In summary, considering all five of Inkeles's traits for individual political modernity, we must conclude that, on balance, Zé Maria has a decidedly "modern" political outlook. We cannot say with certainty that the explanation of this "modern" outlook is a function of his industrial work experiences. Other factors are at work also. Zé Maria has lived in an urban area all his life, and he has had some formal schooling. He does not have a rural village to return to in times of family economic crisis. Organized political action, therefore, becomes more imperative in terms of economic survival. Nevertheless, it is not unreasonable to assume that certain aspects of Zé Maria's political world relate to his work experiences. The connection appears most obvious regarding his feelings concerning the potential roles of labor unions in the political process, and organized political activity in general. In terms of Inkeles's generalized syndrome of individual political modernity and its relationship with factory work, there does seem to be a reasonably good "fit" in the case of Zé Maria.

For the remainder of this essay we move to a deeper analysis of the political world of Zé Maria. We must do so because Inkeles's modernity syndrome is too general. It is almost devoid of value content. It may be that the factory does lend assistance to the development of "modern" political men, *as defined by Inkeles*, but the five traits do not give us much insight into the kind of value changes, if any, induced by the factory work experience.

In his discussion of "work life in the metropolis," Lane finds that work in the factory is compatible with the persistence of a democratic spirit among the "common men" he studied in Eastport.[44] But Lane's analysis involves men living in an affluent society where, speaking comparatively, the rewards for a day's work tend to reach down to the average working class man. In Zé Maria we are looking at the life and political world of a man who shares only slightly in the affluent life and who sees widespread impoverishment all around him. Whether or not the factory job is conducive to "demo-

[44] Lane, *Political Ideology*, pp. 228–249.

cratic spirit" may very well vary with the societal and economic context of that employment. Certainly, the nature of the political regime must be considered as well. Awareness of the specialized form that individual political modernity takes in Brazil, as exemplified by the case of Zé Maria, is crucial for a greater understanding of the processes involved and, eventually, for offering policy prescriptions concerning nation-building on the macrolevel. Let us continue our exploration of the political world of Zé Maria, therefore, in our search for a broader understanding of the overall impact of industrial employment on the basic value orientations of the urban worker in the Brazilian context. It is important to know what kind of "modern" political men the factory job helps to create.

Work in the Factory and Basic Value Orientations: "Modernization" in the Brazilian Context

How might the job in the factory affect such basic Latin American (including Brazilian) value patterns and orientations as: *personalismo, dignidad de la persona (dignidade da pessoa), machismo*, the nature of trust in one's fellow man, as embodied in the Spanish expression *hombre de confianza* and the Portuguese term *pessoa de confiança*, the view of social hierarchy as the natural order of things, the importance of ritualized and institutionalized patterns of friendship bound up in the notion of *compadrazgo (compadrio)*, and attitudes toward work, death, life, and so forth, as they coalesce in an "idealistic" or "transcendental" world view?[45] From an awareness of the kind of factors that make up the modernity syndrome uncovered by Inkeles we cannot draw many easy and direct inferences with respect to the impact of the factory job. We will focus, therefore, on these basic Latin American value patterns and

[45] The cultural themes and patterns discussed here are among those that John Gillin deems essential to consider in any treatment of Latin American culture. See his "Ethos Components of Modern Latin American Culture," in Dwight Heath and Richard Adams, eds., *Contemporary Cultures and Societies of Latin America* (N.Y., 1965), pp. 503–517. John F. Santos also discusses these and other aspects of Latin American culture, as they apply to the Brazilian situation. See his "A Psychologist Reflects on Brazil and Brazilians," in Eric N. Baklanoff, ed., *New Perspectives of Brazil* (Nashville, Tenn., 1966), pp. 233–263.

orientations below in order to shed some light on the *possible* effect of work in the factory upon them, within the context of present-day Brazil.

In his excellent study of political ideology among Malaysian bureaucrats, James Scott borrows a framework for the analysis of basic value orientations from Kluckhohn and Strodtbeck. The framework points to five fundamental problem areas: (1) "what is the character of innate human nature?," (2) "what is the relation of man to man (and supernature)?," (3) "what is the temporal focus of human life?," (4) "what is the modality of human activity? (being, becoming)," and (5) "what is the modality of man's relationship to other men?"[46] In examining the political world of Zé Maria we concentrate on three of Kluckhohn and Strodtbeck's themes, plus one additional area. We focus on: (1) the nature of human nature, (2) the nature of man's relationship with nature, (3) the nature of man's relationship with his fellow men, and (4) the nature of man's relationship with his inner self. We are not interested in these basic value orientations per se, but in their implications for more specifically political outlooks and behavior. That is, a political scientist is most interested in how the basic value patterns translate into political beliefs, feelings, and action. If the factory acts in part as a "school" for microlevel political modernization, and if Zé Maria is representative of urban factory workers in Brazil, then we want to know to what extent, if any, the job in the factory has changed the basic value orientations of Zé Maria. For a change in his basic values implies a change in his political beliefs, feelings, attitudes, and possibly in his behavior. While the following sections of this essay treat the four areas of core value orientations in relative isolation from their political implications, the final parts will consider their political consequences.

On the Nature of Human Nature: Misanthropy, Pessimism, and the Cautious Search for Friendship

Writing about Latin American "ethos components," Professor John Gillin describes how throughout the region "friendship, of

[46] James C. Scott, *Political Ideology in Malaysia* (New Haven and London, 1968), pp. 60–61.

the intimate personal connection, is essential to inter-personal relations."[47] But that friendship is highly restricted: "only persons united by ties of kinship, *compadrazgo*, and real friendship can trust one another. Something like this is, of course, true in all societies. Yet the impersonal confidence which, say a buyer has toward a salesman of a large established corporation in the United States is not yet part of the pattern in Latin America. There, you have to know him as an individual and to understand his 'soul' really to have confidence in him."[48] Outside of kinship relationships, it is only with an *hombre de confianza* or a *pessoa de confiança* that one can feel at ease and trustful. In a study carried out in 1965 by the Department of Sociology and Political Science of the University of Minas Gerais, 89 percent of a sample of 645 residents of Belo Horizonte agreed that "one must be very careful when dealing with other persons"; only 11 percent felt that "one can trust people by and large."[49] The sample included white-collar workers (including professional people and high executives), skilled and unskilled blue-collar workers, housewives, students, the unemployed, and the retired. Breaking the categories of respondents down into "manual" and "nonmanual" workers, the data indicate that fully 94 percent of the 163 manual workers opted for the misanthropic response (84 percent of the 211 nonmanually employed selected the distrustful option).[50]

How does Zé Maria stand against such a background? I gave him a scale used to measure trustfulness in Brazil and Mexico by Joseph Kahl. The scale consists of four items; the range of scores one can receive on the scale are from 0 to 12.[51] Zé Maria scored a "5"—one

[47] Gillin, "Ethos Components," p. 510.
[48] *Ibid.*
[49] Júlio Barbosa in association with Antônio Octávio Cintra, Fábio Wanderley Reis, and José Maria Carvalho directed the research project. I would like to express my appreciation to Júlio Barbosa for giving me permission to use the data, which is archived in the International Data Library and Reference Service of the Survey Research Center at the University of California at Berkeley. Citations hereafter refer to the study as the "Barbosa Study."
[50] "Manual" employment refers to skilled, semiskilled, and unskilled labor; "nonmanual" employment refers to clerical and supervisory white-collar work, along with professional and high executive work.
[51] Joseph A. Kahl, *The Measurement of Modernism: A Study of Values in Brazil and Mexico* (Austin and London, 1968), p. 32.

might say he is about 40 percent trustful, or some 60 percent misanthropic. Fortunately, the interview material is rich enough to explore the depths of Zé Maria's misanthropy in greater detail.

Professor Harold Lasswell considers "the maintenance of an open as against a closed ego" to be the most "outstanding characteristic" of the "democratic character."[52] The term "open ego" involves an "attitude toward other human beings" that "is warm rather than frigid, inclusive and expanding rather than exclusive and constricting."[53] In sum, Lasswell is referring to "an underlying personality structure which is capable of 'friendship,' as Aristotle put it, and which is unalienated from humanity."[54] Another important feature of Lasswell's "democratic character" is a belief in the charitable capacities of man.[55] Commenting and elaborating upon this notion, Fred Greenstein writes that "the cognitive pattern that Lasswell emphasizes is a belief in the benevolent potentialities of mankind. *If not his conception of man's present behavior, at least in his notion of man's potential capacities,* the democrat acts on assumptions that are more Rousseauesque than Hobbesian."[56]

How close does Zé Maria come to having an "open ego"? How does Zé Maria stand with respect to an "underlying personality structure which is capable of friendship," that is "unalienated from humanity"? Is he able to "transcend most of the cultural categories that divide human beings from one another"? Does he possess a "serene outlook that reaches out hopefully and tolerantly toward other human beings"? In sum, has Zé Maria developed "a perspective that fosters inclusive identifications with other people"?[57]

Zé Maria says he has "a lot of friends." At least this is what he claims. But this estimation stems mainly from his perspective on the nature of friendship and his tendencies toward extroversion. Zé Maria considers himself to be a "mixer." He likes to join in

[52] Lasswell, "Democratic Character," p. 495.
[53] *Ibid.*
[54] *Ibid.*
[55] *Ibid.*, p. 498.
[56] Greenstein, "Harold D. Lasswell's Concept of Democratic Character," p. 702 [emphasis added].
[57] Lasswell, "Democratic Character," p. 495.

gatherings of people—"depending upon the people." In general, however, Zé Maria likes to be with others and he enjoys a festive atmosphere. He views himself as "the life of the party," not simply a "listener": "Ah! I am the life of a party—I love to liven up a party!" Among the most important lessons in life that Zé Maria tries desperately to instill in his teenage son is "to be sociable":

> I like to teach him to treat everyone well, y'know? And—because he isn't very sociable at all. He doesn't like to visit his own relatives. He doesn't like to enter into family get-togethers—he's always trying to sneak away. Well, I try to teach him these things—and when someone is sick—he doesn't even like to pay a visit. And I keep telling him he should, y'know—that he should visit people when they are sick....

But extroversion is not always the best indicator of genuine warmth in interpersonal relations. Indeed, it often provides a convenient shield that enables only surface friendships to develop. We must look at the way in which Zé Maria perceives the nature of friendship as well. Friendship involves both giving and receiving. From his responses to certain questions and from personal observations comparing him with other workers, it seems that Zé Maria tends to emphasize the receiving side of friendship. In a social system where friendships provide an important form of "social security," however, this is not unusual. When I asked Zé Maria about the importance of a friend, he answered: "Friends are very important, y'know? A friend—a friend is useful for many things. When things get tight—in times of sickness—in the hour of personal tragedy—well, a friend is useful—very helpful, y'know? ... And one can always visit his friends to exchange ideas—one can express himself frankly. Say exactly how one feels."

Zé Maria is by no means a "cold" individual, but the warmth is usually reserved for his most intimate friends and relations. I detect in Zé Maria a generalized distrust of others combined with a desire and a need for friendship. It is an intense, but cautious, search for friendship in a social setting where connections are necessary for survival. In a society where people often do take advantage of others when the guard is let down and in a social system where friendship is necessary, a rather anxious "alienation from humanity" seems inevitable.

There are many barriers that tend to divide men in society: barriers of race, class, sex, generations, ethnicity, religion, nationalism, and so forth. The "self-system" of the democratic personality is able to transcend most, if not all, of them. Zé Maria, along with most Brazilians, I think, displays a laudable tolerance with regard to those on the other side of the social dividers. Take race, for example, which provides an area for deep divisions in the United States. In a country like Brazil, which has experienced widespread miscegenation, the lines that tend to divide men along racial lines begin to blur. To be sure, racial prejudice is not completely absent in Brazil—blond hair, blue eyes, and fair skin are still preferred.[58] But attitudes are more relaxed than in the United States. The atmosphere is more congenial. Outright racial hostility is absent. Zé Maria boasts about his own family situation: "There are colored people in my very own family—even *very* black ones. I have several black cousins because my aunt married a Negro." Zé Maria holds no hostilities toward Brazilians of darker complexion. In Brazil, "coffee with cream" easily substitutes for "peaches and cream."

Nor do ethnic backgrounds raise insurmountable barriers to smooth interpersonal relations for Zé Maria. I asked him if he had any special thoughts regarding Brazilians of Italian extraction, for example. Somewhat surprised at the question, he exclaimed: "Geez! I think—I don't think anything at all! I think they are just people."

With regard to religious barriers, Zé Maria provides an exceptional case. Since his wife is a Protestant—a Baptist—Zé Maria is under cross-pressures. He harbors no hostility toward the atheist in Brazil. I asked him if an atheist could be a "good person and lead a decent life." Zé Maria replied with assurance: "Absolutely! A man who has character—who is honest—well, he doesn't need religion. Religion is a prop." Zé Maria is somewhat antagonistic toward the Catholic church in Brazil, though he still considers himself to be a Catholic—at least for the present. He has this to say about the church: "I am not very religious—not closely connected

---

[58] See Wagley's discussion of race and class in Brazil, *Introduction to Brazil*, pp. 132–147.

to Catholicism. I am a Catholic, but there is a lot wrong with the church that one can easily see, y'know? I think religion these days is more like a business than a religion—an authentic religion, if you know what I mean." By placing the church in the category of business, Zé Maria is placing it in a category which contains the people in Brazil of whom he is most distrustful—that of the businessman. As far as businessmen are concerned, says Zé Maria, "they only say things to deceive you—they don't ever do anything to benefit anyone else. They just try to take advantage of you."

Our urban factory worker believes that Jews are not well liked in Brazil as a rule, but he denies having any anti-Semitic feelings himself. "I have already done business with Jews—I think they are just like everyone else, y'know? They may even give you a break. No, I don't find any fault with Jews at all."

Turning to the area of social class, Zé Maria sees greater hostility *within* the various classes in Brazil, rather than between them. Instead of a "war between the classes," Zé Maria considers a "war within the classes" to be a greater likelihood. As Zé Maria puts it: "I think there is hostility *within* the lower class itself—and *within* the upper class, too. To such an extent that there are—there are lawyers in this city who are arch-enemies, y'know? And in the lower class, too. There are workers hereabouts who show outright hostility toward one another! I think there is hostility *within all the classes* —but friendships, too. That is the reality."

Another potential source of division in society, witness the United States in the late 1960s and the early 1970s, is that between generations. While Zé Maria is apprehensive about the changing manner of dress and courtship patterns, in a region of Brazil noted for traditionalism and conservatism he takes a rather indulgent attitude toward the young people of Brazil. "I think there are all kinds of young people—some are patient; some are impetuous—all kinds, y'know? . . . But, they are just beginning, y'know? And they have a right to taste life, too."

In a cultural region of the world where male dominance and female submission have long been celebrated—usually by the males —one could hardly expect Zé Maria to be devoid of "sexism." He believes that the woman's place is in the home. "The man has a stronger pulse and a tougher heart—he doesn't give in as easily as the woman." In a region where masculinity is often defined in terms of feminine conquest, which in turn is often explained in terms of deep-seated masculine insecurities, one might expect to find a punishing attitude toward homosexuals and homosexuality. Such is not the case, however, with Zé Maria. He views homosexuality as a "sickness" that "ought to be treated," but the homosexual should never be punished.

Finally, with respect to the boundaries that tend to divide the nations of the world, we find a mixture of nationalistic pride and anxious pessimism. On the basis of firsthand observations in the foreign-controlled and operated plant in which he works, Zé Maria shows justifiable hostility:

> ... the government here helps them. It helps the foreigners. I'm going to tell you something to illustrate what I mean. The head of a foreign-owned industry here—well, let's say a Brazilian is doing the job—and the head brings over a foreigner. ... Now, the Brazilian has more experience, but they always put a foreigner over him—or take the Brazilian out and put the foreigner in his place. I'm damned tired of seeing this? And all the foreign firms do this, y'know?

Summarizing the discussion of his values thus far, we find an admirable ability on the part of Zé Maria to overcome many of the barriers that can potentially divide men in society. Nevertheless, an intense need and a cautious search for friendship seem to permeate the atmosphere. Perhaps if it were not for the material scarcities of underdevelopment, along with an inequitable distribution of the things people value and desire, that renders friendship necessary, we might be able to wipe away the caution as well as the dependence. Perhaps only then can the way be paved toward the development of completely "open egos" among urban workers like Zé Maria. He already has a substantial basis upon which to build.

How about Zé Maria's attitude toward the benevolent potentiality of human nature? Such a belief, according to Lasswell, arises from a warm, expanding, and inclusive ego: it represents an "affirmative trust" that is "very different from the apathetic endurance of life," such as one might encounter in the case of an "apathetic orphan."[59] A question that taps this dimension is: Will there always be war? When I asked Zé Maria this question, he responded vigorously and with assurance: "Ah! So long as the world goes on! All my life there has been war and I believe there will continue to be wars until I don't know when—until the end of the world I guess." I asked him what he thought caused war. After reflecting a moment, Zé Maria answered:

> The cause of war is—I think the major cause is—well, a person wants to be owner of the whole world, y'know? He wants to be the ruler and take things that don't belong to him, y'know? Accordingly, it even happens in our everyday lives. . . . If, for example, I have a house and someone comes to take it, well, I'm not going to let him—and so, I fight with him. I think it is the same with wars. It is the right of the individual to defend what is his.

Obviously, Zé Maria is not very optimistic about the benevolent potentialities of mankind. Aggression and greed are a part of human nature. Zé Maria strongly agrees that "in spite of what some people say, the lot of the average man is getting worse, not better"; he agrees that "it's hardly fair to bring children into the world with the way things look for the future."[60]

On the Nature of Man in Society: Hierarchy as the Natural Social Order

Professor Gillin writes that "the peculiarly Latin American mental pattern or premise of individual worth is . . . involved in a cultural configuration that recognizes and accepts the *social inequality of human beings.*"[61] He continues, "every person realizes that, from the point of view of social structure, he is not equal with everyone else, either in position or opportunity."[62] The "average" Latin American "will readily admit that there are social categories

---

[59] Lasswell, "Democratic Character," p. 502.
[60] These two items are from the "anomie scale" James Scott used in his Malaysian study, *Political Ideology in Malaysia*, p. 282.
[61] Gillin, "Ethos Components," p. 511.
[62] *Ibid.*, pp. 511–512.

above or below him. Yet, he as an individual with a soul in his inner consciousness or unconsciousness, does not have to pay too much attention to the unfair distribution of rights and privileges which the social system imposes upon him."[63] The Latin American "is aware that he is born to a certain social position which is one of the facts of life, but that at the same time he can perhaps improve his position."[64] While "no one pretends (as is ideally the case in the United States) that the son of a common laborer has an equal chance with the son of an old *hacendado* family . . . it is evident . . . that boys and girls with a poor start in life can in certain cases, at least, make the grade, if they really have the soul to do so."[65] Gillin concludes:

> Thus, according to the Latin American pattern, one may rise in the social scale if he has the soul to do so; but at the same time one recognizes and accepts, at least for the time being, his position in society. He has no right to expect more. Strange as it may seem to a North American, the acceptance of the social order as given is not, for Latin Americans, inconsistent with the concept of individuality as they conceive it. At one and the same time, therefore, the average Latin American is motivated to maintain the established order and also to take advantage of it for his own personal ends with the help of his friends, including kinsmen of various types. . . .[66]

These "Latin American" notions of individualism and social inequality are strikingly similar to those encountered by Lane in his study of working-class men in the United States. Lane argues that "many members of the working class do not want equality. They are afraid of it. In some ways they already seek to escape from it. . . . Inequality has values to them that have been overlooked."[67] While American culture and the democratic dogma have given to the "American public the notion that 'all men are created equal,'" other messages are also getting through and they are inequalitarian in nature: "even more insistently, the American culture tells its

---

[63] *Ibid.*, p. 512.
[64] *Ibid.*, p. 513.
[65] *Ibid.*
[66] *Ibid.*
[67] Lane, *Political Ideology*, p. 60.

members: 'achieve,' 'compete,' 'be better, smarter, quicker, richer than your fellow man'; in short, 'be unequal.' "[68] In order to account for their own status in life—lower than many, but higher than some—Lane found the men using a variety of rationalizations.

The most common theme in Eastport was this: " 'All men can better themselves'; the circumstances of American life do not imprison men in their class or station—if there is such a prison, the iron bars are within each man."[69] Only a minority of the "common men of Eastport" resorted to the idea of "moral or spiritual equality," or "I'm just as good as anybody else"; the theme of "differential life chances" was rarely used as well.[70] When the American working-class man looks *up* the social ladder, he "explains" his relatively low position by resorting to such mechanisms as: (1) limiting his focus to those closest to him in the hierarchy—putting the upper classes out of the range of comparison, (2) denying the importance of class position, or (3) reluctantly resigning himself to his fate.[71] When the American "common man" looks *down* the social hierarchy, he can "point with pride to achievement, material well-being, standing in community."[72]

Even for the small number of American upper-lower- or lower-middle-class men who did resort to the theme of "moral or spiritual equality" (or, "I think I'm just as good as anybody else"), Lane believes they were really trying to tell him something else.

> ... O'Hara means, if I may put words in his mouth: "Don't put on airs around me; I'm trying to preserve my self-respect in a world that challenges it; I therefore assert my equality with all. I won't be pushed around; I know my rights;" and, to the interviewer, "Just because you're a professor and I'm an oiler, it doesn't mean you can patronize me." And when Sokolsky, a machine operator and part-time janitor says ... : "The rich guy—because he's got money he's no better than I am. I mean, that's the way I feel," he is not talking about moral or spiritual qualities. He is saying, in effect, to his prosperous older brother and his snobbish wife, "but

[68] *Ibid.*, p. 61.
[69] *Ibid.*
[70] *Ibid.*, p. 62.
[71] *Ibid.*, pp. 62–65.
[72] *Ibid.*, p. 65.

I will protect my self-esteem." These men are posting notices similar to the motto on the early American colonies' flags, "Don't tread on me."[73]

This comes very close to describing what is implied in the Latin American phrase, *la dignidad de la persona*, which Gillin defines as "the inner integrity or worth which every person is supposed to guard jealously."[74]

Let us now take a look at our own urban factory worker and examine his outlook on the nature of man in society. With respect to equality, Zé Maria says, "We are all human beings, aren't we?" But with regard to the social order, he argues: "There are people who think differently—and they are superior to me; there are others who think differently—and they are inferior. . . . This is only natural—only natural." Like the majority of Lane's respondents, Zé Maria feels he could better his social standing: "I could. Definitely!," he exclaims. But at age forty-seven, he has little hope. When I was younger, I didn't have the opportunity. In those days there was no SENAI (National Service of Industrial Apprenticeship), no *ginásio*—and my father died when I was only four and—so, I didn't have a chance to study— or anything. . . . And, in order to get ahead in life, one must study, y'know? . . . Education is the main thing." Here, Zé Maria uses the theme of "differential life chances" to "explain" his own positioning in the social order and as a rationale for resigning himself to his fate. Interestingly enough, such a theme was rarely used by the men of Eastport.

But "differential life chances" is not a sufficient explanation for Zé Maria. In order to protect his inner worth or individual *dignidade*, he, like the men of Eastport, narrows his focus to *within* rather than *between* class comparisons: "I belong to the working class, sure—but, I am better off than most, y'know? [chuckles proudly]" Zé Maria associates himself vicariously with his oldest son in life's struggle: "But, take my son—he could [move up the social ladder] because he is studying. He could move up to a level superior to me, y'know?" Zé Maria would like his son to be a lawyer, or an engineer, or an accountant, but "not to have the

[73] *Ibid.*, pp. 67–68.
[74] Gillin, "Ethos Components," p. 508.

same kind of job I have. . . . My means of making a living—I think it is very hard work—very arduous, y'know?—and I don't desire it for either of my sons—in no way!"

Lane found lower levels of income and status much easier to live with in Eastport, if the working-class man could "believe that the rich are not receiving a happiness income commensurate with their money income."[75] Zé Maria feels this way, too. Are the rich happier than the working-class man? "No! Absolutely not! There are rich people that are unhappier than the poorest of men. Because they may not enjoy good health. They have lots of money, but they may not have good health. They have money, but they can't enjoy it! And a poor man may not have enough money to do anything, but with good health and enough sleep he is strong and able to work." Zé Maria's response closely resembles that of O'Hara in the Lane study. Yet, like O'Hara, Zé Maria believes that happiness is the most important thing that money can buy:

> Many things are important in life, y'know? But money—I think it is the main thing, y'know? I think money is a very important thing because with money you can do anything—provide for family needs—and educate the kids, y'know?—and one can take care of his family's health needs. He can take them to the doctor when necessary. And with money one doesn't have to work so hard, y'know?— one can work less. I think money can take care of everything. It helps in every way, y'know?

Perhaps Lane's analysis of O'Hara fits the case of Zé Maria as well—"that money buys happiness for the average man but not for the rich. In this way he can cope with a mild envy by appropriating happiness for himself and 'his kind.' "[76]

Lasswell has written that "when the fixation on wealth is so intense that other values are almost deprived of meaning, we have miserly, greedy types who are eager to accumulate and to retain goods and services. Such acquisitive and retentive personalities are referred to in the folklore of many cultures with utter disdain, since public service, affection, or other values are rejected in order to

[75] Lane, *Political Ideology*, p. 65.
[76] *Ibid.*

get hold of impersonal and tangible resources."[77] Zé Maria has not reached a stage of complete fixation on material well-being, but he does place considerable emphasis on the value of wealth. It may be that his job in the factory, along with the *relative* "affluence" it has brought him, rather than lend support to the development of a "multi-valued democratic character," has, indeed, been destructive of those ends.

We find, then, in the case of our urban factory worker a basic value orientation concerning the nature of man in society as one that views hierarchy as the natural social order. This orientation remains seemingly unshaken, and perhaps even strengthened, by ten years of work in the factory.

On Man and Nature: A "Transcendental" or "Idealistic" View

When North Americans tamed a continent and industrialized their society, they evolved two "successful formulas," according to Gillin: "hard work and technical ingenuity."[78] These "precepts" have become a fixed part of the culture and they have been palmed off on other cultures in United States' foreign-aid programs. Gillin chastizes United States' decisionmakers for basing aid programs on the presumption that " 'if we give the Latin Americans our technical know-how, and if they will just work as hard as we did, they will enjoy the materialistic benefits these things provided for us.' "[79] He goes on to note that "it is just possible that technology and pragmatism alone do not ring a bell in the Latin American culture."[80] Importantly, however, Professor Gillin believes that the Latin American has the capacity to learn the routines involving pragmatic and utilitarian goals.[81] "They learn the routines, but they are not primarily interested in or attracted by the underlying premises involved."[82] The Latin American needs "something more." He

[77] Lasswell, "Democratic Character," p. 501.
[78] Gillin, p. 514.
[79] *Ibid.*
[80] *Ibid.*
[81] *Ibid.*
[82] *Ibid.*, p. 513.

needs "something beyond the practical affairs of everyday life."[83]

No doubt after some ten years in the factory, Zé Maria has been "programed" into the routines and rigors of industrial employment. We have an opportunity, then, to explore Gillin's argument and relate it to Inkeles's finding that the factory can serve in some measure as a "school" for individual political modernization. Inkeles argues as follows:

> ... we may see the factory as a school in rationality. A factory runs largely according to formal rules guided by impersonal technical norms. Its system of authority and rewards is intimately geared to a more or less objective and precisely graded hierarchy of technical skill which, in turn, rests on formal education. Such an environment might well, therefore, encourage men to carry over to the political realm the expectation that high position should rest on education and skill, and that people should be treated not according to their unique personal qualities or their intimate relations with authority, but rather by rule and according to their rights.[84]

He continues: "Order, rationality, firm organization, effective technical competence, justice in the distribution of rewards and punishment, even intimate personal relatedness, are often much more common in the factory than in the urban milieu which houses it in the developing countries."[85] What, then, have been the experiences of our Brazilian urban factory worker with respect to these factors?

I asked Zé Maria if he preferred working in a large industrial plant to working for a smaller company. He retorted, "The large one—without doubt!" Why? "Because in the large plant—well, people have better opportunities—a better chance to move up, y'know? But in the smaller company, the *patrão* is always peering over your shoulders." Zé Maria feels that when the boss is always breathing down the worker's neck, the worker losses the opportunity of making a good impression on him. "Suppose," he says, "the worker is not feeling so well one day. Well, he has to keep

---

[83] *Ibid.*, p. 515.
[84] Inkeles, "Participant Citizenship," p. 1140.
[85] *Ibid.*, p. 1141.

moving regardless because the *patrão* is always standing right there." But in the large industrial plant, "the *patrões* allow a certain freedom for the workers to get their jobs done. One day he works very hard, the next day he takes it a little easier." In this way, according to Zé Maria, "the worker, if he isn't feeling so well —he doesn't have to work as hard as he does on the days he's feeling good. And, on the days he is feeling strong he works extra hard, y'know?—balancing things off and satisfying the goals of the factory. But with small firms you can't do this—and I have already worked for a small firm—it is really terrible—horrible!"

Zé Maria prefers working in the large factory because it provides an opportunity to hide, in a sense, from the rigors of production. In the large plant Zé Maria finds a certain freedom—a freedom to escape the watchful eyes of the boss whose mind always centers on matters of efficiency and productivity, regardless of the worker's state of health or mood. It should be emphasized, however, that Zé Maria is not out to take advantage of the impersonality and size of the large industrial plant. He has little patience with gold-brickers and loafers. Rather, Zé Maria finds room to maneuver in the large plant. And this maneuverability provides him with the opportunity to balance off a just work output for his employer with the dictates of his own state of health and his own feelings. Perhaps he has the opportunity of getting that "something else" that Gillin believes is so necessary.

Zé Maria's work experiences in the factory have *not* demonstrated to him that "authority and rewards are intimately geared to a more or less objective hierarchy of technical skill which, in turn, rests on formal education." Zé Maria has seen foreigners brought in and placed in management positions over the more experienced Brazilian. Or he has seen the experienced Brazilian removed with the foreigner inserted in his place. As Zé Maria so frequently says when this topic rises, "I'm damn sick of seeing this, y'know?" In a country like Brazil, where so much heavy industry is foreign-controlled and operated,[86] the experiences of Zé Maria can

---

[86] See the discussion of foreign investment in Brazil in Teotonio dos Santos, "Foreign Investment and the Large Enterprise in Latin America: The Brazilian Case," in Petras and Zeitlin, eds., *Latin America*, pp. 431–453.

undoubtedly be multiplied over and over again. Even where industries are owned and operated by Brazilians, the phenomenon of family influence in job placement is by no means absent. And it is not always related to skill, training, or capacity!

While Zé Maria has worked hard all his life, he still seems to feel a need for that "something else" that Gillin writes about. In his younger days, *Carnaval* provided an outlet for him:

> Ah! *Carnaval!* During *Carnaval*—it was the only time I refused to work in my entire life—that is, when I was single. Look! I worked hard the whole year long—overtime, too. I worked to excess, y'know?—whenever I was needed. But on the four days of *Carnaval*, I refused to work. It used to begin on Sunday and, then Monday and Tuesday—one rested up on Wednesday and returned to work on Thursday. On the days of *Carnaval* I refused to work. I would go to the *clubes*, y'know?—the different ones during *Carnaval*, y'know?—leave the "dead" ones and seek out the ones with the most "life"—leave one, go to another.

And this is one thing that Zé Maria dislikes about his job in the factory—the fact that he does not have enough time off to enjoy properly such events as *Carnaval*. He looks forward to his "retirement," but never wants to stop working entirely. "I would like to do something less arduous, y'know?—but I like to work and I hope to do so as long as I am able."

Shortly, we will look at the implication of Zé Maria's factory work experiences, as they effect his more specifically political outlooks and actions. For the present, we can conclude that the experiences of Zé Maria in the factory job indicate something other than that suggested by Inkeles. The experiences seem only to have confirmed in Zé Maria the nature of things he has observed in the general urban milieu of Belo Horizonte—that "pull" and family connections are the surest means of advancement; that hard work and efficiency have their place, but one must have room to maneuver; finally, one must also be able to transcend the work-a-day world—finding relief in the abandonment of such fiestas as *Carnaval* and the excitement of such pastimes as soccer. Undoubtedly, however, his job in the factory has provided Zé Maria with some sense of mastery over the environment and his life. He strongly disagrees that "planning only makes a person unhappy, since your plans hardly ever work out anyway," and he disagrees also that "when a man is born, the success he is going to have is already in the stars, so he might as well accept it and not fight against it."[87]

On the Nature of Man's Relationship with His Inner-Self: The Struggle against an "Impoverished Self"[88]

Two widely discussed aspects of the Latin American cultural tradition may be summed up in two words—*dignidad* and *machismo*. The *macho*, writes Gillin, represents "a highly valued ideal in Latin American culture."[89] He continues:

> In a sense it corresponds to an ideal type of male society personality. Yet, regardless of social position, the *macho* is admired. The cultural concept involves sexual prowess, action orientation (including verbal action), and various other components. But, a "real *macho*" is one who is sure of himself, cognizant of his own inner worth, and willing to bet everything on such self-confidence. There can be no question about his *dignidad*.[90]

In *Five Families*, Oscar Lewis wrote that "*machismo* is much weaker in rural areas than in the cities and weaker among the lower classes than in the middle and upper classes."[91] Perhaps the differential extent of *machismo* on distinct social levels and in different settings is a function of the nature of "white-collar work," as opposed to working with the soil or working with one's hands. The lower-class wage earner and the rural peasant are under less strain to "prove their masculinity" than the middle- or upper-class member who engages in paperwork, conferences, "desk action," and other "less manly" occupations. At any rate, Zé Maria works with his hands. Accordingly, we may expect less emphasis on *machismo* in his case.

Moreover, with respect to Brazil, Santos argues that "there is

---

[87] These two items are from a "control over future and environment scale" that James Scott used in his study of Malaysian bureaucrats, *Political Ideology in Malaysia*, pp. 285–286.
[88] The term "impoverished self" is from Lane, *Political Ideology*, pp. 409–412.
[89] Gillin, "Ethos Components," p. 509.
[90] *Ibid.*
[91] Oscar Lewis, *Five Families* (N.Y., 1962), p. 17.

not the degree of *machismo* that Diaz-Guerrero describes as so characteristic of Mexican males."[92] In a similar vein, Wagley, writing "as if he were a Brazilian," says "We are appalled by the seriousness with which most Spanish-Americans view themselves. They have a sense of 'face' and dignity that works against them. We take life more lightly. We say that you can live in Brazil only with a sense of humor."[93]

While Zé Maria is a proud individual and he does share to some extent in the cultural pattern of *machismo*, he is not "unduly" proud, given the general cultural milieu, nor does he represent the case of an ideal-type *macho*. But what, after all, is "undue pride"? Problems of "abnormal pride" arise out of problems of "abnormal insecurities," which, in turn, arise out of problems of "abnormal scarcities" and "abnormal distributions" of the things people desire. Zé Maria's concern for self-esteem and self-acceptance represent a struggle to overcome an "impoverished self" amidst widespread material impoverishment. An environment of scarcity and a heated competition for survival are bound to produce anxieties and insecurities that may manifest themselves in an "exaggerated" desire for affection in order to bolster sagging estimates of the self.

Zé Maria's job in the factory has helped him in his internal struggles by allowing him to acquire a few worldly possessions, and by providing him with steady work at a salary above those who live about him. But there is nothing special about the factory job per se that could not be provided in another work context offering the worker steady employment along with a reasonable day's pay for a day's work.

Basic Value Orientations and Their Political Consequences: The Case of Zé Maria

What, then, are the political consequences of Zé Maria's basic value orientations? While this topic cannot be treated exhaustively in this essay, we can comment on its most suggestive implications.

---

[92] Santos, "A Psychologist Reflects," p. 244.
[93] Wagley, *Introduction to Brazil*, p. 294.

Let us look first at Zé Maria's generally low estimate of human nature. We may reasonably expect his generally distrustful outlook to apply in the case of politicians. Whether or not Zé Maria is justified in his general distrust of Brazilian politicians is another question, but we can expect him to view them as self-seeking and, perhaps, vindictive.

Who or what is responsible for the problems facing Brazil today? "I think blame must fall on these people who run for office, y'know? —who seek to lead the country. And each one only wants to take his own little piece, y'know? They don't look at matters honestly—and, so, the common people—even those who are well-off—must suffer the consequences. Accordingly, even I have suffered y'know? [laughs sadly or, perhaps, worriedly]." Zé Maria is not at all out of step with his fellow citizens of Belo Horizonte. Some 80 percent more or less agree that "it is not worth it to trust politicians because in general they are not interested in our problems."[94] And that percentage rises to 90 percent among unskilled and semiskilled workers like Zé Maria![95]

The distrust carries over to an abstraction like "government," because Zé Maria tends to view it in personalistic terms. I posed this question: When you think about "government"—the word, "government"—what do you think about? After a short pause, he answered: "I think about—when I hear the word 'government,' I think about leadership—I think about a *person* who is leading the country, y'know?—a *person* who is governing. When things go wrong, he comes along and takes control of the situation—it really doesn't matter if the situation is good or bad."

Since one can only confide in and trust close personal friends, along with ritual and real kin, one can trust only that politician for whom he feels some personalistic attachment. That is why Zé Maria, although a strong supporter of the PTB before 1964, says he always "voted for the candidate, not the party." He argues: "I voted for candidates running on other party tickets, too—because, if one likes a certain candidate, for example, and he happens to belong to another party, well, one votes for the man, y'know?"

[94] Barbosa Study.
[95] *Ibid.*

Once again, Zé Maria is in accord with a great majority (about 80 percent) of the citizens of Belo Horizonte.[96] If, then, one can find a politician for whom he feels some personal attachment, the trust usually reserved for intimate friends and relations is generalized to that political figure. I asked Zé Maria if there was any politician, living or dead, that he especially liked. He replied firmly, "Yes!" It was the man Zé Maria helped to campaign for in the local elections:

> I considered him just like a great friend. . . . He is a very charitable man—and honest, too. He took me to City Hall with him several times. On one occasion he stopped the car right in the middle of the street—to look after an old lady who had keeled over by the curb. He put her in the car and brought her to the hospital and had them make a space for her. And we were almost at City Hall when it happened—he forgot about our appointment! And, so, I admire him a lot for the way he conducts himself, y'know? A great guy!

Earlier in this paper we noted that personalistic attachments can form with respect to national political figures as well. For reasons of local pride and loyalty, Zé Maria was a "real fan" of Juscelino Kubitschek. Similarly, if one can identify with a national political personage, a strong attachment and trust can adhere. I wondered if Zé Maria would feel comfortable or at ease with someone like the late Getúlio Vargas. "Getúlio? Ah! I think so. I think I even would have enjoyed chatting with him—but, of course, this is no longer possible, right?" Could Zé Maria feel at ease "chatting" with Castelo Branco, the rather austere, cold, and aloof general who became the first president of the post-1964 era in Brazil? He could not even imagine the possibility! "Castelo Branco? No.— because Castelo Branco was—Castelo Branco was an army man. The chances of my talking with him were not very likely, y'know? But Getúlio was different. Everytime he came here to Belo Horizonte I was right there to see him. I liked him a lot. I don't know why, but I had a special liking for him. I thought he governed well. He was a good man." While Castelo Branco avoided contact with the people, Getúlio Vargas always "mixed right in":

[96] *Ibid.*

I saw Getúlio conversing with the people. He wasn't too proud to speak with any kind of person—even the "lowliest." He appeared honored talking with even the poorest of men—and, it seems he was a very humble man, y'know?—a man who was both humble and intelligent. I don't know if it is just because I am a simple man myself that I liked him—because he spoke just as nicely to the rich as he did to the poor. And, I don't know if it was just a political 'technique,' y'know? I mean, I was there when he was speaking with a man who was all crippled up—first, he put his hand on the man's head, then he gave him an *abraço*. Wherever he went he behaved this way, y'know? I had tremendous *simpatia* for him.

If, then, you can find a politician whom you can really trust, let him be a leader who can "take charge" and hold everything in check in what is generally regarded to be a jungle world. At least, that is the way Zé Maria feels. After Vargas was ousted by the military in 1945 following fifteen years of rule, General Dutra was elected to the presidency. Zé Maria saw a certain strength in Dutra that appealed to him: "Under Dutra all was calm. Prices didn't rise. It was a balanced situation, y'know? And he controlled the country very well during the same time he was our leader. I liked his government a lot. It was a serene period. I liked him a lot—and he was a general, too." Even though Zé Maria is highly critical of the Costa e Silva regime, which followed the Castelo Branco administration to power in 1967, he admired the courage, conviction, and strength of the late Costa e Silva. While he vigorously attacked the regime for its lack of attention to the problems and needs of the working class, Zé Maria admired the *man*. He displayed his admiration in response to the question: what do you consider to be the qualities of an ideal politician? "What do I like in a politician? What I like in a politician is—honesty and a strong pulse. I like a politician who doesn't go back on his word—like this—this Costa e Silva. He says something and you better believe him. He isn't afraid of his enemies, y'know? Such is my ideal politician...."

Zé Maria has little patience and sympathy for what he views as "weakness" in a person, especially if it concerns a leading national political figure. He views Jânio Quadros's resignation from the presidency in 1961 as a sign of weakness and vacillation: "I don't know much about what happened to Jânio Quadros—but I think he acted like a coward. He should not have left his position like he did, y'know? He should have taken a firm grasp on matters. That's why the people elected him!"

And, if one has a strong, paternalistic, and personable leader, it is a short step to the desire for the elimination of elections altogether. As Zé Maria argues: "If you have an amiable and clearheaded leader—a good President—good for the whole nation—a good leader who can control things as they ought to be controlled, well, I think even if he is not elected he ought to govern the country." The argument extends to the realm of party politics as well. Why have competing parties if you can have just one that can do a good job and "keep things under control"? Better still, no parties at all— it is less expensive: "I think there shouldn't be any political parties in Brazil. What Brazil really needs is—a dictatorship. Just one man to rule. It would be best. At least, that's my impression. And there would be much less expense. Less expense and one head to do the thinking and ruling, y'know? Because too many people giving orders just doesn't work out well at all."

Here is an attitude we can trace directly to Zé Maria's work experience in the factory. Inkeles writes: "The factory is organized hierarchically, and authority in it runs strictly along formal lines. Decisions are made not on the basis of consultation and vote, but on grounds of technical efficiency and position in the power hierarchy."[97] Therefore, one might expect the factory "to reinforce traditional habits and expectations in dealing with authority, rather than to stimulate a man to play a more modern citizenship role."[98] But this need not be the case. Rather, as Inkeles argues, the experience may be viewed as "an important way of schooling men in the acceptance of a central political authority not resting solely on the diffuse basis of kinship."[99] But at times, even in large industrial plants, authority and power "lines" may get "crossed," and

[97] Inkeles, "Participant Citizenship," p. 1139.
[98] *Ibid.*
[99] *Ibid.*

the message that comes through to Zé Maria loud and clear is this: too many cooks spoil the broth; too many chiefs and not enough Indians. When I asked Zé Maria if he ever "flies off the handle," he said, "from time to time." I wondered if he could describe what took place the last time he lost control of himself:

> This is what happened: my boss ordered me to do something. Then the engineer came along and ordered me to stop what I was doing and do something else. Well, then the big boss came along and ordered me to stop what I was doing and do something else. Well, that's when I really got burned up. I said: "Who the hell is the boss in this fuck'n place anyway!?" "Is it you or Fulano or Sicrano?" I thought it was a rotten situation. Well, he got all nervous and angry with me—and I was angry with him, too. It ended up with him agreeing that I had reason to be mad. The three [bosses] were wrong because each one gave me an order—one order from here, one order from there, y'know?—and each one "super-urgent"! Each had to be done immediately! Well, that was the last time I lost my patience.

"Democratic formalism" best describes the political world of Zé Maria and, perhaps, Brazilians in general. Formalism signifies a superficiality of political beliefs, and democratic formalism occurs when a set of political institutions and ideas (separation of powers, popular sovereignty, division of powers, and so on) are imported and "transplanted" in a society whose underlying cultural heritage and everyday life experiences belie its chances of survival. While Zé Maria does give lip-service to western liberal-democratic forms and processes, his belief in them does not run deep. James Rowe has written about democratic formalism in Brazil.[100] Rowe cites Fred Riggs's illustration of formalism in which he "used the apt simile of a city map of impressive appearance and detail—the only trouble being that the streets it depicted either turned out not to be there or to run in a different way."[101] As Rowe writes, the stopping of the capitol clocks in 1967 to insure completion of the

---

[100] James W. Rowe, "Brazil Stops the Clock: 'Democratic Formalism' before 1964 and in the Elections of 1966," *American Universities Field Staff Reports Service*, East Coast South American Series, 13:1 (Brazil), p. 1.

[101] *Ibid.*, p. 14.

final reading of the new constitution before the midnight deadline "was eloquently symbolic of the formalism that so pervades Brazilian political practice—nurtured by the liberal *bacharéis* of the Old Republic (1889–1930), prominent in the Constitution of 1846 and the political institutions of the last twenty years, and never more conspicuous than in the feverish political activity of the past few months (July, 1966, to March, 1967)."[102] In the post-"revolutionary" period there was "a supreme effort by the governing elite of generals and technocrats to alter the Brazilian political model in a drastic and durable fashion, clothing the changes nonetheless in an elaborate juristic formalism."[103] While democratic formalism is by no means absent in the United States where clocks in state legislative chambers are stopped at the end of a fiscal year, it is far more widespread in Brazil.

Here is how democratic formalism filters down to the urban factory worker in Brazil. I asked Zé Maria what the word "democracy" meant to him. "The word 'democracy' means that everything is okay . . . when everything goes wrong you don't have democracy. . . . Democracy indicates everything that is good." Zé Maria is thinking primarily in economic terms when he defines democracy as "everything that is good." I asked him how he would classify Brazil in terms of democracy. "From the point of view of work—concerning earning more money, no—we don't have a democracy. During the time of Juscelino, it seems that more money flowed—more work, too. It was easier to find a job—you could earn a living more easily. Today it is very hard to find a job, y'know? It is harder to earn a living today."

That is why Zé Maria favors "a good leader who can control things as they ought to be . . . even if he is not elected." I think he is trying to say something similar to the sentiments Alexander Pope expressed in his *Essay on Criticism*: "fools admire, but men of sense approve." One can admire the democratic forms, but he must approve of that which works—if he is a man of good sense. Zé Maria approves of elections. He even thinks they are important—when not pressed to evaluate them under special circumstances that in-

[102] *Ibid.*, p. 1.
[103] *Ibid.*, pp. 1–2.

volve his own economic welfare. "Elections are good—because the majority of the people can choose their candidate, y'know?—the one he thinks ought to be ruler of the country." And Zé Maria reflects the outlook and feelings of those about him. Seventy-one percent of his fellow-*mineiros* living in Belo Horizonte regard a "government elected by the people" as the best kind to solve Brazilian problems; even though about half of them feel that "Brazil needs a government capable of undertaking deep changes in the situation of the country"; and in spite of the fact that 64 percent believe "that it is all the same for your *personal* economic situation regardless of the candidate who wins." [104]

James Scott, writing about Malaysian bureaucrats, argues that "it would be difficult to overstate the importance of a man's estimate of human nature in influencing the construction of his political ideology. Seeing human nature as good, bad, or varied has an effect on how one views the motives of others, whether people are given the benefit of the doubt or whether skepticism prevails, and whether co-operation with others for common ends is considered possible." [105] Robert Scott, writing about Mexican political culture, makes a similar point.[106] It is plausible enough to assume that Zé Maria's job in the factory and his association with labor unions has had some impact on him in this sense. He believes there is strength in unified action, and this tends to undermine his basically pessimistic view of mankind. While the factory experiences may have opened the door to a greater sense of mutual trust, pressures against collective action felt under the political regime in Brazil have quickly slammed it shut once more. Zé Maria now prefers "to stay neutral" concerning matters involving organized political activity. For Zé Maria, the "ideal union leader" is one who "works for his class—just for the workers and no other class," but, as he adds sadly, "not one approximates this ideal today because you can't—the government doesn't allow unions to function freely." He reminisces:

[104] Barbosa Study.
[105] Scott, *Political Ideology in Malaysia*, p. 61.
[106] Robert E. Scott, "Mexico: The Established Revolution," in Lucian W. Pye and Sidney Verba, eds., *Political Culture and Political Development* (Princeton, N.J., 1965), *passim*.

"I don't know why, either. They used to be able to function freely and they had a lot of support—today they are worthless."

Combine a skeptical view of human nature with a belief in a natural social order involving a hierarchy of "superiors" and "inferiors," and you find the need for strong leaders even more pressing. How else can the social order be maintained, in terms of relative rankings, in the face of self-seeking individuals and groups taking advantage of one another in order to move up the hierarchy? How can Zé Maria protect what little he has, which he has struggled hard to acquire? How, in the face of a swelling mass of illiterate and unemployed Brazilians who might seek to topple the existing order? Although he would like to see the existing social order maintained, at least in relative terms, he would like to see the level of living for all Brazilians raised as well. I asked Zé Maria what kinds of things an "ideal politician" would do:

> First thing he must do is be honest. Second,—second, look after everything that the country needs: schools, day nurseries for abandoned children, and—he ought to look after the rural people—this is very important—the government ought to look into the situation of those who live and work in the interior and who don't have anything at all going for them, y'know? And end the inflation in the country. And look after the needs of the worker. Look after the needs of the rich, the poor, and those in the middle—balance all these things—this system of life, y'know?—not just representing any one group—not just the rich, not just the poor, not just those in the middle. Try to control the situation, y'know?—without destroying one or the other class. . . . Try to control it. That is what is needed.

Once again, we find another reason why Zé Maria has such fond memories of Getúlio Vargas:

> I think this constant changing of government is responsible for our situation, y'know?—take out one, put in another; cancel the mandate of first one, then another. It keeps things in a constant state of disorder, y'know? And, so, it upsets the entire country! The poor are suffering, and so are the rich—suffering from this endless changing of governments. . . . When Getúlio Vargas was our Presi-

dent—for some fifteen years—it seems that life was much better, much calmer, more balanced, y'know? This business of canceling mandates, canceling mandates—it just makes a mess of things. But I think it will continue for a long time to come [laughs sadly].

Zé Maria's belief in a natural social hierarchy is built on a base sufficiently high for all to share in at least some basic minimum of the things people desire. In sum, hold the existing hierarchy intact, but give it a general uplifting. This is not very different from the welfare state philosophy, as it combines with capitalism, that one finds in the United States. It may be a function of an essentially capitalist economic system compounded in the case of Brazil with the scarcities of a "constant-pie world,"[107] where the game played for the goods and services which society can offer is, relatively speaking, a zero-sum game. What one gets, one must take from the other —there is just so much to go around.

Concerning the fifteen "common men" of Eastport, Lane writes: "It is easier to accept differences one calls 'just' than those that appear 'unjust'; there are the very substantial self-congratulatory satisfactions of comparison with those lower on the scale. Thus the theme of 'just desserts' applies to one's own group, those higher, and those lower."[108] Zé Maria, too, feels that people get pretty much what they deserve. I asked him how he would feel if everyone in Brazil received the same salary, regardless of the nature of his work. "What would I think?—why, I would think it was all wrong—very wrong! Every person has his niche, y'know? There must be some means for differentiating—because if everyone received the same salary, those with greater capacities would not want to work—naturally." Zé Maria does not agree "that the government ought to make sure that everyone has a good standard of living"; he is much opposed to the idea that "every person should have a good house, even if the government has to build it for him"; he strongly agrees, however, that "the government should give a person work if he cannot find another job."[109] Zé Maria believes that "there will always be

---

[107] James Scott explores the notion of a "constant-pie" world and "constant-pie" thinking in his study of political ideology in the Malaysian context, *Political Ideology in Malaysia*, Chap. 6.

[108] Lane, *Political Ideology*, p. 68.

[109] These three items are from the "economic equality scale" that James Scott

poverty, so people might as well get used to the fact" and, in general, he feels that the poverty stricken "deserve their status." I asked him what he thought the cause of poverty was, and he responded:

> There are diverse factors causing poverty, y'know? I think the main cause of poverty—well, one factor is, let's say, when a person gets married and he is irresponsible. That's how it starts, y'know? —the cause of poverty. Because he only wants to—well, he doesn't want to take care of things with responsibility: he doesn't work, he doesn't educate his kids, and he raises his family in this manner, y'know?—and each day he becomes a little poorer. . . . And, so, I believe one of the causes is this lack of responsibility on the part of the man of the house.

But sometimes poverty can befall a family under circumstances that are not entirely within its control. Zé Maria recognizes this, too. Sickness and luck can play important roles as well:

> Another cause is this. A man, for example, gets married and takes sick, y'know? He becomes incapacitated. He *can't* work. And, well, poverty comes to him, too. And another factor is luck, y'know? Because there are many people whose stars never seem to shine at all. They want to do right, but everything they do seems to go wrong, y'know? It's a question of good fortune.

If, however, poverty is caused mainly by factors residing within the individual, especially in his "sense of responsibility," what can the government do to eliminate poverty? "The government? Eradicate poverty? Why,—in order to do this, I think the government would have a big job on its hands, y'know? . . . It would have to seek out those who don't want to work and look after their families and punish them, y'know?—and try to find jobs for those who want to work but can't find a job." I asked Zé Maria how poverty might be handled in an "ideal world." He answered:

> The government ought to take care of those who *can't* work: have hospitals for treatment of people that are sick. Now, when a person has recovered and is able to work again, well, put him to work. Another thing I would be in favor of—that the government

---

adapted from McClosky's work and used in his own study, *Political Ideology in Malaysia*, p. 209.

ought to do—is take these petty thieves, these good-for-nothings, and kill them all—take them to an electric chair like the one that they use in the United States, y'know? Eliminate these good-for-nothing people . . . because there are people in the world who only exist to do evil.

Because of his low estimate of human nature in general and his belief in a natural social order involving superiors and inferiors, Zé Maria has a fear of too much freedom. He prefers too little freedom to too much liberty, lest the balance be upset. "Give people complete freedom and everything will go wrong," he says, "what is needed is liberty in moderation—freedom without excess." He fears the prospect of illiterate Brazilians voting in important elections; so do 63 percent of his fellow citizens of Belo Horizonte.[110] "The ignorant should not be allowed to vote in important elections, because they don't know what they are doing. They are easily influenced." Zé Maria is not completely in step with a majority of his fellow semiskilled and unskilled workers, however, since 52 percent of them believe that illiterates should be allowed to vote in all elections.[111] Could this be the impact of his job in the factory, which has enabled him to move up a notch or two above the average wage earner in Belo Horizonte?

For Zé Maria, the "ideal citizen" is "one who obeys the laws laid down by the President of the Republic—one who is honest and a hard worker." "What else," he asks, "need a good citizen do?" Nevertheless, I believe I detect in Zé Maria a "secret" desire to break the "chains" that bind him. Perhaps his frequent dream-walking episodes, topped off by his tearing open the metal frame on his door and breaking through the glass, are indications of his subconscious at work. When I read Rousseau's famous dictum to Zé Maria, "man is born free, and everywhere he is in chains," he pondered the statement and then reacted:

> I think—the only thing this means is that, let's see—man is born free and everywhere he is in chains—I think—I get the idea this is what he means: a person is born free, right? Well, he grows up, gets married, and has a family. So, from this point of view, if he is a

[110] Barbosa Study.
[111] *Ibid.*

man who loves his family and is responsible, well—he is enchained, y'know? And this man, well—I think he is enchained for the rest of his life. After a person acquires a family, and if he is a responsible person,—well, he is enchained. He cannot do whatever he wants to do. Sometimes he may want to do something, but he can't. This is what I mean when I say he is enchained.

It is not only with respect to domestic affairs that Zé Maria sees the chains on men:

There are many other ways man is enchained from this point of view, y'know? At times one might like to do something at the place he works, but—well, he is afraid to do it and lose his job! So, he doesn't do it because he is enchained. He is afraid—afraid his *patrão* won't like it and afraid he'll send him on his way. So, this worker is enchained—he wants to do something, but he is afraid to try. And so forth, y'know?

If it is true that Zé Maria harbors a subconscious desire to "break the chains that bind him," how must he feel about all the other people who may not have the same degree of self-control that Zé Maria feels he has? Firm leadership that can keep men in their "chains" is a welcome relief from this perspective, as an alternative to social chaos and unleashed selfishness on the part of what is viewed as a generally untrustworthy populace.

John Santos has written that "the realities of Brazil certainly do not encourage confidence. They seem more likely to inspire a sense of helplessness. For the Brazilian, it becomes a necessary mode of adaptation to play the game, to accept the frustration and ambiguity of the system and hope for the best."[112] Santos goes on to discuss the famous *jeito* as the Brazilian means of coping with the realities of life: "The *jeito* and the emphasis upon skills in the ways of life and the intricacies of the system may thus be explained as a carry-over from adaptation patterns developed in the past to cope with the physical environment."[113] The *jeito* is the Brazilian solution to democratic formalism and the underlying political reality. Somehow, one can always find a way. The most important aspect of the

[112] Santos, "A Psychologist Reflects," p. 235.
[113] *Ibid.*, pp. 235–236.

jeito, according to Santos, "is the subtle by-passing of the system through the mechanism of mere 'formal' satisfaction of rules and regulations."[114] Charles Wagley feels that the Brazilian immigrant, Peter Kelleman, "hit the right note" in his bestselling book, *Brasil para principiantes (Brazil for Beginners)*, that "pokes fun, which is not always gentle, at Brazil and Brazilians."[115] Wagley relates one of Kelleman's stories that "begins when the Brazilian consul in Paris recommends that he [a prospective immigrant] declare himself as an agronomist rather than a physician (which he is) because the quota for agronomists is higher. He protests and is afraid, but then he understands."[116] In perfect harmony with the *jeito* is Zé Maria's belief that "there is nothing wrong with getting around the law if you do not actually break it."[117]

Santos, a psychologist, writes that foreigners "are almost inevitably amazed and confused by the number and complexities of rituals that must be fulfilled before even relatively simple things can be accomplished."[118] He argues, however, that "there are . . . undeniable limits to the Brazilian's great tolerance for frustration" and suggests that "a great deal of the frustration is discharged in such behavior as aggressive driving and the mass emotional orgies of *Carnaval* and the football games."[119] Such are the consequences of a political superstructure that has been imposed on a set of basic value orientations that run in different directions. While the *jeito*, *Carnaval*, soccer, and aggressive driving may provide a means for Brazilians to transcend "alien" political forms and processes, they also are supportive of a kind of "amoral familism" that is not unlike that encountered by Banfield among Italian peasants.[120] "Maximize the material, short-run advantage of the nuclear family; assume that all others will do likewise"—this is the basic principle that seems to

---

114 *Ibid.*, p. 236.
115 Wagley, "Introduction to Brazil," p. 294.
116 *Ibid.*
117 This item is from the democratic "rule of the game scale" that James Scott adapted from the work of Herbert McClosky and used in his study, *Political Ideology in Malaysia*, p. 288.
118 Santos, "A Psychologist Reflects," p. 236.
119 *Ibid.*
120 Edward C. Banfield, *The Moral Basis of a Backward Society* (Glencoe, Ill., 1958), p. 85; James C. Scott discusses "amoral familism" at length in his study of political values and beliefs, *Political Ideology in Malaysia*, pp. 48–50.

underlie interpersonal relations among the Montegranesi.[121] Recall here that almost all, if not all, of Zé Maria's political activities involved a concern for his family's health and safety—trying to get sewers installed and trying to have street lamps erected, for example. "The Brazilian," Santos writes, "realizes that he cannot solve all of the problems, so he doesn't expend any appreciable amount of energy trying to do so. He accepts the reality of the situation as he sees it and goes about taking care of himself as best he can, while he overlooks, de-emphasizes or forgets the problems of others."[122]

In the case of Zé Maria, it is an emphasis almost, but not entirely, on the present. One must provide for and protect the immediate needs of his own family; if he does not, who will? So, the *jeito* provides Zé Maria, and other Brazilians, with a mechanism for finding his way through the political maze; *Carnaval*, soccer, and other festive occasions provide the "something else" necessary to escape the realities of Brazilian life and offer relief to the conscience. It is not that Zé Maria is callous about the fate of his fellow man. After all, "God is a Brazilian" and he will see to it that *all* his children are taken care of.[123] What is more, "at night, God corrects the errors that Brazilians make during the day."[124] In other words, while Zé Maria takes care of himself and his family, he can be consoled that God will take care of the others; "Believe in the Virgin and run."[125] About his family, Zé Maria worries "if everything is okay; enough food, clothes, and so forth"; about those "down on their luck," he sympathizes: "but what can I do? I think each one has to follow his own lucky star. . . . But if I could free everyone from poverty, I would do it tomorrow—but, what can I do?"

Conclusion

Its conclusion, unlike the rest of this essay, is short. The study offers ample evidence that Zé Maria is a "modern" political individual, according to the five criteria uncovered by Alex Inkeles in his sur-

---

[121] *Ibid.*
[122] Santos, "A Psychologist Reflects," p. 237.
[123] *Ibid.*
[124] Wagley, "Introduction to Brazil," p. 295.
[125] *Ibid.*, p. 289.

vey of six developing nations. Indeed, one might argue that, on the basis of the qualitative evidence presented above, Zé Maria appears to be "more modern" than one might have imagined, considering solely the five survey items that coalesce in Inkeles's syndrome for individual political modernity. The traits Inkeles presents as descriptive of individual modernity are so broad and free of value content, however, that they are not very helpful unless analyzed carefully within a given cultural, economic, and regime context. Could we have deduced the kind of political world Zé Maria inhabits, as described in the preceding section, from the simple knowledge that he meets Inkeles's "test" for political modernity? Probably not. Perhaps, one may argue, Zé Maria is not "representative" of urban factory workers in Brazil, or other "modern" political individuals in that country. With Lane, I can only say: "In this work of mixed ideas and illustrative evidence, I can suggest, but, alas, I cannot prove."[126]

Like the "farmer who moves to the city or the immigrant who arrives in a new country," Zé Maria's work experience in the factory "does not immediately change the whole complex of beliefs and values associated with his past way of life."[127] As a matter of fact, we have seen over and over again in the preceding pages that the factory job seems only to reinforce certain of Zé Maria's more "traditional" central beliefs and values. Factory work in a relatively affluent and industrialized society like the United States may be perfectly compatible with the development and maintenance of a "democratic spirit," as Lane found to be the case among the "common men" of Eastport. Place the factory in a society characterized by scarcity and widespread impoverishment which nourishes an authoritarian cultural heritage, however, and one finds a rather specialized impact that may act to dampen the democratic spirit altogether. And certainly one cannot overlook the influence, demands, and constraints of the present political regime in Brazil which operate on the outlook and behavior of urban factory workers, such as Zé Maria.

Of course, Inkeles does not claim that his syndrome is peculiar to

[126] Lane, *Political Ideology*, p. 4.
[127] James Scott, *Political Ideology in Malaysia*, p. 55.

"democratic" political development. On the contrary, he argues, it is just as appropriate to the development of modern authoritarian individuals and systems.[128] That is precisely why the present analysis was undertaken—to explore and determine what the "modern" political individual looks like within the confines and context of his natural habitat, which in the present instance happens to be Brazil. I think these findings regarding Zé Maria are not obvious consequences of our having known that he qualifies as a modern individual in Inkeles's terms.

We find in Brazil a situation where most economic, psychological, cultural, and legitimacy factors are exerting pressures in a common direction—toward a form of politics that may be characterized as misanthropic, personalistic, paternalistic, and authoritarian. The present political regime in Brazil, which is authoritarian or quasi-authoritarian in nature (though formally displayed in a "constitutional"/"liberal-democratic" showcase), is in substantial harmony with the basic value orientations and political outlook of our urban factory worker. As we noted at the outset, however, *mere congruence of structure and culture is not sufficient to bring maximum legitimacy and support to the regime.* We suggested that *policy outputs and outcomes must be reflective of and responsive to the material as well as the emotional needs of the people.* I think enough evidence has been presented to establish that the "missing link" in the legitimacy "chain" lies in the realm of unsatisfactory policy outcomes from the perspective of urban workers like Zé Maria.

If authoritarian political leadership can produce material well-being for Brazilian workers (along with emotional satisfactions), there can be little doubt that legitimacy will attach to the political structures and regime that produces such rewards.[129] Urban workers, such as Zé Maria, do not ask for the world on a silver platter. In this regard, they resemble the men of Eastport, about whom Lane writes: "They are not asking for much—they never do; they do not want to be cocoons in a cradle-to-grave web of security (at least they

---

[128] Inkeles, "Participant Citizenship," p. 1123.

[129] For a discussion of the use of learning theory and dissonance theory in the acquisition of legitimacy by a regime, see Richard Merleman, "Learning and Legitimacy," *American Political Science Review*, 60:3 (September, 1966), pp. 548–561.

do not ask for it). They want relief from worries about what would happen if they got sick. How will we see our children through their education? Will my job be there tomorrow? Is my family protected when I'm away? Could we afford another child?"[130] For men like Zé Maria, a latter-day Getúlio Vargas would fill the bill just fine— even if he happened to wear a general's hat. Zé Maria, I think, would agree once more with the poet, Alexander Pope, who during the early eighteenth century wrote in his *Essay on Man*: "For forms of government let fools contest; What'er is best administer'd is best."

[130] Lane, *Political Ideology*, p. 209.

Racial Adaptation in the Modernization of Cartagena, Colombia

Sidney Kronus and Mauricio Solaún

Introduction

Social change generally leads to political crises and to generation of several types of conflict. In the United States, racial conflict has been closely linked with the urbanization of black Americans.[1] A similar line of thought linking social change to increases in ethnic and racial conflict in developing nations has also been made.[2] Some sources have predicted increases in racial conflict in Latin American societies concomitant to their increased modernization. Although a

---

Portions of the material contained in this paper appeared in a paper published in Spanish, "Dimensiones Estructurales del Conflicto Racial en la Modernización-Urbanización de Cartagena (Colombia)," *Aportes*, No. 24 (1972), pp. 22–43. We wish to thank and acknowledge additional financial support given to this project by the Research Board of the University of Illinois. Madeline Gates and Ann Wendell aided us in preparing this paper and we are grateful for their research assistance. Also we acknowledge the helpful suggestions and criticisms of Robert E. Scott and Norman E. Whitten, Jr.

[1] For evidence on this point, see Ray Stannard Baker, *Following the Color Line: American Negro Citizenship in the Progressive Era* (New York, 1908); Elliot M. Rudwick, *Race Riot in East St. Louis (1917)* (Carbondale, Ill., 1964); The Chicago Commission on Race Relations, *The Negro in Chicago: A Study of Race Relations and a Race Riot* (Chicago, 1922); Alfred McClung Lee, *Race Riot (Detroit, 1943)* (New York, 1943); and Otto Kerner, *et al.*, *Report of the National Advisory Commission on Civil Disorders* (New York, 1968).

[2] See, for instance, Samuel P. Huntington, *Political Order in Changing Societies* (New Haven, Conn., 1968), p. 39.

wealth of literature describes relatively racially homogeneous, small agricultural villages in contemporary Latin America, no major empirical effort investigates the potential for racial conflict in a racially heterogeneous, large Latin American urban area. This situation led us to undertake a racial study of such a complex area, the city of Cartagena, Colombia.

This study will explore the structural factors that account for the absence of overt racial conflict in the city. The presence or absence of escalated racial conflict can and will have an important effect on the success of the Latin American efforts to urbanize and modernize. An understanding of the linkages between social change (modernization-urbanization) and racial conflict in Cartagena will be useful for policymakers in Latin America for future developmental planning. Furthermore, any findings about the nature of Latin American racial patterns, which permit these societies to experience social change without substantial racial conflict, may contribute to the understanding and solution of racial problems in the United States.

In Cartagena the process of urbanization is taking place at a rapid pace. It is a very old and aristocratic city where, although racial discrimination has been evident, there has been an absence of a history of major racial conflict and violence. Overall, we found Cartagena to be a city where a pattern of racial tolerance dominates social relations; yet racial discrimination exists also. Further, contemporary social changes seemingly are not producing high levels of racial conflict in the area, nor do we feel that it is probable that conflict will escalate in the near future.

The purpose of this paper is to determine those racial structural characteristics which have permitted the absence of racial violence amidst discrimination in the history of Cartagena. It should be noted here that Colombian history has been characterized by high levels of political and class violence[3] and minimum levels of overt

[3] For a description of recent patterns of violence, which have resulted in over 100,000 deaths, see Mons. Germán Guzmán Campos, et al., *La Violencia en Colombia* (Bogotá, 1962). For the most comprehensive interpretation of Colombia's twentieth-century political history, see Robert H. Dix, *Colombia: The Political Dimensions of Change* (New Haven, Conn., 1967).

racial conflict. In this sense, the setting is optimal for the study of the determinants of nonviolent racial relations.

Basic Colombian Racial Patterns

As we proceed we will discuss more fully those racial patterns which are significant to our investigation. At this stage it is pertinent to single out, for the benefit of the uninitiated, some key characteristics of Colombian race relations. But first, a note on the relationship between them and Latin American racial patterns. While there are variations in interracial relations among Latin American countries and within national regions,[4] their similarities are sufficient to warrant the conceptualization of a Latin American type of race relations. More precisely, it is feasible to categorize an Iberian American variant of racial relationships, as contrasted to a northwest European type.[5] In doing so, the very similar Spanish and Portuguese racial patterns are distinguished from other European types, including the French, and we are allowed to make some broad generalizations from our data.

Although generally adaptive, Iberian American Negro-white relationships are still discriminatory. Race inhibits the upward movements of individuals within the class structure, and the bulk of the blacks are members of the lower class. In particular, Negroid racial characteristics are deliberately employed by gatekeepers to exclude persons from membership in the national socioeconomic elite.[6] Furthermore, Negroid physical characteristics are widely

[4] See, for instance, van den Berghe's consideration of Brazil's greater racial discrimination over that of Mexico, and about regional differences within Brazil itself, in Pierre L. van den Berghe, *Race and Racism, a Comparative Perspective* (New York, 1967), pp. 37, 74–75.

[5] In this sense, see H. Hoetink, *The Two Variants in Caribbean Race Relations, a Contribution to the Sociology of Segmented Societies* (London, 1967).

[6] The criterion of deliberate exclusion from elite membership on racial grounds is a better indicator of discrimination than the concentration of blacks in the lower classes which characterizes Latin American societies, because, assuming low levels of upward mobility in the society and given the historical fact of slavery, it is feasible to interpret black overrepresentation in the lower classes as a historical class phenomenon, not a deliberate racial discriminatory one. Kottack has made this case for differences in land-ownership in a Brazilian village. See Conrad Phillip Kottack, "Race Relations in a Bahian Fishing Village," *Luso-Brazilian Review*, 4 (1967), pp. 35–52.

considered as "ugly."[7] This aesthetic preference is apparent even among some predominantly Negroid slum settings, where sales of products destined to "lighten" their users is common. Racial discrimination notwithstanding, a crucial characteristic of the Iberian American variant of Negro-white relations is that there is some acceptance of coloreds in the dominant segment.[8] That is, a significant number of persons among the exclusivist national socioeconomic elite are considered by other elite members as not being "pure" white, without such consideration altering the elite status of these colored persons. In short, the awareness of racial "impurity" does not entirely preclude inclusion into the national socioeconomic elite.[9] Reference here is being made to the nonwhite segment that normally predominates in these societies—the miscegenated group. (A high proportion of miscegenated population is another fundamental characteristic of Iberian American race relations.) Of course, in the Iberian American variant, membership in the national socioeconomic elite remains virtually closed to "pure" Negroes, that is, persons with highly conspicuous Negroid characteristics.

These preliminary statements on the nature of white-Negro relationships in Latin America suggest the ambiguity or inconsistency of race relations in the area. In contrast to the United States, in Iberian America persons are not either entirely white or black. In the United States the rule of hypodescent prevails. Briefly stated, this racist descent principle is applied to groups which stand in a subordinate-superordinate relationship to one another, as blacks and whites do in the United States. Under this rule any person who has some lineal ancestor in the subordinate group is categorized as a member of that group. Thus, ambiguity is avoided since any discernible Negroid characteristic in a person, regardless of the preponderance of Caucasoid traits, forces him into the "Negro"

---

[7] See Charles Wagley, ed., *Race and Class in Rural Brazil* (Paris, 1952), p. 153, and Hoetink, *Two Variants*, p. 165.

[8] *Ibid.*, p. 161.

[9] As we shall document, what allows a greater degree of "passing" in these societies is not mainly that the Latin elites do not readily recognize Negroid characteristics, but that Latin Americans are more tolerant of them. For a different interpretation, see *ibid.*, pp. 167–168.

category. Marvin Harris states that "the rule of hypo-descent is, therefore, an invention which we in the United States have made in order to keep our biological facts from intruding into our collective racist fantasies."[10] While the northwest European variant of race relations in the Caribbean recognizes an intermediate racial group—the mulattoes or colored—it is in Latin America where this mixed race group experiences more fluid or less discriminatory boundaries. In Latin America a significant proportion of the dominant segment recognizes its miscegenated background, but at the same time exercises racial discrimination to block access to its ranks of nonwhites.

Historical evidence suggests that a fluid racial situation was already present in Iberian America prior to independence. For example, although discrimination existed during the colonial period, racial boundaries were ill-defined. It is well documented that licenses making persons legally white were purchased during this period.[11] Not only did miscegenated persons penetrate the national elites but several national heroes had nonwhite ancestry. In addition, by the time of independence miscegenation had achieved high levels. For instance, it has been estimated that in 1789, 53.6 percent of the population was miscegenated in an area where four-fifths of the slave population of Colombia lived.[12] While the extent and pace of miscegenation throughout the area can be questioned,[13] if we contrast Iberian and northwest European patterns in the hemisphere, miscegenation was higher in the Iberian-American areas. This early institutionalization of racial patterns suggests the need for an historical investigation of race relations in the area, a task beyond the scope of this essay. Nevertheless, given the persistence of some of these patterns, we will be able to extrapolate some of our

[10] Marvin Harris, *Patterns of Race in the Americas* (New York, 1964), p. 56.
[11] See, for instance, Magnus Mörner, *Race Mixture in the History of Latin America* (Boston, Mass., 1967), p. 45.
[12] See Jaime Jaramillo Uribe, *Ensayos sobre Historia Social Colombiana* (Bogotá, 1968), pp. 10–11.
[13] Some sources consider that miscegenation is less common today than in earlier periods. See, for Brazil, van den Berghe, *Race and Racism*, p. 70. However, others consider that Latin American societies experience a progressive racial homogenization through miscegenation that "whitens" people and lifts the color bar. For instance, see Herbert S. Klein, *Slavery in the Americas, a Comparative Study of Virginia and Cuba* (Chicago, 1967), pp. 254–260.

data on current Colombian racial patterns, to explain the reasons for the historical duality of low racial strife amidst intense political-class conflict.

The Setting

Cartagena is a sprawling metropolis of approximately 300,000 inhabitants located on the Caribbean Sea.[14] Founded in 1533, Cartagena became a very important city in the New World for the Spanish Empire. During the colonial period, the Crown exercised a fundamental role in the growth and welfare of Cartagena. The seventeenth century saw a mercantilist colonial policy on the part of Spain in which Cartagena served as a mandatory port city for one of the two prescribed routes between the metropolis and South America.[15] Early in that century, Cartagena was established as one of the major slave markets in the New World; as such, it was an historic port of entry for blacks into Colombia.[16]

The deterioration in the volume of trading between Spain and her colonies which occurred during the first half of the eighteenth century was not conducive to Cartagena's further development, but the general liberalization of colonial trade under Carlos III and the consolidation of Cartagena during his reign as a major port for the Spanish mercantile armada contributed to the importance of the city until Colombia's independence from Spain in the early nineteenth century.[17] Cartagena's role as a military port—*plaza fuerte*—enabled it to receive the *situado*, a subsidy from other colonial territories, which contributed to its economic welfare. During the eighteenth century, Cartagena was a commercial center whose direct influence spread as far south as Quito.[18]

---

[14] According to the latest census, July 15, 1964, it had 242,085 inhabitants. See Departamento Administrativo Nacional de Estadística, *XIII Censo Nacional de Población* (1964), Resumen General (Bogotá, 1967), p. 30.

[15] Rodolfo Segovia, "Teoría de Cartagena: Por qué se Pierde un Siglo," in Donaldo Bossa Herazo, *Cartagena Independiente: Tradición y Desarrollo* (Bogotá, 1967), p. 21.

[16] Aquiles Escalante, *El Negro en Colombia* (Bogotá, 1964).

[17] Segovia, "Teoría de Cartagena," pp. 23, 24. The major fortifications which still beautify the city date from the reign of Carlos III.

[18] Jorge Juan y Antonio De Ulloa, *Noticias Secretas de América* (Buenos Aires, 1953), pp. 158–178. It is interesting to note that according to this source, although Cartagena was a military port, a large share of its trade consisted of contraband.

After independence Cartagena no longer served as an important port and within a few decades its population abruptly declined. Although there is disagreement among sources as to its size around 1810—estimates oscillate between 50,000 and 20,000[19]—there is consensus that in the 1880s, its population was less than 10,000 inhabitants.[20] While the loss of its colonially determined importance was a prime factor in the decline of the city, the literature speaks of additional factors which contributed to this deterioration.[21] In 1815 the Spaniards, in their attempt to reestablish control over Colombia, successfully laid seige to the city. After 108 days, Cartagena surrendered. The Spanish interim governor estimated the civilian dead at 3,000.[22] The combination of the termination of its military role and the violence accompanying Colombia's struggle for independence from Spain took a heavy toll from Cartagena's elite. Bossa has traced the emigration and death of prominent Cartagenians to these events.[23] This initial depletion of its elite has been interpreted as an important cause for the relative economic stagnation of the city during the nineteenth century.[24]

In 1880, a native Cartagenian, Rafael Nuñez, was elected president of Colombia. As a result, the political power of the Cartagenian elite was enhanced, and the city itself benefited by attention from the central government in the form of public works and industrial subsidies.[25] However, as indicated by Table 1, not until the first decade of this century did its population achieve pre-independence levels. For all practical purposes, during the nineteenth century

---

[19] See, respectively, *Almanach de Gotha pour l'anné, 1810*, p. 9, and Bossa Herazo, *Cartagena Independiente*, p. 88.

[20] See *Almanach de Gotha pour l'anné, 1889*, p. 643, and Segovia, *Teoría de Cartagena*, p. 29.

[21] According to one source, during the years immediately prior to independence, Cartagena depended more on its military than commercial, that is, export-import, services. See Martín Alonzo Pinzón, "Zaguán," in Donaldo Bossa Herazo, *Cartagena independiente*, p. 14. In this sense, its welfare was highly dependent on its continuation as a colony.

[22] See Eduardo Lemaitre, *Antecedentes y Consecuencias del Once de Noviembre de 1811. Testimonios y Documentos Relacionados con la Gloriosa Gesta de la Independencia Absoluta de Cartagena de Indias* (Cartagena, 1961), pp. 141–150.

[23] See Bossa Herazo, *Cartagena Independiente*, pp. 47, 48. According to him, three sons of the still socially prominent Pombo family died of hunger during the siege.

[24] Segovia, "Teoría de Cartagena."

[25] Pinzón, *Zaguán*, pp. 16, 17.

TABLE 1. POPULATION OF CARTAGENA
(Census Years)

Year	Population	Year	Population
1905	9,681	1943	97,680
1912	36,632	1951	128,877
1918	51,382	1964	242,085
1928	92,494	1969	297,173
1938	84,937		

SOURCES: *Anuario Estadístico de Colombia, 1943*, p. 30; *Anuario Estadístico de Colombia, 1953*, p. 18; *XIII Censo Nacional de Población, 1964, Resúmen General*, p. 30; and *Boletín Estadístico de Bolívar, Enero y Febrero, 1969*, p. 1.

Cartagena was a "ghost town." In effect, a prominent Cartagenian industrialist and writer reports that in the 1880s there was such a shortage of people that real-estate owners would search for occupants who would merely maintain their buildings.[26] Notwithstanding the efforts made under Nuñez, strategically located Barranquilla on the Magdalena River supplanted Cartagena as the most important port city of Colombia. Throughout this century, Barranquilla has kept this position.

There is no written history of the recent social changes of Cartagena, but official statistics indicate that it is among the most rapidly urbanizing cities of Colombia.[27] Its industrial growth is also visible. The point that must be stressed here is that Cartagena is a city of *abolengo*, that is, of lineage or strong tradition, which has experienced periods of socioeconomic decline, followed by processes of rapid urbanization. Notwithstanding Cartagena's relative socioeconomic deterioration, the importance of aristocratic orientations in Colombian culture[28] has contributed to the high social status of the city's elite in the national society.[29]

Thus, with a large population of nonwhites, a dynamic social and economic history, and high contemporary growth rates, Cartagena

[26] Daniel Lemaitre, *Flor de Corralitos de Piedra* (Cartagena, 1961), pp. 214–215.

[27] Departamento Administrativo Nacional de Estadística (1964), p. 30. Also, see Table 1.

[28] For the prevalence of these orientations, even when contrasted to other Latin American countries, see the important study of José Gutiérrez, *De la Pseudo-Aristocracia a la Autenticidad* (Bogotá, 1961).

[29] See Dix, *Colombia*, p. 46.

provides an optimal site for the study of the relationships between racial discrimination and conflict in societies experiencing rapid social change. Cartagena was selected also because, given our concern with current racial problems in the United States, we were interested in analyzing a location where blacks, as opposed to Indians, constituted the prevalent subordinate racial group. This seemed particularly important to us because previous racial studies of Latin America indicated substantial differences in the relationship between Negroes and other racial groups as compared to Indians. In contrast to blacks, Latin American Indians are mainly differentiated from the rest of the population on ethnic (language, culture, and patterns of dress) as opposed to racial (visible physical) characteristics.[30] Furthermore, there are key differences in the race relations of *mestizos* and *mulatos* to other racial groups. The former group, the largest in Colombia,[31] originally meant the offspring of Caucasians and Indians; the latter, the offspring of Caucasians and Negroes. Although current racial terminology in Colombia has lost some of its biological connotations and is affected by factors such as class,[32] among the educated, *mestizo* and *mulato* have maintained a meaning close to their origins.[33] That is, a *mestizo* is a person who cannot be considered to be "pure" white and has Indian racial characteristics. *Mulato*, on the other hand, is a person with salient Negroid characteristics but who is not a *negro* (Negro)[34] nor a *blanco* (white). Given our interest in black studies, we then selected

[30] In this sense, see John P. Gillin, "Some Signposts for Policy," in *Social Change in Latin America Today*, Richard N. Adams, et al. (New York, 1960), p. 19. According to Mörner, in Indo-Latin America, the criterion for distinguishing groups is "socio-cultural," whereas in Afro-Latin America it is "physical appearance, the phenotype," that is, racial. See Mörner, *Race Mixture*, p. 136. Thus, the Indo-Iberian variant of "race" relations corresponds to American ethnic patterns.

[31] After 1918, Colombian censuses have avoided any racial or color classification. T. Lynn Smith has made the following racial estimate for Colombia as a whole: whites, 25 percent; Indians, 5 percent; Negroes, 8 percent; *mestizos*, 42 percent; and mulattoes, 20 percent. See T. Lynn Smith, "The Racial Composition of the Population of Colombia," in *Studies of Latin American Societies* (same author) (New York, 1970), pp. 56–83. For a similar estimate, see Ernesto Camacho Leyva, *Quick Colombian Facts* (Bogotá, 1962), p. 174.

[32] In a future publication, we will present detailed data analysis from picture tests to document this point.

[33] *Mestizo* is derived from the popular Latin term *mixticius* or mixed, and *mulato*, from mule, which is a hybrid resulting from crossing a horse and a donkey.

[34] In this paper the term "Negro" is used to mean only the polar racial type.

Cartagena because of its conspicuous *negro* and *mulato* presence.

There were other reasons for the selection of Cartagena. As noted, of the largest Colombian cities with a high percentage of blacks, Cartagena has the most aristocratic tradition. This led us to expect the presence of a dominant group defining itself as white and the existence of patterns of relatively pronounced racial discrimination which, given the high proportion of blacks in Cartagena, would be centered against Negroid persons.[35] Finally, Cartagena was selected because of its relatively high rates of social change. As we have seen, the city has gone from a major port city in the colonial period, to a "ghost" town in the early twentieth century, and up again to metropolitan status in the mid-twentieth century.

This combination of racial discrimination, exacerbated by the alleged dominance of a traditional aristocratic elite, and rapid social change which seemed to characterize Cartagena was particularly appealing to us for another reason. Some investigators have interpreted the absence of racial strife in Latin America as being partly the product of a static traditional equilibrium in which paternalistic, economically noncompetitive, quasi-feudal relationships of dependency among the races are highly institutionalized and accepted. For example, according to Beals, "Brazil's reputation for liberality toward Negroes rests largely on the fact that most of them are in the lowest class."[36] While such consideration seems to be an overstatement, the combination of both aristocratic, *Gemeinschaft*-type of relations and social change seemed to us a fertile ground to explore the dynamics of discriminatory mechanisms and processes for interracial integration. The setting seemed propitious to survey "survivals" of traditional discriminatory patterns, and even to study incipient increases in racial conflict impinging upon a traditional order that was starting to crumble vis-à-vis the economic competition brought about by rapid social change.[37] There was yet another

[35] For Brazil, Wagley had established the relation between aristocratic background and attachments to racial discrimination. Wagley, *Rural Brazil*, p. 153.

[36] Quoted in Hoetink, *Two Variants*, p. 38.

[37] The latter case has been made by Whitten for the Pacific littoral of Northwest Ecuador and Colombia. See Norman E. Whitten, Jr., "Ecología de las Relaciones Raciales al Noroeste del Equador," *América indígena*, vol. 30, no. 2 (1970), 345–358. Also, van den Berghe considers that modernization has brought about increases in racial discrimination in Brazil. See van den Berghe, *Race and Racism*, p. 74. Further,

possibility. The particular nature of "traditional" race relations in the area might have produced some basis for obtaining a durable interracial peace in a society experiencing rapid social change and mobilization, mechanisms that deserve systematic consideration.[38] It was to test these diverse observations and forecasts in a complex urban situtation that Cartagena was selected for study.

The Structure of Class and Race in Cartagena

Crucial to our understanding of the potentialities for racial conflict in Cartagena during the contemporary processes of modernization and urbanization is the extent to which racial characteristics are related to positions in the class structure. By definition, if the class hierarchy of the city corresponds almost perfectly to gradations by color, high levels of discrimination are clearly present, and the potential for racial conflict is very great. If, on the other hand, persons of all colors are randomly distributed along the class structure, we must conclude that race has not inhibited the movement from one position in the class structure to another, evidence of an absence of racial discrimination in the society. Sociologists have defined these two systems as the closed and open models of race relations, respectively. Yet another possibility exists. Societies may be characterized by a nonrandom, racial class distribution but, at the same time, also by the infusion of persons of some color throughout the class struc-

---

Blalock has considered that racial discrimination will increase with future modernization in Brazil. See Hubert M. Blalock, Jr., *Toward a Theory of Minority Group Relations* (New York, 1967), p. 170.

[38] In contrast to the preceding pessimistic interpretations, other sources have stressed a more positive interpretation. Klein, for instance, traces "evolutionary" racial patterns in Cuba to the nature of its slave system. Klein, *Slavery in the Americas, passim*. Of course, it has been argued that the Cuban revolution has eliminated or highly diminished prejudice in the country. However, those adopting the "traditional" interpretation could answer by saying that the Cuban revolution was a broad social, not racial, revolution, in which racial progress is but one consequence. Clearly, the Cuban revolution was more a case of class than racial violence. Also, the power and persistence of traditional race relations has been seen in the United States. Blumer has made the case that once patterns of acute racial segregation are well established, as in the United States, they also tend to survive, even in the presence of rapid socioeconomic change (industrialization). See Herbert Blumer, "Industrialization and Race Relations," in Guy Hunter, ed., *Industrialization and Race Relations* (London, 1965), pp. 220–254.

ture. In this model, as is the case in Cartagena, where persons of some color can be found in every stratum of the class structure but whites and blacks are concentrated respectively in the upper and lower levels of the class pyramid, *race can affect but does not totally inhibit the movement from one position in the class structure to another.* For this type of society racial segmentation is low and racial discrimination operates imperfectly, or only in selected areas of life.

The following diagram gives a fairly accurate picture of the relationship between class and race in Cartagena (see Figure 1). From

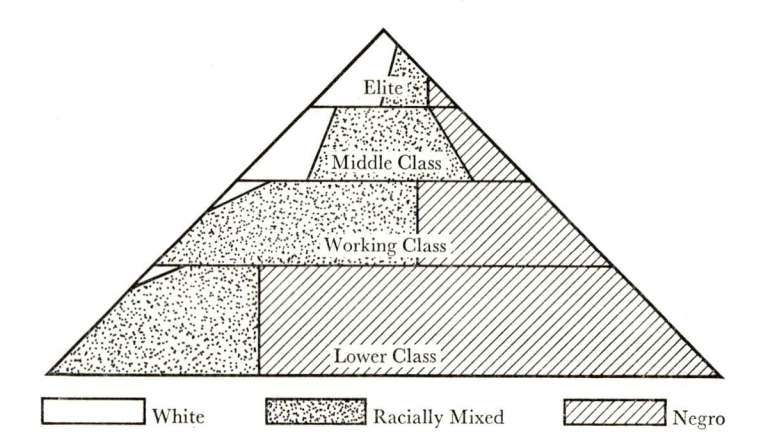

Figure 1. Class and Race in Cartagena

[Pyramid diagram with levels: Elite, Middle Class, Working Class, Lower Class. Legend: White, Racially Mixed, Negro]

its analysis, two clear conclusions emerge concerning the relationship of race and class in Cartagena. First and most important is the fact that, due to an absence of hypodescent, persons of some color (the miscegenated) are found at every class level. Second, only the polar extremes of the class structure are racially "segmented"; that is, virtually no Negroes are found at the elite level and no whites at the lower-class level. As to the first point, in contrast to the United States where, although there are different class levels among blacks, they constitute a sector that is socially segmented from whites no matter how much or how little "black blood" runs in their veins, in Cartagena a substantial proportion of miscegenated persons are found at the top of the class structure. In effect, miscegenated inhabitants of Cartagena have full membership in the exclusive, elite social club, and intermarry freely within this group. The American counterpart of this pattern would be a substantial number of persons with noticeable nonwhite physical characteristics and known black ancestry fully accepted into the most traditional social club of a city and allowed to intermarry freely within its membership. As to the second point—a polarization of races at the top and bottom of the class structure—in Cartagena highly Negroid persons, who in some cases achieve economic or political success, are segmented from the highest social elite realm in that they are not found in the elite social club. In this respect, this pattern closely resembles that in the United States. However, as noted, a substantial number of miscegenated persons are found in exclusive social circles.

Further, in contrast to the United States there is a high rate of interracial mingling between persons with different racial characteristics at every class level. This does not mean, of course, that there is a pattern of Negro-white intermarriage; rather, that persons of close but differing characteristics are intermarrying, the mixture being significantly lighter at the top of the class pyramid and darker at its base.

As our interpretation of race relations in Cartagena rests in large part on the validity of the race-class pyramid described by Figure 1, before we discuss its implications for racial conflict we must present a detailed description of the methods employed to construct it.

The Class Structure of Cartagena

There are no adequate census data to construct a class diagram of the city of Cartagena. The most recent estimate available utilizes a three-category classification and places 7.5 percent of the population in the high socioeconomic stratum, 27.7 percent in the middle stratum, and 64.8 percent in the lowest stratum.[39] Unfortunately, no criteria are given for these determinations, but it seems clear that, as in cities of most other developing countries, the class struc-

[39] Instituto De Crédito Territorial, *Desarrollo Urbano en Cartagena: Filosofía y Critérios* (Cartagena, 1969), p. 2.

ture of Cartagena is composed of a very large and poor lower class and a relatively small middle class. Precisely this preponderance of lower-class and the low ratio of middle-class persons distinguishes the class structure of Cartagena from a comparably sized city in the United States.

It is beyond the scope of our investigation to determine with census precision the class structure of the city. Our goal was to obtain a fairly accurate estimate of the racial distribution among differing layers of the class structure. To this end, we followed a strategy of seeking out the ecological and institutional locations of the distinct social strata.

In order to investigate the elite, we obtained lists of the most exclusive social club of the city, of the local Chamber of Commerce and Association of Manufacturers,[40] and of senators and governors. Thus, we could determine the social elite from the club membership, the economic elite from the economic associations, and of course, the political elite among present or former officeholders. These sectors were combined in order to obtain a cross-classification of the total elite stratum.

In order to determine the middle class, the strategy followed was to analyze educational institutions. Secondary sources have established that the majority of university students in Latin America, in general, and Colombia, in particular, have a middle-class background.[41]

Consequently, we first considered studying graduating classes from the University of Cartagena, but we knew that certain middle-class young people might go elsewhere for higher education, to public or private universities in Bogotá, for instance. After further investigation, we learned that the student bodies of private secondary schools in the area were composed mainly of middle-class youths.[42] Therefore, we analyzed yearbooks and class pictures from

[40] Unfortunately, we were unable to obtain lists of persons belonging exclusively to the agrarian elite. However, given the traditional nature of this elite, most leading agriculturalists are included in the social elite.

[41] For Colombia, see Robert C. Williamson, *El Estudiante Colombiano y Sus Actitudes* (Bogotá, 1962).

[42] Interviews with directors of these institutions established that over 95 percent of their students were from middle-class homes.

these schools. Finally, we made several visits to a local middle-class club in order to familiarize ourselves with its membership.

While the distinctions between the upper and the middle class along the lines employed in this study are relatively clear, the differences between the lower levels of the middle class and the upper working class are much more diffuse. Clearly, the bulk of persons in service occupations, particularly those involving manual work, can be considered members of the working class, but certain portions of this sector, such as salesclerks in major department stores, bank tellers, and so on, should be considered members of the lower-middle class. In order to determine the working class, therefore, we observed service workers and manual workers directly, paying particular attention to status differences within the work groups. Finally, our analysis of the lower class was based upon observations made in the slum areas of the city. Given the conditions of extreme poverty in these areas, the location of their residents at the very bottom of the social pyramid is overwhelmingly evident.

Racial Characteristics of the Class Groups

Research on race relations was complicated because, in addition to the already mentioned impossibility of constructing a class pyramid for Cartagena from census data, after 1918 Colombian censuses have avoided any racial or color classification. Consequently, we utilized our personal assessments of the racial composition of individuals in the four class groups.[43]

Compared to the population of any large North American city either in the north or south the population of Cartagena overall is darker in pigmentation, and clear racial contrasts such as those found in the United States are lacking. One rarely sees very white skin, blond or light brown hair, and green or blue eyes on the streets of the city. With the exception of a small proportion of clearly phenotypic Caucasians and a few Orientals, in most cases it would

---

[43] This description is based on the observations of the authors. One is a native North American with considerable familiarity with the interracial picture in both the North and South, and the other a native Latin American who has traveled and worked extensively in Latin America. Therefore, the observations are tempered by a cross-cultural perspective.

be very difficult to argue that a person with light brown or white skin color was either pure Caucasian or of some mixed ancestry.

There are two reasons for this, one somatic and the other climatic. Practically all Cartagenians with Caucasian ancestry can trace their background to Iberian stock. This means that the somatic norm is straight or wavy black hair, brown eyes, and in many cases a swarthy complexion. Moreover, the Caribbean sun can add many shades to the complexion, even in families where the pigmentation is very white. This results in a reinforced physical likeness to a mulatto—a person with both Negroid and Caucasoid genes. Additionally, the great bulk of the population, at least two out of every three people, and probably more, do have some distinguishing physical characteristic that is Negroid, suggesting the overwhelming presence of Negro blood throughout the entire population.

Now that we have a working picture of the class structure and of the racial mixture of the population, we must put the two together. In order to do this, we applied the following methods to the segments of the class structure described earlier—elite, middle, working, and lower classes. Basically, two approaches were used to determine group racial characteristics: the direct and indirect. The direct method entailed the authors acting as participant observers, systematically counting and categorizing groups in the city by race. The indirect method entailed our racial classification of pictures of *cartageneros*. The use of these photographs provided an efficient method of inquiry, but one with certain drawbacks. The quality of the photos led to some interpretation difficulties, especially with older pictures. Another aspect of our indirect approach was a special elite investigation. In this case, we asked several members of the socioeconomic elite to give a racial designation to our sample of elite members. This approach was necessary because of the relative inaccessibility of the elite to extensive systematic observations by the researchers.

Racial classifications in an area which has experienced such high levels of miscegenation as Cartagena are very difficult to make. It should be noted that in addition to Negroid ancestry, the population under investigation has experienced a significant degree of racial mixture with Indian elements. Given the particular somatic similarity of *mestizo*, not *mulato*, types with Iberians, the task was complicated further. Therefore, in order to classify persons we constructed three categories: white, racially mixed, and Negro. Persons were classified as racially mixed if their pigmentation, their hair type, or their physical facial characteristics denoted non-Caucasian ancestry. Within this group we placed both persons with clear *mulato* and *mestizo* characteristics. Persons were classified as Negro only if they revealed no visible sign of racial mixture. This method probably underrepresents Negroes, since our criteria were more restrictive than those prevailing both in the United States and Cartagena.[44]

Let us begin at the top of the social ladder, with the elite. Our primary source of data for the racial characteristics of the elite comes from the information provided by seven persons belonging to the socioeconomic elite on a random sample of 109 members of social, economic, and political elites. Table 2 summarizes the results. It should be noted that persons were placed into a category on the basis of the majority response. There was not perfect agreement in many cases. A comparison of the findings summarized in Figure 1 and Table 2 is significant.

Table 2 indicates that the Cartagenian elite considers itself as not being purely white. The penetration of the elite includes persons who received classifications of the term *negro*. That is, some persons were sufficiently Negroid so that our respondents employed this polar racial term. However, this does not mean that these subjects were "pure" Negroes. Our observations indicate that with the exception of rare persons among the political elite, there are no somatic Negroes at the elite level, particularly in its social realm. Periodic visits to the exclusive social club—to be a member of this club is to assert that you have arrived socially—indicated the presence of racially mixed persons but not Negroes.[45] Furthermore, our analysis of pictures of the club membership in the late nineteenth century showed a 4 to 1 ratio of whites to racially mixed persons;

[44] This consideration is based on a test of racial designations administered in Cartagena, where we found that local Cartagenians termed persons *negro* that we considered racially mixed.

[45] Most clubs of equal social honor in the United States would almost certainly be restricted; that is, neither blacks nor Jews would be admitted.

TABLE 2. RACIAL CLASSIFICATION OF THE ELITE
(Percentage)

	White	Racially Mixed	Negro	N[a]	Total
Social	63.1	35.4	1.5	65	100.0
Economic	41.0	53.4	5.6	39	100.0
Political	43.9	33.3	22.8	66	100.0
Social and Economic	66.9	32.5	0.6	178	100.0
Social and Political	66.9	31.7	1.4	145	100.0
Social, Economic, and Political	76.1	21.7	2.2	46	100.0

There are seven possible combinations of the different elite types and only one did not exist empirically: a combination of economic and political only. The lack of existence of this type of elite might be explained as follows. Given a high economic and political status, individuals also achieve a high social position: that is, they have been admitted to the exclusive social club.

[a] This is the total number of racial classifications for each category received for our sample of 109 persons.

there were no Negroes. Finally, we viewed twenty-five pictures of past presidents of the club; they were all white. This leads us into the analysis of discrimination.

Table 2 suggests that of all elite sectors, the social realm is the most difficult for nonwhites to penetrate, as evidenced by the higher proportion of whites in all the social elite categories. The political elite seems much more open to nonwhites in that the largest percentage of Negroes appears under the "political only" category. As indicated by the "economic only" group, however, a number of heavily miscegenated persons are economically successful persons.[46] Further, the apex of the class pyramid—the "social, economic, and political" category—overrepresents whites. Two possible factors explain the overrepresentation of whites in the social realm. First, the traditionalist-exclusivist argument maintains that the social elite of Cartagena was established in an early historical period and remains virtually closed to newcomers. The evidence necessary to support this interpretation is that few new persons are admitted into the social elite. Second, the argument of racial discrimination states that nonwhites who are successful in economic and political spheres of endeavor deliberately are excluded from club membership. Evi-

[46] It should be recalled that this category corresponds to the relatively modern industrial and commercial sectors.

dence to support this position must be based on the presence of turnover in the social elite. Our data support the presence of some discrimination, as there has been some mobility within the club. In effect, if we contrast prominent names in the Cartagena of the nineteenth century[47] with the current lists of club members, we find at least a 50 percent turnover of names. Furthermore, our investigation indicated that approximately one-fifth of a random sample of twenty-seven current economic leaders who belong to the club are persons who obtained prominence only recently.[48] Thus, it appears that while there is some mobility in the social elite realm, there are also some racial barriers to social success. Nevertheless, the fact that some racial discrimination exists in these highly exclusive social circles should not obscure the parallel finding that nonwhites do penetrate these circles. Although virtually closed to Negroes, social success is obtainable by a substantial proportion of the miscegenated.

In order to assess the racial composition of the middle class we looked not only at selected educational institutions in the city but also at a middle-class social club. We first classified pictures in the yearbooks from three secondary schools in the area—two men's schools and one for women only. For the first men's school we analyzed the graduating classes for the years 1940 to 1959. During these twenty years slightly over 300 students earned degrees from the school. Less than two-thirds of the graduates appeared to be white and over one-third racially mixed. Most were light-skinned. There were no phenotypical Negroes.[49] For the second men's school, we were able to classify racially the graduating classes from 1919 to 1945. During this twenty-six-year period, the school graduated 229 students.[50] Only three out of every ten students were not white.

[47] The list was constructed from Bossa Herazo, *Cartagena Independiente*.
[48] Actually, 14.9 percent of the leaders were migrants themselves.
[49] It should be noted here that in many cases the quality of the photos, especially the older ones, was not very good. Thus, our classification of racially mixed persons tended to be restricted mainly to persons with *mulato* characteristics. It is very possible that persons who were actually *mestizos* were classified as white. Therefore, our analysis quite probably overrepresents whites, not the miscegenated. As previously noted, our definition of Negro excluded persons that were not somatically Negro, who would probably be termed *negro* by locals.
[50] The reason for the relatively small number of subjects is that during the early

We also obtained three yearbooks from a girls' school, covering the years 1958 to 1960, and all grade levels, from kindergarten through the fourth year of high school. Over 300 students were pictured in these books. The girls' school seems to practice greater racial selectivity, as only two out of ten of the girls were clearly miscegenated and there were no Negroes. Furthermore, the hair type of the girls pictured showed an important difference when compared to that of the boys. While some of the mulattoes at the boys' schools had kinky hair, none of the miscegenated girls had kinky hair.[51]

Our analysis of students at the University of Cartagena was based on the graduating class pictures of its law school, 1943 to 1964. Table 3 contains our racial classification of these lawyers by year. Again, these students are predominantly white (two-thirds), with a fair proportion of racially mixed persons and very few somatic Negroes (less than 5 percent). These racial proportions follow naturally from the evidence presented for the racial composition of the private *colegios*, for if a person must have a secondary school diploma to enter the university and the high schools are predominantly white, it follows that the university will be predominantly white also.[52]

In contrast to the elite social club of Cartagena, the middle-class club is much less elegant. It has no swimming pool or air-condition-

---

years a typical graduating class contained only six or seven students. This figure gradually increased to over twenty in 1945.

[51] In our field observations, we did see some men with their heads greased and tightly wrapped. This used to be a very common practice among Negro men in the United States to make their hair wavy or straight instead of kinky. They usually slept and worked with their hair greased and wrapped in a stocking (it was called a "mammy's leg") so it would stay straight when they engaged in evening social activities. It seems that the use of hair straightener among women in Cartagena is much more widespread. The term *morena alisada* is used to describe such females. One American who lives in the city but sends his children to school in the United States reported to us that when word gets around that he is going to the United States to visit his children, he is besieged with requests from local women to bring back hair-straightening kits.

[52] It should be noted that although virtually free and compulsory, public education in Colombia and in Cartagena is highly inefficient. In 1969, of the 72,985 children between the ages of five and fourteen years, 36,802, or only about half, were registered in the city's schools. See Departamento de Bolívar, *Boletín Estadístico de Bolívar, Enero y Febrero* (1969), p. 7.

TABLE 3. CLASSES OF THE LAW SCHOOL

Year	Negro	Racially Mixed	White	Total
1943	2	6	21	29
1944	3	10	13	26
1946	2	3	15	20
1947	1	4	21	26
1951	1	4	28	33
1952	5	7	28	40
1959	3	15	11	29
1960	0	13	22	35
1961	0	8	17	25
1962	0	5	17	22
1963	0	12	23	35
1964	0	17	20	37
Total	17	104	236	357
Percentage	4.8	29.1	66.1	100.0

ing, though it does have a large, pleasant pavillion. The club has about 200 members. Some are clearly Negro, but the majority of the membership are light brown and brown. Some could easily pass for white. The cost of membership is much less than the elite social club. The relative low cost, coupled with the many light and white persons seen there, leads us to conclude that it is a club for a particular income level and not one for those excluded from other clubs on racial grounds. It is noteworthy that this club clearly contains many persons of color.

The emergent picture of the racial composition of the middle class based on our data is the following. The dominant proportion of middle-class *cartageneros* is white, a substantial minority is miscegenated, and a small percentage is Negro. This contrasts somewhat with the city's general population, in which both *mestizos* and *mulatos* are proportionately much more numerous.

This generalized picture is subject to modification for the following reasons. First, by looking mainly at private high schools and the law school of the University of Cartagena, we are concentrating on the solid middle class. Second, because of the previously mentioned difficulties in utilizing our picture materials, we are fairly certain that we have underrepresented *mestizo* types. Also, the somatic likeness of light *mulato* types with pure Iberian Caucasians leads us to feel that to some extent we have underrepresented *mulatos*. Therefore, we shall qualify our data interpretations concerning the proportions of white and the miscegenated to say that the latter group predominates at the middle-class level. This does not imply that a substantial number of phenotypic whites are not found in the middle class of Cartagena.

The small percentage of Negroes found in the middle class could be interpreted as evidence of a substantial amount of racial discrimination, particularly against polar Negroid types. We do not deny that this may be the case, but this interpretation should be placed in the context of the racial dynamic operating in the class structure. This racial dynamic can be seen as a "two-step" process toward middle-class status. Economically successful Negroes (or highly Negroid persons) tend to marry lighter females. Children of these marriages are financially able to achieve education and their racial classification is of a mixed type. As a consequence, the bulk of Negroes (or highly Negroid persons) found in the middle class at any given point in time are those who are self-made men. Very few of these men reproduce their own racial type. Thus, our educational data reveal few somatic Negroes.

The evidence for this dynamic element in racial patterns is indicated by Table 4, which shows racial-marital values as measured by marriage photographs. It is clear from these data that lightness of skin color is valued in marriage. Men marry women who are either the same shade as themselves or lighter. Two exceptions to this pattern involved white men who married mulatto women. In both cases, the females were very light-skinned and extremely beautiful.

We now turn to an analysis of the working class. In the course of a two-month period, we observed over 500 persons in over sixty business establishments and work groups. Our observations indicated noticeable differences of racial composition among businesses and type of occupation. Employees of the larger and more prestigious businesses, such as national chain stores, as opposed to a small local store, showed a much lighter racial composition. In the former type of establishment, somatic Negroes were virtually absent. A similar marked difference in racial composition also was found along occupational lines. The closer the job was to middle-class

Table 4. Racial Characteristics of Marriage Partners from Four Photo Studios

			Both Partners Negroid		
Studio	Both Partners White	White Male Negroid Female	Male Darker than Female	Same Shade	Total
1	3	—	2	5	10
2	—	—	—	3	3
3	—	—	4	—	4
4	—	2	19	22	43
Total	3	2	25	30	60
Percentage	5.0	3.3	41.7	50.0	100

status, the less the probability that a Negro would hold the position. For example, while in a given hotel somatic Negroes were employed as waiters, the croupiers in its casino were all light. Similarly, bank tellers tended to be darker than policy-level bank employees. The most striking evidence on this point lies in the realm of the purely manual-labor type of employment. Within the working class it was among construction workers, bus drivers, and furniture movers that the largest proportion of heavily Negroid persons was found.

This apparent discriminatory evidence notwithstanding, the case can be made that there is a virtual absence of occupational racial discrimination among particular levels of the working class. Although as we approach the upper occupational levels which approximate middle-class status, somatic Negroes are less likely to be found, it is highly probable that within each hierarchical level there will be a random racial distribution. For example, in a restaurant the waiters can range from Negro to white (or virtually so) and the cashier can be clearly a mulatto, so that a more Negroid person will be in a hierarchical superordinate position to a light person. Our observations indicate that this randomness of race, which produces work situations where light and dark persons work as equals and where darker persons are superior to lighter ones, is a very common pattern in Cartagena. Finally, the overall racial composition of the working class is dominated by miscegenated persons with a substantial proportion of highly Negroid persons (particularly at the lower levels) and a virtually insignificant proportion of whites.

At the bottom of the class pyramid lies what we have termed the lower class. For our purposes, we have defined this group as being formed by the inhabitants of the slums. The abysmal living conditions of this group, which reflect their lack of education and unstable employment, clearly places them on the lowest rung of the social ladder. Most of these people live in what is locally termed invasion *barrios* (or *tugurios*), that is, in areas where the people neither own nor rent the land on which they construct their dwellings. Rather, they simply occupy unused land, build shacks out of wood and waste materials, and inhabit them. Among the cities of Colombia, Cartagena is noted for the geographical preponderance of its slums. This has led to the establishment of a major program of slum rehabilitation by the government. After inspecting several of these *barrios* and noting little difference among them in their racial composition, we randomly selected one for detailed racial analysis.

The *barrio* is located on the northern edge of the city and, like most of the *tugurios* of the city, it is extremely poor in appearance. The houses, one-room affairs made out of wood and salvage materials, provide little more than shade from the sun and minimal protection from the rain. There is no running water, so the inhabitants must buy water from a wagon that passes through the streets during the day. Animals abound in the area—dogs, cats, chickens, and pigs. One can count the ribs on any of them.

In the *barrio*, we observed 106 persons in approximately forty households. The most striking racial characteristic was the darkness of the people. None were white and only ten could be considered light brown. Approximately sixty were dark brown and five out of every six had very kinky hair. Thirty-seven, or slightly over one-third, appeared to be somatically Negro. Where men were observed, adult females, normally consensual wives, were present in the households, so it was possible to compare the racial characteristics of man and wife. Approximately two-thirds of these men were of the same color as the wife and one-third were darker. In only one case was the male lighter than the female.

Although we estimated that only one-third of the people in this *barrio* were somatically Negro, we feel that in fact many more of the inhabitants were of this classification, for the following reasons.

First, because of the predominance of very dark skin color and of kinky hair among *barrio* residents, local Cartagenians term most of these people *negro*.[53] Second, many of these persons may have been "pure" blacks (genotypically Negro) but appear to have some racial mixture. We say this because health deficiencies, especially malnutrition, prevail in these *barrios* and this has a tendency to remove pigmentation from the hair (lighten it) and to pale or sallow the complexion, so that a genotype Negro suffering from malnutrition can appear to be phenotypically racially mixed. These factors lead us to conclude that the bulk of the lower class is heavily Negroid, with a relatively smaller proportion of clearly miscegenated types.

Our conclusion concerning the racial composition of the class structure of Cartagena is represented in Figure 1. Whites dominate at the elite level, particularly the exclusive, social elite sector. Within the elite, however, a significantly visible proportion of persons are of racially mixed ancestry, and persons termed *negros* by the elite have penetrated the political elite sector especially, but also are found in the economic elite sector. Nevertheless, somatic Negroes have not penetrated the social elite realm. The middle class as a whole is dominated by miscegenated persons, with a substantial proportion of whites. Negroes are also found in the middle class in small but significant numbers. These factors make this class the most racially heterogeneous stratum of the class structure. Racially mixed persons also dominate in the working class, but their hegemony within this class is less than in the middle class, because a substantial proportion of Negroes also is found at this level. White persons are a rarity in this class. Finally, the lower class is dominated by Negroes and virtually devoid of whites. In summary, then, we do find racial discrimination operating within the class structure of Cartagena. If we look at the very top and very bottom strata of the society it is possible to conclude that this is a highly segmented society. A closer analysis of the class-race pyramid reveals the penetration of persons of some color (miscegenated) throughout the stratification system, however, with a significant penetration even into the elite.

[53] As previously noted, local Cartagenians term persons *negro* who have these characteristics.

Implications for Conflict of the Class-Race Structure of Cartagena

At the outset of this paper, we established a dual pattern for Cartagena—substantial levels of class-related political conflict amidst a minimum of overt racial conflict. We are now prepared to give a structural explanation for this phenomenon.

In Cartagena, major overt racial discrimination is practiced mainly at the social elite level. It is a fact that somatic Negroes are barred from entry into this realm by gatekeepers. Nonetheless, as previously noted, a significant number of miscegenated persons and even a rare Negro have entered into these exclusive, familistic circles. Under these circumstances, what factors operate against the generation of overt racial hostility among this group? First, although racial discrimination exists, it is of an ambiguous nature because some miscegenated persons have been accepted into the social elite and some whites also are barred from admittance into these snobbish circles. This latter case of denial is most conspicuous among Cartagenians of Arab ancestry. Second, a plausible argument can be advanced that status-seeking, upwardly mobile miscegenated persons tend to marry into the white race to "improve" their race. Obviously, this pattern reduces the level of hostility that can be openly directed toward whites. Third, the lack of economic segmentation between whites and nonwhites at this level of the social system, coupled with the need for economic success in order to knock at the door of the social elite, means that these economically successful, miscegenated persons have both colleagues and clientele that are white. Thus, any overt racial protest by them could prove to be very costly. Except for the fact that no somatic Negroes have been accepted into the social elite, the bulk of the previous arguments pertain to them as well. Further, the number of economically successful Negroes who could attempt penetration into the social elite is small. This factor, coupled with their personal success as measured against the baseline of all of the Negroes of Cartagena, makes it propitious for them to accept their situation with relative complacency.

At the middle-class level racial heterogeneity finds its greatest expression, a factor which contributes greatly to the ideology of equalitarianism that pervades this sector. Racial differences exist here but they are conducive to overt manifestations of class conflict rather than racial conflict. First, whites who find themselves at this class position, rather than in the elite, logically cannot resort to racists' arguments to explain their class position. Second, there are also reasons why the miscegenated—the predominant group of this class—have a low propensity to voice racial protest. Foremost is the fact that the substantial number of whites found at this level are not highly segmented from them. In addition, many of the miscegenated are *mestizo* types who are racially similar to whites and consequently do not experience substantial racial discrimination, a situation that reduces the number of persons available to be mobilized for racial conflict.

In a more negative vein, our data indicate that at this middle level of the stratification system, the more Negroid the person is, the more racial discrimination he is likely to experience. But factors operate to subdue the expression of racial tensions among this group. The more Negroid a person is, the greater the probability that he will, all other factors equal, manifest feelings of racial oppression. Yet, given existing educational and economic constraints, extremely Negroid persons are small in number at this level and can consider themselves relatively successful compared to their racial colleagues in the lower classes. Finally, by following the dominant marital pattern of the city—that is, marrying a lighter person— they can facilitate mobility opportunities for their children.

At the working-class level, as our data indicated, if it exists at all occupational discrimination is minimal, for the juxtaposition of occupational hierarchies on race is quite random. Consequently, the life experiences or deprivations of this group, too, tend to have a class rather than a race manifestation. The same arguments hold for the lower class as well. It should be noted here, however, that some of these slum dwellers are recent migrants from highly homogeneous, heavily Negroid villages and settlements along the Caribbean coast. Although prior to migration these people were probably aware of racial differences and "white" domination in the national society, they experience more direct contact with a larger society for the first time in Cartagena. This experience of direct contact with race differences may be interpreted as conducive to an increase in the racial awareness of this group. If it has this effect, it does not produce socially based action. In order to generate a broad, national social movement based mainly on racial lines, as is currently the case in the United States, leaders who can mobilize support among high proportions of the colored masses must emerge from the middle or upper classes. For the reasons already stated, it is doubtful that potential racial leadership can be recruited from the middle or upper classes or that the levels of racial awareness and oppression will be sufficient to generate much of a following.

Conclusions

We have attempted to explain the structural factors which account for the absence of overt racial strife amidst discrimination in Cartagena. These conditions have coexisted in a country with a history of substantial levels of class-related political violence without producing substantial levels of overt racial conflict.

Some sources have interpreted the absence of racial strife in Latin America as being the product of a static, traditional equilibrium in which noncompetitive, quasi-feudal relationships of dominance between the races are clearly established and accepted. This interpretation cannot explain the absence of racial strife in contemporary Cartagena, for several reasons. First, although a superficial and static comparison of the "white" elite and the "black" lower classes might lead to the above interpretation, the fact is that racial boundaries are quite fluid in Cartagena. The dynamics of race in the area consist of an infusion of persons of some color (the miscegenated) throughout the social structure. Although imperfect, there is a considerable degree of racial integration in Cartagena. Second, in a political and class sense, Cartagena is not a static society. As witnessed by the presidential election of 1970, it has experienced the social mobilization that accompanies urban and industrial growth, forces which in this environment have led to the emergence of class, not racial, conflict ideologies.

We feel that the structural conditions which have inhibited the emergence of racial violence amidst the political mobilization of the population were established in an early historical period in this area. A high level of miscegenation[54] and its corollary, the infusion of persons of some color throughout the entire stratification pyramid, were present in colonial Cartagena. Our data indicate that miscegenated persons were present in the Cartagenian elite of the nineteenth century. Therefore, a pattern of clear, corporate racial groups has not existed in Cartagena. That is, in the city we do not find a white upper class, a mulatto middle, and a black lower class. Of course, it is true that whites predominate at the top of the class pyramid and blacks at the bottom. As we have seen, however, a substantial proportion (one-third) of the upper class is racially mixed,[55] and the same case can be made for other class groups. Thus, from the perspective of racial aggregates—whites, miscegenated, and blacks—only an imperfect correspondence exists between class and race lines. It is precisely the miscegenated aggregate that blurs race and class in Cartagena.

In the final analysis, the race class pyramid of Cartagena, as depicted in Figure 1, indicates that Cartagenians are relatively tolerant in racial matters. In effect, a case can be made that extensive miscegenation requires some racial tolerance. Several explanations have been put forth to explain the lower psychological distance—and this is a necessary condition for substantial miscegenation—that Iberians felt toward nonwhites in comparison to the attitudes of Northwest Europeans.[56] Space considerations prohibit elaboration here, but the miscegenation-tolerance syndrome has been operating

[54] See Jaramillo Uribe, *Ensayos sobre Historia Social Colombiana*, pp. 10–11.

[55] Survey research data compiled in connection with this study indicates that not only do persons at the elite level designate other elite members as nonwhites, but also the racially mixed elite members themselves acknowledge this fact by using terms of self-designation that signify mixed racial background.

[56] The arguments used to explain Iberian racial tolerance focus on seven major factors: the Moorish conquest, the tradition of slavery, the Latin American pattern of colonization, the role of the Catholic church, the Latin American cultural ethos, the colonial economy, and the somatic distance. Detailed accounts on these factors can be found in: Gilberto Freyre, *The Masters and the Slaves* (New York, 1945); Harris, *Patterns of Race*; Hoetink, *Two Variants*; Klein, *Slavery in the Americas*; Mörner, *Race Mixture*; Donald Pierson, "Race Relations to Portuguese America," in *Race Relations in World Perspective*, Andrew W. Lind, ed., (Honolulu, 1955); Frank Tannenbaum, *Slave and Citizen: The Negro in the Americas* (New York, 1947); van den Berghe, *Race and Racism*; and Wagley, *Rural Brazil*.

in Cartagena for centuries. The point to be stressed is that the current structural configuration of race relations, which for the reasons we have covered is conducive to racial harmony, has been maintained with only minor changes throughout much of the history of the city. In this sense, we believe that our structural interpretation for the racial situation can be extrapolated to explain the historical absence of substantial racial conflict in the Cartagenian area. Furthermore, to extrapolate into the future, we predict that it is improbable that Cartagena will experience major racial problems that will severely complicate continuing urban-industrial modernization. While the utopia of a homogeneous, cosmic race in an entirely racially open society appears to be extremely remote, we believe that the processes of modernization which are impinging upon Cartagena will probably increase the levels of miscegenation and racial homogenization in the Cartagenian area. Finally, it is more probable that these processes of social change will be accompanied by major interclass crises, not racial ones.

The racial experience of Cartagena stands in clear contrast to that of the United States, where, for reasons beyond the scope of this paper, a pattern of acute racial segmentation was institutionalized during the colonial period. Since then the processes of urbanization and industrialization in the United States have operated vis-à-vis a highly segmented racial system. As these processes spread to include black Americans, of necessity, racial compartmentalization and barriers are eroded. In the face of this situation, there are two alternatives to racial policy. Either racial groups are allowed to integrate rapidly or segmentation is maintained by force. Conditions of acute segmentation are not conducive to rapid integration because this structural system of inequality and its accompanying social psychological factors describe a situation of acute prejudice. Under these conditions, miscegenation is greatly inhibited and the miscegenated are stigmatized. The society maintains a clear bifurcation among the races. Consequently, there is a strong tendency toward racial conflict. It is precisely this absence of an infusion of persons of some color throughout the social structure, especially in intimate elite social relations, that sustains a polarized racial system in North America. In Cartagena, as we have seen, just the opposite is true; a unifying thread of miscegenated citizens weaves in and out of all class levels.

In conclusion, it is clear that the representation of persons of some color (the miscegenated) at every level of a stratification system which is not highly segmented is the mechanism by which racial harmony has been achieved. Interestingly enough, this has occurred in a society with scarce resources, in which competition for job opportunities is acute. In the United States, where miscegenated persons are not recognized, where only the bifurcated designation of black and white prevails, if racial harmony is to be achieved and the potential for racial conflict minimized, black persons, or those so designated, must be represented substantially in all levels of the stratification pyramid and accepted into intimate social relations. This structural integration describes a situation in which American nonwhites will compete as status equals with whites.

PART II

THE PHYSICAL SETTING

These three case studies deal with a few of the material factors associated with modernization in Colombia, Peru, and Mexico. They review problems of land tenure, of mass population movement from the countryside to the city, and finally, of housing the exploding urban population. Individually, each of these reports offers examples of the inelasticity of Latin America's legal, social, and economic institutions in responding to the problems of speedy change. Collectively, they demonstrate how human beings themselves can discover means of circumventing impediments to resolve their own difficulties.

Roger Findley's discussion of the seemingly endless complexities encountered in trying to administer Colombia's land-reform program may be regarded by social scientists as overly legalistic and detailed. Clearly it is more descriptive than analytical, more factual than interpretive, but this approach may be the most effective way of conveying the nature of the problem to the uninitiated, because complexity, confusion, and delay are the most obvious attributes of the program and, significantly, perceived as such by the people involved. One reaches the reluctant conclusion that in this case land reform was more symbolic than operational, probably because during most of the period under consideration traditional landowners rather than farm workers held the political initiative.

A study of this sort is particularly instructive for the student of Latin American modernization because legal constraints upon solution of basic development problems are by no means limited either to Colombia or to land reform. On the contrary, throughout the region a rigid and formalistic legal system sets up a maze of expensive and time-consuming technical barriers to accomplishment of reform goals. Unless these barriers are removed, enactment of well-intentioned and up-dated government programs, whether in land reform, housing, industrial development, or whatever, may result more in frustration than in constructive change.

In considering internal migration and economic development in Peru, René Vandendries manipulates existing statistical data to make a limited but important point about migrants and their possible contribution to the country's economy. Contrary to the conventional wisdom about such persons in developing states, he suggests, those who come to Lima at least are of relatively high quality. Generally speaking, they are above national average in education, have previous experience in city life, and demonstrate initiative and the ability to compete successfully in the urban labor market, which makes them not unlike the European urban migrants of the earlier Industrial Revolution. Vandendries posits that the real problem in Peru (and by analogy in other late-developing countries) is that excessive population increases have forced urban growth at a rate much faster than industrial expansion could absorb a reasonably well-prepared labor supply, potentially a politically dangerous situation.

If this point is valid broadly, policies dealing with economic development and utilization of manpower resources in emerging countries may have to be re-thought. The difficulty lies in generalizing the finding, for several reasons. The data used may not be reliable, either because of statistically invalid collection methods or because its content was skewed for political reasons. Again, the Peruvian case may not transfer to other national settings, or the situation in a national capital may not exist in smaller or less important cities. In any event, both investigators and policymakers in other countries would be well advised to apply this approach to the study of their own urban migrants.

The comparison of five "shantytowns" near Oaxaca, Mexico, presented by Douglas Butterworth, demonstrates the danger of glib generalizations about the nature of such communities. By applying careful analytical techniques, he shows that these settlements are very different in regard to their formation, development, legal status, and potential growth. Each has its own history and mix of inhabitants. While some are true squatter settlements, others are quasi-legal suburban units, and the social, political, and economic roles of their citizens are just as distinct. As Butterworth suggests, it behooves those studying other such communities in Mexico and elsewhere to define the nature of the settlements involved, in order to devise adequate theoretical bases upon which governmental policy concerning them can be constructed.

Problems Faced by Colombia's Agrarian Reform Institute in Acquiring and Distributing Land[1]

Roger W. Findley

Introduction

One of the most pressing problems growing out of rapid change in Latin America is the need for agrarian reform.[2] As a result of the ubiquitous transistor radio, better transportation, and an occasional village television set, the once isolated peasants have acquired a new social, economic, and political awareness. They have become more

---

[1] Field work for this study was done in Colombia in the summer of 1969, and the manuscript was finalized in November, 1971. The author expresses his gratitude to Dr. Carlos Villamil Cháux, then general manager of the Colombian Agrarian Reform Institute, to Dr. Carlos Sánchez Ramos, the head of the Division of Adjudications, and to the many other INCORA officials in Bogotá and in the Departments of Meta and Tolima for their interest and total cooperation, without which this study could not have been made. Valuable assistance was also received from Dr. Luis Arévalo, a Colombian lawyer and agricultural economist associated with the University of Wisconsin Land Tenure Center in Bogotá, and Dr. José Ignacio Rengifo, Professor of Civil Engineering at the University of the Andes in Bogotá. Despite their generous cooperation, none of the above persons is responsible for the findings in this work.

[2] See generally Thomas F. Carroll, "The Land Reform Issue in Latin America," in Albert O. Hirschman, ed., *Latin American Issues: Essays and Comments* (New York, 1961); Solon L. Barraclough and Arthur L. Domike, "Agrarian Structure in Seven Latin American Countries," XLII, *Land Economics* (1966), p. 391; Oscar Delgado, ed., *Reformas Agrarias en la América Latina* (México, 1965); Kenneth L. Karst, *Latin American Legal Institutions: Problems for Comparative Study* (Los Angeles, 1966), Chap. 4.

modern. As their expectations and demands grow, so do their frustrations, especially as the promises inherent in land-reform laws enacted in the wake of the Cuban Revolution continue to go unfulfilled. Throughout Latin America, agrarian reform remains one of the matters on which public policy seems least successful.

Some observers claim that the inadequate solutions are due to political manipulation, others that the policy process makes impossible meaningful incremental change, and still others that the cumbersome legal mechanisms under which Latin American countries operate are the real culprits because too little can be accomplished speedily enough to meet rapidly shifting demands. This study of the activities and procedures of Colombia's Agrarian Reform Institute (INCORA) suggests that a mixture of all these factors is responsible for the very limited scope of that country's efforts and achievements to date. Although it seemed in 1970 and early 1971 that political pressure from a newly organized peasantry might force an acceleration in the program to redistribute private lands, exactly the opposite has occurred. The future is difficult to predict.

The study is divided into two major parts. The first deals with what many think of as true land reform: public acquisition of private land and redistribution of it to persons with little or none of their own. The second part concerns an even more important area of activity in terms of the numbers of persons and land areas involved: the titling of Colombia's vast public domain.

Acquisition and Redistribution of Privately Owned Land

Article 1 of the Colombian Social Agrarian Reform Law, Law 135 of 1961, which established INCORA, states that purposes of the act are to:

1. Reform the social land structure of the country, eliminating the inequitable concentration of rural landholdings and preventing uneconomic partition; re-establish viable farms in areas where small landholdings predominate and distribute land to persons who have none, with preference to those directly responsible for working the land and engaging in such work themselves.

2. Promote proper economic exploitation of uncultivated or inefficiently worked land on the basis of programmes provided for the ordered distribution of land and its rational utilization. . . .

4. Create conditions such that small tenant farmers and sharecroppers are given more adequate guarantees, and ensure that both they and agricultural workers have greater opportunity to become landowners. . . .[3]

INCORA is authorized to acquire privately owned land in pursuance of these aims, although it is directed first to distribute to peasants any easily accessible public land in the same locality if suitable for "family farms."[4]

The Need for Redistribution of Land Ownership in Colombia

Since Law 135 and debates preceding its enactment emphasized the need to eliminate "the inequitable concentration of rural landholdings,"[5] it came as a surprise in 1964 when INCORA announced its conclusion that, contrary to prior belief, *latifundismo* (the concentration of lands in large estates) was not a problem because small and medium-sized landholdings of less than 100 hectares dominate Colombian agriculture.[6] This determination was immediately attacked by writers familiar with Colombian land-tenure structure, and data now available appear to contradict INCORA's conclu-

[3] FAO translation, *Food and Agricultural Legislation*, Vol. X, No. 4: V/1. For an excellent chronicle of the historical circumstances and events leading to enactment of Law 135 of 1961, see Chapter 2, "Land Use and Land Reform in Colombia," in Albert O. Hirschman, *Journeys Toward Progress* (New York, 1963). A more recent treatment which also discusses some aspects of the implementation of the law is Ernest A. Duff, *Agrarian Reform in Colombia* (New York, 1968). See also Ministerio de Agricultura, *Informe del Comité Evaluador de la Reforma Agraria* (Bogotá, January, 1971); Roger W. Findley, "Ten Years of Land Reform in Colombia," *Wisconsin Law Review*, No. 3 (1972).

[4] Law 135 of 1961, Arts. 54 and 55. Requirements for family farms are discussed below in the text at note 41. It appears that even in the more populous parts of the country there are substantial unclaimed lands. See T. Lynn Smith, *Colombia: Social Structure and the Process of Development* (Gainesville, 1967), pp. 31–33. But as indicated below after note 133, it is difficult to know whether such lands are really in the public domain.

[5] Art. 1; Carlos Lleras Restrepo, "Estructura de la Reforma Agraria," in *Tierra: 10 Ensayos sobre la Reforma Agraria en Colombia* (Bogotá, 1961), pp. 13, 36.

[6] INCORA, *Informe de Actividades de 1963: Segundo Año de Reforma Agraria* (Bogotá, 1964), pp. 7–22.

TABLE 1. FARMS AND LAND IN COLOMBIA, 1959–1960

Size of Farm Units in Hectares	Farms Number	Farms Percentage Distribution	Land in Farms Hectares (Thousands)	Land in Farms Percentage Distribution
Less than 1.0	298,071	24.7	132	.5
1.0 to 2.0	308,352	25.5	546	2.0
3.0 to 4.9	150,182	12.4	561	2.0
5.0 to 9.9	169,145	14.0	1,165	4.3
10.0 to 49.9	201,020	16.6	4,211	15.4
50.0 to 99.9	39,990	3.3	2,680	9.8
100.0 to 499.9	36,010	3.0	6,990	25.6
500.0 to 999.9	4,141	.3	2,731	10.0
1000.0 or more	2,761	.2	8,322	30.4
Total	1,209,672	100.0	27,338	100.0

SOURCE: Dale W. Adams, "Landownership Patterns in Colombia," p. 85. Does not include the department of Chocó or the national territories.

sion.[7] As shown in Table 1, derived from the Colombian Agricultural Census of 1959–1960,[8] only 3.5 percent of the farm units enumerated were larger than 100 hectares, but they comprised 66 percent of the total lands in all farm units in the census.

Table 1 also indicates that Colombia has a serious *minifundio* problem, an overabundance of uneconomically small farms.[9] In addition, though not reflected in the table, many *minifundio*-size segments of larger tracts are operated as separate farms by persons other than the owners; for example, by tenants and squatters. Table 2, also based upon the 1959–1960 agricultural census, indicates the numbers of different types of operators for farms of varying sizes.

Under Law 1 of 1968, amending Law 135 of 1961, INCORA is to acquire the land comprising all farms (both separately owned tracts and separately operated segments of larger tracts) of fifteen

[7] Dale W. Adams, "Landownership Patterns in Colombia," *Inter-American Economic Affairs*, 18 (Winter, 1964), p. 77; Ernest Feder, "El Incumplimiento de la Reforma Agraria," in Delgado, note 2 above, pp. 632–635; Smith note 4 above, at Chap. 2; Comité Interamericano de Desarrollo Agrícola (CIDA), *Tenencia de la Tierra y Desarrollo Socio-Económico de Sector Agrícola: Colombia* (Washington, D.C., 1966).

[8] Departamento Administrativo Nacional de Estadística, *Directorio Nacional de Explotaciones Agropecuarias (Censo Agropecuario), 1960 Resumen Nacional*, Segunda Parte (Bogotá, February, 1964), p. 39.

[9] See also Smith, note 4 above, p. 36.

TABLE 2. FARM OPERATORS IN COLOMBIA, 1959–1960

Size of Farm (Hectares)	Owners	Administrators	Tenants and Sharecroppers	Squatters	Mixed and Other Forms
Less than 2	291,085	2,946	147,625	8,777	38,985
2 to 4.9	148,948	3,160	70,495	7,425	37,159
5 to 9.9	108,442	4,941	32,732	5,787	8,317
10 to 19.9	77,819	5,462	17,305	6,007	10,448
20 to 49.9	61,999	7,137	9,160	7,627	6,144
50 to 199.9	34,214	10,773	4,144	8,921	4,255
200 or more	7,881	8,051	936	2,417	1,310
Total	730,388	42,470	282,397	46,961	106,618

SOURCE: T. Lynn Smith, *Colombia*, pp. 124–133.

hectares or less operated by "small tenants, sharecroppers and the like" (*pequeños arrendatarios, aparceros o similares*) and to redistribute such land to the operators, or to as many of them as can be accommodated thereon in "family farms" or cooperatives of adequate size.[10] This is the so-called *arrepas* program, which in 1969 was one of INCORA's top priorities, in contrast to other types of restructuring activities, which were being cut back.[11] Table 2 indicates that of the approximately 280,000 tenants and sharecroppers in Colombia in 1960, almost 220,000 were farming tracts of less than five hectares, and between 30,000 and 50,000 more were operating tracts of from five to fifteen hectares. As of February, 1969, INCORA's Division of Land Tenures had identified and enrolled a total of approximately 64,000 tenants and sharecroppers as persons working lands which would probably be acquired. Of these, some 51,000 were farming tracts of less than five hectares and 13,000 were operating farms of from five to fifteen hectares. By the end of June, 1969, the number of enrolled tenants and sharecroppers had increased to 76,500, and INCORA was in the process of acquiring 2,275 tracts, though it apparently had not yet obtained title to any of them.[12] It was expected that acquisitions and redistributions for

---

[10] Arts. 59 *bis* and 104 *bis* of Law 135, added by Law 1 of 1968, and implemented by Presidential Decrees 703 of May 10, 1968, and 719 of May 13, 1968. "Family farm" is defined in the text, note 41.

[11] Interviews with Carlos Villamil Cháux, then general manager of INCORA, June 23, 1969, and with INCORA officials in Meta and Tolima, August, 1969.

[12] Data received from Division of Land Tenures on August 13, 1969.

the *arrepas* program could be carried out more rapidly and at less expense than for other types of restructuring activities. No detailed studies were required to determine which lands should be acquired because *all* lands operated by small tenants and sharecroppers were to be acquired. Since most beneficiaries were to receive land which was already being farmed and would continue to be operated in the same way, there would be little cost to INCORA for studies of the productive capacity of the land or for infrastructural facilities, such as new access roads.

Methods by Which INCORA Acquires Land

Private land is acquired by INCORA in four ways: "extinction of the rights of private ownership" (without compensation), expropriation (with compensation), negotiated purchase, and gratuitous transfer.

The doctrine of "extinction" (*Extinción del derecho de dominio privado*) was established by Law 200 of 1936, which provided that rural land of which the owner failed to make "economic use" (planting, occupation with cattle, and other acts of equal economic significance, but not mere fencing or construction of buildings) for ten consecutive years would revert to the public domain.[13] Reversion is not automatic; the government must declare extinction affirmatively and obtain cancellation of the public registration of the title, with the owner having a right to judicial review of the administrative determination of nonuse.[14] Like the provisions of Law 135 of 1961 establishing priorities for expropriation or purchase of private land, discussed in the second paragraph below, Law 200 of 1936 reflects the principle of Colombian law that "ownership is a social function which implies obligations."[15] For a variety of po-

---

[13] Art. 6. A draft law submitted to the Colombian Senate by the Ministry of Agriculture early in 1971 would, among many other changes in Law 200 of 1936 and Law 135 of 1961, as amended, reduce the period of nonuse required for extinction from ten to five years. The draft law, together with a detailed explanation of its background and meaning, has been published by the Ministry in booklet form, *Proyecto de Ley por la cual se Introducen Modificaciones a las Leyes 200 de 1936, 135 de 1961 y la de 1968* (Bogotá, August, 1971).

[14] Art. 8.

[15] Colombian Constitution of 1936, Art. 30. See Karst, note 2 above, pp. 471–475.

litical and administrative reasons, however, little effort was made to enforce Law 200 between 1936 and 1961.[16]

Law 135 of 1961 reiterated the principles of Law 200 and assigned to INCORA the duty of administering the 1936 act. INCORA was directed immediately to survey the degree of use of all farms over 2,000 hectares, and the owners were required to submit certificates describing location, size, and method of operation. Law 135 placed upon private owners the burden of proving that they were making economic use of their lands, and it also simplified administrative and judicial procedures and reduced causes of delay in extinction proceedings.[17]

With respect to acquisition by expropriation or negotiated purchase, Law 135 provides that in regions where there is not sufficient land suitable for "family farms" in the public domain or subject to extinction, INCORA is authorized to acquire private land according to the following priorities: (1) "uncultivated" land not subject to extinction; (2) "inadequately" worked land; (3) land "adequately" farmed by renters and sharecroppers, when in the case of sharecroppers the owner is not himself the manager or responsible for any of the expenses or operation of the farm; (4) "adequately" used land not within category 3 whose owners are willing to alienate it voluntarily; and (5) "adequately" worked land not within category 3 or 4.[18] However, these priorities may be disregarded in acquisitions for the *arrepas* (tenants and sharecroppers)

There is no analogous principle in Anglo-American law; if an owner chooses not to use his land, the government cannot compel him to do so and cannot deprive him of it against his will, except by exercise of the power of eminent domain with payment of just compensation.

[16] See Hirschman, note 3 above, pp. 107–113 and 149.

[17] Arts. 22–24. Art. 23 of Law 135 was amended by Law 1 of 1968, further modifying the procedures.

[18] Art. 55. Art. 56 of Law 135 defines "uncultivated" land as that "which while being economically usable is not used for organized crop farming or stock breeding," and directs that in classifying land as "adequately" or "inadequately" farmed, INCORA shall consider such factors as proximity to urban centers, topography, soil quality, possibility of regular use, type and intensity of farming, capital and labor employed, commercial value and yield, and population density in the particular rural area. As discussed in the text following note 27, the lack of a clearer distinction between adequate and inadequate exploitation has caused serious problems in implementing the land-reform program.

program, establishment of irrigation districts, consolidation of *minifundios*, or erosion control.[19] Expropriation of "adequately" farmed land is authorized only for *arrepas*, irrigation projects, *minifundio* consolidation, transit facilities, and resettlement of small landowners, tenants, or sharecroppers who occupy land which is to be withdrawn from farming.[20] In most cases, owners of "adequately" or "inadequately" used land which is expropriated may exercise a "right of exclusion" to retain up to 100 hectares.[21]

The process for determining the price to be paid by INCORA for land acquired by negotiated purchase or expropriation is rather interesting. As enacted in 1961, Law 135 provided that INCORA should initially seek to negotiate a purchase on the basis of an estimate of the value of the land by expert appraisers from the Augustín Codazzi Geographic Institute, the national cadastral survey office. If negotiations failed and expropriation was necessary, the value was to be determined by three appraisers, appointed by INCORA, the owner, and the Geographic Institute, respectively.[22] Although many people assumed that these various appraisers were to determine the commercial or market value of the property, the act did not so state, and a controversial regulatory decree issued in 1962 provided that their valuation could not exceed 130 percent of the cadastral (assessed) value,[23] usually far below the commercial value. Although the Council of State upheld the legal validity of the decree in March, 1963, political pressures resulted in issuance

---

[19] Presidential Decree 719 of May 13, 1968, Art. 3.

[20] Law 135, as amended, Arts. 58 and 59 *bis*.

[21] Where land is expropriated for the *arrepas* program, the right of exclusion is limited to an area equivalent to a "family farm" if part of the usual 100 hectares is needed to bring the tenants' or sharecroppers' plots up to an adequate size. Law 135, Art. 59 *bis*. In cases of expropriation for irrigation districts, the owners have a preferential claim to 100 hectares or one-third of their land, whichever is less, or to fifty hectares if they own less than 150 hectares; however, unless they own less than fifty hectares, INCORA must acquire their *entire* holdings and then allow the former owners to *buy* back the land to which they have the preferential claim at a price equal to INCORA's acquisition cost, plus the proportional cost of the irrigation works. Law 135, Arts. 68 and 72. Article 19 of the draft law cited in note 13 above, would reduce the right of exclusion to fifty hectares, and would grant it in most cases only to owners of "adequately" used land.

[22] Art. 61.

[23] Presidential Decree 1904 of July 18, 1962, Art. 1.

of another decree[24] eight months later establishing new valuation standards which were expressly approved in the 1968 amendments to Law 135,[25] and are still in effect. These standards require all owners of rural tracts larger than 100 hectares to file with the Geographic Institute by the end of February of each even-numbered year their own estimates of the commercial value of their land. Such "auto-evaluations," which generally may not be less than the cadastral values then in effect or the prices originally paid for the land, serve both as the assessed values for property-tax purposes and as maximum values to be paid by INCORA in negotiated purchases or expropriations. However, at the time INCORA actually seeks to acquire a particular tract of land, appraisers chosen as described at the beginning of this paragraph then make an independent determination of its commercial value. If their valuation is less than the owner's auto-evaluation, INCORA cannot pay more than the value fixed by the appraisers. The result of the 1963 change in evaluation standards has been the payment of higher prices by INCORA[26] and, presumably, higher property taxes, at least by owners who think that INCORA might acquire their lands before they file their next auto-evaluations.

Once the price to be paid by INCORA has been set, the form of payment is determined by reference to the degree of exploitation of the land. Owners of "uncultivated" land are paid in twenty-five-year, 2 percent bonds; owners of land worked "adequately" or "inadequately" by small tenants or sharecroppers receive 50 percent in bonds calling for fifteen equal annual installments, with interest at 7 percent per annum, and 50 percent in twenty-five-year, 2 percent bonds; owners of other "inadequately" used land are paid 20 percent (but not less than 75,000 nor more than 100,000 pesos) in cash, and the remainder in bonds calling for twelve equal annual installments with interest at 5 percent per annum; and owners of other "adequately" used land receive 20 percent (but not less than 150,000 nor more than 300,000 pesos) in cash, and the balance in

---

[24] Presidential Decree 2895 of November 26, 1963, repealing Arts. 1 and 2 of Decree 1904 of 1962.
[25] Law 1 of 1968, Art. 14.
[26] See Duff, note 3 above, pp. 115–117.

bonds calling for five equal annual installments with 6 percent annual interest.[27] (In 1969 a Colombian peso was worth about six cents in United States money.)

It should be apparent that the establishment and application of criteria for determining the degree of land utilization are crucial matters, since the availability of land for acquisition by INCORA, the necessity of paying compensation for it, and the form of payment can all depend on that determination. Unfortunately Law 135 does not clearly define or distinguish between "adequately" and "inadequately" used land. It merely prescribes a number of factors to be considered in classifying the use.[28] To date, the test actually used by INCORA in determining whether particular land is "adequately" used has been a relative and rather vague one, namely, whether the land is as well utilized as the most efficient or productive farms in the same geographic area.[29] Since in expropriation cases INCORA's classification is subject to judicial review, agency personnel have always been concerned that the courts—some of which have appeared more sympathetic to the interests of large landowners than to the goals of the agrarian reform program—might disagree with INCORA's weighting of the prescribed factors. This concern over lengthy appeals and possible reversals has caused INCORA to shun expropriations and to engage in protracted ef-

[27] Law 135 of 1961, Arts. 62 and 59 *bis*, as amended by Law 1 of 1968. Prior to 1968, owners of "inadequately" used land received their deferred payments in eight installments, rather than twelve. Where an owner can show that he obtains from the land in question more than 70 percent of his income and that the land represents more than 50 percent of his total property, he can still receive his deferred payments in eight installments. The validity of deferring any of the compensation was challenged in the courts by a citizen who relied on Art. 30 of the Colombian Constitution, requiring "previous compensation" for expropriated property. In 1964 the Supreme Court of Justice of Colombia upheld the constitutionality of Law 135, stating that the prior compensation could be in bonds rather than cash. Decision of Dec. 11, 1964, VII, *Derecho Colombiano*, No. 37 (January, 1965), p. 5, discussed in *American Journal of Comparative Law*, 14 (1965), p. 118. A requirement that all lands be paid for entirely in cash almost certainly would preclude extensive acquisitions by a developing country. See generally Karst, note 2 above, pp. 542–564; Kenneth L. Karst, "Latin American Land Reform: The Uses of Confiscation," *Michigan Law Review* 63 (1964), p. 327.

[28] See note 18 above.

[29] Speech by Enrique Peñalosa at Urbana, Illinois, April 15, 1971. Peñalosa was General Manager of INCORA from 1961 until 1968 and Minister of Agriculture of Colombia from 1968 to 1969, and is now Executive Director of the Inter-American Development Bank.

forts to negotiate voluntary purchases. The process has consumed a large force of administrative personnel and resulted in great delays, overly generous terms of payment in negotiated purchases, and total failures to acquire some needed land.[30] As will be illustrated later, the incentive to transfer land voluntarily to INCORA is usually a desire to avoid losing an even larger tract in expropriation or extinction proceedings or to obtain a more favorable form of compensation.[31]

Because of such problems, the Ministry of Agriculture has recommended that Law 135 be amended to define "adequately used" land much more precisely, narrowly, and absolutely, and to permit expropriation of adequately used land for some additional purposes for which it cannot now be acquired by INCORA unless the owner agrees to sell it voluntarily. Further, the ministry proposes establishment of an entirely new system of "land courts" which would have exclusive jurisdiction to hear many of the trials and appeals now handled by the regular judiciary, and would be expected to be more sympathetic to the land-reform program.[32]

Methods of Distribution

The method by which INCORA acquires land limits to some extent the methods by which and the persons to whom that land may be distributed.

Lands acquired by extinction either are granted immediately to

[30] Mario Suárez Melo, "Obstáculos Jurídicos para la Realización de la Reforma Agraria en Colombia," in *Hacia una Reforma Agraria Masiva* (Bogotá, September, 1971), p. 87. For an example of some of the difficulties in proving the degree of land utilization in court, see the excerpts from *National Agrarian Institute* v. *Muñoz*, a 1961 Venezuelan case, in Karst, note 2 above, pp. 483–496. At least one knowledgeable writer has urged leaving the concept of extent of utilization out of land-reform legislation altogether, noting that in any event productivity is normally taken into account in appraising the value of the land. Ernest Feder, "The Rational Implementation of Land Reform in Colombia and Its Significance for the Alliance for Progress," VI, *America Latina*, No. 1 (Rio de Janeiro, January–March, 1963), pp. 96–97.

[31] See the case of Hacienda Rey in the text at note 79 and following.

[32] Articles 17, 18, 116, and 117 of the draft law cited in note 13 above. For land to be "adequately" used, the owner would have to permit his workers to share in the profits of the farm, provide vocational training for their sons, comply with all labor laws and laws concerning conservation of natural resources, and earn from the land a net income at least equal to a legally prescribed minimum, which would be based on a percentage of the actual or assessed value of the land.

squatters already established there or are reserved by INCORA for planned settlement areas.[33] In either case, the recipients obtain the land free of charge. In general, squatters who occupied the land prior to the extinction, in the belief that it was publicly owned, and who have cultivated at least two-thirds of the area which they occupy, are entitled to receive immediate "adjudication" (transfer of title) by INCORA, subject to a maximum limit of 450 hectares per recipient. The titles are of the same unconditional character as those given to persons who spontaneously colonize unreserved land in the public domain,[34] and are not encumbered by restrictions like those imposed in grants of "family farms" in planned settlement areas and in parcelization of land acquired by expropriation, negotiated purchase, or gratuitous transfer. However, if granting to each of the squatters title to the segment occupied by him would mean giving disproportionately large farms to some and disproportionately small farms to others, INCORA will instead buy the squatters' improvements and reserve the entire tract for a planned settlement area.[35]

Land which INCORA acquires by expropriation, negotiated purchase, or gratuitous transfer is in general to be distributed to persons of "limited resources" as "family farms" or cooperative farms under the parcelization program.[36] Most distributions to date

[33] Law 135 of 1961, Chap. 9; Accord 11 of May 8, 1967, of the Board of Directors of INCORA. Planned settlement areas, governed by Chapter 9, are distinct from parcelization projects, which are governed by Chapter 14 of Law 135.

[34] See the second part of this paper, beginning at note 118.

[35] Interview with official in INCORA's Division of Adjudications, Bogotá, July 21, 1969.

[36] Law 135 of 1961, Arts. 80 and 81, as amended by Law 1 of 1968. Under Accord 23 of November 27, 1967, of the Board of Directors of INCORA, land acquired gratuitously and occupied at the time of acquisition by persons (other than the grantor) farming at least two-thirds of the area which they occupy is granted to such occupants immediately, free of the restrictions applicable to "family farms" and subject only to a size limitation of 450 hectares per recipient. In effect, the result is the same as if INCORA had acquired the occupied land by extinction. A draft accord proposed by the Division of Adjudications in late 1970 would reduce the rights of such occupants to the privilege of receiving "family farms," although the occupants would not have to meet the test of limited or scarce resources generally required of recipients of family farms. Accord 23 of August 22, 1966, limits recipients to farmers having net assets of less than 50,000 pesos. However, the draft accord referred to above would change that limitation from 50,000 pesos (about US $3,000) to the value of a "family farm" in the locality in question, and would add an income limitation of 24,000 pesos, "exclusive of labor."

have been of individual family farms. However, the numbers of distributions to cooperatives and for communal use have increased since 1969, and the Ministry of Agriculture has recommended amendments to Law 135 which would largely preclude further distributions of family farms intended for individual operation.[37]

Tenants, sharecroppers, and employees already on the land when INCORA acquires it, as well as other farm laborers in the area who have no land of their own, and the heirs, surviving spouses, or permanent companions of deceased grantees of family farms, have preferential rights to family farms.[38] The recipient of a family farm contracts to pay in installments the pro-rata price paid by INCORA, plus the costs of surveying the tract and of any improvements added by INCORA.[39] If INCORA acquired the land gratuitously, the recipient need only pay the cost of improvements and of surveying the area of his farm in excess of fifty hectares.[40]

A "family farm" is one that conforms to the following conditions:[41]

(a) It shall be of such size, considering the soil quality, rainfall, and other individual factors, as to provide a normal family with income adequate for its subsistence, for the payment of debts arising from the purchase of the land and the cost of any necessary development, and for the gradual improvement of housing, farm equipment, and general standard of living; but *in no case shall it be smaller than three hectares.*

[37] See text at notes 52 through 54 and following note 83. According to the Division of Adjudications, only seven distributions were made to cooperatives from 1962 to August, 1969. A summary of INCORA activities through August, 1970, shows a total of 110 cooperative associations comprising 1,996 families and 31,810 hectares, but it is not clear whether all these lands are owned by the cooperatives themselves or whether some are owned by individual members but *operated* collectively. A later summary of INCORA's distributions of lands acquired by negotiated purchase and expropriation through July, 1971, contained in the booklet cited in note 13 above, p. 37, indicates that a total of 654 titles to more than 10,000 hectares had been distributed to cooperatives and for communal use, as against 4,227 titles to 60,000 hectares for individual exploitation. The proposal to cease distributions of family farms is contained in Article 15 of the draft law.

[38] Law 135 of 1961, Art. 81, as amended by Law 1 of 1968. As is discussed in the text following note 105, family farms do not generally pass by inheritance or will.

[39] Law 135 of 1961, Arts. 71 and 82.

[40] Accord 23 of August 22, 1966, note 36 above, Art. 20.

[41] Law 135 of 1961, Arts. 50 and 87; interview with officials of INCORA's Division of Adjudications, July 8, 1969.

(b) It shall normally require for reasonable exploitation no more than the labor of the owner and his family, other than the employment of casual seasonal labor and the occasional mutual assistance which neighboring farmers give each other.

Actual Acquisitions and Redistributions, 1962 to 1969

Table 3 summarizes all completed acquisitions of private lands by INCORA, and all distributions of parcels derived from such lands, through July, 1969.

Among the interesting facts revealed by Table 3 and discussed below are these: the small numbers of farms and hectares actually distributed; the disparities between the relatively large amounts of land acquired and the smaller amounts distributed; the large areas acquired by extinction; the insignificant number of expropriations, especially as compared to the fairly substantial number of negotiated purchases; and the differences among the average sizes of farms distributed, depending on the manner in which INCORA acquired the land.[42]

Few Titles Distributed: Political Reasons

In view of the need, discussed at the beginning of the paper, for redistribution of land to many hundreds of thousands of peasant families—*minifundio* owners, tenants, sharecroppers, and squatters, not to mention farm laborers and others who do not have even bare possession of any land—the distribution during seven-and-one-half years of a total of approximately 7,000 titles comprising 113,000 hectares (out of almost 2,900,000 hectares acquired by INCORA) was not an impressive response to the problem. Why did INCORA not move faster?

The main purpose of this study was to evaluate INCORA's procedures for acquiring and distributing rural land. While it is clear

[42] The last of these points is discussed in the text following note 85. The average sizes of parcels distributed were about eighteen hectares for lands acquired by extinction, 11.6 hectares for lands acquired by negotiated purchase, and 25.5 hectares for lands acquired by gratuitous transfer. The average size of all tracts distributed was about sixteen hectares.

Table 3. Acquisitions and Redistributions of Privately Owned Lands by INCORA through July, 1969[a]

Project	Total Acquisitions Farms	Total Acquisitions Hectares	Total Distributions Farms	Total Distributions Hectares
Antioquia 1-2-3	26	79,070	44 (53)	1,904
Atlántico 3	199	13,449	(701)	5,621
Bolívar 1	126	24,803	277 (395)	4,370
Boyacá 1	50	709,332	(31)	631
Cauca 1	4	124,739	0	
Cauca 2	11	142,623	17	1[c]
Cesar 1	15	140,814	0	
Cesar 2	12	747,036	63 (233)	9,261
Córdoba 1	32	10,330	84 (145)	2,141
Córdoba 2	98	14,059	(768)	6,270
Cundinamarca 1	8	1,791	206 (30)	1,411
Cundinamarca 2			207[b]	1,209
Cundinamarca 3	5	31,356	(7)	98
Cundinamarca 4	17	10,012	261 (64)	1,264
Huila 1-2-3			293[b]	9,656
Magdalena 1	29	53,110	547 (36)	1,288
Magdalena 2	13	26,649	547 (46)	5,712
Magdalena Medio	15	172,235	588 (19)	32,950
Meta 1	6	35,354	0	
Nariño 1—Putumayo 1	30	61,205	148 (349)	4,725
Norte de Santander 1	101	93,622	(251)	7,213
Santander 1-2	28	117,943	156 (75)	4,701
Sucre 1	5	120,056	(100)	1,258
Tolima 1	66	76,918	68 (83)	2,177
Tolima 2	94	51,637	67 (136)	4,089
Tolima 3	13	4,732	90 (68)	2,479
Valle 1	12	3,617	71 (67)	1,015
Valle 2	3	3,430	121	1,408
Totals	1,018	2,869,922	3,308 (3,657)	112,852

TABLE 3 (Continued). ACQUISITIONS AND REDISTRIBUTIONS OF PRIVATELY OWNED LANDS BY INCORA THROUGH JULY, 1969

| Project | Acquired by Negotiated Purchase |||| Acquired by Gratuitous Transfer ||||
| | Acquisitions || Distributions || Acquisitions || Distributions ||
	Farms	Hectares	Farms	Hectares	Farms	Hectares	Farms	Hectares
Antioquia 1–2–3	6	976			3	6,068	44	1,353
Atlántico 3	196	12,991	(53)	551	0		0	
Bolívar 1	122	16,657	(701)f	5,621	1	1,017	277	1,899
Boyacá 1	40	261	(395)f	2,471	0		0	
Cauca 1	2	68	0		0		0	
Cauca 2	1	14	0		1	15	17	1e
Cesar 1	0		0		0		0	
Cesar 2	2	7,034	(233)	6,799	1	9,870	63	2,462
Córdoba 1	29	4,113	?i	1,396	1	3,379	84j	745
Córdoba 2	93	8,178	(145)	6,270	1	3,751	0	
Cundinamarca 1	8	1,791	(768)	1,411	2		0	
Cundinamarca 2			(30)		0			
Cundinamarca 3	0		206		1	18,780		98
Cundinamarca 4	6	1,769	0		0		(7)	
Huila 1–2–3		9,764	261	733		15,170		
Magdalena 1	23	1,245			0		0	
Magdalena 2	4	567	(36)	1,288	1	17,179	547	3,563
Magdalena Medio	0		0		3	116,905	588	32,683
Meta 1	3	5,302	0		1	12,200	0	
Nariño 1—Putumayo 1	20	6,514	148g (349)	3,680	2	626	?g	
Norte de Santander 1	74	13,835	(251)h	7,213	1	463	?h	
Santander 1–2	15	8,696	156 (75)k	4,701	4	15,917	?k	
Sucre 1	1	240	(?)l		2	84,218	(100)l	1,258
Tolima 1	56	9,381	68 (83)	2,177	0		0	
Tolima 2	85	8,415	67 (136)	4,089	3	1,769	0	
Tolima 3	11	3,018	90 (68)	2,479	0		0	
Valle 1	9	587	71 (67)i	1,015	2	2,506	0	
Valle 2	0		0		2	1,430	?e	
Totals	806	121,416	1,067 (3,390)	51,894	29	311,263	1,620 (107)	44,062

TABLE 3 (Continued). ACQUISITIONS AND REDISTRIBUTIONS OF PRIVATELY OWNED LANDS BY INCORA THROUGH JULY, 1969

Project	Acquired by Extinction Acquisitions Farms	Acquired by Extinction Acquisitions Hectares	Acquired by Extinction Distributions Farms	Acquired by Extinction Distributions Hectares	Acquired by Expropriation Acquisitions Farms	Acquired by Expropriation Acquisitions Hectares	Acquired by Expropriation Distributions Farms	Acquired by Expropriation Distributions Hectares
Antioquia 1–2–3	17	72,026	0		0		0	
Atlántico 3	1	125	0		2	458	?f	
Bolívar 1	2	6,550	0		1	579	?f	
Boyacá 1	10	709,061[d]	(31)	631	1	0.17	0	
Cauca 1	2	124,671[d]	0		0		0	
Cauca 2	9	142,594	0		0		0	
Cesar 1	15	140,814	0		0		0	
Cesar 2	8	730,132	0		0		0	
Córdoba 1	2	2,839	0		1	486	0	
Córdoba 2	2	1,644	0		0		0	
Cundinamarca 1	0		0					
Cundinamarca 2								
Cundinamarca 3	4	12,576	0		0		0	
Cundinamarca 4	11	8,243	(64)	531	0		0	
Huila 1–2–3	6	51,865	0		0		0	
Magdalena 1	8	8,902	(46)	2,149	0		0	
Magdalena 2	12	55,330	(19)	267	0		0	
Magdalena Medio	2	17,852	0		0		0	
Meta 1	6	49,628	0		2	4,437	?g	
Nariño 1—Putumayo 1	24	78,896	0		2	428	?h	
Norte de Santander 1	9	93,330	0		0		0	
Santander 1–2	2	35,598	0		0		0	
Sucre 1	8	66,530	0		2	1,007	0	
Tolima 1	6	41,453	0		0		0	
Tolima 2	2	1,714	0		0		0	
Tolima 3	0		0		1	74	?i	
Valle 1	1	2,000	121e	1,408	0		0	
Valle 2								
Totals	169	2,454,373	121 (160)	4,986	12	7,486	?	

a Taken from tabulations maintained by INCORA's division of adjudications in August, 1969. Farms acquired were generally large farms (*fincas* or *haciendas*) intended for parcelation. Farms distributed were generally small "family farms." In columns enumerating farms distributed, numbers in parentheses represent "tentative assignments," and numbers not in parentheses represent "final adjudications." See text at notes 94 to 112 below. In some cases the figures in the "Total Acquisitions" and "Total Distributions" columns cannot be obtained by adding the related subtotals in the other columns. Such discrepancies existed in the INCORA charts from which these data were derived, and were not explained.

b Through May, 1969. No data beyond those shown were available for Cundinamarca 2 or Huila 1-2-3. It is not known whether some of the distributions were tentative rather than final.

c It is apparent that seventeen family farms could not have a total of one hectare or have been formed out of the one fifteen-hectare farm acquired by gratuitous transfer, but that was the result shown by INCORA records.

d Of the ten farms acquired by extinction in Boyacá 1, one had an area of 495,200 hectares. Of the two farms acquired by extinction in Cauca 1, one had an area of 120,000 hectares.

e Of the 121 farms distributed in Valle 2, an undetermined number were derived from the one farm acquired by extinction, and the remainder from the two farms acquired by gratuitous transfer.

f Although most of the 701 farms distributed in Atlántico 3 were derived from thirty of the 196 farms acquired by negotiated purchase, an undetermined number were derived from one of the two farms acquired by expropriation. Although most of the 395 farms tentatively assigned in Bolívar 1 were derived from thirteen of the 122 farms acquired by negotiated purchase, an undetermined number were derived from the one farm acquired by expropriation.

g Of the 148 farms finally adjudicated in Nariño 1—Putumayo 1, an undetermined number were derived from three farms acquired by negotiated purchase, and the remainder from one farm acquired by gratuitous transfer. Of the 349 farms tentatively assigned, most appear to have been derived from fourteen farms acquired by negotiated purchase, and the remainder from two farms acquired by expropriation.

h Of the 251 farms distributed in Norte de Santander 1, most appear to have been derived from thirty-seven of the seventy-four farms acquired by negotiated purchase, and the remainder from one of the two farms acquired by expropriation and the one farm acquired by gratuitous transfer.

i Of the 138 farms distributed in Valle 1, most were derived from seven of the nine farms acquired by negotiated purchase, and the remainder from the one farm acquired by expropriation.

j Of the eighty-four farms finally adjudicated in Córdoba 1, an undetermined number were derived from the one farm acquired by gratuitous transfer, and the remainder from one of the twenty-nine farms acquired by negotiated purchase.

k The seventy-five farms tentatively assigned in Santander 1-2 were derived from six farms of the fifteen acquired by negotiated purchase. Of the 156 farms tentatively assigned, most appear to have been derived from three farms acquired by negotiated purchase, and the remainder from one of the four farms acquired by gratuitous transfer.

l Of the 100 farms distributed in Sucre 1, most appear to have been derived from one of the two farms acquired by gratuitous transfer, and the remainder from the one farm acquired by negotiated purchase.

that the procedures do entail delays, as discussed previously and in later sections, it is apparent that the principal reason for the slow pace of Colombia's land-reform program (and indeed for many of the procedural obstacles) has been the lack of effective political support for the program. The basic problem seems to have been the absence of leadership and focused political action by the peasants themselves.

Ordinarily a governmental program for major social or economic change is adopted and implemented at least in substantial part in response to rather immediate pressures from the group which stands to benefit directly from the change. That was not true in the present case. In the past two decades Colombian peasants have had very little voice in whatever government happened to be in power. Neither did they exert significant extralegal pressures for land reform, such as they did through widespread invasions of large estates during the 1930s.[43]

The immediate circumstances leading to enactment of Law 135 of 1961 seem to have been apprehension among the political elite as a result of the Cuban Revolution and the attendant confiscation of private estates, and the not unrelated respectability and even possible profitability of land reform due to the adoption of the Act of Bogotá by the Organization of American States and establishment of the Alliance for Progress.[44] Another contributing factor may well have been a belief by some that the law would not actually be implemented and was therefore a harmless gesture, a belief supported by the relative ineffectiveness of earlier "progressive" Colombian land legislation.[45] Basically, the act was passed without significant pressure from the peasantry by a combination of con-

---

[43] See Hirschman, note 3 above, pp. 101–106.

[44] *Ibid.*, pp. 156–157. The Act of Bogotá was adopted in September, 1960. Article I-A called for a "wider and more equitable distribution of the ownership of land," more agricultural credit, and tax laws which would encourage "improved use of land, especially of privately owned land which is idle." In August, 1961, the Declaration of Punta del Este established the Alliance for Progress. Title I encouraged "comprehensive agrarian reform . . . with a view to replacing *latifundia* and dwarf holdings by an equitable system of land tenure so that, supplemented by timely and adequate credit, technical assistance and improved marketing arrangements, the land will become for the man who works it the basis of his economic stability, the foundation of his increasing welfare, and the guarantee of his freedom and dignity."

[45] See Hirschman, note 3 above, pp. 107–116, 156–157.

gressmen, some of whom affirmatively favored its implementation, but others of whom would oppose implementation or, at most, support it only so long as failure to do so seemed to pose a threat of even more drastic and distasteful change.

Once it began to appear that INCORA officials would actually move to enforce the act, and that there was no substantial threat of revolution or land seizures by the peasants, the lack of strong support for land reform began to show, particularly in the Conservative party. And under Colombia's unusual bipartisan coalition government, it is difficult for the executive branch to take forceful action in any program which does not have the backing of both parties involved, the Conservatives and the Liberals. The National Front coalition (*Frente Nacional*) was formed in 1958 and is to terminate in 1974.[46] Under the arrangement, the two participating parties alternate in nominating presidential candidates every four years, and the coalition's slate of candidates for the national senate and house of representatives is divided equally between Conservatives and Liberals. Cabinet, department (state), and municipal offices, and even seats on INCORA's board of directors, also are divided equally between the parties.[47] The President tends to govern by consensus or not at all. Even a Liberal like Carlos Lleras Restrepo, who as a senator was chiefly responsible for pushing Law 135

[46] The National Front was formed to end the violence (*La Violencia*) which had wracked the Colombian countryside for a decade, pitting Liberal against Conservative peasants in a massive bloodbath stemming from the assassination in 1948 of Jorge Eliecer Gaitán, the charismatic populist leader of the reform wing of the Liberal party. Although the violence demonstrated the high degree of attachment which Colombian peasants traditionally have felt toward one or the other of the two parties, the affiliations have been determined mainly by heredity and without regard for the parties' espousal of programs of potential benefit to the peasants. In fact, neither party served its poor rural constituents well, both being elitist and representing merely different segments of the Establishment.

[47] See generally Duff, note 3 above, pp. 20–36; Robert H. Dix, *Colombia: The Political Dimensions of Change* (New Haven, 1967). The composition of INCORA's Board of Directors is prescribed by Article 8 of Law 135, as amended in 1968, and Article 14 of the agency's bylaws. Its seventeen members include the Minister of Agriculture, who acts as chairman; the managing officers of several other governmental agencies concerned with rural affairs; representatives of trade associations of the agricultural cooperatives, the agricultural workers, and the large landowners; a member of the General Staff of the Armed Forces; a representative of the Catholic Social Action organizations, "whose presence on the Board shall be disregarded in applying the rule of equal political representation"; and two members from each of the national Senate and House of Representatives.

through the Congress in 1961, was restrained in his power to implement it while he was President from 1966 to 1970.

Another deterrent to an aggressive land redistribution effort during Lleras's presidency seems to have been his concentration on programs for rapid economic development, combined with a belief that, by and large, land reform would not contribute to short-run increases in national income or the production of exportable commodities capable of generating the foreign exchange needed for industrialization. INCORA officials in Bogotá and in the field stated in 1969 that the institute's major concern had shifted from social reform to increased production. The general manager said that the highest priorities were extension of credit, construction of irrigation works for the very best lands, and implementation of the new *arrepas* program.[48]

Why was the *arrepas* program established by Law 1 of 1968 and immediately given such high priority, despite the fact that it promised primarily social rather than economic change, and in the absence of special political pressure from small tenants and sharecroppers? The answer probably lies in the anticipated termination of the National Front in 1974. In 1968 Carlos Lleras Restrepo, the final Liberal President under the coalition, was halfway through his term and attempting to lay the foundation for a Liberal victory, and perhaps his own return to the presidency, in the anticipated wide-open elections of 1974. He wanted to institute programs for which he and the Liberals could claim credit, even after four intervening years with a Conservative President. As discussed earlier, acquisitions and redistributions for the *arrepas* program could be achieved more rapidly than for other types of restructuring activities;[49] hence there should be more political impact in a relatively

---

[48] Interview with Carlos Villamil Cháux, June 23, 1969. In "Carta Informativa" No. 14, published by INCORA in July, 1969, Dr. Cháux said that only 2.8 percent of Colombia was flat, arable land capable of producing crops on a competitive basis for international markets. According to the Ministry of Agriculture, between 1962 and 1969 INCORA expended 3,143 million pesos, including (in millions) 1,171 for credit; 908 for irrigation works; 366 for land purchases; 192 for road construction; 178 for technical assistance; thirty-six for *arrepas*; thirty-five for distribution of titles; thirty-five for construction of operating centers; ten on legal matters; and 208 for other activities. *El Espectador* (Bogotá), April 4, 1971, Agricultural Section, p. 2, col. 3.

[49] Text at note 10 above and following.

short time. The Conservatives apparently decided to go along with the proposed law in hopes that they could either impede or take the credit for its implementation.[50]

The pace of distributions by INCORA of lands acquired by means other than extinction began to increase rapidly in the latter part of Carlos Lleras Restrepo's term, partly but not entirely as a result of the *arrepas* program. Table 3 shows that from 1962 through July, 1969, approximately 440,000 hectares were acquired by expropriation, negotiated purchase, and gratuitous transfer, and about 96,000 hectares of such lands were distributed to 6,200 families. From August, 1969, through December, 1970, INCORA acquired only about 14,000 additional hectares by these methods, but it distributed more titles (7,600) and more hectares (117,000) than during the preceding seven-and-one-half years.[51]

Another significant element of Law 1 of 1968, in addition to establishment of the *arrepas* program, was a provision authorizing INCORA to regulate the organization and operation of cooperatives and other associations of peasants receiving land, credit, technical assistance, or other rural services from the government.[52] By early 1969, at President Lleras's direction, INCORA had undertaken actively to promote the formation of such associations—for example, by distributing land or extending credit to them—in every area where it was operating,[53] and officials acknowledged that the peasants were being organized at least in part for the purpose of making them an effective political force. Lleras's aims may well have been twofold: to build peasant leadership and create the popu-

---

[50] Enrique Peñalosa, who was general manager of INCORA and then Minister of Agriculture, under President Lleras, said in the speech referred to in note 29 above that even now he cannot understand how Law 1 of 1968 got through the Congress.

[51] Letter of February 4, 1971, from Carlos Sánchez Ramos, then head of the Division of Adjudications. The total distributions through 1970 included 9,462 final adjudications (147,303 hectares) and 4,392 tentative assignments (65,550 hectares). Concerning the distinction between final adjudications and tentative assignments, see the text at notes 94 through 105 below.

[52] Art. 28, amending Art. 100 of Law 135 of 1961.

[53] Accord 2 of January 27, 1969, of INCORA's Board of Directors, Art. 7, expressly approved by Presidential Decree 461 of March 28, 1969. This accord also contains the regulations governing the organization and operation of the associations. Enrique Peñalosa, note 29 above, said that credit extended to cooperatives has been better used than that granted to individuals.

lar support and pressure for agrarian reform that had previously been lacking, and (as with the *arrepas* program) to bring Conservative peasants into the Liberal camp by 1974. Whatever may eventuate with respect to the latter aim, it seems clear that the former is being realized. Just before his term ended in August, 1970, Lleras inaugurated a national peasants' union, the *Asociación Nacional de Usuarios Campesinos*, which has been very active in 1971.[54]

The 1970 Colombian national elections left the National Front in a very precarious position. The coalition's presidential candidate, Conservative Misael Pastrana Borrero, barely won over former dictator Gustavo Rojas Pinilla, whose strong showing demonstrated a great dissatisfaction among the poor, especially the urban poor, with the slow pace of social reform. The coalition was left with only a small majority in Congress over Rojas's party, the National Popular Alliance (ANAPO). With Liberals already restive in anticipation of 1974, Pastrana was in trouble from the start.[55]

When Pastrana began to slow down land reform in response to Conservative demands,[56] he was met in February, 1971, with apparently coordinated student riots in Cali, Colombia's third largest city, and invasions by 3,000 peasants of forty-four private estates in the departments of Córdoba, Huila, Sucre, and Tolima.[57] The government's request that the peasants withdraw was rejected, and the *Asociación Nacional de Usuarios Campesinos* issued a statement in which it said, "The land our comrades have taken belongs to the people. We will not return it to the selfish oligarchic exploiters. The people must defend it."[58] Carlos Villamil Cháux, whom Pastrana had held over from the Lleras administration as general manager of INCORA, joined the chorus by issuing a statement that the land seizures were caused by the peasants' "justifiable mistrust of the legal channels of land reform," and Pastrana responded by firing him.[59] These events then evoked an unprecedented statement from the bishops of the Colombian church,

---

[54] V, *Latin America* (London, March 5, 1971), pp. 78–79.
[55] IV, *Latin America* (London, September 25, 1970), p. 311.
[56] *Ibid*.
[57] See note 54 above; *New York Times*, April 26, 1971, col. 13, p. 1.
[58] See note 54 above.
[59] V, *Latin America* (London, March 19, 1971), p. 95.

traditionally one of the most conservative in Latin America and closely allied with the Conservative party, calling for widespread social and economic reforms, including accelerated land reform.[60] The total pressure on the shaky government was enormous, and on April 12, 1971, it announced INCORA's impending expropriation of a large number of estates in the savanna of Bogotá, an action that would have seemed politically impossible earlier.[61]

At that point it appeared that vigorous popular support for social change, coming at a time when the Conservatives could feel compelled to yield in the face of the impending termination of the National Front coalition, might produce an acceleration in the pace of the land-reform program.[62] However, something quite different happened. In July, 1971, the Minister of Agriculture announced that the government had decided to halt the land redistribution program for the time being and concentrate on helping peasants who had already received land from INCORA. He attributed the decision to an expected shortage of food in Colombia due to crop damage from heavy rains and to rural unrest over the ineffectiveness of agrarian reform. "This means," he said, "that INCORA will not be committing itself to new operations until those it already has are functioning properly."[63] And that is where matters stand at the end of 1971, though the Conservative government continues to talk about the need for a stronger land-reform program.

[60] *Ibid.*
[61] Speech by Enrique Peñalosa, note 29 above.
[62] A special task force commissioned by the President in November, 1970, to evaluate the agrarian reform program had just issued its report, cited in note 3 above, strongly criticizing the slow pace of the program and its emphasis on increasing production rather than bringing about social change, and recommending numerous amendments to strengthen Law 135 and related acts. The recommendations had been speedily incorporated into the draft law cited in note 13 above. As compared to INCORA's total expenditures of 3,143 million pesos for 1962 to 1969, summarized in note 48 above, the projected budget for 1970 to 1973 was 5,027 million pesos, including (in millions): 1,294 for credit; 1,067 for irrigation works; 833 for land purchases; 333 for road construction; 266 for technical assistance; sixty-one for distribution of titles; fifty-seven for special programs of parcelization, colonization, and extinction; thirty-nine on legal matters; thirty-seven for construction of operating centers; seventeen for direction of the *arrepas* program; and 904 for other rural development programs. *El Espectador* (Bogotá), April 4, 1971, Agricultural Section, col. 2, p. 3.
[63] V, *Latin America* (London, July 16, 1971), pp. 230–231; John A. Moreau, "Colombia's Agrarian Reform, in Chaos, Has Been Halted," Chicago *Sun-Times*, September 7, 1971, col. 32, p. 1.

What will be done as the 1974 elections draw nearer remains to be seen.

Disparities Between Acquisitions and Distributions

One might expect that after having spent time and effort, overcome political opposition, and in some cases paid large prices in order to acquire private lands, INCORA would move rapidly to distribute them to anxious peasants. However, Table 3 shows very large disparities between the amounts of land acquired and the amounts distributed. This fact did not go unnoticed by Colombia's large landowners, who demanded that INCORA stop trying to devise ways of acquiring more land and satisfy the peasants by distributing lands which the agency was stockpiling.[64]

The most striking disparity between acquisitions and distributions is in the case of lands acquired by extinction. Of the almost 2.5 million hectares acquired, only about 5,000 appear to have been distributed. The magnitude of the acquisitions is explained in the following section, so the question considered here is why so few of the lands were distributed. One explanation given by a former general manager of INCORA is that in fact many of the "undistributed" hectares are in the possession of peasants who were living there and claiming ownership at the times the titles of the other, absentee claimants were declared canceled by extinction, and that INCORA simply recognized the occupants' claims without actually adjudicating or granting new titles to them. In other words, he says that INCORA's official statistics are misleading in that they show the institute as the owner of some lands which INCORA itself considers as belonging to peasants whose titles have been "cleared" by extinction proceedings. The second explanation given was that others of the lands acquired are too remote, of poor quality, or for other reasons not presently attractive for settlement, and were acquired by INCORA because they were eligible for ex-

---

[64] *El Espectador* (Bogotá), March 25, 1971, col. 5-A, p. 4. According to this article, INCORA's acquisitions had risen from those shown in Table 3 to a total of 3,643,700 hectares by extinction and gratuitous transfer and 376,000 hectares by negotiated purchase and expropriation.

tinction and in order to "prevent future problems."[65] No estimate was made of the number of hectares to which either of these explanations might apply. The latter explanation is undoubtedly accurate with respect to some of the lands. As to the first explanation, however, it is difficult to understand why INCORA would maintain its statistics in such a way as to create a misleading and unfavorable impression of the extent of its activities, or why it would forego the opportunity to give the peasant occupants the additional title security which registrable grants from INCORA would provide.

No reason was given for INCORA's failure to distribute approximately 267,000 of the 311,000 hectares acquired by gratuitous transfer, though at least the second explanation given in the preceding paragraph is probably applicable in some cases.

Of approximately 120,000 hectares acquired by negotiated purchase, only about 50,000 were distributed through July, 1969. INCORA also continued to hold some part of the 7,500 hectares acquired by expropriation, but the amount so held could not be determined.[66] The principal explanation offered for these retentions was that in such purchases, INCORA usually acquires entire farms,[67] taking the bad land with the good so as not to leave the seller with a worthless remnant, but distributes only the portions suitable for family farms.[68] Once again, however, the land areas to which this explanation might apply were not known.

In any event, it is clear that the foregoing reasons for INCORA's retention of land do not explain all the disparities between acquisitions and distributions through July, 1969. With respect to lands acquired by gratuitous transfer, negotiated purchase, and expropriation, the explanations offered are, in substance, that the retained lands were not suitable for distribution. Yet, as indicated previously, about 100,000 hectares of such lands were in fact dis-

---

[65] Interview with Enrique Peñalosa, note 29 above, on April 16, 1971, at Urbana, Illinois.
[66] See notes f, g, h, and i to Table 3.
[67] Subject to the owners' "right of exclusion," discussed in note 21 above and the accompanying text.
[68] Interview with Enrique Peñalosa, note 65 above.

tributed between August, 1969, and December, 1970, and statistics through July, 1971, showed that of the total of 270,500 hectares acquired by negotiated purchase and expropriation since 1962, INCORA still retained about 83,500 hectares, of which only 5,500 were classified as "unusable," with the remainder being held for subsequent distribution.[69]

Other factors could account for some delays between acquisition and distribution. For example, INCORA agronomists and economists must conduct studies to determine the proper size for family farms in each area and must, together with surveyors, actually lay out the boundaries of the parcels. Also, if there are more applicants for family farms than can be accommodated on the land acquired in that area, some time is needed to select the recipients. This can be done, however, while the parcels are being laid out. In the public statement which led to his being fired as general manager of INCORA in 1971, Carlos Villamil Cháux said it took 400 days from the time a farm was voluntarily sold to INCORA until it could be redistributed.[70] In some parcelizations and planned settlements where irrigation works, roads, or other improvements are to be constructed, it may be that the acquired lands are not suitable for distribution prior to completion of the improvements. Nevertheless, it is doubtful whether these various factors could account for a large part of the disparities shown by Table 3, especially since most of the acquisitions occurred before 1968.[71]

It is possible, therefore, to conclude that for some unexplained reason INCORA, at least until mid-1969, was not attempting to distribute acquired lands suitable for farming nearly as rapidly as it might have.

Acquisitions by Extinction

Acquisition of large areas by extinction was foreseeable after INCORA conducted the survey of unused tracts larger than 2,000

---

[69] See text at note 51 above regarding the December, 1970, figures. The July, 1971, statistics appear in the booklet cited in note 13 above, p. 37.

[70] Moreau article, note 63 above. See also text, note 59 above.

[71] Dates of acquisitions, though not shown in Table 3, were determined by examination of detailed INCORA records in August, 1969.

hectares called for by Law 135.[72] The institute received 1,238 declarations from persons claiming ownership of tracts in excess of 2,000 hectares. From the declarations INCORA estimated that there were, in the seventeen departments into which the more populated part of Colombia is divided, a total of 7,408,908 hectares in the tracts reported, of which the owners or claimants themselves admitted that 4,569,561 hectares, or 62 percent, were entirely unused. By the end of 1962 INCORA had commenced 108 different legal proceedings seeking extinction of titles or invalidation of claims to a total of 1,128,735 hectares in these estates.[73] As Table 3 indicates, through mid-1969 there had been extinctions of 169 titles or claims representing a total of almost 2.5 million hectares. One tract alone contained about 500,000 hectares, another tract 120,000. Some of the extinctions resulted from proceedings commenced after 1962. Of those commenced in 1962, some may still have been incomplete or on appeal to the courts in 1969, while others were undoubtedly dropped because the land was determined not to be unused or because the owners transferred their rights to INCORA gratuitously.

Acquisitions would have been even greater in number except for a questionable legal position taken by the Council of State in appeals by landowners from INCORA declarations of extinction. In those cases the council, rather than relying on the evidence introduced at the administrative proceedings conducted by INCORA to determine whether "economic use" was being made of the land, ordered new visual inspections to determine the degree of use. Since at least a year had usually passed between the inspections upon which INCORA relied and the new inspections ordered by the Council of State, the landowners had plenty of time after the extinctions declared by the agency, but before the later inspections, to begin making economic use of the land by grazing livestock there

[72] See text following note 16 above. Article 22 of Law 135 also authorized INCORA to require registry certificates from the owners of farms of less than 2,000 hectares. In 1963 INCORA required certificates from the owners of all farms of between 1,500 and 2,000 hectares, and in 1966 it required certificates from the owners of all farms of between 500 and 1,500 hectares. Accord 10 of May, 1963, and Accord 16 of June, 1966, of the Board of Directors of INCORA; Suárez Melo article, note 30 above, p. 77.
[73] Smith, note 4 above, pp. 38, 89, 255.

or making improvements. As a result, through August, 1971, INCORA had lost twenty of thirty-eight appeals to the Council of State in extinction proceedings.[74]

Few Expropriations

One reason for the small number of expropriations completed by INCORA is the complex and time-consuming procedure which must be followed. It is divided into four stages: notification, negotiation, expropriation, and judicial review.[75] The first two are also necessary in acquiring land by negotiated purchase.

Notification involves adoption of a resolution by the general manager of INCORA declaring the need to acquire the farm as part of an overall project, notification to the owner, and examination of the land to determine its size and quality and the degree of utilization.

Next, INCORA is required to conduct negotiations and attempt to arrange a voluntary sale. The issues which must be resolved are the part of the farm which INCORA will acquire and the part which the owner will retain under his right of exclusion, if he chooses to exercise it; the classification of the land as to degree of utilization, which determines its expropriability and the manner in which the compensation will be paid, as well as the purchase price.[76] The land is appraised by experts from the Agustín Codazzi Geographic Institute, but the results of the appraisal are not revealed to the landowners.[77] In no case can INCORA pay more for

[74] Suárez Melo article, note 30 above, p. 79. Article 10 of the draft law cited in note 13 above, would remedy the situation by providing clearly that only the inspection made at the time of the administrative proceedings before INCORA could be considered by the courts in reviewing the agency's finding that the owner was not making economic use of the land.

[75] Except where otherwise noted, the procedure described in the following paragraphs is prescribed by Law 135 of 1961, Art. 61, as amended by Law 1 of 1968, and implemented by Presidential Decree 719 of May 13, 1968.

[76] See text above at notes 18 through 31.

[77] The only scandal involving INCORA since its creation in 1961 occurred in mid-1969 and stemmed from the alleged acceptance of a bribe by José Ignacio Vives Echeverría, a National Senator and member of INCORA's Board of Directors, in return for which Vives was said to have revealed the amount of the confidential appraisal to a prominent landowner, Manuel Ospina Vasquez, whose hacienda INCORA was seeking to acquire. Vives was also alleged to have attempted in other ways to maximize the price which INCORA would pay to Ospina. When the Attorney General

the land than the lesser of this appraisal or the owner's auto-evaluation for cadastral purposes. If INCORA does not complete a negotiated purchase or commence expropriation within two years following notification of the resolution initiating acquisition proceedings, the owner may make a new (higher) auto-evaluation.

The expropriation stage is commenced by INCORA's general manager issuing a resolution declaring the portion of the farm to be taken, the classification of the land as to use, and the method of payment. This resolution must then be approved by the board of directors, with an affirmative vote by the Minister of Agriculture. Notice of the resolution is then given to the landowner, who can petition for an appeal before the appropriate administrative disputes court (*Tribunal de lo Contencioso Administrativo*). If he elects to do so, and if the administrative court decides to hear the appeal, the only matters reviewed are INCORA's compliance with the required formalities and procedures, and the correctness of the determinations as to the degree of use and the land to be retained by the owner under his right of exclusion. If the owner elects not to appeal, or if the administrative court either refuses to hear the appeal or affirms INCORA's actions (including INCORA's compliance with any modifications ordered by the court), the expropriation resolution becomes final. On the other hand, if the administrative court disapproves INCORA's actions, the expropriation proceedings are terminated. Neither party may appeal the decision further. In one early case involving land in Project Córdoba No. 2, the administrative court decided in April, 1965, that an expropriation commenced with notification in May, 1963, was invalid because

---

sought to prosecute Vives, he claimed senatorial immunity and demanded a full debate on the Senate floor before the Senate voted on whether to withdraw his immunity. In the debate, which lasted for weeks and was broadcast by national radio, Vives launched a vitriolic attack on INCORA, President Carlos Lleras Restrepo, and particularly on Enrique Peñalosa, the Minister of Agriculture, who had been general manager of INCORA for seven years. Peñalosa, who presented the government's case in the debate, was forced to resign shortly thereafter. Vives lost his immunity, was prosecuted, convicted and jailed for a short time, but then freed on a legal technicality. He remains a senator and was reported to be promoting his presidential ambitions by attempting to take over ex-dictator Rojas's ANAPO party until Rojas expelled Vives from the party early in 1971. See the Bogotá newspaper, *El Tiempo*, for August and September, 1969; IV, *Latin America* (London, December 4, 1970), p. 391; and V, *Latin America* (February 5, 1971), p. 45.

INCORA, though it had personally notified the owner of all its resolutions and had posted them on the municipal building (*alcaldía*), had failed to post them on the main building of the farm to be expropriated.[78] INCORA had no choice but to start all over again.

Only after the expropriation resolution becomes final can INCORA initiate the final stage by taking the case before the appropriate civil court (*Juez del Circuito*), which puts INCORA in possession of the land and determines the expropriation price after receiving still another appraisal by experts of the Geographic Institute.

As suggested earlier, the expropriation procedure could be improved by clarifying the statutory distinction between "adequately" and "inadequately" used land, thereby removing a major cause of lengthy delays and inordinate consumption of staff time in the negotiation stage.

Negotiated Acquisitions

The technical and time-consuming steps just described are one reason why INCORA has not acquired much land by expropriation. However, the threat of expropriation (or extinction) often enables INCORA to acquire land by negotiated purchase (or gratuitous transfer). A case in point is that of Hacienda Rey in Project Norte de Santander No. 1.[79]

In November, 1962, the general manager of INCORA by resolution declared the necessity of acquiring Hacienda Rey as part of an irrigation district and parcelization approved by the board of directors two weeks earlier. Upon being notified, the apparent owner of the land, Rey Ltda., a limited liability company, by letter from its attorney, Senator Alfredo Rey, advised INCORA that the land in question was not well suited for growing cultivated crops because of poor soil and frequent flooding, that it was being put to its

---

[78] Information obtained by Joseph R. Thome from INCORA files and field visits and summarized in mimeographed class materials used at the University of Wisconsin Law School.

[79] This information was obtained from files in INCORA's Division of Adjudications. Only the names have been changed.

best use, cattle raising, but that if INCORA still wished to acquire the land, the firm was disposed to negotiate a sale and the seven members wished to exercise their right of exclusion and retain a total of 400 hectares.[80] The general manager of INCORA responded, stating that the law prohibited attorney Rey from representing Rey Ltda. before INCORA while he held the office of Senator of the Republic:[81] "I know this stems from an oversight [and] hope the company will designate a new attorney." It did. During 1963 the hacienda was inspected and surveyed by INCORA officials. They reported that of the approximately 1,600 hectares of flat land comprising the hacienda, 500 were used for grazing by 790 cattle, 411 were "pastures in formation," and 683 were forested.

In August, 1964, immediately after INCORA personnel conducted a second inspection of the land and determined its area to be 1,500 hectares, the "first stage of direct negotiations" began and Rey Ltda. was advised that INCORA was not authorized to negotiate for purchase of unused land subject to extinction, which a large part of Hacienda Rey appeared to be. The parties then began bargaining over how the land should be classified as to use. Within a short time they tentatively agreed that 524 hectares would be considered adequately exploited, 411 hectares inadequately exploited, and 565 hectares unused. It was understood that the last item would not be binding, however, if the parties were unable to agree on the price and method of compensation for the lands in the prior two categories.

At that point, in November, 1964, INCORA decided that it could not acquire the land by negotiation because of legal uncertainty over whether the company was still the owner or had been dissolved, and that acquisition by extinction and expropriation would be necessary. The matter was turned over to the Division of National Lands for a determination of the extent to which extinction was applicable. In March, 1965, persons from that division

---

[80] Law 135 of 1961, Art. 64, provides that a farm owned by a partnership or a limited liability company since before September 1, 1960, should be considered not as a single unit but as separate farms corresponding proportionately to each partner's or member's share in the firm. A farm which became the property of such a firm after September 1, 1960, is treated as belonging to a single landowner.

[81] Law 8 of 1958.

conducted another inspection of the hacienda, found the area to be 1,300 hectares, and described the land as flat, 400 hectares of manmade pasture, 200 of potential pasture containing much scrub, 190 with a three-year growth of scrub, and 510 of forest. That same month it was determined that the hacienda was still owned by Rey Ltda., and the company offered to continue negotiations and to grant to INCORA without charge the forest and any other land found to be unused.

In May, 1965, the company formally offered to tranfser to INCORA approximately 510 hectares of forest land. In October, 1965, the company did transfer to INCORA by gratuitous conveyance 463 hectares. In December, 1965, the general manager of INCORA by resolution declared that the remaining portions of Hacienda Rey had been found to be sufficiently exploited so as not to be subject to extinction, and ordered suspension of the extinction proceedings. Negotiations continued over what portions should be classified as adequately used, and what portions as inadequately used. The parties agreed in January, 1966, to classification of 524 hectares as adequately exploited and 506 as inadequately used, including in the latter category ninety-five hectares of forest considered to be reserved for conservation of waters and for service of the farm. As part of the agreement the company and its members renounced their right of exclusion. This ended the first stage of negotiations.

The second stage of direct negotiations took place after the regional cadastral director advised INCORA that the assessed valuation of Hacienda Rey as fixed by the owner's auto-evaluation was 1.3 million pesos, less the value of twenty-three hectares no longer owned by Rey Ltda. INCORA also requested and presumably received an appraisal of the land by experts from the Agustín Codazzi Geographic Institute, but that appraisal is not in the file. In March, 1966, Rey Ltda. entered into a contract to sell the remaining 1,006 hectares to INCORA for a total price of 1,110,647 pesos, with 50.87 percent of that amount being for lands adequately exploited and 49.13 percent for lands inadequately exploited. Each of the seven members was to receive 80,712 pesos for lands adequately used and 77,952 pesos for lands inadequately used, paid in the following form: 150,000 in cash on presentation of the deed, and the remainder of 8,664 pesos, relating to inadequately used land, in eight equal annual installments.[82] The agreement was approved by IN-CORA's Board of Directors in April, 1966, and the transaction completed in June, 1966.

In sum, the process of transferring control of Hacienda Rey from its owners to INCORA took a total of three years and seven months. This was a reasonably straightforward process, but meanwhile land-hungry peasants waited, wondering whether the land-reform law really could satisfy their needs and aspirations.

Special Problems in Distributing Family Farms

The definition of "family farm" and the circumstances under which INCORA distributes such units were discussed earlier in the text, following note 35. Each farm is supposed to be large enough to provide subsistence and a gradually increasing standard of living, but small enough to require only the labor of the owner and his family. The minimum allowable size is three hectares, and many are not substantially larger than that. It has been argued that such farms are merely new *minifundios*.[83] Undoubtedly it is true that some are in fact too small to support a family and that, if operated separately, most are too small to permit capital-intensive agriculture. With high rural unemployment, Colombia is probably right in promoting labor-intensive agriculture at this time. Nevertheless, at some future time it may be desirable to mechanize, and it would be unfortunate if land fragmentation made it impossible to do so. As previously mentioned the proportion of distributions to cooperatives and for communal use has been increasing; with respect to individual family farms, an eventual step may be to encourage their cooperative operation.

The following sections deal with practical problems in the process of distributing family farms. It should be noted that some of

[82] See note 80 above and also note 27 and accompanying text.
[83] Cornelio Reyes, in "La Obsesión del Minifundio," in *El Espectador* (Bogotá), March 22, 1971, made this argument, stressing that while INCORA is granting tracts of three to five hectares in irrigation districts comprising Colombia's best agricultural lands, West Germany has in the last decade eliminated by consolidation more than a million farms of less than ten hectares, and the average farm in the United States has grown to more than 120 hectares.

the most difficult problems—such as determining the proper size for individual farms, formulating a correct legal description for each of them, requiring recipients to prove themselves competent managers before their titles become final, imposing restrictions on each recipient's right to transfer or encumber his land, and limiting the cost per recipient— would be substantially alleviated if the distributions were to cooperatives or for communal use.

Determining the Layout of the Subdivision

The most important step in laying out the individual units in a parcelization project or planned settlement area is determining how large each farm should be. INCORA agronomists and agricultural economists study such factors as the topography, soil, and availability of water, and then decide what type of exploitation seems most appropriate and how much land an average family conducting such exploitation by their own labor would need in order to subsist and gradually to improve their standard of living. Although the law prescribes no maximum size for family farms, none distributed through mid-1969 had exceeded ninety hectares, and many were in the range of three to five hectares. When the size has been determined, INCORA surveyors in cooperation with the agronomists and economists lay out the individual parcels on the site, taking into consideration any special needs, such as access to roads or streams.[84]

Several factors have on occasion caused INCORA to distribute parcels later conceded to be too small to support a family. One is mistakes concerning the type of exploitation which will be conducted on the land. For example, in Parcelization Paticuinde in Project Tolima No. 1, Municipio of Icononzo, a former coffee plantation was divided in 1963 into fifty-nine parcels intended for cultivation (presumably of coffee) and averaging 5.5 hectares, and four parcels intended for cattle-raising and averaging fifty-three hectares. When the smaller tracts were occupied by peasants under tentative assignments, they were used almost immediately for cattle-raising. This was attributable both to the farmers' own preferences and to INCORA's acquiescence, since INCORA has the right to dictate

[84] Interview with officials of INCORA's Division of Adjudications in Bogotá, July 8, 1969.

the use of family farms which it distributes.[85] Since 5.5-hectare tracts were obviously too small for family cattle farms, the parcelization was restructured into a total of thirty-six parcels whose average size was about fifteen hectares, far less than the fifty-three hectares originally determined to be appropriate for cattle-raising in that subdivision.

Other factors which can prejudice INCORA's judgment concerning the proper size of family farms are the number of persons already occupying land when it is acquired for parcelization, and the availability and cost of other unoccupied land nearby. Serious political and social problems could arise if INCORA acquired 500 hectares of land occupied by 100 families, divided it up among only twenty of the families, and made no provision for the other eighty. Therefore, the tendency, according to INCORA officials, is to try to accommodate in a parcelization as many as reasonably possible of those persons who seem to have some kind of moral claim to share the land, even if this means distributing somewhat smaller parcels than would be provided without such pressure. Table 3 shows that the average size of parcels distributed from land acquired by negotiated purchase is about 11.5 hectares, less than half the size of the average parcel derived from land acquired by gratuitous transfer (25.5 hectares) and about two-thirds the size of the average parcel derived from land obtained by extinction (eighteen hectares). Of course, another possible explanation for these facts might be that land acquired without cost is often of poorer quality.

Besides size and the need for access to roads or streams, other factors considered in laying out family farms include ease of boundary identification and the personal security of the inhabitants.

It has been strongly advocated that surveys and boundary identification would be facilitated by having regularly shaped parcels, such as rectangles or at least figures with straight sides.[86] In flat areas parcels frequently are quite regular in shape, but in rough country

---

[85] See text at note 103 below. INCORA officials in Tolima who showed the author through Paticuinde in August, 1969, said the reason for INCORA's acquiescence was that the land and rainfall were not adequate for cultivation (though Paticuinde had previously been a coffee plantation), while an official in Bogotá cited changes in the world coffee market and in Colombia's agricultural policies.

[86] Smith, note 4 above, pp. 158–167.

INCORA personnel generally conform parcel boundaries to roads, streams, ridges, gulleys and other topographical features. In the short run, this system does perhaps make location of boundaries easier in broken terrain, though it makes accurate description of the land by angles and distances very difficult. In the long run, topographical features have a way of changing, and the lack of accurate surveys and of descriptions based on permanent reference points is likely to produce boundary disputes and title insecurity.

In Tolima and Nariño, sites of great civil violence during the decade or more prior to commencement of the land-reform program, INCORA adopted a system of nuclear parcelizations. For reason of personal safety, many distributees of family farms received two parcels, a small one in the central residential *concentración* and a larger one on the periphery for cattle or crops. Besides providing security, such an arrangement has other seeming advantages, such as increasing the social contacts of the inhabitants and reducing the cost of providing electricity and other public services and facilities.[87] Nevertheless, the nuclear system has not been particularly well received by the peasants in Tolima and Nariño, many of whom have abandoned their residential tracts and built homes on the land where they work. For example, in Parcelization Paticuinde only twelve of the twenty lots in the *concentración* were occupied, while all thirty-six farming tracts were being operated. In that case there was an additional consideration: INCORA had constructed on each residential tract a house with two or three bedrooms and running water, for which a distributee had to pay a substantial price if he chose to live in the nuclear area.

Selection of Recipients

Since the number of persons wishing their own family farms far exceeds the number of farms being distributed by INCORA, the matter of selecting actual recipients is of great importance. Once INCORA has acquired land for a parcelization project, agency officials conduct at the site, after prior public notice, a registration

[87] For discussion of the three principal patterns of rural settlement—nuclear villages, line villages, and single farmsteads—see Smith, note 4 above, pp. 257–286. The single farmstead is most common in Colombia.

of persons who wish to apply for parcels. Those eligible include tenants, sharecroppers, laborers, and others who have farmed the land being subdivided, as well as peasants from the surrounding area. All must be of "limited resources."[88] The forms to be completed by or for the applicants call for such information as age, education, dependents, farming experience, claimed interests in and improvements added to land, other assets, liabilities, and sources and amount of income.

When the registration has ended, a board of review (the *Junta de Revisión*) composed of the director of the particular INCORA project or his representative, a representative of the Division of Adjudications, and four persons elected by and from among the applicants, reviews and classifies the applications one by one, recording in each case any additional relevant information known by members of the board about the applicant or his family, such as the level of his ability, whether he is a hard worker, or whether any member of the family has been in jail.[89]

After classification of the applicants by the board of review, the matter passes to a selection committee (*Comité de Selección de Adjudicatarios*), comprised of the director of the particular INCORA project, the official in charge of INCORA's supervised credit program, a representative of the national auditor's office, and two representatives from certain local associations established pursuant to authority of the Ministry of Agriculture by users of state agricultural services. The duties of the selection committee are to approve or revise the classification of applicants by the board of review, to select the persons to receive tentative assignments and final adjudications and, subsequently, to determine whether such recipients have met their contractual obligations with INCORA, or should have their interests terminated.[90]

[88] Accord 23 of August 22, 1966, of the Board of Directors of INCORA, Arts. 1–8. This accord establishes most of the procedures for distributing family farms. Late in 1970 the Division of Adjudications had a draft of a new accord which would replace Accord 23 and modify some of the procedures. For the definitions of "limited resources" in Accord 23 and in the draft accord, see note 36 above.

[89] Accord 23 of 1966, note 88 above. The examples of additional relevant information are contained in the INCORA mimeographed form used for preparing minutes of the meeting of the *Junta de Revisión*.

[90] Accord 7 of September 2, 1968, of the Board of Directors of INCORA, Arts. 1 and 3.

Among eligible applicants, the following groups have preferential rights to receive family farms, in the order indicated:
1. Tenants, sharecroppers, and laborers on the land which is being subdivided.
2. Other peasants from neighboring areas with no land of their own.
3. Owners of farms smaller than three hectares whose lands adjoin the tract being subdivided and can be augmented so as to create integrated family farms.[91]

Within each of these groups, applicants are ranked according to a point system which considers four factors: the age of the applicant and the other members of his family; the number of years for which the applicant has worked on the same land; the character and value of improvements made by the applicant; and the value of all property belonging to the applicant other than the land and improvements in question. With respect to age, the most points are given to persons between twenty-five and forty-five years, and the least to those over sixty. The longer the applicant has farmed the same land, the more points he gets, which may compensate for the age bias in some cases. Improvements which are permanent command more points than temporary ones, and the points also increase with the value of the improvements; but points are inversely related to the applicant's other property holdings.[92]

On the basis of the foregoing factors, the selection committee determines which applicants will receive parcels. A lottery is then held to determine which particular parcel each successful applicant will get, except that a recipient who has previously farmed and made improvements on the land being subdivided has a preferential right to the parcel which includes his prior improvements.[93]

Tentative Assignments

The distribution of a family farm by INCORA is in the form of either a tentative assignment (*asignación provisional*) or a final

[91] Accord 23 of 1966, note 88 above, Art. 9.
[92] *Ibid.*, Art. 10.
[93] *Ibid.*, Art. 13; INCORA mimeo form for the selection committee's minutes of the lottery proceeding.

grant or adjudication (*adjudicación definitiva*). The contractual obligations of an *asignatario* during his provisional period, usually about two years, are to farm the parcel in the manner indicated by INCORA; not to make permanent improvements without prior authorization from INCORA; not to transfer any of his rights under the contract to any other person; to farm the land only with his own labor and that of his family except in occasional special circumstances, when he may employ paid labor; and, if INCORA acquired the land by expropriation or negotiated purchase, to pay an annual user charge equal to 0.4 percent of the total acquisition price divided by the number of parcels created.[94] The selection committee can terminate the assignment if the *asignatario* violates any of these obligations or any other obligations imposed by INCORA in connection with the extension of credit, or if he becomes physically or financially incapable of operating the farm, or dies, and the *asignatario* may not appeal the decision to the courts. Upon terminating an assignment, INCORA must pay the appraised value of any improvements by the *asignatario*.[95] Where the cause of termination is the death of the *asignatario*, his best-qualified heir has a preferential right to receive a tentative assignment of the same land.[96]

Although no administrative regulation prescribed any guidelines for determining when parcels were to be tentatively assigned rather than finally adjudicated, the head of the Division of Adjudications in a 1969 letter to a project director suggested use of tentative assignments in the following cases:[97]

(a) When the boundaries of the parcel cannot be delimited in final form. For example, in an irrigation district the plan may be to have as boundaries canals whose routes have not yet been determined; or if an hacienda with 50 tenants on it is ac-

[94] INCORA Multilith 117.67, Form 1-37, Contract of Tentative Assignment; Accord 27 of October 3, 1966, of the Board of Directors of INCORA.

[95] Accord 45 of November 15, 1965, of the Board of Directors of INCORA, as amended by Accord 21 of November 27, 1967, of the board. Although the termination of a tentative assignment is not subject to judicial review, the *asignatario* is entitled to demand a rehearing by INCORA under a procedure known as *recurso de reposición*, set forth in Presidential Decree 2733 of October 7, 1969.

[96] INCORA Multilith 117.67, Form 1-37, Contract of Tentative Assignment.

[97] Letter of May 7, 1969, from Carlos Sánchez Ramos, to the Director of Project Santander No. 1-2.

quired under the *arrepas* program, but it will make only 25 family farms, each of the 50 tenants can be temporarily assigned the tract he already occupies until other nearby land can be acquired on which to resettle 25 of the tenants.

(b) When the inexperience of the recipients makes advisable a training period for them to learn and to demonstrate their ability to work with new crops and farming techniques with which they have not worked before.

(c) When the distributees must adjust to a radically new social situation in the parcelization from that in which they have previously lived.

The letter said that tenants, sharecroppers, and others with experience in the use of the land who are going to continue to farm it in the traditional way and who constitute a cohesive group should receive final adjudications immediately, except in cases similar to the second example (a) in case.

It should not be overlooked that tentative assignments are advantageous to the recipients in some situations. In case (a), where immediate final adjudications would be impossible or unwise, tentative assignments legitimate the *asignatarios*'s possession and allow them to qualify for credit and technical assistance not otherwise available. In other situations where INCORA personnel, as in Parcelization Paticuinde, underestimate the proper size for a family farm, final adjudication of an inadequate parcel can be a disaster for the recipient. Prior to 1962 the Agrarian Bank (*Caja de Crédito Agrario, Industrial y Minero*) carried out some parcelizations near Paticuinde and gave all recipients immediate final adjudications to seven-hectare tracts. Now those landowners do not qualify for credit because of their presumed inability to repay loans from the product of parcels which are uneconomically small; but neither do they qualify to receive more land under the agrarian reform program because their parcels exceed three hectares and are therefore not legally *minifundios*.[98]

Nevertheless, a proposed new regulation would provide that "as a general rule" family farms should be distributed by final adjudication at the outset, and that tentative assignments should be used

[98] Situation described by INCORA officials in Tolima. See text, note 91 above.

only in exceptional cases.[99] Hopefully, INCORA personnel (who change, particularly out in the field) have had enough experience to avoid more mistakes like those in Paticuinde.

Final Adjudications, with Restrictions

Final adjudications of land acquired by INCORA through expropriation or purchase are effectuated by a deed of sale (*contrato de compraventa* or *escritura pública de compraventa*) in which the recipient (*adjudicatario*) agrees to pay for his parcel a price equal to the sum of INCORA's acquisition cost, the cost of surveying and marking the boundaries (not to exceed ten pesos per hectare, about one-third the commercial rate), the cost to INCORA of its improvements to the parcel, and the proportional cost of all irrigation works if the land is in an INCORA irrigation district.[100]

The total price is amortized over a specified period, usually not to exceed fifteen years, with interest on the unpaid balance at the annual rate of 2 percent during the first two years and 4 percent thereafter.[101] Where INCORA acquired the land gratuitously, a regular deed (*escritura pública*) is used and the *adjudicatario* is obliged to pay only for survey and marking and for INCORA improvements and irrigation works. Violation of any of the preceding terms is cause for INCORA to terminate the grantee's rights and retake possession, paying only the value of his improvements.[102] However, termination of the rights of an *adjudicatario*, for any reason, is subject to judicial review by the administrative disputes court.

The most interesting and important aspect of the final adjudication is the high degree of control retained by INCORA over the use and transferability of the land, even after the grantee has fulfilled his repayment obligations:[103]

[99] Art. 16 of the draft accord referred to in note 88 above.
[100] Law 135 of 1961, Arts. 71 and 82, as amended by Law 1 of 1968.
[101] *Ibid.*, Art. 83. INCORA's land cost is calculated by prorating the price paid for the entire farm being subdivided and taking into consideration any factors which may cause differences in value per unit of area among different parcels.
[102] Accord 23 of 1966, note 88 above, Art. 17.
[103] Law 135 of 1961, Arts. 51, 53, and 81, as amended by Law 1 of 1968; Accord 23 of 1966, note 88 above, Art. 15.

(a) The owner must farm the parcel with his own labor and that of his family, and cannot rent or allow others to operate it without INCORA's prior consent.

(b) He must exploit "a reasonable part" of the land in the manner prescribed by INCORA.

(c) He can be required at the time of adjudication to place the farm under the "family ownership system" (*patrimonio familiar*), which prevents it from being mortgaged or subjected to creditors' liens without INCORA's prior approval. If the farm is not placed under this system, INCORA nevertheless has a right to buy it at the appraised value if it becomes the subject of any foreclosure proceedings brought by creditors.[104]

(d) He cannot convey the land to a third person without the prior consent of INCORA, which has the right to buy the land "at a price to be determined by experts" if in INCORA's judgment the proposed conveyance would "contradict the spirit and aims" of Law 135. INCORA is prohibited from approving transfers to persons other than farmers of "limited resources."[105]

(e) In the event of violation of any of the foregoing obligations *or the death of the adjudicatario*, INCORA may terminate the rights of the owner by paying the appraised value of the farm. The best qualified heir or the surviving spouse or "permanent companion" of a deceased *adjudicatario* has a preferential right to receive a tentative assignment or final adjudication of the farm if he or she qualifies as a farmer of "limited resources."

---

[104] The *patrimonio familiar* is established by Law 70 of 1931 and Articles 24 and 25 of Law 100 of 1944 in pursuance of Article 50 of the Colombian Constitution. It and the various other title restrictions referred to in the text obviously come close to making it impossible for any grantee to obtain loans secured by a mortgage on the land. INCORA officials in Tolima said that so far as they knew, no grantee of a family farm had ever received credit from a commercial bank. However, quasi-public lenders such as the Agrarian Bank, the Cattle Bank (*Banco Ganadero*), and INCORA itself, rely for security on the *prenda agraria*, a pledge of the farmer's crops and movable property, for example, equipment and livestock. Law 24 of 1921, as amended, discussed in INCORA, *Prenda Agraria: Comentarios y Normas Legales* (Bogotá, March, 1969).

[105] See note 36 above. INCORA officials in Bogotá said there had been only two requests for permission to convey family farms to third persons; one was approved and the other denied. Interview, July 8, 1969.

These restrictions raise familiar questions about the supposed need of the Latin American peasant for some sort of paternal guidance and control.[106] To what extent is he incapable of managing his own affairs because for centuries he has not been permitted to do so? To what extent is legal paternalism merely an elitist device for selfishly monopolizing power, and to what extent is it necessary to achieve proper levels of national agricultural production? How real is the risk of new *latifundios* if family farms are not subject to restrictions on alienation and mortgaging? How great is the danger of new *minifundios* if fractional interests in the farms are permitted to pass by inheritance to multiple heirs of the deceased owners?[107] If protective restrictions are so important, why are they included only in conveyances of family farms, and not in grants of land in the public domain, or in grants to squatters on land acquired by extinction or gratuitous transfer?[108]

Most Latin American nations with land redistribution programs have resolved these kinds of questions by limiting in some way the beneficiaries' control over lands distributed. Some countries have done so by granting land to cooperatives or communities and regulating them.[109] Cuba, for example, established cooperatives to take over large sugar plantations in 1960. However, the Agrarian Reform Institute retained the power to name all the administrators, and members were not allowed to sell their rights, though they could voluntarily withdraw and relinquish their shares or exchange them with members of other cooperatives. The Mexican *ejidos* are communities which have received land under the agrarian laws growing out of the Revolution of 1910. A community's rights in the land may not be transferred or made subject to any mortgage or other lien. Most *ejidos* operate their noncrop lands (that is, pastures

[106] See Karst, note 2 above, at 572.

[107] Interestingly, when a landowner whose title is not restricted dies in Colombia and his property passes by inheritance to multiple heirs, it is customary for his heirs, and even succeeding generations of heirs, not to partition or divide the land among themselves, but to remain cotenants (*indivisos*), owners of undivided fractional interests in the entire tract. In the extreme this can produce a kind of communal ownership, as it has in parts of Brazil. See Smith, note 4 above, p. 154.

[108] See text at note 34 above; note 36 above; text at note 125 below.

[109] See generally Karst, note 2 above, pp. 573–591, from which the following information is derived.

and forests) collectively, but allocate to each member (*ejidatario*) an individual parcel which he and his family cultivate. His usufructuary rights in the parcel may not be conveyed or subjected to any liens, nor may he permit anyone else to farm the land, but the usufruct may pass by will or inheritance to the person whom the *ejidatario* designates to succeed him as head of the family.[110]

INCORA believes that restrictions of the types included in its deeds to family farms are necessary to achieve the aims of the land-reform program and prevent the creation of new *latifundios* and *minifundios*. This may well be true with respect to restrictions on conveyances, liens, and passage at death. As for the requirement that *adjudicatarios* exploit their land in the manner prescribed by INCORA, agency officials concede that this may be unduly paternalistic, but they expect enforcement of the requirement to decline as the program expands and as peasant associations or unions grow and achieve greater bargaining power.[111] Hopefully, this will happen. In addition, relaxation of the requirement that the *adjudicatario* himself must farm his land might also be desirable.[112]

Title Documents

Each deed used in a final adjudication is prepared by a notary in the notarial circuit where the land is situated.[113] The deed is then exe-

[110] *Ejidatarios* are also subject to some control by elected *ejido* officials, who have frequently exercised it for partisan political purposes. A recent law seeks to reduce the power of entrenched *ejido* bosses, and of the state governors to whom they are usually answerable, by requiring secret ballots in future elections of *ejido* officials, by limiting them to two successive terms in office, and by making the President rather than the governors the final authority in agrarian matters. V, *Latin America* (London, January 29, 1971), pp. 34–35.

[111] Speech by Enrique Peñalosa, note 29 above.

[112] Governmental paternalism toward landowners is not limited to Latin America. See *United States v. Forrester*, 118 F. Supp. 401 (W. D. Ark. 1954), in which the Farmers Home Administration loaned a disabled veteran $6,000 to buy a seventy-seven–acre farm, and then sought to foreclose the mortgage because the debtor did not plant row crops which the administration recommended, and because he leased part of the farm to someone else in violation of the terms of the mortgage. After finding that all payments on the mortgage and for taxes and insurance had been made on time, that the farm had not depreciated in value, that the land was not suited for row crops, and that thirty-seven acres were leased for pasture because the debtor had a broken leg and mangled ankle and could not work, the federal district court decided that it would be "inequitable" to permit foreclosure.

[113] On the notarial and registry systems in Colombia see Luis Arévalo, "The Legal

cuted by the parties, notarized, and recorded in the notary's office. (If the particular INCORA regional office has its own draftsmen and prepares drawings of the subdivision locally rather than sending the surveyors' notes to Bogotá so that the drawings can be made there, a separate drawing of the parcel to be adjudicated may also be prepared and submitted to the notary to be recorded in his office with the deed. This was not done in Tolima No. 1, nor did the *adjudicatario* himself receive a drawing of his parcel.) The notary then issues two copies of the deed, one for INCORA and one for the grantee.[114]

To be legally effective, the deed must then be inscribed in the Registry Office for Public and Private Documents for the registry circuit in which the land is located. This means that at least one of the copies must be delivered to the registrar so that he can extract it in the registry book. Since all notary and registry fees are to be paid by the grantee, the practice in Tolima No. 1 prior to 1968 was to place on him the responsibility for picking up the copies (and paying the fees) at the notary's office, taking them to the registry office (again paying the fees), and subsequently going back there to get his copy after the inscription had been completed and the date, book, and page number noted on each of the two copies. (INCORA's copy was and is sent from the registry office to the cadastral office with jurisdiction over the land, where it is noted and then returned to the INCORA regional office.) However, notarial and registry circuits usually cover several counties (*municipios*), and the registry office may be in a different town from the notary who prepares the deed; and both may be a hard trip from where the grantee lives if he must go on foot or by mule. The result was that many deeds were never registered. The grantees either took them directly home from the notary's office or did not even pick them up there. Of

---

Insecurity of Rural Property in Colombia: A Case Study of the Notarial and Registry Systems" (Ph.D. dissertation, University of Wisconsin, 1970); Pablo Garzón Muñoz and José Edmundo Morato R., *Notariado y Registro* (Bogotá, 1960). The systems were modified in some important respects by Presidential Decrees 1250, 2156, and 2163 of 1970, discussed and set out in full in 37, *Legislación Económica*, No. 435 (Bogotá, November 30, 1970), pp. 259ff.

[114] The factual information in this section concerning title documents was obtained from interviews with INCORA officials in Project Tolima No. 1 on August 18, 1969, and from personal observation.

approximately ten grantees with whom we talked in Parcelization Cafrería in the Municipio of Icononzo, where final adjudications were made in 1964, only one had a copy of his deed, and it bore no registry notation.

Since 1968 the copies of each deed are delivered by the notary or INCORA to the registry office, and after inscription the grantee's copy is returned to the notary, from whom the grantee can get it by paying all fees. The fees average about 150 pesos per parcel.

The procedure could still be improved. It seems that INCORA could easily deliver the grantee's copy of the deed to him after registration and add the fees to his other repayment obligations if he has no cash. If at all possible, a drawing of each parcel should be recorded in the notary's office with the deed, and a copy given to the grantee, showing the shape and dimensions, the location of the numbered stone or concrete markers set at the corners, and any other natural or artificial physical features referred to in the description, or otherwise of importance. Many deeds simply describe parcels in terms such as these: "Beginning at the southwest corner at marker no. 241, thence 400 meters north to marker no. 242, thence 385 meters east to marker no. 243, thence. . . ." Without a drawing, the owner will have difficulty identifying his boundaries if the markers disappear, as many already have.

Large Cost of Parcelizations

Particularly where INCORA must pay for the land which it acquires for redistribution, the costs of parcelization projects can be great. For instance, from 1962 through 1968 virtually all money and effort expended in Project Tolima No. 1 related to parcelizations which in 1969 accommodated a total of approximately 600 families —350 *adjudicatarios* and 250 *asignatarios*—on family farms with an aggregate area of about 9,000 hectares and an average size of fifteen hectares.[115] To obtain INCORA's average cost per family, including the cost of new roads and other improvements and the provision of credit and technical assistance, INCORA officials in Cunday said

[115] Data in this section were obtained from interviews with INCORA officials in Tolima No. 1 on August 18, 1969, and from INCORA's *Boletín de Estadística*, September, 1968, pp. 132–133.

it was reasonable to divide the total budget of Tolima No. 1 for the period 1962 to 1968 by 600. That budget is shown in Table 4. Since

TABLE 4. FINANCIAL AND HUMAN RESOURCES COMMITTED BY INCORA TO PROJECT TOLIMA NO. 1, 1962–1968

	1962–1967	Budgeted for 1968	Actual Jan.–Sept. 1968
Expenditures (thousands of pesos)	57,117	14,472	9,283
Agricultural development	5,894	75	78
Legal	14,716	3,418	773
Titling of public domain lands	344	108	95
Legal counsel		109	23
Land purchases	14,372	2,807	367
Arrepas program		394	288
Engineering	22,571	6,439	5,511
Irrigation			
Works	488		
Studies	1,719		
Roads	16,634	5,500	4,954
Supervision	685	414	303
Hydrology		30	19
Engineering studies	297	225	110
Various constructions	2,748	320	125
Specific projects	5,123	3,508	2,178
Cooperatives	940	223	21
Rural development	968	600	230
Technical assistance (credit)	3,215	2,685	1,927
Regional administration	8,813	982	743
Personnel			
Director's office			
Director	1		1
Assistants	1		1
Agricultural scientists			
Professionals	8		10
Assistants	28		31
Legal			
Professionals	1		3
Assistants	1		1
Engineering			
Professionals	1		2
Assistants	10		26
Administration			
Administrators			2
Assistants	19		23
Planning personnel			43

SOURCE: *Boletín de Estadística*, September, 1968, p. 133.

the total expenditures through 1967 were a little over 57,000,000 pesos, and about 14,500,000 pesos were budgeted for 1968, the cost per family to INCORA was almost 120,000 pesos, or US $7,500. Major items of expense were approximately 17,000,000 pesos for purchase of 12,000 hectares of land and 22,000,000 pesos for road construction. The land consisted of sixty farms obtained by negotiation and nine by expropriation.[116] (Much more land was acquired by extinction, but none of it was distributed.)[117] Even without any land acquisition expenses at all, INCORA's cost per family for the parcelizations would have been about 90,000 pesos.

Distribution of Land in the Public Domain

In Colombia the public domain (*terrenos baldíos*, or *baldíos*) includes lands never adjudicated, and lands which were adjudicated but subsequently reverted to the state because they were not exploited to the extent required by law or by the terms of the original grants.[118] Except for those portions specially reserved for such purposes as planned settlement areas, conservation of natural resources, and provision of public services,[119] the public domain is open to spontaneous colonization by Colombian citizens, each of whom can acquire a right to adjudication of up to 450 hectares (or up to 1,000 or even 3,000 hectares in remote areas in the eastern part of the nation lacking any roads or other public services) by bringing under cultivation, or sowing with artificial pastures and exploiting by grazing, at least two-thirds of the area to which he seeks title.[120] In order to avoid creation of new *minifundios*, the law provides that tracts of less than twenty-five hectares shall not be adjudicated ex-

---

[116] The author does not know why these figures differ from those in Table 3 above.
[117] See Table 3 above.
[118] Código Fiscal, Art. 44; Laws 34 and 200 of 1936. See Josefina Amézquita de Almeida and Wenceslao Tovar Mozo, *Régimen Legal de Baldíos en Colombia* (Bogotá, 1961), pp. 9–10.
[119] Articles 31, 39, and 43 of Law 135 of 1961, as amended by Law 1 of 1968.
[120] *Ibid.*, Arts. 29 and 30. However, Article 31 of Law 135 and Articles 45 and 107 of the Código Fiscal prescribe more stringent restrictions on lands very close to roads, railroads, navigable rivers, seaports, or urban centers of more than 10,000 persons. Prior to 1961 tracts up to 5,000 hectares were adjudicable in the vast eastern plains. Law 97 of 1946, Art. 11.

cept where adjacent settlers or private lands or the nature of the terrain do not permit compliance with this minimum.[121]

The *baldíos* of Colombia are enormous. Of the total national area of 113.8 million hectares, approximately 60 million lie east of the *cordillera oriental*, the most eastern of the three mountain chains extending north and northeast from the southwest corner of the country. This land is mostly *baldíos*. In addition, much land west of the *cordillera oriental* is also *baldíos*, most of which are mountainous and unsuited for agriculture. Although reliable evidence is scarce concerning the real agricultural possibilities of the eastern plains (*llanos*), this has not deterred thousands of hopeful people from extending the frontier to acquire their own land, nor has it prevented opponents of land redistribution in the heavily populated Andean region from advocating that INCORA concentrate on promoting settlement of the public domain.[122] Although INCORA has generally refrained from such promotion, it has nevertheless distributed far more *baldíos* than land acquired from private persons.

Methods of Distribution

There are two procedures—"ordinary" and "special"—for adjudicating unreserved *baldíos*. Both require an application by the claimant; publication of various notices of the application; a visual inspection and a survey or measurement to establish occupancy, boundaries, extent of exploitation, and other factors relevant to the applicant's claimed right to adjudication; and a resolution of adjudication by INCORA, having the effect of a deed.

The "ordinary" procedure antedates INCORA and the "special" procedure but probably will no longer be used much, except

[121] Law 98 of 1946, Art. 9; Presidential Decree 547 of February 17, 1947, Art. 12. To discourage accumulation of new *latifundios*, Law 135 of 1961, Art. 37, provides that if a person receives public domain land and transfers it, neither he nor his grantee may receive any further adjudication for five years.

[122] Duff, note 3 above, pp. 95–96. Enrique Peñalosa, note 29 above, said that most settlers are doomed to subsistence living because Colombia's unused lands are of only marginal quality, and that the government therefore should not and would not actively encourage colonization. Nevertheless, he said, population pressure will inevitably result in colonization which will require the government to provide public facilities and services, including agricultural credit.

in areas in which there is little new settlement and in which IN-CORA therefore does not maintain its own titling commissions. Under the ordinary procedure, an application for adjudication, describing the land in question, is made at the local mayor's office (*alcaldía*), or to the territorial judge or commissioner in the national territories. Intially, a notice of the application must be posted for thirty days on the door of the *alcaldía* or the judge's or commissioner's office and proclaimed aloud in the public market on three consecutive market days (usually held once a week); if the land exceeds fifty hectares, the notice also must appear in a newspaper published in the capital of the department or in the official governmental journal (*Diario Oficial*). Then the presiding official sets the date for the inspection and measurement and orders that personal notice be given to the government attorney, the inspector of forests, and the occupants of adjacent lands. The inspection and measurement are conducted by two "experts," one chosen by the presiding official and one by the applicant, accompanied by the presiding official, the applicant, and any others who are interested. If this inspection substantiates the applicant's claim, a notice of proposed adjudication must be posted at the presiding official's office for ten days. Thereafter, if there is no opposition by competing claimants, the file, including a detailed report of the results of the inspection and a drawing of the tract, both signed by the experts, is sent to INCORA in Bogotá for review. If INCORA finds no errors and has no questions, the resolution of adjudication is prepared, signed, and returned to the presiding local official. The experts' fees, the cost of the drawing, and legal expenses if the applicant has a lawyer are all borne by the applicant.[123]

Under the "special" procedure, applications for adjudication are submitted directly to the chief of a local INCORA titling commission. If the area exceeds fifty hectares, he arranges to have a notice of the application announced on three different days over a local radio station and posted for ten days at his office, at the *alcaldía*, and

[123] The ordinary procedure is prescribed by Law 97 of 1946 and Presidential Decree 547 of February 17, 1947. Examination of a substantial number of files indicates that in many if not most cases the "experts" are not surveyors; however, Article 3 of Law 97 requires that drawings of tracts larger than 200 hectares, a small minority of all tracts adjudicated, be made by licensed surveyors.

at the police station or territorial commissioner's office. In all cases he arranges for personal notice of the inspection date to be given to the government attorney, the inspector of forests, and the occupants of adjacent lands. The inspection and a boundary survey are conducted by the titling commission, after which a notice of proposed adjudication is posted at the commission's office for ten days and the chief submits the file, including inspection report and survey notes, to the INCORA project office. Either there or in Bogotá, a drawing is prepared from the survey notes, the file is reviewed, and if all is in order a resolution of adjudication is executed and delivered to the appropriate registry office for inscription. The only costs payable by a recipient of less than fifty hectares are the registry fee and a documentary tax of one peso per hectare; if the tract adjudicated is larger, he also must pay the cost of the radio notices and fifteen pesos for each hectare beyond fifty to cover some of the survey and drawing costs.[124]

Actual Adjudications, 1962 to 1969

Table 5 summarizes by departments the numbers of titles to unreserved *baldíos* granted by INCORA through May, 1969, and the

[124] The special procedure is now prescribed mainly by Presidential Decree 810 of May 23, 1969. Accord 9 of October 20, 1969, of the Board of Directors of INCORA adds a few details concerning tracts of more than fifty hectares, including the survey fee of fifteen pesos per hectare, about half the commercial rate according to INCORA officials. Originally, Presidential Decree 1415 of July 8, 1940, Art. 10, authorized the Ministry of National Economy to adjudicate *baldíos* not exceeding fifty hectares, and Decree 198 of January 29, 1943, established the procedure for titling commissions. Law 135 of 1961 and Presidential Decree 3337 of December 29, 1961, transferred to INCORA the duty of adjudicating *baldíos*, and INCORA commissions were established to handle tracts of up to fifty hectares pursuant to Decree 198 of 1943. Article 42 *bis*, added to Law 135 by Law 1 of 1968, provided that INCORA through its own officers could collect all information necessary to adjudicate tracts of more than fifty hectares. Decree 810 of 1969 repealed Decree 198 of 1943. In August, 1969, there were fifty-three INCORA commissions titling tracts of fifty hectares or less, and seven new and entirely distinct commissions were just being formed to handle larger tracts. The former were generally composed of a surveyor (usually not licensed), who was the chief, and one or more assistants; the latter were to be composed of a legally trained person, who would be the chief, and one or more surveyors and assistants. Accord 9 of 1969 designates the following as the areas in which INCORA commissions will title tracts larger than fifty hectares: the Departments of Antioquia, Bolívar, Boyacá, Cesar, Caldas, Guajira, Norte de Santander, Meta, Magdalena, Nariño, and Santander, and the Intendencias of Aráuca, Caquetá, and Putumayo. In other areas applicants will have to use the "ordinary" procedure.

TABLE 5. TITLING OF UNRESERVED PUBLIC DOMAIN LANDS[a]

Department	1962 Titles	1962 Hectares	1963 Titles	1963 Hectares	1964 Titles	1964 Hectares	1965 Titles	1965 Hectares
Antioquia	216	17,068	479	42,892	1,296	100,816	1,103	46,346
Atlántico	—	—	1	1	—	—	—	—
Bolívar	11	1,720	14	2,997	50	8,572	244	5,352
Boyacá	66	5,738	420	8,361	542	13,152	783	19,001
Caldas	122	13,744	35	816	—	—	103	1,823
Cauca	75	2,783	132	3,590	451	7,800	474	13,051
Cesar	—	—	—	—	—	—	—	—
Córdoba	32	1,662	365	21,955	381	33,746	575	28,374
Cundinamarca	107	7,084	31	3,650	188	12,815	158	8,856
Chocó	12	1,139	1	50	4	618	660	11,569
Huila	543	11,086	839	20,582	545	8,688	779	7,961
Magdalena	184	27,496	457	40,432	554	52,365	362	17,770
Meta	509	14,470	360	21,017	840	23,616	1,879	54,311
Nariño	176	4,137	710	8,759	782	8,302	59	734
Norte de Santander	1	323	124	15,114	153	15,601	307	16,197
Santander	327	16,379	660	62,170	390	26,710	594	28,386
Tolima	508	22,849	363	8,862	484	8,637	535	12,157
Valle del Cauca	388	7,024	6	873	231	4,094	625	10,347
Guajira	143	16,101	128	12,520	135	14,774	663	30,031
Caquetá	533	31,818	744	39,975	807	44,376	929	41,781
Putumayo	362	8,313	230	2,199	532	8,371	230	5,200
Aráuca	2	1	11	3	106	7,798	334	8,941
Vaupes	—	—	—	—	—	—	—	—
Quindío	—	—	—	—	—	—	—	—
Amazonas	7	180	—	—	1	26	2	3
Risaralda	—	—	—	—	—	—	—	—
Sucre	—	—	—	—	—	—	—	—
Totals	4,324	211,115	6,110	316,858	8,472	400,607	11,398	368,192

[a] Through May, 1969. Data received from INCORA's Division of Adjudications on July 8, 1969.

TABLE 5 (Continued). TITLING OF UNRESERVED PUBLIC DOMAIN LANDS

Department	1966 Titles	1966 Hectares	1967 Titles	1967 Hectares	1968 Titles	1968 Hectares	1969 Titles	1969 Hectares	Totals Titles	Totals Hectares
Antioquia	634	24,445	487	28,905	870	29,239	757	21,272	5,842	310,984
Atlántico	—	—	—	—	—	—	—	—	1	1
Bolívar	317	10,037	1,017	75,804	840	21,884	84	1,662	2,577	134,028
Boyacá	1,081	21,657	919	30,502	1,023	22,728	398	9,217	5,232	130,356
Caldas	148	1,834	76	340	137	1,345	35	453	656	20,355
Cauca	610	7,213	348	3,012	409	4,658	764	3,356	3,263	45,463
Cesar	—	—	4	313	707	20,445	123	4,031	834	24,789
Córdoba	103	3,354	156	8,392	303	17,674	55	5,799	1,970	120,686
Cundinamarca	565	7,713	623	11,725	665	7,735	332	5,350	2,669	64,927
Chocó	459	10,264	153	3,738	438	13,591	64	2,661	1,791	43,629
Huila	2,628	18,499	3,075	15,674	1,471	15,029	228	3,333	10,108	100,852
Magdalena	429	22,483	802	41,015	748	17,558	189	6,015	3,725	225,134
Meta	1,084	41,801	1,117	51,319	1,153	37,052	301	10,244	7,243	253,832
Nariño	194	1,847	550	4,212	687	4,896	401	2,659	3,559	35,538
Norte de Santander	435	12,837	301	10,170	718	21,600	141	3,700	2,180	95,542
Santander	1,215	29,191	2,044	57,962	1,920	44,925	497	13,630	7,647	279,400
Tolima	459	4,624	466	7,252	944	10,790	637	7,296	4,396	82,465
Valle del Cauca	176	1,537	157	3,216	815	6,910	734	4,533	3,132	38,533
Guajira	314	15,517	134	9,073	177	6,234	30	548	1,724	101,797
Caquetá	1,314	54,090	696	44,238	400	14,947	123	4,056	5,546	275,281
Putumayo	371	9,066	343	28,961	185	5,965	118	2,557	2,371	70,632
Aráuca	355	10,497	189	7,393	73	2,350	4	70	1,074	37,053
Vaupes	—	—	13	42	10	50	3	50	27	191
Quindío	1	49	6	89	3	17	6	310	16	421
Amazonas	—	—	—	—	—	—	—	—	10	209
Risaralda	—	—	19	89	380	3,522	13	142	412	3,754
Sucre	—	—	13	625	57	1,610	5	253	75	2,488
Totals	12,893	314,559	13,708	444,060	15,133	332,755	6,042	111,037	78,080	2,499,182

total areas of the lands. It is obvious from comparison with Table 3 that the numbers and total areas of tracts distributed from the public domain dwarf those of parcels distributed from lands acquired by INCORA through extinction, expropriation, negotiated purchase, and gratuitous transfer.

Table 6 relates only to 1968, and classifies by size the individual tracts adjudicated during that year and referred to in the 1968 column of Table 5.

The purpose of obtaining the data in Table 6 was to determine to what extent new *minifundios* or *latifundios* are being created. As stated earlier, titles granted to settlers of unreserved public domain lands are not subject to any of the restrictions imposed upon recipients of family farms in parcelization or planned settlement projects.[125] This means, for example, that fractional interests in a tract may pass by inheritance to multiple heirs of the *adjudicatario*. With almost half of all the tracts adjudicated from unreserved *baldíos* in 1968 being less than ten hectares, and over two-thirds being less than twenty-five hectares, it appears that there is already a *minifundio* problem, and that it will become worse. Since twenty-five hectares generally is supposed to be the minimum size of such tracts, the question naturally arises whether INCORA is seriously attempting to comply with this requirement.[126] The answer of a former general manager is that there are thousands of cases of de facto occupation of small farms over many years which do fall within the legal exception to the twenty-five-hectare requirement, and that INCORA has no choice but to grant the occupants titles.[127] In considering this explanation, it should be noted from Table 5 that while the number of adjudications increased each year—by an average of almost 40 percent per year from 1962 to 1965 and 10 percent per year from 1965 to 1968—the average size of the tracts decreased in the later years, dropping from almost fifty hectares in 1962 to 1964 to twenty-two hectares in 1968 and only eighteen in 1969. It seems that the backlog of cases from years prior to INCORA's crea-

[125] See notes 103 to 108 above.
[126] See note 121 above.
[127] Interview with Enrique Peñalosa, note 29 above, on April 16, 1971, at Urbana, Illinois.

TABLE 6. TRACTS TITLED FROM THE PUBLIC DOMAIN IN 1968, CLASSIFIED BY SIZE[a]

Department	Less than 10 Hectares	From 10 to 24.9 Hectares	From 25 to 49.9 Hectares	From 50 to 99.9 Hectares	From 100 to 199.9 Hectares	From 200 to 449.9 Hectares	450 Hectares & Larger	Totals
Antioquia	85	181	541	57	3	3	—	870
Bolívar	350	200	213	56	18	2	1	840
Boyacá	394	306	272	41	3	4	3	1,023
Caldas	101	23	11	1	1	—	—	137
Cauca	247	116	39	1	5	—	1	409
Cesar	247	201	180	45	22	10	2	707
Córdoba	92	72	37	40	55	5	2	303
Cundinamarca	540	83	32	4	5	1	—	665
Chocó	63	130	219	21	5	—	—	438
Guajira	88	27	28	18	15	1	—	177
Huila	963	293	198	14	3	—	—	1,471
Magdalena	268	190	238	43	3	6	—	748
Meta	454	234	313	90	46	13	3	1,153
Nariño	481	118	78	10	—	—	—	687
Norte de Santander	160	148	352	52	6	—	—	718
Quindío	1	2	—	—	—	—	—	3
Risaralda	218	126	33	2	1	—	—	380
Santander	822	419	581	71	24	3	—	1,920
Sucre	28	7	10	7	3	2	—	57
Tolima	651	217	68	3	5	—	—	944
Valle del Cauca	578	156	75	4	2	—	—	815
Aráuca	8	19	24	22	—	—	—	73
Caquetá	93	94	165	30	18	—	—	400
Putumayo	98	22	31	10	21	3	—	185
Vaupes	7	2	1	—	—	—	—	10
Totals	7,037	3,386	3,739	642	264	53	12	15,133

[a] Data specially compiled for the author by INCORA's Division of Adjudications and received in September, 1969.

tion may have been handled in the earlier years covered by Table 5, and that many adjudications in the later years may have been to persons who settled after 1961 and whom INCORA could have discouraged from occupying and seeking titles to inordinately small tracts. The general lack of planning or direction in connection with the colonization of *baldíos* will be discussed in the final section of this paper.

As for the possibility of new *latifundios*, Table 6 indicates that, at least in 1968, few if any such holdings were created by the initial grants. The real danger, made possible by the free transferability of the adjudicated lands, is that many grantees eventually will be forced by lack of sufficient credit, technical assistance, public facilities, or land itself, to sell out to others who will be able to accumulate large holdings, perhaps at a very low cost.[128] The author believes that the preferable way to forestall such a contingency is not by imposing new restrictions on alienability, but by subjecting spontaneous colonization to more planning and supervision and by providing the settlers with adequate credit, technical assistance, roads, and other facilities. It appeared from a visit to Meta that this was not being done and that most *adjudicatarios* were barely subsisting.[129]

Titling Problems

Insecure land titles can produce serious economic and social problems. They can discourage improvements, make it difficult to obtain credit or to sell the land for its full value, and generate expensive litigation and even physical violence.[130]

Observation of INCORA's adjudication procedure in actual operation in Meta disclosed several respects in which it could be improved. Some of the shortcomings of the current practice are likely to cause title insecurity, while others are matters of inconvenience.

---

[128] See Feder, note 30 above, p. 97; Smith, note 4 above, p. 255.
[129] INCORA officials there in August, 1969, shared this view.
[130] See Joseph R. Thome, "Title Problems in Rural Areas: A Colonization Example," in A. Eugene Havens and William L. Flinn (eds.), *Internal Colonialism and Structural Change in Colombia* (New York, 1970), p. 146.

Lack of Permanent Reference Points for Locating Lands Adjudicated

Describing the shape and area of a piece of land is one thing; locating that land in relation to other tracts, or on a map of the state, is something else. To do the latter, one must be able to locate all the tracts with respect to the same reference points.

The rectangular survey system generally is regarded as the most effective method of permanently locating individual tracts. A region such as a state is divided into roughly rectangular segments whose corners are at the intersections of geographic coordinates known as meridians and parallels of latitude. The beginning point of the survey and description of each individual tract is then located by reference to such coordinates.[131]

There has been no rectangular survey of Colombia's public domain. Although the law does require that in the adjudication of tracts larger than 1,000 hectares at least one of the corners of the tract must be fixed by reference to geographic coordinates,[132] Table 6 shows that the number of tracts of this size is negligible in comparison to the total number of adjudications. In 1944 and again in 1959, a bill was introduced in the Colombian Congress which would have required rectangular surveys of all adjudicable public lands, but for apparently extraneous political reasons it was not enacted.[133]

The result is that in Colombia surveys of adjudicated tracts do little more than establish their size and shape. If the description in a resolution of adjudication expressly refers to markers placed by the surveyors, or to other objects such as buildings, fence posts, trees, ridges, or streams, it may be possible for a surveyor later to relocate the boundaries *if* some of the markers or other objects are still there *and* in the same places. In five or ten years they may well

---

[131] Meridians are true north-south lines, and parallels are east-west lines. They should be run astronomically with a solar compass because a magnetic compass does not generally point due north but varies from place to place and time to time. See Frank E. Clark, *Law of Surveying and Boundaries* (3rd ed., Indianapolis, 1959), pp. 79-85.

[132] Código Fiscal, Art. 55; Law 64 of 1915. INCORA officials in Project Meta No. 1 said that their surveyors comply with this requirement.

[133] See Smith, note 4 above, pp. 160-167 for the text of the proposed law.

not be. Nothing in the surveyor's notes or the resolution of adjudication locates the land with reference to any other parcels (except perhaps adjacent ones with common boundaries which are expressly mentioned in the description, for example, "bounded on the east by the land of Carlos Rodriguez") or any geographic coordinates. Neither INCORA nor its grantees can locate adjudicated tracts on any map, nor can anyone determine from INCORA files or recorded title documents what lands have not been adjudicated and thus are still in the public domain.

This means that INCORA sometimes adjudicates lands owned or claimed to be owned by others, especially where the claimants are not in possession.[134] Although the law expressly provides that the state does not guarantee that lands were *baldíos* prior to adjudication, and that the act of adjudication by INCORA does not guarantee the title of the *adjudicatario* or prejudice the rights of third-party claimants,[135] INCORA's practice is to refuse adjudication wherever it learns of a claim inconsistent with a pending application for adjudication, requiring the applicant and the other claimant to go into court to settle the dispute, after which INCORA will adjudicate if the applicant prevails.[136]

Where INCORA does not learn of a conflicting claim and adjudicates land to the occupant, two legal doctrines may enable the occupant to prevail in a later court dispute with the other claimant, even if the latter actually did own the land. One is the conclusive presumption (*presunción de derecho*) that land was in the public domain if its adjudication was based on at least five years' prior exploitation by the *adjudicatario* and the opposing claimant does not assert his claim within one year after the resolution of adjudication is inscribed in the proper registry office.[137]

Of course, not all adjudications are based on five years' exploitation, since a person is entitled to receive adjudication of unreserved

---

[134] See Arévalo, note 113 above, p. 135.
[135] Código Fiscal, Art. 47.
[136] Interview with INCORA officials in Project Meta No. 1, August 20, 1969. For a discussion of judicial and nonjudicial methods of resolving boundary disputes in Colombia, see Arévalo, note 113 above, pp. 152–160.
[137] Law 97 of 1946, Art. 6.

baldíos as soon as he has cultivated or planted pasture in two-thirds of the area claimed, even if that is after only one year. There is naturally a desire by some settlers to obtain title at the earliest possible time. On the other hand, there is also an incentive to delay for the five-year period because of the above presumption (assuming the settler is advised of it), and because of the rule that governmental and semigovernmental agencies extending credit upon the security of real-estate mortgages must accept as valid the titles of only those *adjudicatarios* having the benefit of the presumption.[138]

The second doctrine which may enable an *adjudicatario* to prevail over an actual owner of the land is that of "prescription" (*prescripción adquisitiva del dominio*).[139] Where a squatter occupies and exploits vacant but privately owned land for five years in the belief that it is in the public domain, he acquires title to it even without any purported adjudication by INCORA. Although most nations have a similar legal doctrine, a general prescriptive period of five years is unusually short. For instance, the typical period for acquiring title by "adverse possession" in the United States (where each state has its own statutory rule) is twenty years, though it may be less where the occupancy is based upon a deed or other instrument which appeared on its face to convey good title.[140]

As suggested above, the best way to prevent such problems would be a rectangular survey of Colombia's public domain. The longer this step is delayed, the more additional tracts will be adjudicated and the more future title disputes will be assured. An alternative, also expensive, would be an aerial survey.[141] Although frequent cloud cover in parts of Colombia is a handicap to photogrammetry, some aerial cadastral surveying already has been done by the Agus-

---

[138] *Ibid.*, Art. 8. Most such agencies, however, seem to rely more on the *prenda agraria*, a pledge of crops and movable property, than on real estate mortgages. See note 104 above.

[139] Law 200 of 1936, Art. 12. Originally Article 15 provided that Law 200 did not apply in the *intendencias*, *comisarías*, and *llanos* of Casanare, but Article 15 was repealed by Law 1 of 1968, Art. 8.

[140] See John E. Cribbet, *Principles of the Law of Property* (Brooklyn, 1962), p. 233.

[141] See Frank Osterhoudt, "Land Titles in Northeast Brazil: The Use of Aerial Photography," *Land Economics* 41 (1965), p. 387; "The Use of Aerial Photography in Cadasters for Developing Countries," in Organization of American States, *Physical Resource Investigations for Economic Development* (Washington, 1969), p. 307.

tín Codazzi Geographic Institute, but it appears that INCORA is not utilizing such surveys in its titling activities.[142]

Failure to Mark Boundaries Adequately

Even though an adjudicated tract cannot be located on a map because of lack of reference to geographic coordinates or aerial photos, the chances of being able to relocate the boundaries in the future are enhanced if the description of the land in the title documents refers to relatively permanent artificial or natural markers on the ground. Earlier there was brief mention of the practice of placing numbered markers (*mojones*) at the corners of family farms and describing the land partly or entirely by reference to such markers.[143] In the case of adjudications of unreserved *baldíos*, although the beginning point of the survey of each tract is supposed to be marked by a *mojon* of stone, cement, or metal set at least fifty centimeters into the ground, with a cross-section large enough to allow identifying letters or numbers to be placed on it,[144] such markers are in fact set by INCORA titling commissions only for tracts larger than fifty hectares, a small minority of all tracts titled.[145] In smaller parcels, the only *mojones* set are small pegs cut from saplings, an inch or two in diameter and four or five inches long.[146] They are not really intended as boundary markers at all, but rather as one-day devices enabling the operator of the transit to see where his assistant set up the leveling rod, and vice versa. The pegs almost certainly disappear in a matter of days or weeks.

INCORA commissions are also supposed to locate the beginning point of each survey by describing the distances from it to such relatively stable objects as buildings, roads, and streams,[147] but in two surveys which the author observed no effort was made to fix the

[142] A letter in the INCORA file from the attorney for Hacienda Rey stated that the entire farm had been aerially photographed by the Geographic Institute.
[143] In the text preceding note 115 above.
[144] Resolution 1699 of December 13, 1955, of the Ministry of Agriculture, Arts. 6 and 9.
[145] See Tables 5 and 6 and accompanying text.
[146] Interviews with INCORA officials in Project Meta No. 1 and observation of surveys near San Martín, Meta.
[147] Resolution 197 of November 8, 1965, of the Board of Directors of INCORA, Art. 1.

beginning points or any of the corners with respect to anything more permanent than the small pegs referred to above and some wooden fence posts, although there were a house and a road both within seventy-five yards of the beginning point.[148]

In many cases INCORA's descriptions do refer to physical features such as streams, ridges, and roads, particularly where they actually form boundaries of the land in question.[149] Such references are, of course, better than none at all, but long experience in Colombia and elsewhere has demonstrated that such markers are not sufficiently permanent and that their use in legal descriptions eventually breeds disputes and title insecurity.[150]

Clearly, INCORA practice regarding the marking of the point of beginning of each survey should be amended to conform to the legal requirements. An experienced surveyor should be responsible for setting a substantial concrete, metal, or stone monument and describing its location by reference to the bearing and distance from several nearby and relatively permanent physical structures or features. Beyond that, it would be preferable to mark *all* principal corners in the same way.

Inaccurate Surveys and Drawings

A major reason for adoption of the "special" procedure in which INCORA personnel inspect, measure, and prepare drawings of *baldíos* prior to adjudication was the unreliability of work performed by "experts" selected by local governmental officials. (For the same reason INCORA commissions, rather than independent surveyors contracted by INCORA, now perform these functions in connection with the layout of family farms.) There were many cases not only of inaccurate work but also of outright fraud, including the fabrication of drawings without examination of the land.[151]

[148] Surveys, note 146 above.
[149] For example, the western boundary of the tract adjudicated in File No. 140326 of the Division of Adjudications is described as follows: "Oeste: En 200.00 metros con [name of adjacent landowner], *aguas abajo*, puntos 1 al 3 [emphasis added]."
[150] See Smith, note 4 above, pp. 150–153; Arévalo, note 113 above, pp. 136–145; Orlando Fals-Borda, *El Hombre y la Tierra en Boyacá, Bases Socio-Históricas para una Reforma Agraria* (Bogotá, 1957), Chap. 5.
[151] Interview with official in INCORA's Division of Engineering, Bogotá, August 6, 1969.

Under the "ordinary" procedure the experts are not required to have any surveying training where less than 200 hectares are involved, and the prescribed technical standards, particularly for measuring tracts under fifty hectares, are very crude. For example, the angle formed by two intersecting boundary lines can be determined without using a compass or transit, by fixing a point on each line ten meters from their intersection and measuring the distance between the two points.[152]

Under the "special" procedure, INCORA uses different personnel, standards, and equipment for measuring tracts of more than fifty hectares than for measuring smaller tracts. In both cases the chief surveyor (usually not licensed) of each titling team is ordinarily a high-school graduate whose training in surveying may be limited to a two-month course given by INCORA, plus field experience. Officials of INCORA's Division of Engineering concede that some of the surveyors are not adequately prepared to do the work required of them. The survey assistants may have little or no training or experience; on some jobs involving tracts of less than fifty hectares, the prospective *adjudicatarios* themselves serve as the assistants or "rod men."[153]

The shapes and sizes of tracts smaller than fifty hectares are determined by a method known as "direction and distance" (*rumbo y distancia*). Rather than using a transit to measure the angles directly, the surveyor measures the angle between each boundary line and a north-south line as indicated by magnetic compass; the angle between the two boundary lines is computed later by the draftsman, who prepares the drawing from the surveyor's field notes. Distances in both large and small tracts are determined by tachymetry, taking a single reading through the telescope of the graduated scale on the leveling rod, rather than by direct measurement with a tape. Because the transits used in surveying tracts of less than fifty hectares are considerably less accurate than those used for larger tracts, and because of the shortcomings of the direction-and-distance method and the inadequate training of personnel, the measure-

[152] Resolution 1699 of 1955, note 144 above, Art. 2.
[153] Interview, note 151 above.

ments by INCORA titling commissions of tracts of fifty hectares and less are acknowledged to be only approximate.[154]

Deficiencies in surveys may become apparent when draftsmen attempt to prepare drawings of the tracts from the surveyors' field notes. As of 1969, almost all such drawings were either prepared or reviewed by the Bogotá office of INCORA's Division of Engineering.[155] During the preceding one and a half years that office had received approximately 30,000 files requiring such preparation or review of drawings in connection with proposed adjudications of fifty hectares or less under the "special" procedure. Of these, about 12 percent, or 3,500 files, were returned for new surveys because of errors which prevented the boundaries from closing.[156]

Recommended improvements in surveying tracts to be adjudicated include the following. All surveyors should have adequate training and experience. Those who do not have formal education in civil engineering prior to coming with INCORA should receive more training than at present before being placed in charge of survey teams. Equipment and technical standards should be upgraded where necessary, so that errors will not exceed fifteen minutes in the measurement of angles and 1:1000 in the measurement of distances. The direction-and-distance method of measuring angles should be abandoned.[157]

Adjudication of Irregularly Shaped Tracts

The granting of irregularly shaped tracts makes surveys and descriptions much more difficult and enhances the likelihood of title insecurity. Nonetheless, INCORA makes no effort to require or even to

[154] Interviews, note 151 above, and in Project Meta No. 1, August 20, 1969.

[155] In 1969 two regional offices, at Bucaramanga and Palmira, had the power to adjudicate lands without review in Bogotá. Several other regional offices, such as the one in San Martín, Meta, prepared the drawings but sent their files to Bogotá for review and execution of the resolutions of adjudication. Under the decentralization plan discussed in note 166 below, most adjudications under the "special" procedure will eventually be done entirely at the regional level without participation by Bogotá.

[156] Interview, note 151 above.

[157] Dr. José Ignacio Rengifo, Professor of Civil Engineering at the University of the Andes, Bogotá, states that the error in distances measured by tachymetry can be

encourage that settlers occupy or accept adjudication of rectangular or other regularly shaped parcels.[158]

A bill introduced in the Colombian Congress in 1944 and 1959 would have required that *baldios* be adjudicated in rectangular parcels; further consideration should be given to adopting such a law.[159] Even under existing law INCORA could regularize many tracts by encouraging if not requiring straight boundaries and easily measurable angles wherever they are not precluded by the lines of adjacent private tracts or streams or roads intended to form boundaries. Since an applicant is entitled to adjudication of 50 percent more land than he has exploited, it seems that this additional land could in many cases be so located on the periphery of the exploited portion as to regularize the shape of the entire tract.[160]

Title Documents

Resolutions of adjudication of unreserved *baldios,* in contrast to deeds to family farms, are prepared by INCORA rather than by notaries. In cases where adjudication is based on at least five years' exploitation, that fact is recited in the resolutions.[161] After a resolution relating to a particular tract has been signed by the appropriate officials in the central or regional office,[162] the original and a copy are sent to the INCORA project office or the *alcaldia* where the application for adjudication was received initially. The applicant is notified and asked to examine the resolution and, if there are no inaccuracies, to sign it and pay a documentary tax of one peso per hectare of land involved. The original and copy are then sent by INCORA or the *alcaldia* to the proper registry office for inscription, which is particularly important if the *adjudicatario* is to have the benefit of the conclusive presumption that the lands were in the

---

reduced to 1:1500 by taking a double reading of the leveling rod, rather than the single reading now taken. According to INCORA officials in Meta, the transits used in measuring angles in tracts not exceeding fifty hectares are accurate only to within about thirty minutes.

[158] Interviews in Meta, note 154 above.
[159] See note 133 above, and accompanying text.
[160] See note 118 above.
[161] See text at note 137 above.
[162] See note 155 above, and text at note 166 below.

public domain.[163] He is advised that he can obtain his copy of the resolution and two copies of the drawing of the land at the registry office after a specified period by paying the registration fees.[164] The original resolution is returned by the registry office to INCORA and deposited in Bogotá. INCORA officials in Meta said they believed that most *adjudicatarios* do pay the registry fees and pick up their title papers.

Although recording of the resolution and drawing at a notary's office is not necessary for the instrument to be legally effective, it does give the *adjudicatario* two advantages: the copies retained by the notary are on file and available locally if the *adjudicatario* should lose his own copies; and if he should later want to sell his land, he will be able to show a complete chain of "public" title documents starting with the adjudication resolution, which probably will be required if the purchaser is represented by a lawyer. Despite these advantages, INCORA apparently does nothing to see that resolutions of adjudication are recorded with notaries. If the *adjudicatario* wishes to have the additional protection, he must arrange and pay for it. INCORA officials said they had no idea what proportion of *adjudicatarios* do so.

When all the foregoing steps are completed, copies of the resolution and drawing are located as follows: the *adjudicatario* has a copy of the resolution and two copies of the drawing (if he got them from the registry office), except that if he recorded a copy of the drawing it is on file in the notary's office along with a copy of the resolution made by the notary; the originals and all other copies of the resolution and drawing are at the INCORA offices in Bogotá. No copies are available for public inspection in the INCORA project office or elsewhere in the locale where the land is located.[165]

---

[163] See text at note 137 above.

[164] Where the tract exceeds fifty hectares, INCORA publishes an extract of the resolution in the *Diario Oficial* before having it registered. Presidential Decree 810 of May 23, 1969, Art. 10. Resolution 197 of November 8, 1965, of the Board of Directors of INCORA, Art. 1, requires that each *adjudicatario* receive without charge two copies of the drawing showing the boundaries of his land.

[165] Documents in notarial offices are not open to inspection by the general public. Interested persons may examine or obtain copies of the resolutions at INCORA's Bogotá office, for a fee. The factual information in this section was obtained through interviews with INCORA officials in the Division of Adjudications

At least two improvements in the procedure seem desirable. First, copies of the resolution of adjudication and the drawing of the tract should be available for public inspection at some convenient place in the area where the land is situated. Second, because of the advantages to the *adjudicatario* of having his documents recorded at a notarial office, INCORA should probably see that this is done, perhaps by having the registry office deliver them directly to the notary.

INCORA has begun putting into effect a program of decentralization of its adjudication activities under the "special" procedure. Increasingly, adjudications will be finalized by the regional offices without the need for sending files to Bogotá for review or execution of the resolutions.[166] It may be that under this program the original resolution and drawing will be kept at the regional office and available for public inspection there.

Delays Between Application and Adjudication

Under the "ordinary" procedure, where applications for adjudications are received and the notice, inspection, and survey functions performed by the local mayors' offices, it commonly takes from one to two years from the time of application to secure final adjudication of a tract, though in some cases the procedure may be completed in as little as six months.[167] The long delays are attributable to a number of factors: lack of prompt action by local officials, the necessity of mailing files to and from Bogotá, and time spent by the division of adjudications reviewing every aspect of each case to ascertain whether local officials complied with all legal requirements and technical standards.[168] These factors were among the reasons for establishment of the "special" procedure and its recent extension to tracts larger than fifty hectares.

---

in Bogotá on July 8, 1969, and in the regional office at San Martín, Meta, on August 20, 1969. See also the sources cited in note 113 above.

[166] Resolution 19950 of August 13, 1968, issued by the general manager of INCORA.

[167] Interviews with officials in the Division of Adjudications, Bogotá, July 8 and 15, 1969.

[168] File No. 31244 in the Division of Adjudications was a case where local officials failed to publish the requisite notices. In File No. 41639 the survey and drawing were found to be inaccurate, and File No. 18717 was being reviewed for possible fraud by the persons who certified, apparently wrongly, that the applicant had exploited at least two-thirds of the land claimed.

Under the "special" procedure the time from application to final adjudication is generally between five and ten months, with some cases taking longer but very few being completed in less time.[169] A study of the 102 files ready to be sent from Project Meta No. 1 to Bogotá on August 22, 1969, for review and execution of the resolutions of adjudication, revealed that in 85 percent of the cases the initial applications were dated between two and seven months earlier, with four months being the average.[170] Meta officials said that ordinarily it required three more months from the time the files were sent to Bogotá for personnel there to review them and return the signed resolutions of adjudication or, in about 2 percent of the cases, to return the files for correction of errors. As the decentralization plan advances, the review of files and signing of resolutions of adjudication will be done locally, and the delays attributable to having to send files to Bogotá will be eliminated. Residual delays in adjudicating *baldíos* under the "special" procedure will presumably be attributable to shortages of titling commissions and draftsmen.

Lack of Planning or Direction

During the author's visit to the *llanos* in 1969, the most striking fact, and the one most regretted by INCORA officials there, was the lack of an affirmative national policy for planning and directing the region's development. If the country could be said to have any policy, it was one of hands off, as suggested by the term "spontaneous colonization," used officially to describe the settlement of *baldíos*. Anyone who wanted to settle on any unreserved part of the public domain could do so, and only after he worked and invested to bring the land under some type of exploitation (chosen entirely by him) did the government enter the picture through INCORA.

---

[169] Interviews note 167 above, and with INCORA officials at San Martín, Meta, on August 20, 1969.

[170] Meta officials said that inspections and surveys of tracts were being made within five days after receipt of applications for adjudication; that a titling team could inspect and survey about six tracts of fifty hectares or less each week; that titling commission chiefs stationed outside San Martín came there once a month to deliver the surveyors' notes; and that each of the three INCORA draftsmen in San Martín could prepare about eighty or ninety drawings per month.

But the agency's role was a limited one. It determined only whether the tract was within the size limitations prescribed by law and whether the claimant had planted at least two-thirds of it. No effort was made to determine whether the nation or the settler himself would be better served by having him settle elsewhere or by adjudicating to him a larger tract or one of a different shape. Where an *adjudicatario* received a tract that was uneconomically small, others usually acquired titles to the adjacent land before he realized his situation and could enlarge his farm. Even in connection with the supervised credit program, under which INCORA extends credit and technical assistance to settlers after they receive their titles, it appeared that agency personnel did not direct the recipients in the way in which they applied the money or exploited their land, certainly not on a coordinated or regional basis.[171]

Opening virgin lands provides a rare national opportunity. Common obstacles to progress in established rural areas—undersized tracts, absentee landlords, a subservient tenantry, high rents, clouded titles—are absent. But the opportunity can easily be wasted with grievous and inexcusable results if past errors, or unique features of the new lands, are disregarded. Opening Colombia's vast, tropical eastern plains to wholesale, unregulated settlement and clearing by persons whose entire agricultural experience is in farming totally different types of soil in temperate, mountainous regions could be an irredeemable disaster. Research is required, with the results being utilized to educate the settlers and to plan and direct their activities.[172]

Initially, Colombia's *baldíos* could be divided into different zones on the basis of such factors as similarity of soil, water, and weather conditions. Instead of one large project, such as Meta No. 1, a number of smaller ones could be established, each comprised

[171] Interviews with INCORA officials in Meta, August 20 to 22, 1969. It was also indicated that credit was being channeled on the basis of where it would contribute most to short-run increases in national agricultural production, particularly of exportable commodities. Thus in Meta much of the credit went to large prosperous farmers rather than to the vast majority of *adjudicatarios* struggling at the subsistence level. On the credit program, see Dale W. Adams, Antonio Giles, and Rodrigo Pena, *Supervised Credit in Colombia's Agrarian Reform* (Madison, 1966).

[172] See Rainer Schickele, *Agrarian Revolution and Economic Progress* (New York, 1968), pp. 218–236.

of lands with similar development problems. Within each such project a definite policy could be adopted concerning what type of colonization was to be permitted, how large the farms should be, what kinds of crops would be encouraged and financed, and what technical assistance was necessary. There could be strict coordination of technical assistance and credit from all sources, including INCORA, the Caja Agraria, and the Banco Ganadero.

Apparently a small start has been made since 1969. According to a former general manager, INCORA personnel now go out into the plains and jungles of Aráuca, Caquetá, Meta, and Sararé ahead of the settlers and set stakes to mark the locations and sizes of desirable tracts. Further, he said that the agency sometimes ignores the legal requirement that two-thirds of the land claimed be cultivated before the tract can be adjudicated. Thus, to avoid granting an uneconomically small tract, INCORA may adjudicate fifty hectares to a settler who is farming only fifteen of them.[173]

If such steps are indeed being taken on a wide scale, they are a promising sign. But much more needs to be done.

Conclusion

In evaluating INCORA's program for acquiring and redistributing private lands, several factors stand out: the small number of titles actually distributed; the complexity of acquisition procedures; the failure to distribute much of the land acquired; the stringent restrictions imposed on recipients' freedom to exploit, transfer, and encumber their family farms; the fact that some of the parcels distributed appear to be uneconomically small; and the emphasis on *arrepas* and irrigation programs, and disregard for peasants who are not tenants, sharecroppers, or residents of areas to be irrigated. Although there is room for clarification and simplification of legal procedures, particularly those prescribed for expropriations, the principal reason why the program has not achieved greater success has been the lack of strong governmental support for it since its inception. This is most obvious in the present administration of

[173] Interview with Enrique Peñalosa, note 29 above, on April 16, 1971, at Urbana, Illinois.

Conservative President Pastrana, who has suspended all redistribution activities since July, 1971. The lack of governmental support is due partly to the lack of political organization and pressure by the peasants themselves, and partly to the inherent unresponsiveness of the National Front coalition. With the help of INCORA during the presidency of Carlos Lleras, peasant associations were formed, and they have given indications of becoming a significant political force. Because the Conservative and Liberal parties both need popular rural support in the face of the impending termination of their coalition and the challenge from ex-dictator Rojas's ANAPO party, such associations may give the peasants some leverage to stimulate and reshape the land redistribution program.

With respect to INCORA's distribution of lands in the public domain, the major problems are inadequate planning and supervision of the settlement process, adjudication of too many small tracts, and title insecurity stemming from the lack of permanent reference points in the descriptions of parcels granted. There are reports that INCORA has begun adjudicating larger tracts where physically possible, by ignoring the legal requirement that two-thirds of each tract must be under cultivation before it is adjudicated. This suggests a need for revision of the law. Some small steps are also said to have been taken toward planning and supervision, but they are at best only a beginning. The title problem remains untouched. Each year more than 10,000 grants are made, and many of the recipients or their successors eventually will become involved in boundary disputes or be unable to obtain credit or to sell their land at a fair price because of uncertainty over who owns what.[174]

[174] In an interview on June 23, 1969, Carlos Villamil Cháux, then general manager of INCORA, minimized the title insecurity problem, saying that the doctrine of prescription, text at note 139 above, would cure any defects. However, absent a court decree applying prescription in the particular case, disputants and third parties tend to rely on the written title documents rather than on the fact of possession.

Internal Migration and Economic Development in Peru

René Vandendries

Introduction

During the 1960s the rate of economic growth in the less developed world has been far from satisfactory. Especially in Latin America, progress has been painfully slow; as a rule, rates of growth were below those of the preceding decade and the overall record fell substantially short of the objectives of the Alliance for Progress. As the decade of the 1970s sets in, the threat of an ever deepening crisis is unmistakable. A major source, if not the root cause, of the difficulties to come is obvious to the most casual visitor to a less developed country—the rapidly growing numbers of urban dwellers. Many of these people live in conditions of extreme poverty in center-city slums or in squatter settlements surrounding the city, and on the average are very inadequately employed and impatiently waiting for their governments to do something about it.

Internal migration has an important role to play in the process of economic development, but it can cause serious though temporary dislocations. The very fast growth of cities over large parts of the less developed world is the result of a combination of rapid rates of growth of population and vast rural-urban migration. The relative decline in the importance of the agricultural sector as development takes place, coupled with equal or more generally higher rural than urban fertility rates, requires a gradual reallocation of the labor force from agriculture to other sectors of the economy. Rural-urban migration therefore is imperative in any developing economy, and also has been an integral part of the development process in the now developed world. There is, however, an important difference between the process as it occurred during the early stages of development in western Europe or North America and as it presently is occurring in most underdeveloped economies. In nineteenth-century western Europe and North America urbanization took place in response to increasing agricultural productivity as well as new industrial employment creation. In other words, urban growth came subsequent to industrial development. Moreover, while large parts of many cities may have had all the appearances of slums, their inhabitants could find employment and thus a basis for future improvement of their situation. In presentday less developed countries, the sequence has been reversed. The cities have grown before industrial jobs have been created, and urban unemployment and underemployment have increased correspondingly, while agricultural production has not expanded markedly. Rural-urban migration of the labor force is turning out to be not as much a requirement of industrial economic growth as it is a result of stagnation in the rural sector, coupled with rapid population growth. The above does not imply that many of the theoretical explanations of migration presented in the literature are no longer valid today, but that the conditions existing in present less developed countries are different to the extent that our traditional thinking about the urbanization process, shaped by events as they occurred in western Europe and North America, has to be modified.

Some of the most cited analyses of migration in the presently developed countries are contained in the works of Ravenstein,[1] Sjaastad,[2] and Kuznets and Thomas.[3] While focusing on different aspects of the migration process, these various analyses are in fact quite similar, and especially unanimous in their emphasis on the

[1] Ravenstein, E. G. "The Laws of Migration," *Journal of the Royal Statistical Society*, Vol. 48, No. 2 (June, 1885), pp. 167–227.

[2] Sjaastad, Larry A. "The Costs and Returns of Human Migration," *Journal of Political Economy*, Vol. 70, No. 5, Pt. 2 (October, 1962).

[3] Kuznets, S., Thomas, D., et al., *Population Redistribution and Economic Growth, United States, 1870–1950* (Philadelphia, 1957, 1960, 1964), 3 vols.

positive contribution migration may make to the rate of economic growth. Ravenstein looks at patterns of migration and discusses the process in terms of pull and push. The pull might consist of growing modern urban employment opportunities but also of other factors, such as educational or medical facilities, entertainment opportunities, or similar services while, on the other hand, the push of rural poverty alone might be sufficient to induce people to migrate, even if the prospective city job is unstable and poorly remunerative. Sjaastad discusses migration in terms of a costs-and-returns model. One of his conclusions is that particularly the younger people may be more likely to move because of higher expected returns. Kuznets studies migration in terms of its selectivity, finding that the migrants are a very distinct group, and primarily from among the younger members of society. On the basis of this selectivity, Kuznets concludes, the migrants are those segments of the population which adapt themselves readily to a new environment, so that migration is bound to have very positive effects for economic growth. This is not to imply that the migration literature concerned with the presently developed countries is not at times very critical of the migration process. Whenever large external diseconomies are present, for instance, urban and industrial concentration may involve serious misallocations of resources and thus fail to produce maximum social welfare. In this event, the desirability of continued migration has come to be questioned. A better assessment of the social costs of and returns from migration may provide the answer. Notwithstanding these criticisms, internal migration undoubtedly remains one of the primary requirements of economic progress. The economic literature has emphasized this idea repeatedly, with the Ravenstein, Sjaastad, and Kuznets migration studies as prime examples.

In contrast to the commentary on the development process in the West, the literature on underdeveloped economies has a tendency to discuss migrants and migration almost exclusively in terms of negatives. It is assumed that upon arrival in the cities migrants join the ranks of the unemployed and in general fail to adjust to city life. Migrants are considered to be poorly educated and therefore of no use for modern industry; they are thought to be very poorly motivated, even to the extent that they do not take advantage of the educational and other opportunities existing in the cities. In sum, urban migrants are described as a burden on society.

The purpose of this paper is to show in the case of the city of Lima, Peru, to what extent the migration process and the migrants have characteristics consistent with one or the other schools of theoretical literature mentioned, to what extent the migration process is of positive value for development, and what can be done in order to maximize the returns from migration. In general terms, the findings of this short study suggest a much more positive role for migrants, consistent with the "western" experience, than the melancholy rhapsody played by many commentators on the experience of emerging countries.

Causes, Magnitude, and Major Pattern of Migration in Peru

We have noted that economic growth generates changes in the composition of national output and thus in the geographical location of economic opportunities, and that therefore internal migration is required for growth to materialize. The major shift in the sectoral composition of output in question is the declining relative importance of agricultural production and the corresponding relative increase in industrial output leading to parallel changes in the sectoral composition of the labor force. These changes in Peru, from 1950 to 1966, can be seen in Table 1.

The relative drop in agricultural employment from 1950 to 1966 is impressive. It should be noted, however, that over this time period the total labor force in Peru increased at a very rapid pace from 2.58 million in 1950 to 3.72 million in 1966. This meant that, even though relative employment in agriculture declined, the absolute number of agricultural workers increased from 1.52 million in 1950 to 1.85 million in 1966. The relative contribution of the manufacturing sector to employment has increased only insignificantly over the same time period. As a result, the proportion of the labor force employed in tertiary activities is growing ever larger. Whereas as a rule in the developed countries a larger proportion of the labor force is employed in the manufacturing sectors than in the services sectors, the opposite appears to be true in Peru. Paralleling these

TABLE 1. SECTORAL COMPOSITION OF VALUE ADDED AND
OF THE LABOR FORCE
(Percentages)

	Value Added		Labor Force	
	1950	1966	1950	1966
Agriculture	23.0	18.1	58.9	49.6
Mining	4.5	5.7	2.2	2.2
Manufacturing	13.6	19.3	13.0	13.7
Construction	5.1	4.5	2.7	3.8
Electricity, Gas & Water	.6	1.0	.2	.3
Government	8.8	8.3	4.0	6.4
Services	44.4	43.1	19.0	24.0
Total	100.0	100.0	100.0	100.0

SOURCE: Banco Central de Reserva del Perú, *Cuentas Nacionales del Perú, 1950–1967* (Lima, Peru, 1968).

changes in the sectoral distribution of the labor force is the gradual shift of the population from a rural to an urban environment, as shown in Table 2.

The limited absorption of labor in modern manufacturing throws doubt on the hypothesis that migration was a requirement for economic growth in Peru over the last few years. The manpower already available in the cities probably was large enough in order to fulfill the needs of manufacturing. Rural-urban migration does

TABLE 2. URBAN AND RURAL POPULATION
(Census Information: Percentage Composition)

		Lima-Callao	Rest of Coast	Sierra	Selva	Total
1940	Urban	9.9	8.1	15.0	2.4	35.4
	Rural	.5	9.1	50.1	4.9	64.6
	Total	10.4	17.2	65.1	7.3	100.0
1961	Urban	18.0	11.5	14.7	3.2	47.4
	Rural	.6	8.2	38.0	5.8	52.6
	Total	18.6	19.7	52.7	9.0	100.0
Yearly Growth Rate (in %)	Urban	5.2	3.9	2.2	3.6	3.7
	Rural	3.4	1.7	.9	3.0	1.2
	Total	5.0	3.0	1.2	3.4	2.3

SOURCE: Ministerio de Hacienda y Comercio, Dirección Nacional de Estadística y Censos, *Boletín de Analisis Demográfico*, Nos. 4–5 (Lima, Peru, 1967), Table 10, p. 50.

take place because of better overall opportunities in the cities than in the countryside, but both rural and urban areas are characterized by unemployment and underemployment. Peru's National Planning Institute has estimated that rural underemployment in 1965 was of the order of 50 percent.[4] In other words, half of the available manpower in agriculture would be sufficient, given present technology and cultivated area, in order to produce the present output, and the other half of the labor force is in surplus.

A similar situation can be found in the cities, but the order of magnitude is much smaller. Thus, surveys undertaken in Lima-Callao in 1967 and in Arequipa in 1965 found open unemployment to be of the order of 4 percent and 7 percent, respectively, whereas rates of underemployment of respectively 27 percent and 32 percent were found.[5] The latter are defined as including all those whose income is below a given minimum level (1,200 soles per month for Lima, 800 soles per month for Arequipa) and/or those who work less than thirty-five hours per week and want to work more. The net outcome of these observations is that whereas migration may not have been a requirement of Peru's industrial growth in the last few years in view of the un- and underemployment in the cities, it did occur probably in response to "relatively" better opportunities in the urban than rural areas. In this situation it seems more appropriate to emphasize the push from the countryside rather than the pull from the cities in describing the migration process. The essential difference from the kind of migration experienced in nineteenth-century western Europe and North America lies in the very rapid rate of growth of population and the inability of the economy as a whole to provide adequate employment. Migrants in Peru as migrants everywhere respond to differences in opportunities, even if often the choice open to them is only a more versus a lesser degree of underemployment.

The discussion thus far and the information contained in Tables

[4] Instituto Nacional de Planificación, *Bases para un Programa de Desarrollo Nacional a Largo Plazo* (Lima, Peru, 1969).
[5] Centro de Investigaciones Sociales por Muestreo, Servicio del Empleo y Recursos Humanos, *Encuestas de Hogares de Lima y Callao 1967* (Lima, Peru, 1968), and Centro de Investigaciones Sociales por Muestreo, Servicio del Empleo y Recursos Humanos, *Encuesta de Hogares en el Area Metropolitana de Arequipa 1965* (Lima, Peru, 1966).

1 and 2 might lead one to conclude that internal migration in Peru consists of farm residents moving to urban areas and that the cities, unable to provide sufficient industrial employment, absorb the rural migrants mainly in the services sectors. As will become clear from the analysis presented below, however, a more detailed look at Peru's internal migration reveals that the above conclusions present far too simple a picture of the migration process.

Table 2 shows that Peru's population grew at a yearly rate of 2.3 percent between the census years of 1940 and 1961. Since 1961, the yearly growth rate is estimated to be at least 3 percent because of a faster drop in death rates than in birth rates. Whereas the 1940 birth rate and death rate were estimated to be respectively 50 and 33 per thousand, yielding a natural population growth rate of 17 per thousand, estimates for about 1968 place the two rates at 41.8 and 11.1 per thousand respectively, yielding a population growth rate of 30.7 per thousand.[6]

Urban population increase from 1940 to 1961 was considerably more rapid than rural growth, 3.7 percent versus 1.2 percent per year. If one assumes the same natural rates of increase in population in both rural and urban areas,[7] the difference in observed growth rates must be due to migration. Table 2 shows that the rural-urban migration is paralleled by a movement from the Sierra to the Coast. Furthermore, the very rapid rate of population expansion in Lima-Callao (about 5 percent per year) is especially noteworthy. According to the 1961 census, of Peru's total population of 9.91 million, 2.28 million, or 23 percent were migrants (that is, they had moved from one province to another); of these, 43 percent had moved to the department of Lima or to Callao. The census also indicates that 47 percent of metropolitan Lima's residents are mi-

[6] Oficina Nacional de Estadística y Censos, *Informe de la Encuesta de Fecundidad en el Agustino* (Lima, Peru, 1969), p. 1.

[7] Precise information is lacking, but rural, natural population-growth rates probably were larger than urban ones. Rural and urban mortality rates cannot be compared very well because of insufficient data, but urban fertility definitely is lower than rural fertility. The 1961 census estimates the difference at about 20 percent. It is of interest to note that while fertility rates for Lima migrant women are higher than for Lima natives, they are, among the migrants, lower for those women who arrived in Lima before the age of twenty than for those who arrived after that age (see note 8, No. 1, p. 35). Earlier exposure to urban living conditions appears to have a decided effect on fertility.

grants. In view of the overwhelming importance of Lima and Callao as points of destination for Peru's migrants and because of the availability of the results of a sample survey of metropolitan Lima-Callao's population taken around the end of 1965 and early in 1966,[8] this study will concentrate on the capital city area. In this survey Lima's migrants are defined as all those people living in but not born in the metropolitan area at the time the survey was taken.

Whereas Peru's overall migration pattern is of a typical rural-urban nature, the migrants to the capital city could represent any one of three distinct movement patterns, or a mixture of them. These new *Limeños* could come directly from the rural areas, or they could move from the rural areas to a small town, migrate subsequently to a larger city and, ultimately, settle in Lima, or finally, the Lima migrant might originate in a smaller urban area while the place which he vacated in that unit on moving to the capital is filled by a former resident of an even smaller urban or rural area. The last pattern appears to predominate. A similar pattern has been observed elsewhere in Latin America.[9]

Table 3 shows that while 64.4 percent of Peru's population outside Lima-Callao (1961 census data) resided in sparsely populated areas of less than 1,000 inhabitants, only 6.1 percent of Lima's migrants originated in similar places. One-third came from cities of

TABLE 3. DISTRIBUTION OF PERU'S POPULATION (EXCLUDING METROPOLITAN LIMA) AND DISTRIBUTION OF LIMA MIGRANTS BY PLACE OF ORIGIN SIZE

City Size	Percent Population	Percent Migrants
> 20,000	8.1	33.3
5,000–19,999	10.6	17.2
1,000– 4,999	16.9	43.4
< 1,000	64.4	6.1
Total	100.0	100.0

SOURCE: Dirección Nacional de Estadística y Censos. *Encuesta de Inmigración Lima Metropolitana* (Lima, Peru, 1966), No. 2, Table 5, p. 9.

[8] Dirección Nacional de Estadística y Censos, *Encuesta de Inmigración Lima Metropolitana* (Lima, Peru, 1966), 3 vols.

[9] Bruce Herrick, *Urban Migration and Economic Development in Chile* (Cambridge, 1965).

more than 20,000. At the same time, about 80 percent of the migrants of ages fourteen and above who arrived in Lima during the decade 1956 to 1965 moved only once in their lifetime. In other words, a very large number of Lima's migrants came from other urban areas, very few came from a real rural origin, and most made only one movement during their lifetime. Furthermore, other urban areas outside of metropolitan Lima also were experiencing fast population growth, while the rural areas were losing people. The migration pattern appears, therefore, to a large extent to be one where the place vacated by the Lima migrant in the smaller cities is filled by migrants from the countryside.

Selectivity of Lima's Migrants

This pattern of migration to the capital means that many of Lima's migrants have been exposed to an urban environment before moving to the capital, so that in urban "skills" they equate more easily with Lima's native residents and adapt themselves more speedily to Lima's environment than would be the case for persons whose origins were predominantly rural. The 1966 sample survey allows us to study the migrants with respect to age, level of education, and employment pattern as well as to make some comparisons between them and Lima's native residents. Table 4 gives the age structure of Peru's total population and contrasts it with the age structure of the migrants in the survey at the time of their arrival in Lima. Clearly the migrants are young, more than half of them between the ages of ten and twenty-four. Furthermore, the relatively large number of migrants below the age of ten indicates the movement of whole families. Of the total number surveyed 51.7 percent were women and 48.3 percent were men, which leads one to believe that among those moving to the capital there is very little sex differentiation.

In terms of education the migrants are considerably more educated than the averages for the country; in fact, as shown in Table 5 they compare quite favorably with Lima's native residents, especially those who arrived in Lima before the age of fifteen. The latter finding implies that the migrants definitely do take advantage of the educational opportunities offered in Lima. The information of Table 5 can be compared with 1961 census data which, for instance, show that of the total of Peru's population over the age of fifteen only 16 percent of the men and 10 percent of the women received any secondary or university education.

TABLE 4. AGE STRUCTURE OF PERU'S TOTAL POPULATION, 1961, AND OF LIMA MIGRANTS AT TIME OF ARRIVAL
(Percentages)

Age Group	Peru's Population Men	Peru's Population Women	Lima Migrants at Arrival Time Men	Lima Migrants at Arrival Time Women
0–4	17.1	16.7	11.9	10.4
5–9	15.0	14.6	11.0	12.4
10–14	12.1	11.2	15.3	18.7
15–19	10.0	9.6	25.4	23.1
20–24	8.5	8.6	15.0	12.1
25–29	7.3	7.7	6.7	6.2
30–34	6.3	6.2	3.9	4.4
35–39	5.3	5.6	2.8	2.6
40–49	7.8	8.0	2.9	4.6
50+	10.6	11.8	3.7	4.0
Unknown	—	—	1.4	1.5
Total	100.0	100.0	100.0	100.0
Total number observations	4,925,518	4,981,228	2,069	2,219

SOURCE: Dirección Nacional de Estadística y Censos. *Encuesta de Inmigración Lima Metropolitana* (Lima, Peru, 1966), No. 2, Table 1, p. 3; Population Census, 1961.

TABLE 5. EDUCATIONAL LEVEL OF PERSONS IN LIMA
(Percentages)

Level of Education	Native Lima Residents Men	Native Lima Residents Women	Migrants Arrived before Age 15 Men	Migrants Arrived before Age 15 Women	Migrants Arrived after Age 15 Men	Migrants Arrived after Age 15 Women
Cannot read	.2	.3	.5	4.2	1.3	8.8
No instruction	.3	1.2	.7	5.2	2.1	7.7
4 years elementary	4.6	6.1	9.4	16.5	12.3	20.0
4–7 years elementary	23.7	30.0	29.2	34.4	40.0	34.7
Secondary or university	69.1	61.0	58.1	38.6	43.1	27.5
Other unspecified	1.1	.8	1.4	.7	.6	.4
Unknown	1.0	.6	.7	.4	.6	.9
Total	100.0	100.0	100.0	100.0	100.0	100.0

SOURCE: Dirección Nacional de Estadística y Censos. *Encuesta de Inmigración Lima Metropolitana* (Lima, Peru, 1966), No. 1, Table 15, p. 38.

Table 6 compares migrants and native Lima residents in terms of socioeconomic groups. As might be expected, relatively more migrants are manual workers but again, especially for the men, their occupational distribution is not drastically different from that of Lima's native residents.

Income comparisons give a similar picture, as can be seen in Table 7. If incomes below 1,500 soles per month are considered to represent underemployment, the situation of the migrants is not very different from that of the natives of Lima, the major exception being very young, recent migrants. This last group includes an unusually large proportion of people earning incomes below 1,500 soles per month and an unusually small proportion receiving incomes over 3,000 soles per month. The explanation may be that this group includes a number of very young (starting at age fourteen) and therefore inexperienced migrants who only recently moved to Lima. Furthermore, not only do the young, recent migrants have less bargaining power than others in the labor force, but they probably also command a smaller amount of accumulated savings which could assist them during their job search. As a result, they are forced to take the least remunerative jobs. Especially in the thirty to fifty-

TABLE 6. ECONOMICALLY ACTIVE POPULATION OVER FIFTEEN YEARS OF AGE
(Percentages)

Socioeconomic groups	Native Lima Residents		Migrants	
	Men	Women	Men	Women
Nonmanual workers	*49*	*67*	*41*	*40*
Professionals	7	21	8	10
Administrators	6	2	3	1
Office employees	23	34	14	15
Vendors	13	10	16	14
Manual workers	*47*	*31*	*54*	*56*
Craftsmen	37	20	42	15
Personal services	3	8	5	40
Other workers	7	3	7	1
Agricultural workers	*2*	*1*	*2*	*1*
Other	*2*	*1*	*3*	*3*
Total	100	100	100	100

SOURCE: Dirección Nacional de Estadística y Censos. *Encuesta de Inmigración Lima Metropolitana* (Lima, Peru, 1966), No. 1, Table 23, p. 55.

TABLE 7. INCOME-GROUP DISTRIBUTION OF MALE MIGRANTS AND NONMIGRANTS
(Percentages)

Age Group and Status	Monthly Income in Soles					
	<1000	1000–1499	1500–2999	3000–3999	>4000	Total
14 and above						
Migrants of 1956–1965	12.1	27.7	35.6	12.2	12.4	100.0
Migrants with > 10 years residence in Lima	5.5	13.3	42.8	16.4	22.0	100.0
Native residents	7.1	13.3	32.6	17.0	30.0	100.0
30 to 54 years						
Migrants of 1956–1965	4.3	7.4	35.1	23.4	29.8	100.0
Migrants with > 10 years residence in Lima	4.0	11.4	41.7	18.6	24.3	100.0
Native residents	2.6	7.1	29.5	18.9	41.9	100.0

SOURCE: Dirección Nacional de Estadística y Censos. *Encuesta de Inmigración Lima Metropolitana* (Lima, Peru, 1966), No. 1, Table 20, p. 50.

four age group, underemployment as defined above is very similar for the two groups; whereas 10 percent of Lima's natives received in 1965 incomes below 1,500 soles per month, the corresponding percentages for migrants were 15 percent for those who arrived in Lima before 1956 and 12 percent for more recent migrants. It must be noted, too, that about 70 percent of the migrants found work in Lima within three months after their arrival, and virtually all did so within one year.[10]

The general conclusion to be derived from all these data is that it is incorrect to think of Lima's migrants as a separate group of unemployed, unemployable, and poorly motivated members of the labor force. In fact, they represent very select elements of Peru's society, individuals who adapt themselves quickly to the new environment to which they have moved.

These observations can have very important policy implications for the future. Peru's and Lima's major tasks are the creation of adequate industrial employment opportunities for the large numbers of underemployed. In trying to find a solution to this problem, there is no need to consider migrants, to the capital at least, as a special group, for they can be shown to be no less prepared for industrial jobs than the natives of Lima.

[10] See note 8, No. 3, p. 41.

Consequences of Migration and Conclusions

There is little doubt that the move to Lima is, on the average, very beneficial for the migrant involved. A 1967 survey[11] found that only 4 percent of the migrants felt that they were worse off after having migrated to Lima than before. Furthermore, the movement to Lima is essentially one-way, there being virtually no evidence of return migration. The higher rates of rural than urban underemployment, discussed previously, may be expected to lead to continued migration to the cities and especially to Lima during the immediate future.

Equally important as the effect of migration on the migrant, is its effect upon the economy as a whole. Clearly, the present rural-urban migration in Peru simply transfers underemployment from the countryside to the cities. Neither before nor after the take-over of the nationalistic-reforming military regime in 1968, has the industrial sector been providing jobs at a rate fast enough to absorb the migrants into highly productive employment. As we have seen, the net result is that Lima's migrants often are considered a poorly educated, unemployable, burdensome group of rural origin with severe adjustment problems to the urban environment, swelling the ranks of the un- and underemployed. We know, however, that Lima's migrants do not fit this description, that the great bulk of Lima's migrants already have been exposed to an urban environment before coming to Lima, and that they adjust very well to their new surroundings. They have come to stay, and the selectivity of their recruitment to the Lima-bound group allows them to compete rather favorably with native Lima residents for the better jobs. In other words, the socioeconomic problem is not migrants who are underemployed after moving to Lima, but rather general underemployment in Lima, a condition shared by both native residents and migrants.

The fact that urbanization came ahead of industrial job creation in Peru, as opposed for example to nineteenth-century western Europe or North America, can be explained on the basis of the

[11] Centro de Investigaciones Sociales por Muestreo, Servicio del Empleo y Recursos Humanos, *Algunos Aspectos de Estratificación, Movilidad y Migración en Lima e Iquitos* (Lima, Peru, 1968).

much more rapid rate of growth of Peru's population. Lack of adequate employment exists throughout the economy, giving internal migration an altogether different character from the way it took place in the past. The findings of this study, however, in general do not contradict the findings of some of the major studies of migration in the West. The fact that migration takes place in a very orderly manner, being very selective and, in the case of Lima, mainly of an urban-urban nature, does mean that the whole process is operating as an efficient resource allocator, moving the more adaptable people to the better jobs, even if many of these jobs have to be created in the future. The continually changing composition of GNP as development takes place would require the eventual movement of people from rural to urban areas in any event. The present lack of employment in the Peruvian economy everywhere simply means that large numbers of people swamped the city's economy (as well as the countryside's), resulting in massive underemployment, an experience virtually unknown in the economic history of the presently developed world.

Obviously, the major task ahead for Peru is the creation of more job opportunities. While it is not the purpose of this paper to discuss possible avenues toward this goal, it does seem appropriate to elaborate somewhat on an overall strategy to be followed and to add a few remarks regarding some additional positive aspects of the migration process. It clearly would be a major achievement if Peru's population could be provided at least with decent housing and adequate food. The "Green Revolution" now in progress in Asia has shown that tremendous technological breakthroughs in agriculture are feasible. This has led to the conviction that, eventually all over the less-developed world, the agricultural sector will be able to produce sufficient quantities of food, at least when and if adequate price, tax, and other indirect policies are followed. In view of the overall employment situation in Peru, however, policymakers would be well advised to select those production techniques in agriculture which provide maximum employment. It is interesting to note in this connection that the authors of a recent study on employment and output prospects in Peru and Guatemala[12] con-

[12] Erik Thorbecke and Ardy Stoutjesdijk, *A Methodology to Estimate the Rela-*

clude that, at least within agriculture, no conflict needs to exist between output and employment, and that agricultural growth through land expansion and yield increases without mechanization is preferable both in terms of production growth and employment creation.

In the area of housing, the selectivity of recruitment and resulting high level of motivation of Lima's migrants is proving to be an invaluable asset. While most migrants originally settle in the center city slums, the 1965 sample survey shows that within metropolitan Lima there is a net movement on the part of the migrants (as well as native residents) from the center city to the *barriadas*, or squatter settlements, surrounding the city. The land involved in these settlements was mostly owned by the state and has come to be a free good for the settlers. Housing construction takes place little by little as the settler accumulates savings, and with a minimum of outside assistance many of these squatter settlements have organized themselves in order to build streets, churches, and schools, to install water pipes and the like, relying heavily upon local labor input. The last fact is an excellent example of self-mobilization by the underemployed which assists in the country's capital formation. Somewhat more government assistance than has been provided in the past would greatly accelerate this process of urban infrastructure creation. Clearly both food and housing, the people's most basic needs, can be provided given a minimum amount of planning on the part of the government, and both of these activities could provide substantial employment.

One additional aspect of Peru's internal migration process is the likely effect of migration on the country's overall population growth. The available evidence in Peru suggests that urban fertility rates are below their rural counterparts. The 1961 census gives 20 percent lower urban than rural fertility. If this pattern holds constant as urbanization proceeds, the rate of population growth is bound to decline. The urgent need to reduce Peru's birth rate can, of course, not be overemphasized.

---

tionship Between Present and Future Output and Employment, Applied to Peru and Guatemala (Paris: OECD, Development Centre Working Document, December, 1969).

Squatters or Suburbanites? The Growth of Shantytowns in Oaxaca, Mexico

Douglas Butterworth

Probably the most conspicuous aspect of urbanization in Latin America is the rapid, seemingly haphazard growth of the shantytowns which ring cities south of the Rio Grande. Usually referred to in English as "squatter settlements," these urban conglomerates have attracted the attention of both policymakers and social scientists. Government officials and city planners are concerned about the effect of such settlements on the social and economic life of the city and nation, yet they have so far done little to meet the challenges presented by shantytowns. Anthropologists have been slow to direct their research interests to these urban communities, but the prospect of collaboration between policymakers and researchers in anthropology and other disciplines makes the study of shantytowns exciting.

Recent investigations of "squatter settlements" quite reasonably move us away from the image of these communities as "festering sores" on the urban body and point out the positive aspects

With the assistance of John Chance, Donald Foster, Cheleen Higgins, and Michael Higgins, this investigation was made possible by support under a program sponsored by the Center for International Comparative Studies and the Center for Latin American Studies, both of the University of Illinois. Supplementary funds were provided by the Department of Anthropology, University of Illinois. The authors express their appreciation for comments by William P. Delaney.

they exhibit. Observations by Morse, Turner, Mangin, and Leeds[1] are especially pertinent in this respect. However, a word of caution seems to be called for at this juncture in our research on shantytowns in Latin America. The enthusiasm which inspires many of the generalizations about "squatter settlements" may be premature and might need to be tempered by more detailed studies of the development and structure of these urban communities. The study of cities and the sociocultural segments within and around them must be committed to the same fine sense of detail and analysis that has characterized some of the better anthropological investigations of small tribal societies and peasant communities. This is not to say that urban anthropologists should "rediscover" sociology, but to suggest that we be wary of building theory and proposing policy on the basis of inadequate data.

As I see it, a basic weakness in the literature which attempts to summarize our knowledge of "squatter settlements" in Latin America is a tendency to overgeneralize from data which are not only meager in the extreme but also poorly classified and defined. In the conclusion of his review of research on "squatter settlements" Mangin notes that:

> despite the talk about urban anthropology, anthropologists have done very little urban work. Other than those on East Africa the number of studies has been very small and mostly unpublished. The few anthropologists, architects, sociologists, and political anthropologists (Latin and North American) who have worked in squatter settlements have to a large extent been responsible for some of the policy changes [of some Latin American governments]. . . . Whether or not influencing policy is anyone's goal, the need for more research on squatter settlements is apparent.[2]

---

[1] Richard M. Morse, "Recent Research on Latin American Urbanization," *Latin American Research Review*, Vol. 1, No. 1 (1965), pp. 35–74; John C. Turner, "Carriers and Channels for Housing Development in Modernizing Countries," *Journal of the American Institute of Planners*, Vol. 33 (1967), pp. 167–181; William Mangin, "Latin American Squatter Settlements: A Problem and a Solution," *Latin American Research Review*, Vol. 2, No. 3 (1967), pp. 65–98; Anthony and Elizabeth Leeds, "Brazil and the Myth of Urban Rurality: Urban Experience, Work, and Values in the Squatments of Rio de Janeiro and Lima," in *City and Country in the Third World*, ed. Arthur J. Field (Cambridge, Mass., 1970), pp. 229–285.

[2] Mangin, "Latin American Squatter Settlements," pp. 89–90.

The purpose of this paper is to contribute to our knowledge of "squatter settlements" by describing five case studies of shantytowns in the city of Oaxaca, Mexico. Specifically, it points up the remarkable differences which exist among communities which a casual observer would be tempted to group together under the rubric "squatter settlements," and sets forth some of the dangers inherent in such gross classifications. Lest we have a hand in replacing popular myths with an academic mythology about shantytowns, we must take a more critical look at our tendencies to lump together dissimilar phenomena. With that view in mind, this paper will limit itself to certain aspects of the formation, growth, and political evolution of the shantytowns of Oaxaca.

The city of Oaxaca is a provincial center and state capital of some 100,000 inhabitants. It has little industry, serving more as a transportation nexus, commercial trading point, and tourist center than as a locus of manufacturing. In spite of the relative lack of industry, migration to the state capital has been heavy, and the last two decades have seen a burgeoning of shantytowns on the hillsides which surround the city. With the assistance of four graduate students from the University of Illinois, I undertook a nine-month study of these suburban communities of Oaxaca.

Oaxaca was selected for this study because very few investigations had been conducted in "squatter settlements" of small and middle-size cities in Latin America. The selection of Oaxaca was felicitous since there is a relatively wide range of diversity in the shantytowns within a reasonably narrow geographical area, thereby facilitating preliminary reconnaissance of the settlements and fairly easy access to those communities we eventually chose for study.

The research team intially surveyed the dozen or so settlements which ring the city to note size, age, and apparent differences in economic position as reflected in construction of homes. We then narrowed our possible choices to eight of the communities and surveyed them to determine the presence or absence of selected social, economic, and political variables.[3] On the basis of the range in these

[3] These variables included local political organizations, internal business, non-political voluntary associations, public transportation, electric service, water, schools, churches, markets, sewers, street pavements, doctors, telephones, brick houses, bars or restaurants, and status of land tenure.

variables, we eventually selected five outlying settlements for investigation: Santa María, Benito Juárez, Linda Vista, San Juan, and Mirador.[4]

The Shantytowns of Oaxaca

Most of the lands which comprise the outlying *colonias* of Oaxaca were unoccupied farmlands or wastelands until about twenty-five years ago. In the 1940s speculators began to buy the lands adjacent to the newly completed Pan American Highway. This was a time of significant population movement in Mexico, stimulated by World War II, expanding trade and industry, improved communications, and the *bracero* program. The Pan American Highway linked, directly or indirectly, many formerly remote villages in southern Mexico to urban centers. In the state of Oaxaca, communities began to feed the migration streams which found their way to state and national capitals such as Puebla, Mexico City, and Oaxaca.[5] In the decade 1940 to 1950 the *municipio* of Oaxaca grew by 56.9 percent, from 31,839 to 49,953.[6] Similar proportional increases in population occurred during the succeeding decades.

As Waterbury has demonstrated, however, Oaxaca's change since the 1940s has been in size, not in kind. It is still principally an administrative, commercial, and cultural center and is "overurbanized," in the sense that its population increase has not been met with a corresponding growth of industry, although there has been some gain in small industries. Inmigration of rural unskilled laborers seeking employment continues, but jobs are becoming increasingly scarce. Thus there is a large population of poor, unemployed, underemployed, and even unemployable adults. "With the paucity of industry, most people have little choice but to work as low-paid,

---

[4] The universe composing the sample consisted of 260 households containing 1,347 members. Because of the nature of the problems presented in each settlement, distribution of the sample was uneven.

[5] Douglas Butterworth, "A Study of the Urbanization Process Among Mixtec Migrants from Tilantongo in Mexico City," *América Indígena*, Vol. 22 (1962), pp. 257–274.

[6] México, Dirección General de Estadística, Sexto censo general de población, Resumen general, 1940 (1948), and Séptimo censo general de población, Resumen general, 1950 (1953).

unskilled assistants in commercial houses, construction, and transportation; as servants; and as market vendors."[7]

Many of the newly arrived migrants to Oaxaca settled in or near the center of the city, living in crowded rooms or run-down old homes deserted by members of the urban elite during earlier natural and political upheavals.[8] Others built rude shacks and adobe huts to the east and west of the city near the banks of the Atoyac River.

As the population of the city increased and housing became scarcer and more expensive, some of the inhabitants began to look toward the hillsides for opportunities to build their own homes on privately owned lots. The businessmen, professionals, and politicians who claimed to own the large tracts of land surrounding the city divided the land into small plots to sell to the land-hungry dwellers of innercity slums. The purchasers usually bought their plots in good faith, believing that the sellers had clear title to the lands. Only occasionally were the new arrivals literally "squatters" —people who settle illegally on government or privately owned land.

Today rude shacks mixed with occasional sturdy brick homes dot the hillsides above and below the Pan American Highway which rims the north edge of the city. The homes extend down into the city to the south and up near the northern peaks of the hills. On the opposite side of the city, across the Atoyac River, the slopes of the southern hills are also filled with similar makeshift and permanent structures.

Linda Vista is the largest, "richest," and most complex of the communities studied. A progressive settlement of some 3,000 inhabitants, it is one of the first *colonias* a traveler sees as he enters the city from the northwest. A dirt road leading from the Pan American Highway traverses level ground as it enters Linda Vista, passing small shops, brightly painted cement houses, and a new school. The road begins to rise at the school and rapidly turns into a steep

---

[7] Ronald Waterbury, "Urbanization and a Traditional Market System," in *The Social Anthropology of Latin America: Essays in Honor of Ralph Leon Beals*, eds. Walter Goldschmidt and Harry Hoijer (Los Angeles, 1970), p. 128.

[8] Norman S. Hayner, "Differential Social Change in a Mexican Town," *Social Forces*, Vol. 26, No. 4 (1948), pp. 381–390.

ravine-filled path. Cars and trucks can enter and circulate in the *colonia* on level ground, but even though the communal labor force (*tequio*) struggles to maintain the higher roads, each summer's rains wash them out and it is months into the dry season before they again resemble anything more than donkey trails.

The community is divided physically into two parts, officially designated as Section One and Section Two, separated by a *barranca* running north and south through the *colonia*. Most of the homes have electricity and easy access to water. A significant proportion of the houses, particularly in the lower part, are substantial dwellings. As in all the *colonias*, the houses become poorer as one ascends the hillside. Many of the inhabitants of the lower reaches of Linda Vista are professionals and skilled laborers.

Linda Vista was first occupied in the mid-1950s, when a schoolteacher purchased the lands which now form the *colonia* from a lawyer and sold plots to those who wanted to settle on the hillsides. The lawyer claimed to be sole owner of the territory under discussion, but it turned out that he did not possess title to all the land he had sold. Thus the new owner had sold property to settlers which was not his to sell.

This situation later came to light and the president of Linda Vista's most powerful political group preferred charges of land fraud against the teacher and had him jailed. The charges were never proved, however, so the teacher was released after spending two years in prison. He still claims legal ownership of the land he purchased and sold.

Meanwhile, as these events were transpiring, two more individuals, a local manufacturing firm, and a group of businessmen emerged with claims of ownership to territories in Linda Vista. So there are now five rivals competing for the lands and, at the time of the study, three law suits concerning the property were in the courts.

While individuals, corporations, and government officials squabbled among themselves, migrants flooded into Linda Vista, acquiring land from whomever could convince them that they were the legal owners of the property. Some of the new arrivals paid for their lots in cash; most made a down payment and agreed to make periodic payments on the balance. Others have refused to make any payments until the law suits are settled. Some "owners" now pay taxes; others do not. Competing politicians have made contradictory promises and claims about land tenure which serve only to confuse the already insecure settlers of Linda Vista. In desperation, the ruling political body of the *colonia* is trying to have the government federalize all the land in order to untangle the problem of land tenure and settle the ownership claims. In view of the volatile politics involved, it is likely that a solution to the land question in Linda Vista will not be forthcoming for some time.

The settlements of Santa María and Benito Juárez, which lie to the east of Linda Vista along the Pan American Highway, belonged until recently to a single *colonia* (Santa María) bifurcated by the highway. Now separate communities, Santa María lies below the highway, Benito Juárez above. The two *colonias* are essentially different. Many of the homes in Santa María, a settlement of some 1,100 people, are firm structures inhabited by middle-income families. A few stores supply minor items to the populace. The community is provided with both water and electric services, and a serviceable road wends from the highway through Santa María toward the city of Oaxaca below.

On the north side of the highway, steep and narrow footpaths lead to the *colonia* Benito Juárez. This settlement, with less than half the population of Santa María, is much poorer than its neighbor to the south. It has no electricity and, until recently, had no potable water. Many of the houses are flimsy and perched precariously in niches carved out of the precipitous terrain. Automobiles cannot enter the community. Foot travel is difficult and, in the rainy season, even dangerous.

Thirty years ago, the lands which now comprise the *colonias* Santa María and Benito Juárez were unoccupied. During the period 1940 to 1946 this terrain was bought by a local lawyer from three separate owners. The Pan American Highway construction around the rim of the Cerro del Fortín was completed in 1944 and passed through the middle of these lands. The purchase of the lands may have been stimulated by the new highway. In 1946 the lawyer sold the terrain to a politician from the state of Durango, but was retained as administrator by the new owner. The lawyer died in 1959 and the administration of the lands was taken over by his sons, who have a law firm in Oaxaca.

In 1960 the lands above the road were settled illegally by a group of about 100 family heads led by a primary schoolteacher from the city. This is one of the rare instances of organized invasion by squatters in Oaxaca. The lawyers administering the territory protested the occupation to the state government. The government intervened and helped the lawyers convince the new settlers that the lands were privately owned and their occupation illegal. The settlers were evicted. It is reported that government intervention was prompted by the desire of the governor of the state to keep the slopes of the Cerro del Fortín unoccupied, since squatter settlements would give a bad impression to visitors entering the city.

In the following year the lands below the highway were opened for development by the lawyers. Lots were laid out and sold to individual residents on installment plans. Homes were erected and the new urban conglomeration became known as Colonia Santa María.

Then the lands above the road were again settled upon illegally. Representatives of the city government declared the land municipally controlled communal property and attempted to collect rents from the approximately fifty squatter families. But this scheme to increase revenue was thwarted once again by the intervention of the state government, which evicted the squatters. The governor, perhaps responding to pressure from influential sources in the state capital, still favored the policy of keeping the lands above the highway free of settlement.

Shortly after this second attempt to settle the terrain above the Pan American Highway, a third group occupied these lands. This group was led by an official of the Marquesado market, one of the city marketplaces. Individuals who had businesses in the market were led to believe that they were to be given lots above the highway by the government free of charge. Coinciding with this invasion, and perhaps partially as a result of the harassment, a different attitude developed on the part of the state government toward housing for the poor.

A new governor had taken office and he did not place such a high premium on keeping the Cerro del Fortín free of settlement. Whether for political reasons or from personal feelings for the less fortunate, he did not intervene to remove the new settlers and thus forced the lawyers to deal directly with the squatters. The lawyers elected to subdivide the land and sell plots to persons from the market who wished to stay and pay. This new section became known as Colonia Santa María, Section Two; the part below was called Section One of the *colonia*. Land tenure in Santa María is reasonably secure and this *colonia* is the more urban of the two. In Benito Juárez, however, land titles are relatively ill-defined as a result of the political vicissitudes.

Mirador is the poorest shantytown in Oaxaca. A small settlement of about 200 people, it lies below the Pan American Highway to the southeast of the communities previously described. A steep footpath leads from the highway into the *colonia* itself. Discarded trash and animal and human excrement clutter the ground. None of the adobe huts and *carrizo* (reed grass) shacks has electricity; there is no water available in the community; only a few homes have an outhouse. The tiny *milpas* (cornfields), the pigs and chickens, and the *temazcales* (sweatbaths) give Mirador an air of rusticity.

The first settler in Mirador was a migrant originally from the *municipio* of Tilantongo, in the Mixteca Alta region of Oaxaca, who squatted on the land in 1938. A lawyer from the city of Oaxaca claimed to be legal owner of the land and demanded that the squatter either pay $1,000 pesos for title or abandon the property. The migrant had lived in the state capital for a decade, however, and had become a bit wise to city ways. He inquired at government offices about title to the land and was told that the land was public, not private, real estate. According to the man from Tilantongo, he thereupon purchased the land for $600 pesos. Today, however, the government claims that it has no record of the transaction and considers Mirador municipal property, officially unoccupied.

As the squatter's children grew and married, they were presented with small plots in Mirador by their father. The squatter also advised friends and relatives from Tilantongo living in Oaxaca that he had land in Mirador that he was willing to sell or rent. Gradually the *colonia* became a small enclave of Tilantongo migrants.

Then, a number of years ago, one of the sons-in-law of the original settler announced that he would like to sell his property in Mirador to some migrants from Tidáa, a neighboring village of Tilantongo in the Mixteca Alta. The father-in-law was at first shocked at the idea, for Tidáa and Tilantongo had been arch enemies for centuries. In their native habitat the citizens of these two communities had been assaulting each other since at least the time of the Spanish conquest.

But the son-in-law convinced the old settler that past enmities should be forgotten and the migrants from Tidáa be allowed to settle in Mirador. The owner relented, and when there proved to be no friction between the two groups, later sold some land plots to more of his former enemies. Soon the families from Tidáa were sending word to their fellow villagers that one could live well and cheaply in Mirador by renting or buying property in the *colonia*. Nevertheless, the land titles in the *colonia* have absolutely no validity in the eyes of municipal officials.

On the southwest edge of the city lies San Juan Chapultepec, a community of about 3,500 people. San Juan is ecologically split into two divisions by a road leading to the archeological zone of Monte Albán. The sector below the road is the old part of the village with four dirt streets and a plaza flanked by a church and cemetery, a small school, local government offices, a reading room used for literacy classes, four private homes, and two stores. The houses in the lower sector of the community are often of substantial materials, such as brick or cement, and reflect the relatively higher economic status of some of the residents. Water and electricity are available to all residents below the road.

The part of San Juan which lies above the road is much newer. The abrupt hillside contains a fairly dense settlement of one- and two-room houses, mostly of cheap materials like adobe, and is crisscrossed by a number of footpaths. It is poorer than the section below the road; only a minority of the families have water and electricity.

San Juan is different from the other settlements under consideration, for it has been in existence since at least the time of the Spanish conquest. Originally a small village jurisdictionally apart from the town of Antequera (now Oaxaca), San Juan has undergone several political and legal changes of status since the coming of the Spaniards. Today it has the legal status of *agencia municipal* and is listed in the 1960 census as a *ranchería*. It is one of the thirteen dependencies of the city of Oaxaca and lies within the *municipio* of Oaxaca. Population trends indicate that it was a small and probably unimportant settlement until the 1950s when it began to grow rapidly by receiving part of the overflow of population from the central city. In 1950 the census listed a population of 403 inhabitants of the community. By the following decade San Juan had grown to 1,391 people, and a 1969 school census gave a population of 3,537 for the *agencia*.

Most of the inhabitants of the upper part of San Juan—the sector of the community with which we are concerned in this study—have come within the past fifteen years. While the majority of the residents of the lower part own their own lots, with few exceptions, families living on the hillside do not. About 1933 the *agente municipal* began to give away free plots of land above the road in an effort to attract more people to the village. This was apparently done without the consent of the municipal officials in Oaxaca, but despite the fact that the land belonged to the *municipio* of Oaxaca and not to the village itself, there was no opposition. Lots were not given away on a large scale until about 1955 when the *agente* launched another campaign to attract new residents. From then on the hillside began to fill rapidly. Today there is no land left to distribute to upper San Juan.

The lots given away by the *agente* are called *donaciones*. The possessor of a *donación* has usufruct rights to it in perpetuity and may do what he wants with it. His descendants may inherit it, he may pass it on to relatives or friends, or he may sell rights to its use to someone else and charge for whatever structures he has erected and improvements he has made on the land. But he may not sell the land itself, which is legally the property of the *municipio* of Oaxaca.

To obtain a *donación* a family must demonstrate to the *agente* that it is lacking in economic resources and in need of a house lot. In most cases families were given the land for nothing, or for a small gratuity. Possessors of *donaciones* do not pay taxes on their land.

In contrast to the other *colonias*, land tenure is well defined in the upper part of San Juan, both from the point of view of the government and from that of the residents themselves. Land titles or rights to the *donaciones* are clearly indicated in the official records and residents are aware of their rights and limitations insofar as land and services are concerned. Everyone realizes that, in return for their lots, each household head is expected to work the Sunday *tequio* or pay a fine of $10 pesos, and to pay monthly sums for water and electricity.

Thus, the processes which have contributed to the formation, fission, and fusion of the shantytowns in Oaxaca are different in each case studied. The result is a series of settlements whose legal statuses range from complete outlaw to official incorporation into the municipal structure. At the one extreme is Mirador, composed of true squatters with no official recognition whatsoever. In fact, government authorities deny that anyone lives there! At the opposite extreme is San Juan, an *agencia municipal* with clearly defined land titles and rights to municipal services.

Linda Vista has quasi-recognition from municipal authorities in the sense that some government agencies have admitted its right to certain services, including water, electricity, and a school. Nevertheless, the situation with regard to land titles is chaotic. A few squatters have taken advantage of the unstable land situation to encroach upon lots which they have no intention of paying for, but the great majority of families in the *colonia* are anxious to pay for their land titles as soon as they are certain that these payments will not be arrogated by persons who themselves have no legal title to the land. Linda Vista will no doubt eventually become a legal subdivision of the city, with lots and streets laid out in accordance with municipal specifications and with rights to services.

The status of Santa María is similar to that of Linda Vista. The main difference is that, because of clearer land titles and more level terrain, incorporation will be achieved earlier.

The situation in Benito Juárez is less well defined. The *colonia* has not gotten support for installation of services, the knotty problem of land ownership remains unsolved, and it has not been granted recognition by the government. Its physical existence is recognized by the authorities, but its legality is questioned.

Thus there are four rather well-defined types of shantytowns in the Oaxaca sample: clandestine squatter (Mirador), quasi-outlaw (Benito Juárez), quasi-legal (Linda Vista and Santa María), and *agencia municipal* (San Juan).[9] These differential statuses carry important political and demographic implications. For one thing the status and phase of development of a shantytown helps to determine what kinds of people are attracted to them.

Residents of the shantytowns of Oaxaca are typically from rural areas in the state of Oaxaca. Contrary to popular local opinion, however, the settlers of the *colonias* are not peasants who have come directly from rural villages, but are overwhelmingly people who have lived in the city of Oaxaca for some time before moving to the hillsides. Almost nine out of ten household heads in the sample had spent a period of residence in the center city (often in slum tenements) before their exodus to the outlying *colonias*. This was not usually just a short stopover in town; household heads averaged ten years in the city before their move. This phenomenon is thus a kind of poor man's suburbia movement. The Oaxaca data are in accord with Mangin's analysis of squatter settlements and with the recent findings of Flinn and Converse in Colombia.[10]

Factors which help to determine the decision to move to the peripheral shantytowns are both objective and subjective. Among the former are considerations of income and savings, place of employment, space, family expansion, and the welfare of children. Outstanding among the latter is the desire for personal freedom (*libertad*)—a wish to escape the psychic (apart from physical) confines of crowded city life.[11]

---

[9] William L. Flinn and James W. Converse, "Eight Assumptions Concerning Rural-Urban Migration in Columbia: A Three-Shantytowns Test," *Land Economics*, Vol. 46 (1970), pp. 456–466, divided the peripheral shantytowns in Colombia into "at least three types": *barrios piratas* or *clandestinos*; *invasiones* or *tugurios*; and *urbanizaciones*. While the typology is helpful for their discussion, I find it somewhat less so for the Oaxaca study.

[10] Mangin, "Latin American Squatter Settlements," p. 68; Flinn and Converse, "Eight Assumptions," pp. 464–465.

[11] The basis for these statements are interviews conducted with informants after their move to the shantytowns. The validity and reliability of these data are therefore subject to the same kinds of criticism which may be levied at all such studies which involve recall and reconstruction by respondents. Nevertheless, the generalizations about subjective considerations made here by informants are strengthened by a high

Once the decision to leave the city for the suburbs has been made, the choice of which settlement the family or individual moves to depends basically upon three things: wealth and place of employment; the status of land tenure and public services in the *colonias*; and the presence of friends or relatives in the shantytowns. The last factor may be an overriding consideration and seriously modifies attempts to construct a neat model of decisionmaking in centrifugal movements of the population in Oaxaca.

Keeping this in mind, some generalizations about these movements may be proposed. Families with some cash on hand and/or with a reasonably high income (by Oaxaca standards) have demonstrated a strong tendency to choose Linda Vista or Santa María in which to settle. These *colonias* had been billed as housing developments and the newcomers were prepared to make what they believed would be a safe investment in real estate. They were not only relatively well off, but had high aspirations for the future. The opportunities in these *colonias* seemed almost unlimited.

Because of the campaigns launched to attract new residents to San Juan, the early settlers of Linda Vista and Santa María almost certainly knew of the opportunities to obtain a free *donación* in San Juan, but the settlement was known to be poor, less accessible than Santa María or Linda Vista, and lacking in services. Further, the traditional obligations of *tequio* service and police or guard duty in San Juan appeared onerous to some.

So the initial wave of settlers in Linda Vista and Santa María claimed among its membership a contingent of "middle-class" citizens, many of whom had never experienced life in a center-city slum. They did, nonetheless, feel the same impulse to escape the restrictions of urban overcrowding and to pioneer on the outskirts of town. Later, when problems of land tenure arose, particularly in Linda Vista, poorer families moved into these *colonias* to take advantage of possible opportunities to acquire lots without substantial economic investment.

These various influxes have produced a strikingly heterogeneous population in Linda Vista and Santa María. Each of these *colonias*

---

degree of consensus among them. The need for "before-and-after" diachronic studies of movements of people within cities and to their peripheral shantytowns is apparent.

has five rather clearly delineated socioeconomic strata: "professionals" (teachers, doctors, secretaries, accountants); skilled laborers; "entrepreneurs" (tradesmen, storekeepers, cottage craftsmen); unskilled laborers; and domestics.

In contrast to the early settlers of Santa María and Linda Vista, the migrants to Benito Juárez were poor, albeit somewhat adventurous, persons who moved onto the craggy lands above Santa María. It will be recalled that the first two waves of migrants to Benito Juárez were squatters who invaded the terrain and were evicted. Although the third wave of invaders was allowed to stay and purchase land, they were not the solid investors who had gone to Linda Vista and Santa María. The absence of official recognition of Benito Juárez by municipal authorities, lack of services, uncertainty of land titles, and construction and communication problems presented by the terrain have, for the most part, discouraged settlement in that *colonia* by "middle-class" migrants. There are some "professionals" living there (a few teachers and secretaries), but the majority of the inhabitants are unskilled laborers.

As mentioned previously, the lower part of San Juan is an ancient settlement dating back to pre-Columbian times; it has not been considered in this study. The upper sector of San Juan was designed for poor people. The major decision involved in moving there was whether one was willing to give up a certain degree of autonomy and live in a rather remote area of town in order to acquire a free parcel of land which would never be his own. Interviews with residents of San Juan suggest a relatively low level of sophistication and expectations among this population. Nevertheless, as in all the *colonias*, social stratification exists in San Juan, but it is simple. There are few professionals, skilled laborers, or home entrepreneurs. Almost two-thirds of the employed adults work as unskilled laborers or domestics.[12]

Mirador represents the stereotyped "festering sore" type of squatter settlement. Residents of this community are desperately poor, unskilled, and mostly illiterate. Social stratification is extremely simple. There are no professionals, skilled laborers, or home entre-

[12] Detailed quantitative data on income, employment, education, religion, civil status, and so on, of the Oaxaca sample will be presented in a future publication.

preneurs. Most adult men work as *cargadores* in the market or railroad station. Most people in Mirador also lived at one time in the central city, but a larger proportion has come directly from rural areas to the squatter settlement than is true of the other *colonias*. With few exceptions, the migrants who move to Mirador have low aspirations for themselves (though not necessarily for their children); in view of their low levels of literacy and skills, this is a realistic outlook. They have little hope of ever legally owning their land or acquiring services.

Politics

The selective processes involved in migration to the shantytowns of Oaxaca and the status of land and services determine to a significant degree the amount and type of political activities carried on in the settlements. Most politics in the *colonias* revolve around acquisition and/or legalization of land titles and attempts to get community services. Three of the settlements (Linda Vista, Santa Maria, and Benito Juárez) have a *mesa directiva* for this purpose. A *mesa directiva* is a form of local government that acts in a lobbying capacity as it represents the needs of a *colonia* in dealings with official government structures. Since the *colonias* must depend upon the city for water, electricity, and other services, the *mesa directiva* tries to apply pressure to obtain these amenities.

Although from *colonia* to *colonia*, these groups differ in specific aims, organization, and operation, they share certain similarities. For one thing, membership in them is voluntary. Most offices are filled by residents of the communities who offer to stand for election; other offices are appointive, but their holders fill them voluntarily. Second, the groups have no legal or judicial powers. They could not, for example, impose an involuntary tax on members of the *colonia*, or punish them for offenses. They do, however, take up collections for political and social activities and exert pressure on people to perform *tequio* service. In Benito Juárez, nonparticipants in the *tequio* are expected to supply a replacement or pay a fine, although most of them do not do this. Third, the groups derive their power from the support of the community. They can carry out their programs only if they have the backing of the *colonia*. Finally, most of the *mesas directivas* have their origins in the problems of land tenure and services which the *colonias* have suffered.

The specific offices and their functions are variable, but there is always a president, who is the executive officer of the *colonia*, a vice-president, a secretary, and a treasurer. There may also be officers in charge of conflicts, organization, political action, social action, public works, and sanitation. The offices of the *mesas directivas* are normally elective for a period of one year, with re-election prohibited. No salary or stipend is attached to the offices.

The formation of *mesas directivas* has been in response to the need for services and the desire to settle problems of land title and tenure. Since these needs and desires—and the possibility of meeting them—differ from *colonia* to *colonia*, political organization and activities in the settlements are correspondingly different.

As an *agencia municipal*, San Juan has a formal political structure fixed by the national constitution and the state laws of Oaxaca. The *agente* appoints assistants in the *colonia* to aid in administrative chores. Thus there is no *mesa directiva* in the community. Informal groupings of residents have formed in attempts to rectify specific wrongs or pressure the *agente* into acting more energetically on their behalf. In general, however, their efforts have been ineffectual. Perhaps it would be fair to say that, with exceptions to be noted below, the citizens of San Juan have been content to forsake political activism for security of land. This attitude is congruent with the type of migrant that has been attracted to the *agencia municipal*.

The rapid development of Santa María and Linda Vista (in terms of acquisition of water and electrical services, roads, a school in Linda Vista, and so forth) is explained by three factors: the problem of land tenure; political factionalism; and the dynamic citizenry which forms an important segment of the population.

In Linda Vista, when the questionable real-estate transactions of the lawyer and teacher became public, a *mesa directiva* was formed to protect and promote the interests of the residents. As noted above, this group has been extremely successful, obtaining a school, services, and quasi-recognition of the *colonia* from municipal authorities, even though it has not yet been able to unravel the knotty land problem. Its success lies in the influence and abilities of its members to exert considerable political pressure on government agencies. The former president of the *mesa directiva* (who is still the ruling force in the *colonia*) is a local radio announcer and *diputado suplente* (alternate deputy) in the state legislature.

A *mesa directiva* cannot, of course, always respond satisfactorily to the diverse needs of a heterogeneous population. Thus political factionalism tends to take place. Indeed, factionalism is one of the salient characteristics of all the *colonias* with *mesas directivas*. In Linda Vista, for example there were three *mesas directivas* vying for political power at the time of the study. The oldest, formed upon the discovery of the fraudulent land sales, has followed a more-or-less consistent policy of trying to protect the property of those in the *colonia* who had acquired their land in good faith, whether or not the sale was fraudulent. This group has the backing of the majority of citizens, is provided with dynamic leadership, and has farsighted plans for the future, including mail delivery into the upper sector of the *colonia* and construction of a small marketplace in the community.

The two other groups have not acquired large followings, but harass the dominant *mesa directiva* by pointing out its failings to the inhabitants of Linda Vista and thereby help to keep it responsive to the needs of the people. This positive function of competing political organizations carries with it, however, the danger of segmenting the *colonia*. This, in fact, occurred in Santa María, where schisms became so deep that the community was literally rent in two.

It will be recalled that during its growth Santa María had become divided into two parts, Section One, below the highway, and Section Two, above. In order to promote the development of facilities in the *colonia*, a *mesa directiva* was elected at a general meeting of the *colonia* residents. The officers were predominantly from Section One. The first order of business concerned the installation of electricity in Santa María. For this to be accomplished, each household would have to pay a quota so the *colonia* could pay its share of the cost of installations. The municipal and federal governments would contribute the balance. However, the residents of Section Two felt that the government should install the electricity free of charge and declined to cooperate.

After the installation of electricity in Section One the executive committee voted to levy another quota for materials to install running water in the *colonia*. Again, those representing Section Two could not agree to the terms of the program and refused to cooperate in the purchase of the needed materials. Section One went ahead on its own and provided the capital for the water installation.

Feeling that the wishes of Section Two were being ignored by the *mesa directiva*, a small group of individuals declared themselves an ad hoc committee to represent the exclusive interests of Section Two. The *mesa directiva* invited the ad hoc committee to join it in its program and not to fractionalize its efforts. First, however, the *mesa directiva* demanded that the ad hoc committee demonstrate that it had been duly elected by the residents of Section Two to represent them. The ad hoc committee could not prove its own legality, but insisted upon its right to represent "the people below."

The schism between the upper and lower sections of Santa María had now become so deep that the next step seemed inevitable. A new ad hoc committee was formed and declared Section Two to be a completely autonomous *colonia*, renaming it Benito Juárez. The committee has not received good support from the people, but has been able to construct two water tanks fed by an independent water line. Also, a small group of men has come out every Sunday for *tequio* service to improve the paths in the community. Otherwise there has been little development in Benito Juárez.

The question of land tenure has been revived by the committee, which is trying to convince residents of Benito Juárez that the lands are not really privately owned but are municipal or federal communal properties. It attempts to induce the people to discontinue payments to the administrators and donate the money for community projects. The administrators scoff at the suggestion that the lands are public property and are able to provide proof of their client's title to the territory in question.

Much of the time of the ad hoc committee has gone into efforts to persuade the government to recognize Benito Juárez officially as an independent *colonia*. So far these endeavors have met with but limited success.

Once again, the characteristics of the population go a long way to explain the differential success of the *mesas directivas* in Santa María and Benito Juárez. The *mesa directiva* of relatively affluent and socially complex Santa María has resolved most of the problems involving land titles, has acquired basic services, and has received recognition from various government agencies. In contrast, Benito Juárez—poor, simply stratified, and lacking dynamic leadership—has proceeded very slowly in its development.

Mirador offers another contrast. The squatters there are aware that they have no legal rights to the lands they occupy. Therefore disputes over proper title have not arisen. Furthermore, they despair of ever acquiring municipal services. The extremely simple social structure has failed to produce charismatic leaders to espouse the needs of the *colonia*. In the absence of litigation over land, expectation of services, and competing interest groups, no *mesa directiva* has been formed and political factionalism has not occurred. An individual in Mirador is grudgingly recognized as "president," but he has no constituency or power and has made no contributions toward the betterment of the *colonia*. The residents of Mirador are almost completely apathetic toward political activity. This settlement may be described as an unstructured network of families living in ignorance and abject poverty who are content to "squat" and hope that they will not be disturbed.

It should be pointed out that the absence of formal political organizations such as *mesas directivas* in no way assures that factionalism will not take place. In San Juan, for instance, an energetic *agente municipal* took office in 1966 and immediately took steps to provide residents of the upper sector with water and electricity. Each household on the hillside had to pay $100 pesos, plus provide *tequio* service to install the water tubing; but, even though it had paid its share, one section of the *colonia* lay too far up the hillside to be reached by the tubing, so it did not receive the service. Residents of that section were vexed and formed a committee to investigate how the money had been spent.

The committee found that there was little it could do, and decided to drop the matter. One individual, however, led a crusade to oust the *agente municipal*. His efforts were not successful, but the wrangling and bitterness erupted in several ugly incidents and for a time San Juan was added to the route of city patrol cars. The *agente* mollified the dissident elements and San Juan settled back to its somnolent existence. Worth mentioning in connection with these incidents is that they were actions taken by individuals against the *agente*, not the result of groups in competition.

To recapitulate, the immediate aims of the *mesas directivas* are to establish legal land titles, acquire services, and seek improvements for the *colonias*. The ultimate goal is official incorporation of the settlements into the urban structure. It may be asked if, from the point of view of the residents of *colonias* like Linda Vista, Santa María, and Benito Juárez, incorporation into the city or *municipio* is desirable. Once incorporation takes place, local action groups such as the *mesas directivas* lose their effectiveness. Government officials are supposed to be responsive to their constituency, but their first loyalty is to the political party, and without the organized initiative provided by a community based *mesa*, local interests may be lost in the mass of citywide problems. Upper San Juan may serve as an example of the stagnation which can occur when a settlement is under control of municipal authorities. It has made less progress—measured in terms of housing, roads, and utilities—during its four decades of existence than have Santa María and Linda Vista in a quarter of that time. A quasi-legal status may be better for the people—at least during the early developmental stages of the community—than formal incorporation into the official political structure.

These case studies of shantytowns in Oaxaca may not be representative of the development of poor suburbs elsewhere in Latin America or, for that matter, in Mexico itself. National and local contexts are obviously important determinants of urbanization and modernization processes. Nevertheless, our findings for Oaxaca might be generalized to other small cities in Latin America. Future studies of such entities will reveal whether or not this is true. In any event, the data presented here should provide a contribution to the growing body of comparative materials on urbanization in

Latin America from which we hope to construct more sophisticated urban theory.

Conclusions

This paper has traced the development of five shantytowns on the outskirts of the city of Oaxaca. It has attempted to show how these settlements, which on casual observation might be lumped together as "squatter settlements," are very different in respect to their formation, growth, organization, legal status, and potential for development. These case studies argue that we should exchange over-inclusive models of urban shantytowns for more precise ones built upon empirical investigation, as has been attempted by Turner and Flinn and Converse.[13] This is essential since proposed solutions to the problems posed by these settlements must take their diversity into account. The present study emphasizes variation, but this in no way implies that generalizations cannot be made; instead, its findings demonstrate that such generalizations must come to grips with the complexity of the subject matter.

In Oaxaca, for example, there are at least four distinct types of outlying shantytowns: "true" squatter settlements, which are illegally occupied lands owned by the government or private parties; "quasi-outlaw" shantytowns, whose existence is acknowledged by government authorities, but which lack official recognition; "quasi-legal" suburban communities which are partially or wholly incorporated into the urban structure; and officially designated municipal agencies. (There are also, of course, fully incorporated *urbanizaciones*.) All but the municipal agencies have been designated "squatter settlements" in various places in the literature on Latin American cities.

Such overzealous lumping together of essentially disparate entities tends to vitiate attempts to formulate theory and policy on urban conglomerates. To illustrate, the validity of Mangin's contention that "the problem [of squatter settlements] is the solution

[13] John C. Turner, "Three Barriadas in Lima, Peru, and a Tentative Typology," paper prepared for the Comparative Urban Settlements Seminar, Syracuse University, October 21, 1968; Flinn and Converse, "Eight Assumptions," pp. 456–466.

to the problem" depends entirely upon one's definition of what squatter settlements are, and Mangin neglects to provide us with this datum. He maintains that squatters make important contributions to national and city economies.[14] This is valid for Oaxaca if we consider Linda Vista and Santa María to be squatter settlements—a dubious assumption. It is doubtful for most of the residents of Benito Juárez and quite untrue for almost the entire population of Mirador. In fact, the sizable proportion of adults in Mirador and Benito Juárez who seek work in the city marketplace help to depress severely the incomes of the permanent venders and laborers there.[15]

The proposition, then, that the problem of squatter settlements is the solution to the problem cannot be tested until we have more refined analyses of suburban shantytowns. If we equate Mangin's "squatter settlements" with what I have termed "quasi-legal suburban communities," the results of this study suggest that such settlements do indeed offer advantages to the settlers and the government as well. The most important benefits accruing to families who build their own homes on the outskirts of the city on land which they own or have reasonable hope to own are mainly economic in nature, although the psychological security should by no means be overlooked. With low-paying jobs and periods of unemployment, the builders can construct their dwellings at their own pace, without the necessity of meeting rent or mortgage payments. Thereby they have little concern about losing their homes or land because of insufficient income.

The most obvious advantages to the government are that squatter settlements provide planners with temporary relief from the urban glut, offer a step toward the goal of home-ownership for the poor, and take some of the burden to build public housing for the needy off the government's shoulders.

However, as Cardona has warned, by magnifying the positive characteristics of squatter settlements, we run the risk of an evasion of responsibility by the government to attack the structural barriers to urban improvement.[16]

---

[14] Mangin, "Latin American Squatter Settlements," pp. 85, 74.
[15] Waterbury, "Urbanization," pp. 126–153.
[16] Ramiro Cardona, "Aspectos Sociales: Mejoramiento de Tugurios y Asenta-

I feel that local and/or national governments might do well to encourage the formation of squatter settlements like Linda Vista, Santa María, and Benito Juárez, provided that governmental assistance is not merely a device to placate potentially dissident elements by bringing them into a political structure in which they have little freedom or power. Land titles could be secured by the settlers through small payments and government agencies could help finance building materials. Most important, the people could undertake construction in their own manner and at their own speed.

A salient aspect of "self-built" settlements which often is overlooked by city planners is the order of priorities which the inhabitants establish for themselves. The first concern of the settlers is security of land tenure. Community facilities are usually the next item of importance. Schools, water, and electricity are considered more urgent than a completed home. The initial investment in housing may involve no more than the construction of a temporary shelter. Capital investment in a more permanent structure then follows, but at a pace determined by an individual's own resources. Only when a family has achieved a certain degree of economic stability and has constructed a reasonably permanent dwelling will there be expenditures for more luxurious items.

The order of priorities concerning the basic components of housing as seen by official planners is thus the reverse of those established by "squatters." The state offers "a modern (but minimal) house in the first place, some community facilities (generally at later stages) and, eventually, title to the property after the mortgage has been paid off."[17] The "squatter" solution involves securing the land, followed by community facilities, and finally an adequate dwelling.

In Oaxaca, the official solution to problems of housing and squatter settlements may be the encouragement of needy families to acquire *donaciones* in San Juan and other *agencias municipales*. However, from the point of view of most of those desirous of moving out of the central city slums, this policy is unsatisfactory because

---

mientos no Controlados," *Revista de la Sociedad Interamericana de Planificación*, Vol. 4, Nos. 13–14 (1970), p. 56.

[17] Turner, "Carriers and Channels," p. 179.

their primary goal (ownership of land) can never be met. A more viable solution is encouragement of "quasi-legal" shantytowns. But such a step should be viewed as a stopgap measure—an intermediate solution to urban overcrowding—since these settlements cannot in the long run resolve the demographic problems posed by stagnant rural economies and the attraction to cities by peasants and town dwellers.

PART III

HANDLING TRANSITIONAL PROBLEMS

These three studies show national-level units confronting the massive dislocations which accompany disruptive change—Brazil's federal authorities trying to capture control of São Paulo, Peru's central planning agency attempting to rationalize economic growth and to distribute its payoffs more widely, and various military regimes seeking national integration through the imposition of broad-based political systems. Together they demonstrate that in the short run government can exert surprisingly little pressure to speed up, slow down, or coordinate change among the multifold factors which throw the economic, social, and political systems out of balance as modernization proceeds. Reform by legislative fiat or even authoritarian decree must wait the slow adjustment of existing institutions or the gradual growth of complementary action patterns where the traditional relationships have been wiped out.

In relating forty years of the history of intergovernmental relations between Brazil's central administration and the state of São Paulo to external and internal marketing data and to information on the nationality of credit sources, Joseph Love offers a lesson that would have been useful in the Katanga or Biafra situations. He shows convincingly that as long as the principal economic activities and self-interest of a powerful political subunit are externally oriented it can reject subordination to a national governmental system and to the more general interests it represents. When foreign economic ties weaken and when the subunit becomes more dependent upon other sections of the country for raw materials and for markets, it will become a working part of the whole. The degree to which such a state or region will dominate the nation depends in large measure on how much economic and political strength other units develop to counterbalance its influence.

The use here of statistical materials and social science methodology to supplement traditional historical analysis offers a valuable new dimension for understanding the development process. This approach underlines the fact that neither constitutions nor conscience can of themselves bring about integrated change or systematize the consequences of uneven shifts in the basic material and human elements which make up a given environment. The point is elaborated in the next case study.

René Vandendries's appraisal of reformist development strategy in Peru during President Belaúnde's administration tests the hypothesis that the extent to which reforms can be implemented is a function of economic, social, and political realities. A twenty-year time series of budgetary data on government income and expenditures by regions and functional sectors (productive, infrastructure, social, general services, financial services, and so on) show relatively stable proportions of public support allocated to competing interests and geographic areas, no matter what the central regime's political complexion. Focusing on the last part of this period, Vandendries demonstrates that neither national planning nor large-scale foreign aid programs, and not even widely supported, presidential populist-reformist proposals, can do much to alter material conditions or deeply internalized human attitudes. He shows that for all the talk of "structural realignment," social justice, and making the inhabitants of the *altiplano* participants in national life, the principal economic institutions that provided most of the government's income and the incumbant dominant power groups continued to exercise primary influence over public fiscal policy.

The final paper in this volume is a comparative study of attempts by several Latin American military regimes to impose solutions to national integration problems. In it Robert E. Scott suggests that despite initial successes in improving administrative efficiency, in mobilizing popular awareness, and in forcing some traditional power elements to accept the implications of change, as the years go by these new-style, authoritarian-populist, and highly nationalistic *juntas* are unable to accomplish their goal of setting up a continuing and self-regulating national integrating political mechanism that can handle the conflicting pressures of speedy change. Here again, the conclusion seems to be that there are no quick or easy mechanistic solutions to the problems of modernization.

It might be argued that the theoretical approach employed in the study assures this conclusion, for systems analysis posits an equilibrium model under which the disruptions of quick and unbalanced development are viewed as departures from the norm and disfunctional to the system. An alternative approach would be to adopt a conflict model that views the political process as a continuous confrontation among competing interests. In the present case, two reasons might be advanced for not using this approach. First, a conflict model obscures our understanding of the development process as much as does systems analysis, but from another perspective, for it tends to reject the possibility of stability. Second, and more pragmatically, most Latin American political leaders—civilian as well as military—see politics as a means of achieving stable and peaceful change. To describe their actions in a conflict model would be to misrepresent their own conception of the political process and to deny their legitimate aspirations.

In any case, and no matter within which frame of reference they are organized, the three studies included in this section should help the reader to recognize how complex and difficult a task the peoples of Latin America face in trying to resolve their modernization problems.

External Financing and Domestic Politics: The Case of São Paulo, Brazil, 1889-1937

Joseph L. Love

Political integration is a complex and lengthy process, and as a major aspect of modernization, it should be studied over a series of decades or even longer periods. In Brazil a critical aspect of this problem has been the difficulties posed by recalcitrant subunits which refused to subordinate their particular interests to the national interest—a situation best exemplified by the quasi-autonomy the state of São Paulo long exercised with respect to the national government.[1]

The study of this problem is complicated by external linkages:[2] São Paulo was not only a political subunit in a federation, but an element in an international financial system as well. São Paulo's relative independence from the central government of Brazil was prolonged by the economic dependence of the state on foreign investment. The independence from the government in Rio de Ja-

---

[1] This paper is preparatory to a four-volume study of Brazilian regionalism with Robert M. Levine and John D. Wirth, covering the period between the fall of the Empire in 1889 and the Estado Nôvo coup d'état in 1937.

[2] For a theoretical statement on the significance of external linkages in the Latin American context, see Douglas A. Chalmers, "Developing on the Periphery: External Factors in Latin American Politics," in James N. Rosenau, ed., *Linkage Politics: Essays on the Convergence of National and International Systems* (New York: 1969), pp. 67–93.

neiro and the reliance on foreign financing provided the state with weapons against attempts to subordinate Paulista goals to national ones. The fact that the principal cash crops, especially coffee, were destined for external markets further reduced the likelihood of Paulista collaboration in efforts toward national political and economic integration. Only when Paulista agricultural investments definitively spilled across state boundaries and the state moved into industrial production requiring a national market did São Paulo's recalcitrance yield to tacit reconciliation. Perhaps in their search for national integration other nations of the Third World can learn from Brazil's experience with São Paulo, since many such countries also have a "primate region."

São Paulo state has commonly been described by its inhabitants as an engine pulling twenty empty boxcars—the other members of the Brazilian federation. Since the 1880s São Paulo has been the most economically dynamic region of Brazil. The period 1889 to 1937 has been chosen for study here because it opens with the rise of a federal republic which replaced a highly centralized imperial government, and closes with a new, centralized, authoritarian regime called the Estado Nôvo (New State). Under the federal constitution of 1891 São Paulo obtained a high degree of financial and political autonomy, and subsequently experimented in financial and commodity-marketing operations which the central government in Rio was unwilling to undertake. In the period under study, São Paulo became the nation's leading industrial producer as well as the foremost state in agricultural output. Yet Paulista growth was heavily dependent on foreign investment, and São Paulo's political leaders joined with business leaders in promoting financial dependence on foreign sources. Perhaps paradoxically, São Paulo's statesmen were more "colonial" in their outlook than those of other states. Their concern about foreign reactions to domestic politics led them to favor narrow and inflexible policies; they consistently supported stable, oligarchic, yet constitutional governments.

São Paulo's place in the national economy was far and away the most important among the states by the time of the first comprehensive economic census in 1920. Its gross agricultural and industrial output amounted to 2,125,538 contos (thousands of milréis, the unit of currency), equivalent to about US $446,363,000 in 1920. This figure represented more than two-sevenths the value of production for the nation as a whole, and more than double the value of output for Minas Gerais, the second most important state.[3] This leadership persisted. By 1939, the first year for which data on state-by-state gross domestic product are available, São Paulo accounted for slightly more than two-sevenths of national output, and over three times the output of Rio Grande do Sul, which was now the second state.[4]

São Paulo had an even more lopsided lead in exports. In the period from 1908 to 1912, São Paulo accounted for 42 percent of Brazil's exports by value, and by 1935 its share had risen to 53 percent.[5] Brazil prospered by counting on a favorable (visible) balance of trade, and São Paulo's coffee (and later cotton) shipments, virtually all from the port of Santos, made that policy work. Rising from about 50 percent of foreign exchange earnings in the years 1901 to 1920, coffee sales reached 70 percent of the value of exports in the decade 1921 to 1930. And of coffee exports in the 1920s, Santos exported 70 percent of the nation's total.[6]

In population, São Paulo was second only to Minas Gerais during most of the period under study, and it passed Minas in the 1930s. The population of São Paulo increased by 419 percent between 1890 and 1940, while Brazil as a whole increased only 188 percent.[7]

In the pre-Vargas era, when political parties were confined to

---

[3] João Lyra, *Cifras e Notas (Economia e Finanças do Brasil)* (Rio, 1925), p. 44. Lyra's figures are from the 1920 census. Unfortunately, the data omit the tertiary sector (services). Exchange rates from Julian Smith Duncan, *Public and Private Operation of Railways in Brazil* (New York, 1932), p. 183.

[4] *Conjuntura Econômica*, XXIV, 6 (June, 1970), p. 95.

[5] Direction Générale de Statistique, *Annuaire Statistique du Brésil: 1ère Année (1908–1912)* II (n.p., 1917), p. 100; Instituto Nacional de Estatística: Commissão Central de Recenseamento, *Sinopse Estatístico do Estado*, no. 2 (São Paulo, 1938), p. 224. Figures apparently refer only to visible exports and include some goods from landlocked Minas Gerais.

[6] In the years 1924 to 1926, the value of coffee exported from Santos represented over half the value of all Brazilian exports. Instituto de Café do Estado de São Paulo, *Exposição Apresentada ao Conselho Director* (São Paulo, 1927), pp. 25–26; Instituto Brasileiro de Geografia e Estatística, *Anuário Estatístico do Brasil: Ano V–1939/1940* (Rio, n.d.), p. 1380.

[7] Estimates from *Anuário Estatístico do Brasil–1969* (Rio, 1969), p. 37.

state boundaries,[8] the state's wealth and large population alone would have sufficed to make it a major factor in national politics. The Paulista Republican party (Partido Republicano Paulista— PRP) was one of the best organized in the country, and vied with the Republican party of Minas Gerais in delivering the largest vote totals, followed by the political organization of Rio Grande do Sul. Together the three states usually accounted for half the vote in the all-important presidential elections.

In the first direct election for the presidency in 1894, São Paulo and Minas had an almost exactly equal share of the total vote (8.8 percent for São Paulo and 8.9 for Minas). São Paulo took a narrow lead in 1898, after which Minas topped the list, reaching a high of 26.1 percent in 1922. By 1930, São Paulo's demographic growth brought the two states almost even again (19.3 percent for São Paulo and 19.5 for Minas). In the 1934 congressional elections, the last simultaneous nationwide contests before 1945, São Paulo took first place in the number of votes cast (20.9 percent of the total, compared to 19.7 percent for Minas Gerais). São Paulo widened its margin over the other states in the postwar era.[9]

In congress, Paulista deputies were able to influence other deputies through lavish lobbying expenditures,[10] and São Paulo and Minas were notorious for their control of the executive during most of the Old Republic (1889 to 1930). This was the "politics of coffee and cream," so-called since both states grew coffee and Minas also produced dairy goods. Between 1894 and 1930, Paulistas were elected to the four-year presidency six times, though presidents

[8] New parties arose after 1930, but major political organizations (new and old) were still largely confined to single states down to 1937 (for instance, the Partido Constitucionalista in São Paulo and the Partido Republicano Liberal in Rio Grande do Sul).

[9] Compiled from *Diario do Congresso Nacional*, June 22, 1894; June 28, 1898; June 27, 1902; June 20, 1906; July 1, 1914; May 26, 1918; July 10, 1919; June 8, 1922; June 8, 1926; May 21, 1930; *Annuaire . . . (1908–1912)*, I (Rio, 1916), p. 66; Instituto Nacional de Estatística, *Anuário Estatístico do Brasil: Ano III—1937* (Rio, 1937), p. 831; on postwar registration by state, see *Anuário Estatístico do Brasil—1960* (Rio, 1960), p. 411.

[10] For instance, see Dep. Carlos Maximiliano Pereira dos Santos to Gov. Antônio Borges de Medeiros (of Rio Grande do Sul), Rio, September 27, 1914, Archive of Borges de Medeiros, Pôrto Alegre, Rio Grande do Sul.

from São Paulo directed the government for only sixteen years.[11]

The presidency was the key to controlling the seventeen satellite states, since the president could and frequently did use the federal army to intervene in these units of the federation. Not so in Minas Gerais, Rio Grande do Sul, and São Paulo. These three states not only were the most powerful in terms of voting and economic output, but they also had state police organizations that amounted to armies. São Paulo's was the largest and best equipped. Varying in size from year to year, the Força Pública of São Paulo had its own foreign military mission, its own military academy, and in the 1920s it added artillery and an air corps. With this sort of force at its disposal, the government of São Paulo had little to fear from federal military intervention, no matter who was president. Minas Gerais and Rio Grande do Sul also could count on important state forces, though smaller than São Paulo's.

In politics, then, São Paulo was quasi-autonomous with respect to the central government, but its economy was anything but autonomous in the international context, and foreign participation in the economy had important consequences for Paulista political behavior. The degree of foreign penetration of the economy was extensive. Of the banks with headquarters in the state capital, foreign institutions held almost two-thirds of the total assets in 1911, as they did in 1920. By 1935, some 45 percent of all foreign-owned banks operating in Brazil were domiciled in São Paulo. At the end of 1936, deposits in foreign banks accounted for one-quarter of the total deposits in the state as a whole (as opposed to those in the capital).[12]

Nor was foreign influence limited to banking. By the late 1890s foreign exporters at Santos already had control over the overwhelming bulk of coffee shipped abroad. The American consul in Santos reported that of the 6 million bags exported in the year ending in June, 1898, the amount exported by Brazilian firms amounted to a pittance of the total value. Of the twenty-three firms listed by name in this consular report (exporting more than 99 percent of

[11] Rodrigues Alves died shortly after taking office for a second term in 1918, and Júlio Prestes was prevented from assuming power by the revolution of 1930.

[12] Repartição de Estatística e Archivo do Estado, *Annuario Estatístico de São Paulo (Brasil): 1911* (São Paulo, 1913), II, pp. 94–99; *Annuario . . . 1920* (São Paulo, 1922), II, pp. 90–91; *Sinopse*, pp. 130, 223.

total sales), six firms were American-owned or controlled, eight German, three French, one Belgian, and four British. The twenty-third and smallest, accounting for only a quarter of 1 percent of total sales, was Brazilian.[13] Another report for the period 1895 to 1907 listed "only" 87 percent of Santos's international coffee trade in foreign hands. In 1927, two-thirds of the coffee trade was still in the hands of foreign firms.[14] Despite fluctuations in the exact percentage of the foreign share, the reality of external control seems indisputable. Furthermore, London bankers financed shipping operations.[15]

A related development was the replacement of traditional local middlemen (*comissários*) by foreign coffee exporters in financing coffee production and storage. In 1905 a British-financed warehousing operation called the Registradora de Santos was created, followed the next year by another foreign-owned venture called the Companhia Paulista de Armazens Gerais. In 1909 the Brazilian Warrant Company, backed by a European consortium, took over and consolidated the Companhia Paulista and the Registradora. The appearance of these concerns was a response to an overproduction crisis discussed below; they did in fact provide a more effective credit system, but one which, in Pierre Monbeig's words, "accelerated the penetration of foreign interests." All this produced a system under which "the profits left the national economy."[16]

The celebrated policy of "valorization" of coffee prices in 1905–06 was in part a Paulista rather than a foreign answer to the oversupply of coffee, one which was by no means viewed with universal favor by the state's foreign creditors. It is noteworthy that in an age of triumphant laissez-faire economics in Latin America, a state gov-

[13] George Rosenheim to Secretary of State William Day, July 27, 1898, in National Archives and Records Service, Microcopy T–351: Dispatches from United States consuls in Santos, 1831–1906: Vol. 5, roll 5.

[14] A [mour] Lalière, *Le Café dans l'Etat de Saint Paul (Brésil)* (Paris, 1909), pp. 346–347; Edgard Carone, *A República Velha (Instituições e Classes Sociais)* (São Paulo, 1970), p. 38; Associação Commercial de Santos, *Boletim: Edição Especial Dedicada ao 2.° Centenario do Café* (Santos, 1927), pp. 35–36.

[15] David Joslin, *A Century of Banking in Latin America* (London, 1963), p. 160. A monograph is needed on the subject of shipping and insurance charges in international coffee sales.

[16] Monbeig, *Pionniers et Planteurs de São Paulo* (Paris, 1952), p. 98. See also Andre Gunder Frank, *Capitalism and Underdevelopment in Latin America: Historical Studies of Chile and Brazil* (New York, 1967), p. 169 and *passim*.

ernment would be eager to flaunt economic orthodoxy even when the federal government was not.

Valorization was a program designed to keep the price of coffee stable and high; in a period of rapidly mounting stocks, the state government of São Paulo purchased coffee from Paulista planters and stored it until it could be released on the market in a period of less abundant supply (for example, owing to drought or frost). The scheme presupposed a virtual Brazilian monopoly on world output, a not unrealistic assumption at the time.[17] Yet valorization inevitably brought more and more producers into the market—in São Paulo, in other states, and abroad—who took advantage of artificially high prices. A Paulista attempt to limit the planting of new coffee trees within the state in 1904 proved only partially effective.

Valorization in 1905–06 has been interpreted as a response to the challenge of foreign control of coffee marketing.[18] This judgment is cast into doubt, however, by the fact that Paulista coffee producers managed to escape more thoroughly from the price manipulation of importers in New York, London, Le Havre, and Hamburg than from the pressures of foreign bankers. The valorization program was financed by an international consortium consisting of the Brasilianische Bank für Deutschland of Berlin; the Nordeutsche Bank um Hamburg; Schröder of London; the Société Generale de Paris et des Pays Bas; and the National City Bank of New York. In 1907 Rothschild of London also came into the scheme.[19] Brazil's largest coffee-exporting firm, Theodor Wille of Hamburg, presided over—that is, policed—the liquidation of coffee stocks and the repayment of the valorization loan. It may be more than coincidence that Wille's share of coffee exports tripled in the first year of valorization.[20] By the late 1930s the Wille concern had become a holder of "vast domains" of coffee trees in São Paulo, and foreign-owned ex-

---

[17] São Paulo managed to coordinate strategy with Minas Gerais and Rio de Janeiro State, despite the fact that the latter two pulled out of the tristate plan for valorization signed in 1906.

[18] Antônio Delfim Netto, *O Problema do Café no Brasil* (São Paulo, 1959), p. 53.

[19] Monbeig, *Pionniers*, p. 99.

[20] Lalière, *Le Café*, pp. 346–347. Thomas H. Holloway has recently shown that the international syndicate financing valorization made large profits from the program. See "The Brazilian Coffee Industry and the First Valorization Scheme of 1906–07" (Unpublished M.A. thesis, University of Wisconsin, 1971), pp. 111–114.

porting firms even went into manufacturing.[21] Furthermore, the all-important São Paulo Railway Company, which shipped coffee from the plateau to the port of Santos, was British-owned. Until 1937, this highly profitable concern, opened in 1867, faced no competitors.[22]

In a list of coffee growers published in 1913, the three largest producing groups were controlled either by foreigners or by immigrants associated with foreign banking and commercial interests. The census of 1920 demonstrates that more than twice the value of rural properties was in the hands of foreigners and foreign-born owners in São Paulo than in all the rest of Brazil.[23]

Local business and political elites alike supported the valorization program, and the means by which São Paulo's government chose to fund valorization was part of a general pattern of financing. During the Old Republic all state governments complained of insufficient revenues. Clearly, their plight was due in part to the general condition of economic underdevelopment in Brazil, as well as to the indirect (and regressive) taxation policies prevailing then, as now. There were three general solutions to the revenue problem: (1) aid from the national government, which became increasingly difficult to obtain as the republican regime developed, since the central government was expanding its own public works programs; (2) unconstitutional taxation, principally on interstate transfers of goods; and (3) foreign loans. The poverty-stricken states of the northeast relied as much as possible on central government assistance; Minas Gerais relied in part on legal and illegal export (and transfer) taxes, having common frontiers with six other states; São Paulo, more than the rest, chose the route of foreign borrowing.[24]

[21] Monbeig, *Pionniers*, p. 99; Warren Dean, *The Industrialization of São Paulo: 1880–1945* (Austin, Texas, 1969), p. 55.

[22] Odilon Nogueira Matos, "O Desenvolvimento da Rêde Ferroviária e a Expansão da Cultura de Café em São Paulo," in *Boletim Geográfico*, 33 (1956), p. 380.

[23] *Impressões do Brasil no Seculo Vinte: Sua Historia, Seu Povo, Commercio, Industrias e Recursos* (London, 1913), p. 632; Directoria Geral de Estatistica, *Recenseamento do Brazil Realisado em 1 de Setembro de 1920: Synopse do Censo da Agricultura: Superficie Territorial, Area e Valor dos Immoveis Ruraes, Categoria e Nacionalidade dos Proprietarios, Systema de Exploração Pecuaria—Producção Agricola* (Rio, 1922), pp. 20–21. Regrettably, no distinction is made here between the foreign-born, as to foreign nationals and naturalized Brazilians.

[24] Dalmo de Abreu Dallari, "Os Estados na Federação Brasileira, de 1891 a 1937"

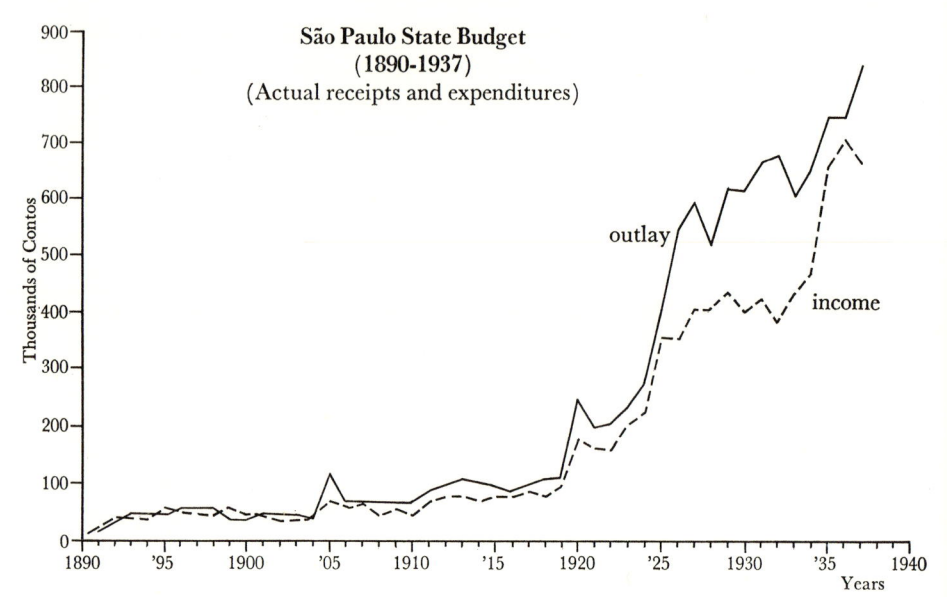

**São Paulo State Budget
(1890-1937)
(Actual receipts and expenditures)**

Departamento Estadual de Estatística, *São Paulo: 1889-1939* ([São Paulo, 1940]), p. 7 (current figures).

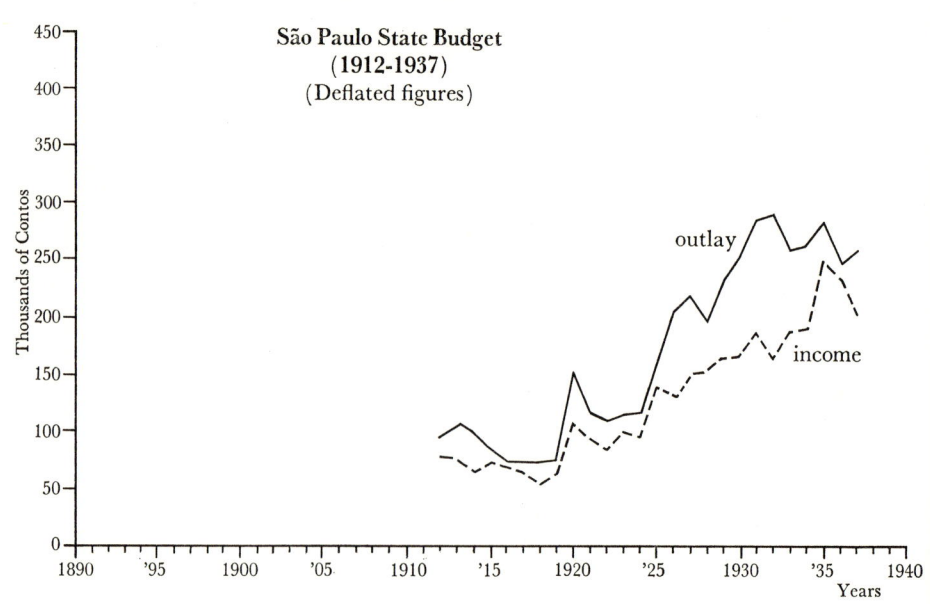

**São Paulo State Budget
(1912-1937)
(Deflated figures)**

Deflator is cost of living index for the city of Rio de Janeiro (1912 = 100). See Instituto Brasileiro de Geografia e Estatística, *Anuário estatístico do Brasil: Ano V 1939/1940* (n.p., n.d.), p. 1384.

From 1905 through 1937, state government expenditures in São Paulo always exceeded revenues (see graphs), despite the fact that the Paulista government generally collected more than one-third of all Brazilian state revenues combined.[25] As the graphs illustrate, the gap between revenues and expenditures widened in the late 1920s, and was not readily adjusted in the 1930s, in spite of expenditure-slashing policies. Data collected on the twenty state budgets between 1897 and 1937 show that São Paulo had more deficit years than any other state (thirty-seven of forty-one years). São Paulo's share of total state outlays rose from 29.2 percent in the decade 1897 to 1906 to 42.9 percent in 1927 to 1936.[26] A state constitutional reform to control deficit financing in 1911 had no effect.

For state revenues, the Paulista leaders depended on the export tax (overwhelmingly derived from coffee exports), which produced 60 to 75 percent of state income from 1890 to 1915, and remained the largest single revenue earner until its abolition in 1936, owing to federal limitations on the tax in 1934.[27] This dependence on the export levy had a major advantage for the Paulistas—apparently the tax on coffee was at least in part passed on to the foreign consumer.

In the state's authorized budget—available in more detailed form than the realized budget—the fact that São Paulo was a "big spender" is evident. Huge amounts were spent on coffee protection, but significant sums also were allocated for state police, sanitation operations, and elementary education (though funds spent for education were inadequate).[28] Debt servicing, however, became the largest single item in the budget from 1917 through 1937 (see be-

---

(manuscript, 1970), p. 21 and *passim*. Rio Grande do Sul uniquely developed a fourth pattern of budget-balancing, by limiting public expenditures and relying much more heavily on rural property taxes and sales taxes.

[25] São Paulo's share of total state revenues rose steadily from the decade 1897–1906 (29.3 percent) to 1927–36 (37.8 percent). *Anuário . . . 1939/1940*, p. 1416.

[26] *Ibid.*, pp. 1415–16. (There were twenty states until 1960, when the old Federal District, containing the city of Rio de Janeiro, became the state of Guanabara.)

[27] Departamento Estadual de Estatística, *São Paulo: 1889–1939* ([São Paulo, 1940]), pp. 11–28. This includes the coffee export tax of 1932–1935 called "impôsto de emergência sôbre o café."

[28] See Eugênio Lefevre, *A Administração do Estado de São Paulo na República Velha* (São Paulo, 1937), pp. 27, 41–42, 66–67, 90–91; Dean, *Industrialization*, p. 46.

low).[29] The rapid expansion of the state economy from the 1880s onward had created a "pay tomorrow" mentality, since the initial growth of São Paulo was financed extensively by domestic and foreign borrowing.

The state government purchased the Sorocabana Railway in 1905, partly to terminate fixed interest rate charges, and partly to open new coffee lands. A year later the state established the first valorization program, financed by an international consortium, as we have seen, so that by 1906 São Paulo had incurred more than half the combined foreign debts of the twenty states (£9.2 million of £17.7 million).[30] Another loan to São Paulo of £15 million in 1908, consolidating obligations for valorization operations and other debts, underscored the reliance of the state government on foreign credit. Again, in the 1920s state borrowing rose rapidly as responsibility for coffee valorization reverted to São Paulo after the central government had directed the program for three years. In 1926 the Paulista government contracted a £10 million loan for valorization, and another loan for £20 million to finance stockpiled coffee in 1930. In São Paulo's authorized budget, external debt servicing rose 150 percent between 1905 and 1906, and by 1931 one-third of the budget was earmarked to pay off debts, with 20 percent of the state's expenditures expressly tagged for foreign debt servicing.[31] From 1892 to 1929, the external-funded debt of São Paulo rose from £1.2 million to £11.9 million, plus US $43.0 million and Dutch Fl. 10.7 million. As in 1906, São Paulo at the time of the revolution of 1930 had more than half the total state debt owed to foreign creditors. In 1937, São Paulo still accounted for approximately half the overall state debt owed abroad.[32]

The valorization program begun in 1905–06 brought other

---

[29] *Leis e Decretos do Estado de São Paulo, 1890–1936* (São Paulo, 1890–1937) (authorized figures). Debt servicing here includes "diferenças de câmbio."
[30] J. P. Wileman, *The Brazilian Year Book* (Rio, 1908), p. 432.
[31] *Leis e Decretos do Estado de São Paulo de 1904* (São Paulo, 1905), pp. 33, 52; ... *de 1905* (São Paulo, 1906), pp. 50, 75; ... *de 1931* (São Paulo, 1932), pp. 754, 847.
[32] Lefevre, *A Administração*, p. 8; Getúlio Vargas, *A Nova Política do Brasil*, I (Rio, 1938), p. 247; *Anuário ... 1939/1940*, pp. 1424–1425. In addition, the *municípios* (roughly counties) of São Paulo and Santos had contracted foreign loans worth several million pounds. As *municípios* were legal subdivisions of the state, the latter was ultimately responsible for the debt incurred.

changes in financial and fiscal policy. New taxes were introduced during that period which might have made it possible to finance a major portion of the state's new obligations domestically. The potentially most important of the new levies was a rural property tax (*impôsto territorial*). But this tax was limited to one-tenth of 1 percent of assessed property value per annum, and specifically excluded all properties planted with coffee trees! At the time of the law's passage, noncoffee lands were estimated at only a fifth the value of coffee properties. Not until 1935 did the *impôsto territorial* become even the fourth largest revenue producer.[33] Rio Grande do Sul's taxation of rural property showed that such a source of revenue was a feasible choice in the period under consideration, but the Paulista government chose to ignore it as a major revenue earner.

As shown above, São Paulo's taxation policy was centered around the coffee export tax. Paulista statesmen fulminated about the unconstitutional interstate taxes exacted by the government of Minas Gerais and many other states, but in part their defense of constitutional norms and relatively modern fiscal policies was hypocritical, for a portion of the coffee tax collected at Santos was itself an interstate duty that benefited São Paulo. Minas Gerais, having no port of its own, shipped most of its coffee through São Paulo's main port.

What were the economic gains and losses of São Paulo's financial behavior? Clearly, São Paulo did not fare as badly as the classical colony, where foreign investment sought only to develop mines and plantations. Part of the foreign investment (direct and indirect) in São Paulo went into railway and port development; but moving coffee was undeniably the major concern, and rail lines tended to follow the coffee frontier in the rich deposits of soil called *terra roxa*. Highways remained pitifully undeveloped; even in 1939, some 90 percent of São Paulo's roads were classified as "unimproved dirt roads."[34]

---

[33] Camara dos Deputados do Estado de São Paulo, *Annaes da Sessão Ordinaria de 1904* (n.p., 1905), p. 386; Eugenio Egas, *Impostos e Taxas de São Paulo (Synthese Historica de Sua Evolução)* (São Paulo, 1926), p. 87; *São Paulo: 1889–1939*, pp. 21–22. The *impôsto territorial* was introduced between 1901 and 1905 in Rio Grande do Sul, Minas Gerais, and São Paulo. Only in Rio Grande did it become a major revenue producer during the Old Republic.

[34] Gordon Wright Smith, "Agricultural Marketing and Economic Development:

On the positive side, São Paulo was industrializing, and by the 1930s São Paulo had become a net exporter to other states.[35] Yet it remains unclear to what extent public foreign borrowing contributed directly and indirectly to industrial expansion. Whether the valorization program on balance provided net economic benefits for São Paulo is also questionable;[36] but Paulista political leaders and their planter constituents definitely believed there was a net benefit.

In a sense, the state government did brilliantly, given its limited bargaining power in the international financial arena. The Great Depression forced the state to turn its foreign debts over to the central government, which partially defaulted on the debt in 1934 and again in 1938. Consequently, the Paulistas got off at less than the full cost of the capital they borrowed for valorization. Yet interest rates on foreign loans were high in the 1920s—up to 8 percent from a 5 percent rate at the turn of the century—and foreign loans were always subject to an initial discount for prepaid interest and carrying charges. We also already have seen that foreign investment was related to a loss of control of the financing of the coffee industry. It seems clear too that the state government's commitment to agriculture sacrificed alternative strategies of economic development. For example, despite the fact that industrial output in São Paulo declined in 1924, in the same year the state government devoted its extensive resources to coffee protection, assuming the burden of valorization from the central government. Paulista industrialists made strictures on the state as well as federal governments in the late 1920s for neglecting manufacturing interests.[37]

As for the mechanics of valorization itself, it seems in retrospect extremely shortsighted of the Paulista government to have encouraged new entrants into coffee production through price supports in

---

A Brazilian Case Study" (Unpublished Ph. D. dissertation, Harvard University, 1965), mimeo., p. 130.

[35] Dean, *Industrialization*, pp. 193–194.

[36] J. W. F. Rowe, *Markets and Men: A Study of Artificial Control Schemes in Some Primary Industries* (Cambridge, 1936), p. 33.

[37] Werner Baer, *Industrialization and Economic Development in Brazil* (Homewood, Ill., 1965), p. 21; Centro das Industrias de Fiação e Tecelagem de São Paulo, *Relatório sobre a Crise Textil: Suas Causas; Seus Effeitos; Seus Remedios* (n.p., 1928), pp. 32–41.

the late 1920s. The collapse of the rubber industry in the Amazon Valley in the decade 1910 to 1920 should have been ample warning, since a rubber valorization scheme there was a total failure.

No coherent picture of São Paulo's financial and fiscal operations can be presented without a discussion of federal policies, since programs at the two levels of government were often interdependent. The federal government collected about a third of its total revenue in the state[38] and, given the existence of Paulista political autonomy, whoever led the government in Rio could ill afford to ignore the economic demands of established interests in São Paulo.

It is a well-accepted notion that federal fiscal and monetary policies were tailored to meet the needs of coffee planters and their allies during the Old Republic.[39] This is not the whole story, however, since numerous other pressures were exerted on the federal government. Coffee interests wanted falling exchange rates, because they calculated their costs in milréis and received payment in "hard" currencies. Industrialists also wanted falling exchange rates, because a cheap milréis made foreign manufactures more expensive, though this motive was partially offset by the need to import capital goods. On the other hand, there were groups—hardly negligible in their influence on government—who wanted stable or rising exchange rates. Importers of all types fell into this category, as did foreign investors who wanted to remit profits to their home countries; consumers (effectively, urban workers and middle groups of the major cities) also favored a strong milréis, since this made imported manufactured goods cheaper. Finally, and most important, the national treasury favored a hard unit of currency, since the union's foreign debts had to be paid back in ever more expensive pounds, dollars, and francs.[40]

The coffee bloc generally wanted federal support for valorization, and whether this was obtained or not, coffee interests also sought

[38] In 1935, for instance, the federal government collected 32 percent of its total receipts in São Paulo—*Sinopse*, p. 230.

[39] For example, see Celso Furtado, *The Economic Growth of Brazil: A Survey from Colonial to Modern Times*, trans. A. Aguiar and E. Drysdale (Berkeley, Calif., 1965), p. 197.

[40] For a discussion of pressure groups, see Carone, *A República Velha*, pp. 96–99. An important monograph on the federal foreign debt is Valentim F. Bouças, *História da Dívida Externa* (2nd. ed., Rio, 1950).

ever-depreciating exchange rates. When the value of the milréis was rising—because of favorable trade balances—coffee groups were willing to settle for stable exchange rates.[41]

In addition to pressures from domestic groups, the central government had to face external pressures as well. By the late 1890s civil war, contradictory financial policies, and the desire to buy out foreign-owned railways with fixed interest guarantees, induced President-elect Manuel Campos Sales to travel to London to refinance Brazil's foreign debt personally. Campos Sales later wrote, with no apparent disapproval, that the directors of the House of Rothschild conjectured that "beyond the total loss of credit of the country, [suspension of Brazil's international debt payments] could gravely affect national sovereignty itself, provoking claims that would perhaps go to the extreme of foreign intervention."[42]

The Rothschild Funding Loan of 1898 consolidated Brazil's foreign obligations in exchange for a planned amortization of the outstanding debt and a lien on Brazilian customs if the government should default on its gold remittances. The lien was aimed at a jugular vein, since import duties remained the largest source of national government revenue in the period under study, just as export and transit taxes were the bedrock of state revenues.[43]

Campos Sales and his successor, Francisco Rodrigues Alves, were both anxious to meet the treasury's obligations abroad and thus to avert foreign intervention, such as occurred in Venezuela in 1902. Indeed, Campos Sales was so committed to his expense-slashing and budget-balancing policies that he allowed the federally controlled Banco da República to fail in the depression of 1900 to 1902. Rodrigues Alves was understandably reluctant to bring the national government into the uncharted seas of valorization in 1905, despite his earlier defense of coffee interests as governor of São Paulo.

It is an ironic fact, but perhaps more than a coincidence, that the

[41] As I have remarked elsewhere, a study of intragroup conflict of coffee interests is still lacking. Exporters and bankers would clearly gain more from depreciating exchange rates, at least directly, than planters. But these groups were closely tied together by kinship networks, and members of the uppermost social stratum were sometimes simultaneously bankers, planters, and exporters.

[42] [Manuel] Campos Salles, *Da Propaganda á Presidencia* (São Paulo, 1908), p. 186.

[43] As late as 1937, import taxes still provided 34 percent of federal revenues. *Anuário... 1939/1940*, pp. 1411, 1417.

only three presidents of Brazil during the Old Republic who repeatedly managed to balance the budget were all Paulistas—Campos Sales, Rodrigues Alves, and Washington Luís Pereira de Sousa. The timing of the external financial pressures on the federal government, plus the domestic tranquility prevailing during their administrations, may account for the success of the three Paulistas. Campos Sales and Rodrigues Alves headed the government in the early years of the Funding Loan, and Washington Luís was president in 1927, when amortization of the principal of the loan, refinanced in 1914, was due. In general, the requirements of the treasury (to minimize external financial burdens) and those of the Paulista coffee groups had to be balanced. The national government was dependent on massive coffee exports to bring in foreign exchange that could offset federal debt servicing and profit remittances made by foreign firms operating in Brazil. Nonetheless, for the reasons cited above, whenever possible the federal treasury tried to prevent a decline in the value of the milréis, to the potential disadvantage of the Paulista coffee interests.

It should not be assumed that state and national governments responded in like fashion to the dangers of foreign borrowing and exchange manipulation. In certain ways foreign pressures decidedly affected policies of the men who ran the state government. But the central government clearly had greater responsibilities vis-à-vis the rest of the world than did the states, for it was the Union that would be held accountable by foreign investors for the states' wayward behavior. Another reason for a different response at the state level was that however powerful they may have been at the national level, coffee interests obviously were proportionately much stronger in São Paulo. Finally, the tremendous success of the Paulista "borrow as you grow" economy made it seem perfectly natural and proper to depend on foreign financing.

External financing of coffee valorization and the extensive penetration of São Paulo by foreign capital led to a degree of foreign political control, at least to the extent of restricting São Paulo's political options. Local politicians often had significant links with foreign capital. More than a third of the state secretaries of finance for whom biographical data are available had direct ties with foreign interests, as did an even greater proportion of the governors.[44] Presumably, such links affected their views on the role of foreign capital in São Paulo.

The first major political response to external financial pressure, however, came at the national government level. The notorious *política dos governadores* (politics of the governors), which cast in permanent form the corruption of liberal democracy in the Old Republic, was a crystallization of a pattern of rule by increasingly stable state oligarchies. Yet the triggering factor was President Campos Sales's desire to ensure that a pliant congress would meet the chief executive's demands for the unpopular austerity measures required under the terms of the 1898 Funding Loan.[45] In 1901 the Paulista Republican party suffered a major schism as a result of the application of the *política*. Former President Prudente de Morais led many prominent politicians out of the PRP, now dominated by Governor Rodrigues Alves and President Campos Sales, who insisted on controlling the party from the top. The *política dos governadores* was a corrupt form of patronage politics, in which incumbent groups remained in office indefinitely; its implementation was a coup de grace by one of the Republican movement's leading ideologues, Manuel Campos Sales.

As one member of the 1901 PRP *dissidência* put it, the national Republican coalition led by Campos Sales was "a party without faith, without creeds, without ideas."[46] But the mainstream of the PRP went along with the *política*, and in the following years the state government's external debt obligations also forced it increas-

---

[44] Of a total of twenty-seven secretaries of finance who served at least ninety days in the years 1889 to 1937, information was obtained for twenty-three; and of these, nine were found to have had foreign ties. Of the twenty governors, eight also could be shown to have had foreign connections. Of course these proportions are minimal figures, since other officials might have had overseas links that were not listed in the available biographical data.

[45] Campos Salles, *Da Propaganda*, pp. 236–250, 278. The implementation of the *política dos governadores* involved rules changes in congress and changes in vote-counting procedures in the states; the term referred to an understanding between the president and the governors of the leading states to perpetuate the tenure of incumbent machines at all levels of government. For a fuller description, see Francisco de Assis Barbosa, "A Presidência Campos Sales," *Luso-Brazilian Review*, V, 1 (Summer, 1968), pp. 3–26; and Joseph L. Love, *Rio Grande do Sul and Brazilian Regionalism, 1882–1930* (Stanford, Calif., 1971), pp. 95–96.

[46] P[artido] R[epublicano] P[aulista], *A Scisão de 1901* (São Paulo, 1901), p. 211.

ingly to adjust its domestic policies to square with its financial obligations abroad.

It bears repeating that 1905–06 was the critical period in the state's financial and fiscal development. The crisis of excess coffee production was apparent by 1905. The 1906–07 crop was predicted to be more than 20 million bags—in a period of depressed prices and with a 10 million-bag inventory against an annual world consumption rate of 16 million bags.[47] At the same time, foreign firms were rapidly taking over coffee financing. The Paulista elite's response was valorization, with its attendant dependence on foreign loans, the beginning of a continuous resort to budgetary deficits, and a foreign military mission to assure São Paulo of independence from the central government. The accompanying tax reforms of 1905 were conspicuous only for their complete inadequacy to provide for domestic financing of government operations. Two loans in 1905–06 totaling £6.8 million were the beginning of a debt cycle from which the state did not recover until dictator Getúlio Vargas suspended state as well as national government payments of foreign debts in 1938.

What were the constraints imposed by foreign financing on the political posture of São Paulo's leaders? First of all was the necessity to support "legality," that is, constitutional government, though this principle was subject to extensive distortion. In the minds of both Paulista leaders and foreign creditors, stability was a more basic concern than constitutionality. When it was impossible to support an unambiguously constitutional government (in Paulista *municípios*, in other states, and at the national level) because of rival claims to authority, Paulista politicians backed claimants who would offer the best prospects for stability. A basic reason for this pattern of behavior was that Paulista politicians believed—as their European creditors emphatically did—that irregular (nonconstitutional) governments produced upheavals, to the detriment of foreign creditors and investors. At the worst, this situation might lead to gunboat diplomacy at the expense of the central as well as state governments.

An early but important instance of such pro-"legality" behavior

[47] Delfim Netto, *O Problema*, p. 55.

occurred in 1891. During the attempted coup d'état of Marshal Deodoro da Fonseca, state deputy Cincinato Braga, later to be São Paulo's financial expert in congress, argued that the House of Rothschild would have nothing to do with an illegal government (and in fact Rothschild did oppose the coup). "Foreign bankers have no alternative," Braga declared in the state assembly, "when they know that once constitutional norms (*legalidade*) are violated, revolts break out; given a revolutionary situation, the foreign creditor cannot foresee which faction will win, and which will make good on the debt."[48]

Another example of preoccupation with stability is provided by Campos Sales after his term in the presidency (1898 to 1902). When his candidacy for election for a second term began running into opposition in 1905, he urged his chief backer, Senator José Gomes Pinheiro Machado, to abandon the effort; Campos Sales argued that any disturbances might exacerbate the nation's "administrative" problems, by which he clearly meant difficulties in meeting international financial obligations.[49]

A further instance of Paulista concern about "legality" and foreign investors' attitudes can be found in São Paulo's role in Brazil's first contested presidential election in 1910. The Paulista Republican party (PRP) and part of the establishment machine of Bahia decided to oppose the odds-on favorite, Marshal Hermes da Fonseca, who was backed by the states of Minas and Rio Grande, as well as the army. It is a well-known fact that Brazilian newspapers were sensitive to foreign bankers' opinions on the possible outcome of the election,[50] so the decision to run Senator Rui Barbosa of Bahia may well have arisen from Paulista fears about foreign investors' reactions if Hermes won. Witness the remark of *The Economist* of London soon after Hermes's selection as the "official" candidate: "Enormous amounts of British capital have been placed in Brazil,

[48] Camara dos Deputados, *Annaes da Sessão Ordinaria de 1891* (n.p., 1895), p. 891. On this occasion the anti-Deodoro faction lost, having won a close vote on a related issue the previous day. The anti-Deodoro group now withdrew from the assembly, and, after the would-be dictator was overthrown, his supporters were purged from the new legislature.

[49] A. C. de Salles Júnior, *O Idealismo Republicano de Campos Salles* (Rio, n.d.), p. 209.

[50] For example, see *Correio da Manhã* (Rio), October 1, 1909.

and should Marshal Hermes be elected we must be prepared for the worst. . . . [His election] would lead in all likelihood to revolution." Furthermore, warned *The Economist*, Hermes was "a strong partisan of war with Argentina," and could be expected to spend huge sums on an armaments program. The attitude of *The Economist* and other British opinionmakers was apparently the cause of a drop in the value of São Paulo state bonds on the London market.[51]

During the campaign Rui tried to laugh off suggestions that he had received 700 contos (about US $217,000 in 1909) from the government of São Paulo, with the blessing of the coffee and banking firm of Theodor Wille. But his platform did include the defense of "the honor . . . of our credit, as civilized and free men."[52]

Two years later, when the wily Pinheiro Machado, now *éminence grise* of the Hermes regime, toyed with the notion of provoking central government intervention in São Paulo, Governor-elect Rodrigues Alves issued a warning to the federal authorities: "Those who speak out against the autonomy of the states and rashly preach armed intervention as a normal means of settling local political disputes do not understand our financial situation; neither do they realize the influence that the threat of disorder exercises over public credit abroad." São Paulo beefed up its Força Pública from 5,044 men in 1910 to 7,757 in 1914, when Hermes's term ended, and the Hermes regime never did attempt to intervene militarily in the state.[53]

Still another example is found in a 1930 publication entitled "The Point of View of the PRP." This establishment party document stated that "Foreign bankers are wary of doing business [in Brazil], and their reticence is natural. In 1922 we had a revolution; in 1924, another that lasted until 1926, and one in which the damage done to the property of foreigners living here was far from negligible. . . [now] yet another revolution is announced for 1930. . . [We therefore live] . . . in an unstable South American republic,

---

[51] *The Economist*, June 5, 19, 26, 1909, pp. 1178–79, 1283, 1314, 1359.

[52] Rui Barbosa, *Escritos e Discursos Seletos*, ed. Virgínia Côrtes de Lacerda (Rio, 1960), pp. 314, 338.

[53] Rodrigues Alves, in Eugenio Egas, *Galeria dos Presidentes de S. Paulo* (São Paulo, 1922), II, p. 416; Euclides Andrade and Hely F. da Camara, *A Força Publica de São Paulo: Esboço Historico 1831–1931* (São Paulo, 1931), p. 33.

where there are no guarantees for foreign capital, given the continual uprisings of the *natives*."[54]

The revolution of October, 1930, was in fact a reaction to an international economic system that no sector of the Brazilian elite had defended as conspicuously as the politicians of São Paulo. For many Brazilians, the collapse of the international economy was also the failure of São Paulo, whose politicians would have continued to run Brazil if President-elect Júlio Prestes had been inaugurated in November, 1930. And it was consistent with Paulista political tradition that the most violent civil conflict in this century was São Paulo's "constitutionalist" rebellion against the Vargas dictatorship in 1932.[55]

While consistently legalist over the course of the Old Republic, the Paulistas altered their position on a related issue. This was the question of revision of the federal constitution of 1891. For almost twenty years, the PRP joined forces with other establishment parties to defend the constitution as it stood, but by the time of the presidential campaign of 1909–10, Paulista leaders had shifted their ground. They now backed Rui Barbosa's revisionist program, which would have allowed the national government to discipline the financially "irresponsible" states. (Paulistas obviously did not expect such action to endanger their own autonomy, given the professional military character of the state's new Força Pública.)

Following Rui's defeat, the revision issue was shelved for more than a decade. The Mineiro President Artur Bernardes picked it up again in the early 1920s, emphasizing that foreign intervention might take place if the central government were not given the authority to bridle the extravagances of various state governments which were verging on bankruptcy—for one, Amazonas.[56] Paulista

[54] "Natives" in English in original. Percival de Oliveira, *O Ponto de Vista do P. R. P. (Uma Campanha Política* (São Paulo, 1930), p. 34. (Article originally in *O Diario de S. Paulo*, September 3, 1929.)

[55] A Marxist historian has described the revolution of 1932 in part as a reaction of British capital to increasing American domination. For this writer, the thesis is a little too neat. However, as another historian has noted, it may be more than coincidence that President-elect Júlio Prestes took refuge in the British Consulate during the revolution of 1930. See Leônicio Basbaum, *História Sincera da República*, III (São Paulo, 1962), p. 64; and Boris Fausto, "A Revolução de 1930," in Manuel Nunes Dias *et al.*, *Brasil em Perspectiva* (São Paulo, 1968), p. 273.

[56] Love, *Rio Grande do Sul*, p. 125.

congressmen now embraced the proposed series of revisions for several reasons. One factor was that PRP leaders were well aware of the need to bring federal finances into line to meet Funding Loan obligations falling due in 1927; a related consideration was that a Paulista would have the presidency for the next four years (partly in exchange for supporting the constitutional amendments). Another major factor was the growth of Paulista investments and markets beyond São Paulo's frontiers (especially in coffee production), which made PRP leaders more amenable to a greater degree of central authority. Furthermore, a series of disruptive revolts in the early and mid-1920s had made strengthening the national government much more palatable to the "law and order" Paulistas. A probable final element was São Paulo's sense of security against federal intervention, since the state's Força Pública rose from less than 9,000 men to 14,000 between 1924 and 1925.[57]

In the constituent assembly of 1933, São Paulo's delegation became the bastion of conservatism in its aspiration to reproduce the constitutional system of 1891. The Paulistas objected to central government attempts to control the states' authority to contract foreign loans, though the delegation did stand by the PRP decision in 1925 to allow national intervention in sharply restricted instances of state financial misbehavior.[58] Paulista politicians hoped to sit out the mandate of Getúlio Vargas, who was elected president by the constituent assembly for the term 1934–38, and to replace him with Armando de Sales Oliveira, who governed São Paulo from 1933 to 1936. Sales Oliveira was a leading candidate in 1937, and represented the cause of legality and orthodox liberalism; his campaign was rudely terminated by the centralizing Estado Nôvo coup of November of that year.

From the Paulista political elite's point of view, one unfortunate result of the continued recourse to foreign borrowing was the fact that the Great Depression brought such crushing burdens that, in assuming São Paulo's financial obligations, the national govern-

[57] Andrade and Camara, *A Força Publica*, p. 33.
[58] *A Ação da Bancada Paulista "Por São Paulo Unido" na Assembléa Constituinte: O Programa da "Chapa Unica" e a Nova Constituição* (São Paulo, 1935), p. vi; Thomas W. Palmer, Jr., "S. Paulo in the Brazilian Federation: A State Out of Balance" (Unpublished Ph.D. dissertation, Columbia University, 1950), p. 83.

ment also found it convenient to chip away at the state's political autonomy. During 1931 São Paulo had to turn coffee valorization over to the Vargas government in Rio, and the same year Vargas decreed that states could no longer borrow money abroad. In 1937 state autonomy was formally suppressed.

In a more speculative vein, one might hazard that the Paulistas' well-developed sense of superiority over Brazilians from other parts of the nation—already apparent by the 1880s but reaching a zenit' in the 1920s and early 1930s—was due in part to their fuller recognition of the neocolonial economic status of Brazil. Because of their trading and financial transactions abroad, the Paulistas were the most "internationalist" sector of the Brazilian economic elite, and as a consequence knew the extent to which the success of their coffee and industrial enterprises were dependent on European and American capital and markets. Even during the depressed 1930s, the sale of primary materials abroad (now cotton as well as coffee) was critical for continuing development in São Paulo.[59] Yet manufacturing grew rapidly under the Estado Nôvo, and industrialists in São Paulo began to appreciate more fully the advantages of a powerful central government in their search for national markets.

In São Paulo we find a political elite representing, *grosso modo*, Brazil's economic elite. The Paulista political elite was preoccupied with maintaining autonomy within the nation rather than autonomy in an international context.[60] In fact, international dependence increased through foreign loans and budgetary deficits, which were due in part to the Paulista leaders' desire to maintain their independence of the federal executive. In relying on foreign financing, they restricted their options in national politics by consistently supporting the superficial "legality" of the *política dos governadores*.

In the years 1889 to 1937, at least, it seems clear that the political elite of São Paulo was unwilling to come to grips with such issues as

[59] Carlos Manuel Peláez, "A Balança Comercial, a Grande Depressão e a Industrialização Brasileira," *Revista Brasileira de Economia*, XXII, 1 (March, 1968), pp. 45–47.

[60] Cf. Holloway's judgment on the early years of valorization that "Politically, the state government lost relative to the power of the foreign capitalists, and gained relative to the other states of Brazil and the national government"—"The Brazilian Coffee Industry," p. 109.

domestic financing of public works and state intervention in the economy (valorization). The daring experiment of valorization was paid for by foreign investors, even though it was directed against foreign manipulation of coffee prices overseas; moreover, foreigners were allowed to take over coffee marketing and financing within São Paulo. Alternative formulas that could have provided the impetus toward more autonomous economic growth, such as direct taxation and consistent support of industry, were never seriously entertained. The locomotive pulling empty boxcars was fueled abroad. Major strides toward political and economic integration were achieved only when the international financial system was in crisis, and when Paulista economic interests were more fully oriented toward the rest of Brazil. Even so, to the extent that a government-assisted program of industrialization was undertaken at the national level before 1945, it was directed by non-Paulista political and military leaders, led by Getúlio Vargas of Rio Grande do Sul.[61] Among the important state political elites, only that of Rio Grande was not discredited by the collapse of the international economy in 1930; consequently it was uniquely qualified to lead a modernizing revolution, aimed in part against São Paulo and what it represented.

If São Paulo is viewed as one of the notable successes of economic growth in underdeveloped countries, one may still question the extent to which traditional economic elites and their political leaders in such countries are capable of the hard decisions required to subordinate local to national economic priorities, and to transform neocolonial social and economic structures sufficiently to achieve self-sustained growth.

[61] On the economic decisions of the central government in the 1930s, see John D. Wirth, *The Politics of Brazilian Development, 1930–1954* (Stanford, Calif., 1970), pp. 1–129.

An Appraisal of the Reformist Development Strategy of Peru

René Vandendries

Problems can be stated only in terms of objectives. Since the end of World War II economic development problems have become major issues in world affairs, not because of any sudden discovery of poor countries in the world but instead because of a rather abrupt increase in the desire to develop. The objectives of every country seeking rapid economic development generally are pretty much alike. First and foremost is the attainment of a high rate of growth of gross national product per capita. Other major objectives usually are reasonable price and balance of payments stability, employment creation, improvement in income distribution, and balanced internal regional development. The problems encountered in trying to achieve each one of these objectives are, during the early stages of development, formidable, and the success record of less-developed countries thus far has not been very encouraging.

The rate of per-capita GNP growth continues to be below expectations. Acceleration in the rate of population growth is a partial cause of this phenomenon, of course, but the major sources of difficulty lie much deeper. Agriculture still constitutes a large proportion of GNP; and productivity in this sector has been lagging because, among other reasons, of the land-tenure system. Stagnation in agriculture, in turn, is one of the factors limiting industrial development. Industry has generally been built behind highly protective tariff walls and the domestic markets are too small to sustain the growth of a modern industrial sector. Whatever industry has developed has tended naturally to concentrate around the main urban market centers, thus aggravating the already substantial regional disparities in the economy. These factors, together with the high-capital–intensive nature of the small amount of modern industry that does exist, severely limit the creation of work opportunities, so unemployment and underemployment are rapidly becoming some of the major problems in development.

Few indications of any overall improvements in the distribution of income can be found. Wage earners in modern industry may be experiencing substantial increases in their incomes, but their numbers have been too small to have any overall impact on income distribution. One of the main factors, but by no means the only factor, contributing to the sustained inflationary pressures which have been especially severe in some Latin American countries is the already mentioned stagnation in agriculture, often leading to agricultural price increases. Inflationary pressures are intensified by the tendency of government budgets to run into a deficit, due to a combination of strong demands for increased expenditures and an inelastic tax system, the latter largely because of the prevalence of regressive taxes. Furthermore, chronic inflation leads to chronic balance-of-payments difficulties, regularly followed by devaluation, which in turn contributes to further inflation. It should also be noted that many less-developed economies are vulnerable to this kind of cycle because they are highly dependent on foreign trade and especially because of the primary product nature of their exports.

Clearly, then, the economic difficulties arising in the development process are many and of a highly complex nature. Problems such as low agricultural productivity, inflation, or budget deficits are furthermore not purely economic but also a result of deep-seated structural and institutional factors. The governments of less-developed countries are increasingly assuming a more important role in the planning of development, and their tasks are proving to be extremely difficult. Agricultural productivity has to be increased, industry has to be created or expanded, and social overhead facilities have to be built. At the same time pressures to improve income distribution continually grow stronger while much needed tax reform is strongly opposed. Recent urban migration far ahead of adequate industrial development has intensified the urgency of job creation.

It is unreasonable to expect a quick or simultaneous solution to all these problems. While examining the limited achievements of the less-developed countries in terms of their objectives, bear in mind that during their take-off periods, under generally much more favorable conditions, the presently developed countries repeatedly ran into great difficulties with respect to income distribution, price stability, and the like. Even though one can fairly say that the economic growth of less-developed economies often falls short of plan objectives simply because the plans are overly ambitious, from a purely economic point of view the situation is often puzzling. Quite often apparently sound and realistic economic development policies have produced disappointing results. Alternatively, governments have proposed development strategies with plainly unrealistic economic content; failure to achieve publicly trumpeted goals leaves the citizens whose expectations were aroused with a sense of frustration and unwilling to pay the price in tears and taxes of new development programs.

The source of these difficulties may be that the study of economic development often has been approached in a narrowly technical way, disregarding the whole set of noneconomic conditions affecting the country. Thus, a policy which appears highly rational from an economic standpoint may fail simply because under the given circumstances it is not very rational politically, or vice versa. The formulation of a development strategy requires more than an analysis of purely economic variables. Development takes place in a historical, social, and political setting which is continually subjected to changing internal and external pressures. Important examples of these pressures include geographic population movements, changes in the dualistic structure and in the relative strength of power groups in the economy, and shifts in the international economic position. The relationship between a development strategy and these various pressures is one of interdependency: development policy will affect the internal and external forces operating in the society while at the same time being affected by them.

The following discussion of development policymaking in Peru during the last few years focuses especially on one example of interdependency between a development strategy and the environment in which it operates. It tries to determine the way in which specific conditions in Peru influenced the process of economic decisionmaking. It is a case study of the attempt on the part of a government to plan for development and of the difficulties and limitations encountered in the process. The analysis has implications which go beyond the borders of that country, because similar experiences and patterns probably would apply to other economies with similar structural characteristics. Problems such as dualism, dependency on exports, and vast internal migration are shared by a number of countries in and out of Latin America, so the Peruvian experience may be transferable to several economies of the world.

Introduction

After seven years of exchange-rate stability and uninterrupted high rates of GNP growth, economic conditions in Peru started to deteriorate toward the end of 1967. Until August 31, the exchange rate had remained at 26.8 soles per dollar, but by December the rate had devalued to 39.7 soles per dollar. Also, compared to an average rate of GNP growth of 6.1 percent per year for the period 1961 to 1966, and 4.6 percent for 1967, GNP grew by only 1.7 percent during 1968.[1] The worsened economic situation reemphasized the urgency of many of the problems plaguing the Peruvian economy, including such important issues as the backwardness of the agricultural sector, the relative lack of government revenues, and the very uneven income distribution. In October, 1968, the military deposed the civilian government of Fernando Belaúnde, and the new president, General Velasco, embarked upon a program of economic and social development to be achieved through a series of structural reforms. The major steps taken by the new administration thus far

[1] Banco Central de Reserva del Perú, *Economic and Financial Review*, No. 25, *Fourth Quarter, 1968* (Lima, Peru), p. 1.

include nationalization of the International Petroleum Company, a United States subsidiary, a new agrarian reform law, some foreign exchange control, the acquisition of several leading banks by the government, and an industrial reform law.

It has always proven to be quite difficult in the Latin American environment to anticipate the nature and outcome of reform movements. Peru is no exception. The Velasco government, however, is not the first reformist regime. In fact, a number of the development policies proposed earlier by the deposed government of President Belaúnde, which was in power from 1963 until 1968, were quite similar to those of General Velasco. Many of the differences can be explained by changes in the underlying conditions, such as the weakening of exports as an impetus of growth toward the end of the 1960s. It is the purpose of this paper to try to gain insights in the recent process of economic policymaking in Peru through an examination of the reform movement under the Belaúnde administration. It is hoped that the conclusion of the analysis may provide some bases for evaluating the policies of the new government. Fernando Belaúnde was elected president of Peru in June, 1963, succeeding Manuel Prado, a close friend of the upper classes who had been in office from July, 1956, until June, 1962. Elections in mid-1962 had been called fraudulent by the military and annulled, though many felt the real cause for the action was the apparent success of the APRA party, a traditional enemy of the army. A military caretaking government had been in power from mid-1962 until the 1963 elections. Two years earlier, in 1961, the Alliance for Progress, of which Peru is a charter member, had been created. This was viewed as a new policy approach designed to accelerate economic growth in Latin America subject to certain constraints with respect to the distribution of the gains, that is, the incorporation of the "forgotten masses" in the mainstream of development was actively sought. Belaúnde was a reformer who fitted ideally into this new design for development.

Under Belaúnde's guidance and with encouragement of the Alliance for Progress, economic policies for the 1960s were meant to be very different from earlier Peruvian experience. Some of the more prominent components of the new strategy were the following. A National Planning System was created in 1962 to elaborate development plans. The public sector was to become a dynamic force in economic growth through increased public investments. The long-neglected development of the Peruvian highlands (Sierra) and jungle (Selva) was to be tied in with the development of the coastal area. After extensive political maneuvering, an agrarian reform law was passed in 1964 and tax reform was promised.

One way to evaluate Belaúnde's development policies would be through a study of the degree to which the different reforms and strategy changes have influenced economic events in Peru. As will be explained below, however, many of the reforms were only partially implemented, if at all. Therefore our analysis will examine the hypothesis that the extent to which reforms were carried out was itself a function of economic and other developments. To do so, we must review briefly the major economic and related social and political events in Peru during recent years.

Brief Description of the Peruvian Economy: World War II to 1968 Military Coup

Economic Characteristics

Our description of postwar Peru starts with the year 1950 because the only consistent set of national accounts, recently revised and published by the Central Reserve Bank, does not cover earlier years. Judging from Table 1, economic growth from 1950 to 1967 was impressive. Real GNP increased at a yearly cumulative rate of 5.5 percent, one of the highest in Latin America.

With population growing at about 2.6 percent per year, real per-capita income grew at about 2.9 percent. The rate of inflation, 8.4 percent per year, was modest by Latin American standards. On the other hand, Peru is one of the relatively poorer countries of the region. Per-capita Gross Domestic Product in 1965 in current dollars was estimated at US $372 for Peru, compared with US $971 for Venezuela, US $670 for Argentina, US $575 for Chile, and US

TABLE 1. GROSS NATIONAL PRODUCT, BY TYPE OF EXPENDITURE
(Millions of Soles at 1963 Prices)

	1950	1967	Yearly Growth Rate Percentage
Private Consumption	27,605	72,715	5.9
Government Consumption	3,860	9,909	5.7
Gross Investment	7,942	25,204	7.0
Exports	5,915	18,799	7.0
Imports	6,366	29,160	9.4
Gross National Product	38,956	97,467	5.5

SOURCE: Banco Central de Reserva del Perú, *Cuentas Nacionales del Perú, 1950–1967* (Lima, Peru, 1968).

$482 for Mexico, but also with US $273 for Brazil and US $166 for Bolivia.[2]

Recent studies of the Peruvian economy[3] generally show that the main stimulus to growth was provided by the export sector. Exports in constant prices grew at an annual rate of 7 percent and accounted for almost 20 percent of GNP in 1967. While exports have always consisted mainly of raw materials, very important changes took place in the composition over the postwar period. As shown in Table 2, Peru's merchandise exports increased from US $193.6 million in 1950 to US $757.2 million in 1967. However, the share of four major agricultural products, which in 1950 had been 55 percent of the total, by 1967 had fallen to 19 percent. On the other hand, by 1967 fishmeal and minerals had taken the lead. This changing composition has important implications for Peru's development strategy, as will be seen below.

Imports in constant prices rose at 9.4 percent per year over the same period, considerably more rapidly than exports. Even though a slight improvement in the terms of trade had taken place by 1967 compared to 1950, the current account deficit in the balance of pay-

[2] E. E. Hagen and Oli Hawrylyshyn, "Analysis of World Income and Growth, 1955–1965," *Economic Development and Cultural Change*, Vol. 18, No. 1, Pt. II (October, 1969).

[3] Erik Thorbecke and Apostolos Condos, "Macroeconomic Growth and Development Models of the Peruvian Economy," in I. Adelman and E. Thorbecke, eds., *The Theory and Design of Economic Development* (Baltimore, 1966), and René Vandendries, "Foreign Trade and the Economic Development of Peru" (Ph.D. dissertation, Iowa State University, Ames, 1967).

TABLE 2. VALUE OF PRINCIPAL EXPORT PRODUCTS, 1950 AND 1967
(Current Million Dollars)

	1950	Percentage	1967	Percentage
Major Agricultural Products	106.6	55	145.2	19
Cotton	68.0		54.8	
Sugar	29.7		53.1	
Coffee	1.0		29.1	
Wool	7.9		8.2	
Fishmeal and Fishoil	5.7	3	204.0	27
Petroleum	25.3	13	8.5	1
Major Minerals	40.8	21	368.6	49
Copper	10.2		198.3	
Silver	8.0		42.3	
Lead	12.3		30.2	
Zinc	10.3		35.7	
Iron Ore	—		62.1	
Other	15.2	8	30.9	4
Total Merchandise Exports	193.6	100	757.2	100

SOURCE: Banco Central de Reserva del Perú, *Cuentas Nacionales del Perú, 1950–1967* (Lima, Peru, 1968).

ments, financed by long-run capital inflows, was growing very large toward the end of the 1960s. The composition of imports changed very little during this period. In 1967, 18 percent of total imports consisted of consumer goods, 46 percent of raw materials and intermediate products, and 36 percent of capital goods. The only notable change in the percentage composition of imports occurred during the latter part of the period under consideration; it consisted of a relative decline in the imports of consumer goods, offset by a relative increase in the imports of raw materials and intermediate products. This development was largely a function of Peru's drive toward industrialization through the establishment of assembly or processing plants which perform the "final touches" on almost finished imported products. The net result is that many consumer products formerly imported as "consumer goods" now enter as "intermediate goods."

Geographically Peru consists of three main regions: the coastal area, the mountains or Sierra, and the jungle or Selva. The modern sector is located predominantly in the coastal area, the main exception being part of the minerals production which takes place in "enclaves" in the Sierra. Fishing, cotton, and sugar production all are located along the coast. Furthermore, with the exception of agricultural and export production, whose location for obvious reasons is resource-oriented, economic activity is heavily concentrated in the Lima-Callao (capital) area. Regional income figures, as published by the Central Reserve Bank for the year 1961, show that 42.5 percent of national income is accounted for by the Lima-Callao area where, also in 1961, slightly over 20 percent of the population resided.[4] Per-capita income in Lima-Callao is about 2.6 times per-capita income of the rest of the country. A recent preliminary study by the National Planning Institute on regional development in Peru shows that in 1963 metropolitan Lima-Callao alone accounted for about 60 percent of industrial production, a proportion which has been increasing over time. According to the same source, income and employment opportunities in Lima-Callao have been rising at much faster rates than in the rest of the country. The Sierra, which covers 30 percent of Peru's land area, is, with the exception of minerals production, an exceedingly poor and backward sector of the economy. Its main activities are very low productivity agriculture and handicrafts. In 1961 about 53 percent of the population resided there. The unusually large differences in income and existing methods of production between the advanced coastal area and the backward Sierra always made Peru an excellent example of a dual economy. The third region of the country, the Selva, plays a very minor role in the economy. It contains 60 percent of Peru's land area, but only 9 percent of the population in 1961. Much of the Selva is untouched, spoken of as a promised land, target of some development policy on the part of the government through road-building aimed at redirecting internal migration to some extent away from the coast. Whether the promise really is valid remains to be seen.

Some additional characteristics of Peru's economy deserve mentioning in order to aid the analysis. Available information on functional income distribution is very incomplete, but whatever does

[4] Banco Central de Reserva del Perú, *Cuentas Nacionales del Perú, 1950–1967* (Lima, Peru, 1968), p. 28.

exist indicates a very uneven distribution, with definitely no tendency toward improvement over the last few years.[5] Data on sectorial developments over the postwar period, as published by the Central Reserve Bank,[6] reveal the following. Fishing, mining, and manufacturing industry, the most dynamic subsectors of the latter being fishmeal plants and minerals refining, grew substantially while agriculture lagged considerably. Finally, the information on central government income and expenditures in Tables 3 and 4

TABLE 3. PERCENTAGE DISTRIBUTION OF CENTRAL GOVERNMENT INCOME

	Profit Taxes	Income Received from Individuals			Indirect Taxes		Non-tax Income from Firms
		Direct Taxes	Social Security Contributions	Other	Import Duties	Other	
1950	46	6	3	—	13	21	11
1951	43	5	3	—	24	20	5
1952	38	6	3	—	24	25	4
1953	29	6	3	—	25	34	3
1954	31	6	5	—	23	31	4
1955	30	6	5	—	22	32	5
1956	28	5	5	—	23	34	5
1957	28	5	5	—	23	34	5
1958	27	7	6	—	21	34	5
1959	25	7	8	—	21	34	5
1960	29	6	7	—	20	34	4
1961	27	6	6	—	20	36	5
1962	26	6	7	—	19	37	5
1963	24	5	10	—	18	38	5
1964	21	4	10	—	23	38	4
1965	18	5	12	—	26	34	5
1966	15	7	12	1	25	35	5
1967	18	7	11	1	25	33	5

SOURCE: Banco Central de Reserva del Perú, *Cuentas Nacionales del Perú, 1950–1967* (Lima, Peru, 1968).

shows among others these developments: a persistent strong dependence on indirect taxation revenue and a fluctuating but, over the whole period, essentially unchanged distribution between current and capital outlays.

[5] René Vandendries, "Foreign Trade," pp. 102–105.
[6] Banco Central de Reserva del Perú, *Cuentas Nacionales del Perú, 1950–1967* (Lima, Peru, 1967), p. 24.

TABLE 4. CENTRAL GOVERNMENT INCOME AND EXPENDITURES
GROSS PUBLIC CAPITAL INFLOW
(Data in Current Terms)

	Central Government Expenditures (Million Soles)			(2) (3) %	Central Gov't. Current Income (Million Soles) (4)	Gross Public Capital Inflow in Million		(5) (4) %	Current Account Savings (4)–(1)
	Current (1)	Capital (2)	Total (3)			Dollars	Soles (5)		
1950	1,476	166	1,642	10.1	1,950	—	2.0	.1	474
1951	1,904	203	2,107	9.6	2,421	.8	12.1	.5	517
1952	2,066	500	2,566	19.5	2,692	3.7	57.5	2.1	626
1953	2,506	460	2,966	15.5	2,959	15.2	257.5	8.7	453
1954	2,621	380	3,001	12.7	3,347	1.5	29.5	.9	726
1955	3,001	917	3,918	23.4	3,720	60.3	1,156.6	31.1	719
1956	3,956	782	4,738	16.5	4,374	27.4	526.9	12.0	418
1957	4,368	690	5,058	13.6	4,803	27.6	526.3	11.0	435
1958	4,630	844	5,474	15.4	4,761	24.0	561.6	11.8	131
1959	5,747	630	6,377	9.9	6,122	16.1	445.0	7.3	375
1960	6,645	591	7,236	8.2	8,151	12.8	349.4	4.3	1,506
1961	8,120	1,150	9,270	12.4	9,666	25.0	670.3	6.9	1,546
1962	9,531	1,447	10,978	13.2	10,924	51.2	1,372.7	12.6	1,393
1963	12,311	884	13,195	6.7	13,111	77.2	2,070.5	15.8	800
1964	16,032	1,640	17,672	9.3	15,843	89.0	2,387.0	15.1	–189
1965	20,095	2,819	22,914	12.3	19,669	98.0	2,628.4	13.4	–426
1966	23,809	3,754	27,563	13.6	23,231	244.1	6,546.8	28.2	–578
1967	28,037	4,619	32,656	14.1	25,967	203.5	5,457.9	21.0	–2,070

SOURCE: Banco Central de Reserva del Perú, *Cuentas Nacionales del Perú, 1950–1967* (Lima, Peru, 1968).

Dualism and Internal Migration

The very uneven economic development within Peru (the coast and mainly Lima-Callao versus the rest of the country) is probably the major factor responsible for the large internal migration which has taken place during the postwar period. Population in urban Lima-Callao has been growing at about 5.2 percent per year versus about 1.8 percent per year for the rest of the country (Table 5). This has given rise to the phenomenal growth of squatter settlements surrounding the capital, and has had a definite effect on the dualistic structure of Peru.

The traditional notion of dualism in Peru refers to the split between the modern coastal areas and the backward agricultural high-

TABLE 5. REGIONAL URBAN AND RURAL POPULATION
(Census Data, in Thousands)

	1940 Urban	1940 Rural	1961 Urban	1961 Rural	Yearly Growth Rate in % Urban	Yearly Growth Rate in % Rural
Lima-Callao	614	31	1,784	62	5.2	3.4
Rest of Coast	502	566	1,137	808	3.9	1.7
Sierra	934	3,106	1,459	3,764	2.2	0.9
Selva	148	307	318	575	3.6	3.0
Total Peru (Urban and Rural)	6,208		9,907		2.3	

SOURCE: Ministerio de Hacienda y Comercio, Dirección Nacional de Estadística y Censos, *Boletín de Análisis Demográfico*, Nos. 4–5 (Lima, Peru, 1967), Table 10, p. 50.

lands where it was feared that sooner or later agrarian revolt would erupt. Over time, unrest in the Sierra did become more pronounced, especially in the early 1960s, implying that as a social force the mass of landless peasants certainly has gained in importance. As a result, an agrarian reform law was passed in 1964.[7] Whether the peasants of the Sierra have become a nationally important political group is much more doubtful. Even though the passage of agrarian reform legislation may be called a victory for Peru's landless, a close examination of the circumstances reveals that agrarian reform in the Sierra interferes to a much smaller extent with the interests of Peru's dominant groups than may appear at first. In one way or another, Peru had to respond to the growing rural agitation in the beginning of the 1960s. The objective of the peasants— land ownership—was very well defined and directed specifically against the local landlords. The power of these landlords in Peru's national decisionmaking process has become marginal over time, largely because of continued poor management and low productivity. (The circumstances surrounding agrarian reform in the efficient coastal farms will be discussed later.) Therefore, although land redistribution in the Sierra does take place at the expense of the local landlords, by itself it has little effect on Peru's national power groups. Consequently it provides a very acceptable placebo for the ills of agrarian unrest. Under Belaúnde,[8] Peru's poor peas-

[7] A new agrarian reform law was passed by the Velasco government in June, 1969.
[8] So far also under Velasco.

ants have been unable to move much beyond this in obtaining the benefits of a larger share of the government's budget or otherwise winning policy battles involving conflicts of interest on a national scale.

On the other hand, the tremendous migration from the Sierra to the coast during the last two or three decades gave rise to a different kind of dualism in Peru which has very significant implications for policymaking. Especially important has been migration to metropolitan Lima-Callao, which in 1968 had an estimated population of about 2.5 million. According to the 1961 population census, 47 percent of metropolitan Lima's residents were migrants and of all people ever to migrate in Peru, 43 percent had done so to the department of Lima and to Callao. Upon arrival in Lima, the migrant usually settles somewhere in the old central areas of the city, thereby contributing to the already existing overcrowding in those sections. As a result, large numbers of both migrants and native Lima residents have started a movement away from the center city slums, creating the so-called *barriadas*, or squatter settlements, surrounding the city. It is estimated that presently about 20 percent of Lima's population resides in these squatter settlements. The lower classes of Lima form a very small part of the regularly employed industrial labor force. Unlike the case of the landless peasant who has remained in the highlands, the objectives of Lima's poor are as yet vaguely defined but potentially competitive with the interests of Peru's dominant groups. Already, Lima's urban growth is placing severe pressures on public sector services and scarce government finances. Also, unrest in Lima and in other coastal urban centers is considerably less tolerable than in the Sierra, as it would interfere directly with the smooth operation of the export economy. Obviously, Lima's poor could very quickly become an important political force. In other words, the vast social mobilization of the last two decades has altered drastically the constraints imposed upon Peru's development strategy.

Politics and Economics

There has always been relatively little doubt about who dictates economic policy in Peru: the exporters. Export groups are predominant in the upper classes of the country.[9] Ever since independence in 1821, the one major characteristic of Peruvian economic conduct has been its relatively unrestricted trade and exchange policies, the only exceptions being a period of exchange controls during the postwar recovery from 1945 through 1948 and some foreign exchange controls introduced by the Velasco government in May, 1970, after the period under consideration here. When in September, 1948, the existing government decided to make controls even stricter, the large Gildemeister sugar enterprise officially expressed its determination not to recognize the new foreign exchange controls. In October, 1948, the Odría military coup overthrew the government and one of its first measures was to eliminate the system of exchange controls.

The 1948 military coup was clearly supported by the exporters. The armed forces have taken power in Peru quite often. As a result, it is frequently assumed that the military, although verbally resentful of the upper classes, have in fact always been their close allies and defenders. This, however, is an oversimplification. For instance, toward the end of his regime in 1956, Odría came increasingly under fire from the export groups because of budgetary deficits, among other reasons. Manuel Prado, a firm believer in budgetary equilibrium and free-trade principles, was elected president in 1956 and served until 1962. It appears that if it wants to stay in office, any regime in Peru, whether military or not, has to abide by the rules of the export economy. A major reason is that government revenue depends very heavily on the performance of the foreign sector. In 1967 import duties alone constituted one-fourth of the total tax revenue of the central government. Also, the 1966 list of principal taxpayers[10] shows that seven of the top ten taxpayers are foreign firms (including the top four), five of them major exporters.

Interestingly enough, Peru's upper classes have never been able to organize an effective conservative political party, except for a feeble effort in the beginning of the twentieth century. The two main political parties, APRA, created in 1924 by Victor Raúl Haya

---

[9] For an excellent description of power structures in Peru, see François Bourricaud, *Power and Society in Contemporary Peru* (New York, 1970).

[10] *El Peruano* (Official Gazette of Peru) (May 5, 1967).

de la Torre, and Acción Popular, created in 1956 by Belaúnde, are both reformist parties who see development as an active effort toward integration of the Sierra and the modern coastal region of Peru. This is in contrast to the traditional approach of the upper classes who see development as an expansion of the modern sector.

A large part of the strength of APRA lies in mine-workers and sugar-workers' unions. From their very origin the *Apristas* have been branded as communists by certain conservative groups, a charge which they have denied consistently and which their political alliances belie. In the early 1930s APRA and the military became archenemies and have been ever since. From 1933 to 1945 (except for a short period in 1934) and again from 1948 to 1956 the APRA party was simply outlawed. The suppression of the party by the military obviously is a major explanation of its failure ever to seize power. But it also can be attributed to the fact that their objective—the integration of the Sierra and the modern coastal sector —lacked realism until very recently because of the almost complete absence of national awareness on the part of the Sierra peasants.[11]

By the time of the elections in 1956 and especially of 1962, circumstances had changed. Rural agitation had become common and the Sierra peasants as a whole were becoming an important social group within Peru. By now, however, a new reformist party under the leadership of Belaúnde had come into being, also with the basic objective of integrating the Sierra and the modern sector of Peru. Thus, as unrest grew in the Sierra in the early 1960s, APRA's objective was becoming more of a realistic issue, but the party now had to deal with the rivalry of Belaúnde, a much more acceptable candidate, not only to the military but also to large segments of the upper classes. Furthermore, Peru's urban growth and problems would come to challenge the priority given by both parties to the Coast-Sierra issue in the first place.

As it turned out, Manuel Prado, who reflected the interests of the upper classes, was elected to the presidency in 1956. His main activities were to bring the central government budget back into

[11] It was reported that at the time of the Bolivian revolution and land reform in the early 1950s, scores of Peruvian peasants went to La Paz in order to claim their land titles, apparently unaware of the fact that they were Peruvians, not Bolivians.

equilibrium, following Odría's excessive expenditures, and to get Peru through the 1957 to 1958 depression. By 1960 Peru's export sector and the economy had started a boom period which was to last for several years. The 1962 elections, in which APRA came out ahead with a very small plurality, were annulled by the military as fraudulent.[12] A junta ruled until new elections were called in 1963, when Belaúnde was elected president.

To conclude this section on background before turning to a detailed discussion of Belaúnde's economic policies, it can be said that the upper classes somehow managed to keep Peruvian economic policy to their advantage, in spite of the absence of a conservative political party. The major opposition party, APRA, has effectively been denied the presidency. Odría (1948 to 1956) outlawed APRA, and his economic policy was directed at fostering export and income growth. Exchange controls were eliminated and new mining legislation designed to attract foreign investment was introduced in 1950. Policies aimed at increasing employment and improving income distribution in Peru were enacted but concentrated on metropolitan Lima-Callao. When budget deficits arose and the fear of monetary instability spread among the exporters, the 1956 elections put Prado in power. During his term of office, economic policy was essentially a continuation of the past, except that unlike Odría he followed a very balanced budgetary policy.

Belaúnde and Structural Reforms, 1963 to 1968

Belaúnde became president in 1963 with a program designed to introduce drastic changes in development strategy. Development was no longer to be looked at primarily as an expansion of the modern sector, the benefits of which were to spread slowly into the backward sector. Instead, through a number of structural reforms the backward sector, especially the Sierra, was to become an integral part of the object of economic policy. Agrarian reform, tax reform, and development planning were all part of this new design. An ex-

[12] It is widely speculated that the main motivating factor of the military coup of October, 1968, again was the high probability of success of the APRA party in the elections which were to be held in 1969.

amination of the progress toward these different reforms will demonstrate to what extent development strategy did change, and why.

It was already suggested that a common misconception about Peru is the assumption that the landowning class and the ruling class are and have continued to be the same.[13] In the first place, the landlords of the Sierra have always been much more locally than nationally oriented and their influence on national policymaking has always been small. Over time, the low productivity of their haciendas and of the agricultural sector producing food for the domestic market in general has eroded the power of these landlords even more. In the postwar period economic policy has more often than not been to their disadvantage. Basic food prices in Peru are usually under some form of government control. Price policy differs for different food items, but the issue generally relates to the relative weights to be attached to the goal of low retail prices on the one hand and to the goal of fair farm prices on the other. A number of studies on food-price policies in Peru[14] lead to the overall conclusion that the objective of low retail prices for the urban consumer traditionally has received the heaviest weight. Whereas industrial production is protected, food production as a rule is not, and imports help maintain low prices. Low food prices are of great interest to the exporters; inexpensive consumer provisions allow them to keep wages low and maintain political stability in the urban centers.

Moreover, Table 2 shows the decreasing importance of the agricultural share of total exports, reducing the political power of even the efficient coastal export haciendas. The declining national power of Peru's landowning class made it relatively easy for the Belaúnde

[13] François Bourricaud, in *Power and Society in Contemporary Peru*, provides an excellent description of the difference between the absentee, inefficient, and nationally rather powerless landlords, and the nontraditional efficient class of exporters who spend little time dreaming about Peru's traditions but instead are concerned about economic growth, balance of payments problems, and the like. The sugar and cotton farmers of the coast belong to the latter group.

[14] Iowa Universities Mission to Peru, *Peruvian Macroeconomic and Agricultural Prospects and Strategy, 1967–1972* (Lima, Peru, 1967), pp. 167–181; William C. Merrill, *Establishing Rice Prices in Peru*, Iowa Universities Mission to Peru (Lima, Peru, April, 1966); and René Vandendries, *An Analysis of the Evolution of Peru's Beef Imports from 1950–1966*, Iowa Universities Mission to Peru (Lima, Peru, October, 1967).

government to start the agrarian reform process. The regime's policy was facilitated because the 1964 congress, which was controlled by Belaúnde's opposition, in passing the agrarian reform law involving land distribution, gave high priority to breaking up the comparatively more inefficient haciendas and for all practical purposes exempted the sugar haciendas.[15]

Attempts by Belaúnde, in conjunction with the Alliance for Progress, to initiate policy shifts in such other areas as tax reforms, obtaining a larger fraction of the government's budget for the agricultural sector and for the Sierra, and increasing the government's savings and investment through foreign capital inflow and planning achieved limited success at best. In very general terms the explanation appears to be as follows. Any development strategy involves more than simply making a choice among alternative means to achieve a given long-run rate of income growth subject to certain distributional constraints. In the short run the planners are subjected to an extremely important political constraint, namely, they have to stay in power.[16] The weight of different social groups in national affairs may change over time as the influence of older groups wanes or new social groups whose demands must be met arise. In Peru, the export-dependent character of the economy implies that the exporters as a group have had and will continue to have majority rule in economic policymaking, barring occurrence of a

[15] The fact that the new agrarian reform law passed in 1969 by the new military government does not exempt the sugar haciendas but rather has subjected them to immediate expropriation can best be explained as follows. The hatred between the military and APRA continues to be very vivid. One way in which the military can attempt to seriously undermine the APRA party is through collectivizing the sugar haciendas, whose labor unions traditionally have been a major source of APRA strength.

Another possible explanation of the inclusion of the sugar haciendas in the 1969 agrarian reform law and of their immediate expropriation is the following. After the expropriation of the International Petroleum Company in Peru (a United States subsidiary) it was feared that the United States might cut Peru's sugar quota in the United States market. Once the haciendas were part of the agrarian reform efforts, the United States would have been in the very uncomfortable position of damaging Peru's agrarian reform process, which, on the other hand, the United States had been advocating for several years.

[16] See for instance, Charles W. Anderson, *Politics and Economic Change in Latin America* (New York, 1967), Chap. 7.

Cuban-style revolution, where the objective is not to reform the existing economic order but rather to eliminate it and put a new order in its place.

This does not imply that the export sector cannot or should not be made to contribute more to the overall development of the economy than it has in the past, through such measures as higher taxes, efforts to increase the proportion of profits reinvested in the country, and the like. Instead, it suggests that because of Peru's vital dependence on exports, the exporters will continue to be a power group. Furthermore, whereas the economy presently depends largely on raw material exports, it is virtually inevitable that future industrial development will likewise have to be largely export-oriented, in view of the relatively small size of the Peruvian domestic market even if the masses' purchasing power is vastly increased. The effects of the vast internal migration since 1940 and the growth of metropolitan Lima-Callao have furthermore led to the growth of a new class of poor with great political potential. The demands of these urban poor have affected economic policymaking (and may be expected to do so increasingly over time) much more than the demands of the rural poor.

Any attempt to quantify the limited success of the reform proposals of Belaúnde and the Alliance for Progress is difficult because of inadequate information, but enough data are available to provide some rough guidelines. One important stated objective of the

TABLE 6. COMPOSITION OF TOTAL PUBLIC EXPENDITURES, BY SECTORS
(Percentage) *

	1960	1961	1962	1963	1964	1965	1966
Productive Sectors	5.1	12.6	8.8	10.4	9.8	8.0	9.1
Agriculture	1.7	2.8	2.4	2.5	3.0	3.5	4.1
Industry	2.8	8.5	6.0	7.5	5.6	3.7	4.5
Infrastructure	13.7	12.3	13.2	14.3	14.4	13.9	13.3
Social Sectors	30.3	31.0	35.7	32.0	35.0	39.6	41.4
General Services	26.3	23.2	26.8	25.9	23.3	21.1	23.5
Financial Services	24.6	20.9	15.5	17.4	17.5	17.4	12.7

* Includes semiautonomous public sector.
SOURCE: Instituto Nacional de Planificación, *Bases para un Programa de Desarrollo Nacional a Largo Plazo*, Documento de Trabajo (Lima, Peru, April, 1969), Capítulo IX–1B.

1960s was to increase agricultural output through an expansion of public expenditures in agriculture, with special emphasis on the Sierra. According to one source,[17] the share of the budget spent on agriculture, about 3 percent, has fluctuated somewhat but basically changed little since 1950, with most of it consistently going to the coastal area. Central government budget data for 1968 show the budget for agriculture at 2.9 percent.[18] A recently published working document by the National Planning Institute[19] provides information and analysis of government expenditures by sector, some of which is reproduced in Table 6. According to that study, agriculture's share of the national budget would have increased somewhat in 1966 (to 4.1 percent), but even this percentage is exceedingly small for a country where about 50 percent of the population are engaged in subsistence agriculture. On the other hand, the share of expenditures on infrastructure has virtually remained unchanged during the 1960s, even though emphasis on infrastructure was part of the development program proposed by Belaúnde. Furthermore, a very large increase took place mainly in the metropolitan area in the share of public expenditures on social services —education, public health, and so on—according to the same source. With respect to agricultural price policies, the Belaúnde government essentially continued along past lines.

In other words, while the government did little to increase productivity or income of agriculture, it did through low food prices and increased social programs cater to the needs of Lima. This pattern reflects the realities of the situation. A debilitated class of landlords together with a politically weak peasant society whose demands appear to be, at least thus far, easily satisfied through little more than a start in land redistribution compete for government benefits with a growing group of poor in Lima, potentially threatening the overall stability of the economy. Belaúnde's government

---

[17] Programa de Investigaciones para el Desarrollo, *Peru, Long Term Projections of Demand for and Supply of Selected Agricultural Commodities Through 1980* (Lima, Peru, 1968).
[18] Banco Central de Reserva del Perú, *Economic and Financial Review No. 22, First Quarter 1968* (Lima, Peru), Table VIII.
[19] Instituto Nacional de Planificación, *Bases para un Programa de Desarrollo Nacional a Largo Plazo*, Documento de Trabajo (Lima, Peru, April, 1969).

was thus forced to deviate considerably from the original intent of its program.

Tax reform, planning, and attracting public foreign capital in order to increase the supply of investment funds for the government were also part of the Belaúnde program. Problems of tax reform have been disregarded so far, with a few minor exceptions.[20] A few examples of fiscal measures taken during 1967 and 1968 are indicative of the restraint exercised in changing the tax structure and of the continued reliance on traditional forms of taxation. Import duties were increased; some of the import duty exonerations extended under industrial promotion laws were revised and rationalized, and a surcharge on profit taxes was added. The 1968 introduction of urban and rural real-estate taxes did, however, constitute a definite change in structure. Table 3 reveals the very limited changes in the structure of tax revenue under Belaúnde, compared with earlier years. Indirect taxes continue to be the main source of income, with some increase in the relative importance of import duties. The declining share of profit taxes is being offset largely by increased social security contributions. Central government revenue did increase as a percentage of GNP. Table 4 shows that capital expenditures as a percentage of total central government expenditures was subject to substantial fluctuations during the period from 1950 to 1967, but was not significantly higher under Belaúnde than it had been during earlier regimes.

This last is of special interest because from 1962 on, a substantial increase took place in the inflow of public foreign capital, largely with the intended purpose of increasing the government's supply of investment funds. Both public gross capital inflow as a percentage of government current income and central government capital expenditures as a percentage of total expenditures are presented in Table 4. The effect of public capital inflow on the investment effort of the government, which can be measured by relating these two percentages, turns out to be almost negligible. Furthermore, Table 4 shows that the current account savings of the central government (income-current expenditures) during the Belaúnde-Alliance for Progress

[20] Banco Central de Reserva del Perú, *Economic and Financial Review No. 22, First Quarter 1968* (Lima, Peru), pp. 2–13.

period decreased and actually became negative. In other words, public foreign capital inflow, rather than supplementing domestic government resources for capital formation, simply replaced them. The explanation again may be found in the difficulty of any government to stay in power. The demands on the Belaúnde regime, especially strong inasmuch as the opposition parties had a majority in congress, were met by increasing both the number and the salaries of public employees and by increased social expenditures. Public foreign capital was one of the factors facilitating Belaúnde's stay in power, but it fell far short of its purpose of increasing the supply of Peru's investment funds. Regarding the nature and source of public foreign capital, mention should be made of the relatively unfavorable structure of Peru's foreign debt and foreign borrowing. When the Alliance for Progress was formed, it was hoped that loans carrying low rates of interest and easy repayment terms would make up the bulk of foreign financial assistance. As Table 7 shows, the amounts of loans obtained by Peru from the major international lending agencies and from the United States government are not predominant in the total. Instead, Peru has relied heavily on suppliers' credit and foreign bank loans, both of which are a generally much less favorable form of borrowing. As a result Peru's debt-service payments have become a very heavy burden on the economy and the government recently has had to engage in substantial refinancing of the debt.

TABLE 7. EXTERNAL PUBLIC DEBT, BY LENDING INSTITUTIONS
(Million US Dollars)

Lender	December, 1967
Agency for International Development	67.4
Eximbank	36.5
World Bank	115.5
Interamerican Development Bank	54.0
Other*	407.6
Total	681.0

* Mainly suppliers credit and foreign bank loans.
SOURCE: Banco Central de Reserva del Perú, *Economic and Financial Review*, No. 22. First Quarter, 1968 (Lima, Peru), Table XX.

Finally, planning and the National Planning Institute, created in 1962, have had virtually no effect on national policymaking. Thus far, Peru's development plans have been little more than elaborate statements of objectives prepared mainly for the purpose of satisfying one of the requirements of the Alliance for Progress, namely that a member country should have development plans in order to be eligible for funds.

Conclusions

The evolution of economic policy and the limited success of a number of structural reform proposals during the Belaúnde administration should not come as a surprise if due consideration is given to such factors as the relative strength of different power groups in Peru and regional shifts in population. Reforms were carried out to the extent that they did not interfere in any major way with the dominant interest groups. Thus an agrarian reform law was passed as an inevitable concession to the peasants of the Sierra, but the commitment to its implementation was limited. Similarly, elaborate development plans were prepared, reflecting the government's desire and efforts to bring about change, yet the relation of the plans to the effective decisionmaking process was very small. On the one hand, little or no changes occurred in agricultural price policies or government tax and expenditure policies. In fact, while earlier governments on the average managed to direct almost 14 percent (Table 4: average from 1950 through 1961) of central government expenditures into capital formation without substantial foreign assistance, the Belaúnde government, with substantial amounts of foreign assistance, on the average spent less than 12 percent (Table 4: average from 1962 through 1967) of the budget for investment purposes. Total tax revenues as a percentage of GNP have risen during the last few years, but a good deal of the increase was due to extra import duty revenues. On the other hand, foreign capital provided the government with funds for capital investment, which allowed it to use domestic resources for current expenditures. If, as Hagen and Hirschman maintain, a certain amount of stress or tension is necessary for societies to be entrepreneurial, the experience of Peru indicates that public foreign capital inflow may have a decidedly undesirable effect. Certainly it did not increase capital investment but allowed the postponement of tax reform.

The military regime, which came to power in October, 1968, again proposed to carry out drastic structural reforms. It is never easy to anticipate the outcome of a new development program, yet the experience of the past may provide some insights into the future. Major policy measures thus far include the expropriation of the International Petroleum Company, a United States subsidiary, a new agrarian reform law which no longer exempts the sugar exporters, some foreign exchange controls, banking reform, and an industrial reform law. Some of these actions are much less radical than might appear at first. A legal conflict between the Peruvian government and the International Petroleum Company had existed for a long period of time without substantial progress toward a solution. Furthermore, partly as a result of this, petroleum production in Peru had been relatively stagnant for the last few years, and the country, which used to be a net exporter of petroleum and petroleum products, had become a net importer. The above factors combined to increase the tension surrounding the issue and make it a matter of national dignity. Expropriation became a most expedient solution.

The inclusion of the sugar haciendas in the agrarian reform process can be explained on the basis of the continually declining relative importance of sugar as an export crop[21] and on purely political grounds, as a means of trying to break the power of the strongest opposition party in Peru. A continuation of land redistribution as such can be expected and does not conflict with present-day major economic interests in Peru. On the other hand, the continuing demographic growth of metropolitan Lima-Callao undoubtedly will make the problem of increased food supplies for the capital a much more important target of future development strategies. The vast external debt and the weakened international credit position

---

[21] The apparent increase in sugar-export earnings in 1967 as compared with 1950 (Table 2) is not evidence of a long-term trend. Peru's sugar earnings during the 1960s have been above earnings during the 1950s, largely because Peru, as well as other Latin American countries, benefited from the disappearance of Cuba as a United States supplier.

of Peru will probably provide a more favorable climate for tax reform.

It is too early to judge the importance of some of the other reform legislation initiated by the Velasco government, as its extent is not yet very clear. It may be pointed out, however, that in general, during its first year in office, the military regime has shown itself to be remarkably practical. It has fully recognized the importance of exports to the economy. The case of the International Petroleum Company has been called a "unique," "a singular case . . . of a company that has transgressed and offended our laws, usurped our rights,"[22] the expropriation of which was not intended to discourage foreign investors. On the contrary, statements by Peruvian officials on investment opportunities and legislation relating to it seem to be geared principally toward attracting foreign investment, especially for export production.[23]

[22] General Bureau of Information, *Petroleum in Peru. For the World to Judge: The History of a Unique Case* (Lima, Peru, 1969).
[23] "Review of the Week Section," *The New York Times* (September 29, 1969).

National Integration Problems and Military Regimes in Latin America

Robert E. Scott

Lately technology has so speeded up and expanded the modernization process around the world that fast and significant changes in social and political conditions often accompany economic growth. In most cases the specific effects are good—improved health and a longer life span, urban amenities, vastly better communications and transport, involvement of the popular masses and of entire regions in national concerns. For some developing countries whose institutions are not equipped to handle massive change, the collective consequences of these same accomplishments may be unexpected and unwelcome—spiraling populations, snowballing demands upon society and economy to provide education, housing, social benefits, and regular employment for unassimilated multitudes. New values confront old action patterns, claims of human beings challenge vested property rights, formerly isolated and quiescent regions begin to compete with each other. Where at one time quite different peoples could live together in the same country, province, or city with a minimum of conflict, the increased rate of change, accompanied by much more intense interaction among all sectors of the populace, has caught many emerging countries in a major crisis of national integration.

Ironically, in attempts to deal with integration problems the advantage lies with the more advanced nations which have longer experience facing shifting conditions, for they can rely not only on greater material resources but also on more effective unifying social and political structures than can most developing states. In the emerging world, the same rapidly changing conditions which upset interpersonal relations among individuals exert implacable pressures upon governmental institutions, breaking down previously accepted relationships between the established and the challenging interests and overwhelming existing political control mechanisms in the process.

Not unexpectedly, in those Latin American states most affected by technology the traditional ruling elites seem much more interested in system maintenance to assure stability and protect their advantageous position than in solving national integration problems. For them, a country's unity is best assured by co-opting emerging popular elements into the ongoing national governmental system, with consensus built around the values and practices of the incumbent central power group rather than on some more inclusive set of norms growing out of a process of continuous compromise with the new interests as they enter the political arena. Increasingly as society and economy become more complex and political life more intense, however, established value patterns prove inadequate and traditional political structures too unyielding and particularistic to contain the disruptions of drastic change. Maintaining the governing elites' political arrangements becomes ever harder because the machinery they favor never was intended to handle the broad range of competing demands now appearing. But the difficulty here is not simply one of scarce resources in a period of rapidly rising expectations, though widespread material need does vastly complicate the fundamental task confronting the political system in such countries.

That task—transforming burgeoning raw demands into generally acceptable policy alternatives to be ratified by the formal constitutional agencies—is very nearly impossible to accomplish under present Latin American conditions because the values motivating the operations of certain legal and extralegal political structures are mutually incompatible. This problem arises because the written constitution setting up the government units usually is based on a foreign model, one delineating a governmental system in which slow and incremental political evolution has encouraged the informal political structures to perform in ways which not only complement each other's goals but also legitimate the actions of the legislative and executive agencies. In fact, the model most commonly followed is that of the United States, with some British and French touches. Whether in a given Latin American state the constitutionally imposed legal mechanisms be federal or unitary, presidential or parliamentary, the political norms enumerated by the basic law to determine their operations call for liberal, representative, and responsible government, in a word, for democracy.

In practice, Latin America's constitutions do not really define the full decisionmaking process, for in most states many of the traditionally oriented political structures—functional interest associations or political parties, for instance—long have acted quite independently of formal government. Historically, as long as important policy questions were settled mainly in the extralegal structures and merely affirmed constitutionally by the legal units, which at this time also were controlled by the ruling elites, few major difficulties arose. During this period the popular masses were too isolated and too ignorant to bring sustained political pressure, a situation complicated by the fact that not only the constitutional agencies but also the informal political structures and action patterns which delimit governmental functions had been formed under conditions in which large sections of the populace really were not considered part of the governmental apparatus. Today, with new political leaders representing challenging popular interests taking over the constitutional organs of government, the traditional elites dominating the established informal political structures discover not only that the interests they represent contradict those motivating the formal government's agencies but also that when applied literally the democratic norms enunciated by the fundamental law sharply restrict long-established, extralegal political action patterns.

If evolution toward mass political involvement could be carried to its logical conclusion, the traditional, informal action patterns necessarily would have to adjust to new conditions under pressure from popularly supported government decisions. Despite growing awareness on the part of the lower classes, reinforced by improving leadership representing mass interests, greater and more sustained popular political input is required if constitutional democratic norms are to be translated into effective legal controls over the established informal political structures. Unfortunately, to date the vast majority of citizens are not motivated to play an activist role in national politics. In political science jargon, they are "parochials," not really aware of the national polity, or "subjects," accustomed to accept the consequences upon their lives of central government policy decisions, rather than "participants" who share in the give-and-take that makes up the political process. This being the situation, the extralegal political structures and the legal government mechanisms probably will continue to operate in a conflicting rather than complementary manner.

The likelihood of resolving this difficulty is reduced because neither the traditional ruling elites nor the popular elements themselves tend to think in terms of positive political action by the lower classes. Members of the masses, often suspicious and fearful of government, usually are brought into national political life through co-optation of functional groups instead of as individuals practicing the concept of one man-one vote. The leaders of these specialized groups, whether traditional or challenging, generally act like conventional Latin American *patrones*, so that even the best intentioned reformers are less interested in what the masses want than in what they believe the masses should have. Because the average citizen relates politically to his primary reference group, playing a reciprocal role of subordinate to its paternalistic leader, the basic units for political confrontation and adjustment are not individuals or value neutral political parties but specific functional interest associations. Intergroup penetration or multiple memberships across class lines, which might encourage evolutionary adjustments between old and new interests, seldom occur.

This problem is exacerbated because many of the most important informal political mechanisms, established or challenging, do not adjust readily to new conditions, resulting in a kind of structural rigidity that seriously impedes their constructive participation in any effectively operating, general decisionmaking process. To a large degree such mechanisms perform less to unite disparate elements in the shifting environment than to encourage destructive competition that emphasizes and reinforces conflicting values in the political culture. In short, under the pressures of speedy and drastic change, internal inconsistencies in the policy-determination process make national integration impossible, causing instead what Huntington has termed "political decay."[1]

Faced with a situation in which constitutional formalism no longer provides a facade for advantageous informal decisionmaking, the older ruling elites have resorted to a variety of devices to maintain the ongoing system. One approach is constitutional tinkering, perhaps to weaken regionalism and enhance central authority, or to contain the influence of emerging political interests or the political movements which represent them. Capturing a preponderance of revenue sources for the national government, or failure to implement provisions for provincial consultative councils, are examples of this tactic; so is the outlawing of an *Aprista* or communist party because it has "international ties."

Another approach is to concentrate expanded national government authority in the president by legal fiat or even by executive decree, rather than to share power with the legislative bodies, in which disparate interests may capture an increasing number of seats, even a majority. Late in 1968, near the end of his term, outgoing President Carlos Lleras Restrepo forced through the Colombian congress a series of bills greatly strengthening the executive's authority over finances, public appointments, and other matters. During 1969 President Frei of Chile obtained extensive new power for his successor, power used effectively by President Allende in his economic and social reform program. During 1970, President Ve-

---

[1] See Samuel P. Huntington, *Political Order in Changing Societies* (New Haven, 1968). See also Huntington and C. H. Moore, *Authoritarian Politics in Modern Society: The Dynamics of Established One Party Systems* (New York, 1970). A selective bibliography of other works dealing with nation-building and its problems is included in K. W. Deutsch and W. J. Foltz, eds., *Nation-Building* (New York, 1963). Two of the many works dealing with change in Latin America are W. R. Duncan and J. N. Goodsell, eds., *The Quest for Change in Latin America; Sources for a Twentieth Century Analysis* (New York, 1971), and Douglass A. Chalmers, "Crisis and Change in Latin America," *Journal of International Affairs*, XXII, 1 (1969), pp. 76–88.

lasco Ibarra of Ecuador engineered a curious *golpe* against members of his own congress to expand the executive's powers when he was unable to win legislative approval for fiscal reform authority he deemed essential. Confronted with serious disruption and guerrilla activities, the presidents of Uruguay and Guatemala recently have assumed much more extensive personal authority, though with less than outstanding results. President Caldera of Venezuela has taken a like stance, with greater success, perhaps because the army backs his efforts.

In some cases the traditional elites' holding action may involve a formal coalition among the established political movements, as occurred during the 1950s when Colombia's Liberal and Conservative parties cooperated in amending the national constitution to set up a "National Front," under which the two parties divide equally between themselves all elective positions except the presidency, which they hold alternately. This approach was copied during 1971 by Honduras. Nonetheless, experience has demonstrated over the years that all these mechanistic, semilegal devices for expanding central government power and presidential authority to maintain unrepresentative political systems ultimately fail, because they do not resolve the problem of discontinuities in the decision-making process. As a consequence, the established ruling elites have turned to the armed forces to provide short-term authoritarian stabilization, with the tacit understanding that political power will be restored to civilian leaders after conditions become stabilized.

Resort to this unconstitutional intervention has proved a two-edged sword, affecting the political power of the vested interests as well as that of their challengers. Because repeated instances of breakdown in the civil government mechanisms have socialized the officer corps into the role of final moderating force in the politics of various countries, the military has assumed an expanded and more permanent responsibility for imposing compromise upon the contending elements and even, in a few cases, for attempting to organize a more broadly based civilian political movement that can provide the means of aggregating particularistic interests. Meanwhile, the armed services themselves act as such a mechanism, assuming power as a mobilizing-integrating military regime with strong overtones of nationalism and a peculiarly Latin version of paternalistic populism.

In a region encompassing twenty-odd states, it would be folly to predicate a single cause for any political phenomenon, or even to suggest one predominant influence over the political experience of different countries. During recent years, however, a kind of pattern has taken shape in a series of Latin American republics whose political systems are inundated by the tides of rapid change—Brazil, Argentina, Peru, Bolivia, Panamá, Ecuador, among others. One can even posit a like pattern in Mexico a half-century ago. Because of commonalities in historical background, in infrastructure organization, and in the nature of the difficulties arising out of technological development's side effects, the integration crisis confronting each of these states is rather similar, and so is the operation of the military regime that has appeared to resolve it. This is not to say that their style or their standard of performance is identical, for human and material resources in each country are different and the traditions of popular, responsible government even more distinct.

Significantly, in the Latin American states just mentioned, the military-dominated governments represent a new departure, for they are not the short duration, caretaker-type administrations of earlier days which imposed a temporary stabilization, only to turn back control to established civilian *políticos* after a few months. Neither are their leaders old-style military *caudillos*, the sort who looked to the presidency as the logical culmination of a military career, with the titles of President of the Republic and Commander-in-Chief as the highest officers' rank. This does not mean that every army general or air force colonel who participates in a new-style military regime is an unwilling victim of circumstances, sucked into the political vacuum left by an overwhelmed civilian administration. Many ambitious officers have been waiting in the wings, eager to move onto the national stage, but new conditions limit severely the possibility that a single strong man can exercise power very long and at the same time fix the direction in which any armed forces–dominated government must move.

Leadership in the mobilizing-integrating military regimes usually falls to a collective *junta* of officers representing the several services, individuals who respond to the imperatives of disruptive change by assuming power for a longer period, at times indefinitely, and by accepting responsibility for reordering government priorities in an effort to reorganize the society and economy to meet shifting demands. In doing so, the collective leadership mobilizes previously underrepresented popular elements, though it does not necessarily accord them immediate access to the input side of the policymaking process. The *junta* also attempts to force the established interests to compromise their demands with those of the new claimants, but with both sets of interests subordinate to the regime's interpretation of national goals. If the military does not succeed immediately in legitimatizing a single set of norms that all the disparate interests can accept as representing a unified national social and economic system, at least it can use its preponderance of physical force to "authenticate" a set of operating rules within which the competing factions must act.

To the degree that the new-style regimes do achieve compromise among disparate elements, they can be termed national integrating mechanisms, but in most cases it is not yet possible to offer any definitive judgment on the effectiveness of their mobilizing-integrating function. Perhaps only time can bring about an evolutionary shift in the deeply ingrained, divisive habit patterns which must be altered before the widespread value-sharing that produces an integrated polity can come into being. Recall that it is precisely the institutionalized nature of dividing factors throughout the region that leads to extraordinary attempts to change them.

This particular mobilizing-nationalizing function of Latin America's armed forces has become evident only in the fairly recent past as the consequences of technology reach out to stir the masses, in whom they engender a desire for popular participation that in turn sparks attempts to mold and channel expanding expectations. Most studies of the nondefense activities of the region's military were made in the 1950s and early 1960s, before the effects of mass communications, easy geographical mobility, and general education had made themselves felt so strongly. Therefore, historical analyses of even relatively recent civil-military relations may not offer a complete picture of the present role of the armed forces in Latin America's politics, though some of the latest studies have begun to shift toward a more inclusive and positive interpretation of the military's contribution.[2]

Genesis of the Integration Crisis

Problems of national integration are nothing new in world history. King Saul struggled with them in trying to unify the Hebrew tribes; so did Charlemagne when he set up his Frankish empire in the eighth century. The United States fought a bloody civil war to assure its continued existence as a national whole, and many present-day Asian and African leaders face the same dreary prospect. Nor has Latin America been immune from integration problems, though for a period it seemed that the worst of the region's nation-building problems might be resolved with the emergence of a series of independent states. In fact, during the first century of independence many geographic integration problems were solved by the breaking off of isolated entities and the formalization of national boundaries. But continuing economic regionalism in existing countries reflects failure to develop nationally oriented economies because of emphasis on export-dominated extractive mineral and plantation agricultural production. Additional barriers to easy so-

---

[2] Compare, for example, the differences in emphasis offered by these two groups of works. The first presents a traditional, essentially negative evaluation of armed-forces activities in politics: Victor Alba, *El Militarismo* (Mexico, 1959); Hans Daalder, *The Role of the Military in the Emerging Countries* (The Hague, 1962); Victor Villanueva, *Un Año Bajo el Sable* (Lima, 1963); José Luis de Imaz, *Los Que Mandan* (Buenos Aires, 1964); John J. Johnson, *The Military and Society in Latin America* (Palo Alto, 1964); Edwin Lieuwen, *Arms and Politics in Latin America* (New York, 1960) and *Generals vs. Presidents* (New York, 1964); Irving L. Horowitz, *Three Worlds of Development* (New York, 1966); Américo Ghioldi, *El Ejército y Política* (Buenos Aires, 1967). A significant change occurred between the original edition of Victor Villanueva's *El Militarismo en Perú* (Lima, 1962) and his *Nueva Mentalidad Militar en Perú* (Buenos Aires, 1969); the author's shift from outright condemnation of military government in his country to a somewhat less negative analysis suggests a transition toward the findings discussed in the second group of studies: Robert D. Putnam, "Toward Explaining Military Intervention in Latin America," *World Politics* (October, 1967), pp. 83–110; L. A. Costa Pinto, "Nacionalismo y Militarismo" (Mimeo., 1969); Douglass A. Chalmers, "Crisis and Change in Latin America," *Journal of International Affairs* (1969), pp. 76–88; Alfred Stepan, *The Military in Politics: Changing Patterns in Brazil* (Princeton, 1971); Harry Bienen, ed., *The Military and Modernization* (Chicago, 1971).

cial and political integration are raised by strongly held and intractable class and cultural differences.

Prior to independence, Latin America consisted of four Spanish vice-royalties and a major Portuguese colony. Soon afterward, Gran Colombia, the Central American union, upper and lower Peru, and a few other larger entities broke into separate states; only Brazil managed to maintain its territorial and political integrity fairly intact. Over the next seventy-five years various areas which sought to separate from existing countries did so—Texas and California, Ecuador, Uruguay—and those which had thought to do so but failed appeared reconciled—Charcas, Yucatán, Buenos Aires, and so on. Other domestic regional differences, in Colombia and Brazil, for example, did not much bother national leaders who were more concerned with external relations, perhaps because low levels of internal development meant that the subunits in most countries were neither very dependent on each other nor disruptive of the governing roles assumed by the central authorities. By the end of the nineteenth century, two final entities—Panamá and Cuba—became sovereign, and the twenty Latin states appeared to enjoy conditions which would permit evolution of a sense of national identity.

It would be naive to assert that Latin America's masses were blissfully happy in a premodern, pastoral Golden Age, but prior to the turn of the century the ruled as well as the rulers were relatively content, or at least innocently unaware. The first fruits of technology improved the lives of most citizens, and later, when difficulties multiplied, the symbol of foreign economic colonialism, identified mainly with "*Yanqui* imperialism," obscured the evils of internal colonialism, exploitation of the popular majorities by the region's ruling elites. A growing sense of nationalism which seemed to cut across regional, class, ethnic, and other divisive lines supplied a feeling of community that damped down the fires of resentment of the have-nots for the haves. During this period, therefore, with geographic boundaries reasonably secure, with few European political pressures because of distance and the built-in protection of the Monroe Doctrine, with a relatively passive population, the governing elites could deal confidently with the earliest challenges to their hegemony, maintaining the ongoing political system with little difficulty. But the seeds of the integration crisis already were planted.

About the time of World War I in the more advanced countries, and a few decades later in the others, some of the changes induced by the industrial revolution began to reach Latin America, but in this early stage the disruptions were minimal. The new individuals and interests which had to be absorbed by the national political process were small in number and concentrated in the middle sectors of the larger cities. In many cases increased national income reflecting more efficient, mechanized agriculture and expanding light industry permitted improvement in the economic status of the challenging middle class without unacceptable decline in that of the traditional elites. If members of the upper class did not welcome the emerging middle-sector participant citizens socially, new parties or ambitious individual spokesmen could appear to represent them politically. The Radical-type parties of Argentina, Uruguay, and Chile served this function, as did certain factions among the Liberals in Colombia, Venezuela, and other countries. Personalistic leaders without institutionalized parties to support them—Colonel Sánchez Cerro in Peru or Colonel Batista in Cuba during the 1930s, for example—also acted to expand middle-class influence. Some members of the new elite found a place in the traditional, functional interest organizations; others formed their own associations and worked out a modus vivendi with the existing groups.

Contrary to the European and North American historical experience, however, Latin America's political integration process did not continue much beyond the urban middle-middle sectors so as to include the newly aware, more popular masses, and middle-class dissidents helped provoke the resulting crisis. Over the years as the middle sectors moved into the national decisionmaking mechanism, a certain amount of political in-fighting took place, for sharing out of power did not always occur smoothly and emergent interests could not automatically be assured an acceptable or even a permanent role in the operation. Inability to satisfy all claimants had profound consequences in the region's politics, for it produced frustrated middle-class leaders to organize the emerging lower classes just at the time they were beginning to capture some formal role in the constitutional system as voters. Members of the newly enfranchized popular sectors soon discovered that their access to the full, national decisionmaking process was blocked because the ruling elites believed, probably correctly, that infusion of long pent-up mass demands would mean that there simply was not enough power, status, or material goods to go around without seriously disrupting the privileges of the establishment. Furthermore, the politically successful middle-class leaders who for tactical electoral reasons might have been expected to provide entrée for the popular elements into formal constitutional politics had first to consolidate the position of their own party *militantes*. Meanwhile, they preferred to retain real decisionmaking authority in the traditional informal political structures, whose unwillingness to compromise under the new conditions effectively thwarted the hopes of the mass challengers.

Precisely at this stage in Latin America's political development the inherent discontinuities in the region's political systems became manifest in the power struggles between the formal agencies of government and the traditional informal political structures. The breakdown in the pattern of incremental inclusion of new participants in the entire political process meant that the constitutional models on which the governmental systems were based had failed, because the representative, responsible, democratic norms they espoused could not be implemented. Increasingly knowledgeable urban masses and awakening rural citizens knew that voting, capturing control of congress, even electing a president who purported to speak in their name, had little real effect on public policy if the major decisions were made elsewhere, in the "private governments," as we shall term them presently. Here it is that the dissident middle-class elements came into their own, providing the leadership that has provoked the present-day national integration crisis.

In any given country, the dislocations to the political system caused by integrating the relatively limited middle sectors into national life and politics depended upon a variety of factors—for example, availability and ease of exploitation of natural resources, amount and nature of penetration by foreign social, economic, and ideological influences, size and quality of the middle class and of the general population. Similarly, the kind of disruption evoked by demands for access to the full decisionmaking process by the awakening popular masses depended not only on the speedy economic growth potential of the particular state but also upon the rigidity of attitudes found in the upper- and middle-sector citizens who made up the traditional, informal political structures.

In Mexico during the first years of this century demonstration effect from the United States reinforced the domestic social and economic consequences of massive foreign investment; in the resulting unstable situation, President Díaz's refusal to permit emerging middle-class interests to play effective political roles set off an early revolt. This Revolution of 1910 so undermined the dominance of the traditional elites that new, more open middle-sector political structures appeared, operating under the aegis of an army-backed "Revolutionary party" that also implemented reformist concepts of greater material benefits for the popular elements. A rapidly expanding economy that permitted a constantly improving standard of living for most members of the lower-middle and the lower classes delayed for many years the political participation crisis that has bobbed up sporadically since 1965 because in the present Mexican political system the popular masses have little direct access to the policy-deciding process.

The Chilean case is much the opposite; isolation from major currents of world thought, together with economic advantages growing out of large mineral reserves and easily exploited nitrate deposits obtained during the War of the Pacific, enabled a relatively large upper and middle class to manipulate urban workers and freeze the rural majorities out of meaningful participation in the country's affairs until very late. By the time any real effort was made to face up to the need for national integration, mass awareness of social and economic inequities was so great and popular frustration so strong that the constitutional government agencies were voted a mandate to impose basic structural reform. The pressures for change so dominated public concern that when relatively drastic but incremental steps taken by President Frei's Christian Democratic party were slowed down and partially blocked by established interests, President Allende's Marxists were voted into power late in 1970. Despite serious economic dislocations caused by capital and management flight and illegal seizures of agricultural lands, evidence suggests that popular support for Allende's regime continues strong.

In most other Latin American republics experiencing the effects of technical change no true revolutionary situation has occurred to break up the traditional political infrastructures in such a way that an evolutionary national integration process can take place. In both Bolivia and Cuba, for instance, most members of the established elite, together with many of the technically trained, middle-class citizens who had serviced the traditional ruling group, elected to leave the country. Elsewhere, many persons in the urban middle sectors are involved in the ongoing political system but most of the structures representing such interests have had little opportunity to mature before demands for access from the popular masses challenge them.

These new claims descend at an inopportune time, because not only are new, middle-class participants entering the decisionmaking process but the very changes which brought them into being also make the limited range of policy options open to the ruling groups less adequate. With development, both society and economy become more complex, so even the long-established elites and their interests no longer are quite so monolithic. Interests which once enjoyed a dominant role in (or exception from the consequences of) the decisionmaking process have fragmented with the increasing functional specialization that accompanies development, producing a multitude of competing groups made up of establishment members who understand the national policymaking process and have access to it. In this sort of situation, even the influential and well connected can believe that government is no longer as responsive to their needs as in earlier days and therefore become more rigid about admitting additional, lower-class mass participants into the decisionmaking circle. We already have seen that neither economic growth nor social adaptability have been sufficiently great in most parts of the region to allow full popular participation in the national life and wealth without serious financial loss and psychic threat to the existing dominant elites.

This does not mean that no sense of moral responsibility to bring the general citizenry into the mainstream of national life exists, or that certain civilian and military strong men have not attempted to mobilize mass supporters over the years. We need merely recall the Brazilian *tenentes* rebellion and the long march during the 1920s, the so-called Communist peasant rebellion of 1930 in El Salvador, the short-lived Socialist Republic of Colonel Marmaduke Grove in Chile during 1931, or Colonel Toro's 1936 Bolivian Socialist Republic, followed a year later by Colonel Busch and his leftist government, not to mention General Lázaro Cárdenas's efforts to popularize Mexico's revolutionary regime at about the same time. A somewhat similar pattern emerged in Brazil with Getulio Vargas and his *Estado Novo* during this period and, a few years later, in the activities of the *Apra*-style political parties of Peru, Bolivia, Venezuela, and Costa Rica. In certain situations strong men took over in the name of the people, only to be ousted by a regrouped establishment; Arévelo and Árbenz in pre-1954 Guatemala are a case in point. In other situations a leader assumed authority in the name of law and order, only to broaden his power base by seeking popular support against the traditional interests, which in turn acted to oust him. General Perón in Argentina, with his *descamisados*, General Rojas Pinilla in Colombia, and General Odría in Peru come to mind, for each adopted Latin America's special brand of personalistic, demogogic, but essentially politically nonparticipant "populism."

In spite of their popularizing tendencies, or perhaps because their populism represented the region's deep-rooted, *patrón*-client relationship, many such leaders who remained in office any appreciable time turned their regimes toward old-line dictatorships—Batista, Vargas, Perón, Odría, Rojas Pinilla, among others. It is my contention that new conditions resulting from technologically induced change make a repetition of this pattern today much less likely, for the *caudillo*-style leader is not much in vogue in the more advanced states.

Some of the popularistic leaders of the 1930s, 1940s, and 1950s undoubtedly believed sincerely that they could assimilate the general citizenry into their country's life and politics by simple fiat.

Others were merely opportunists utilizing the inchoate dreams of half-aware peoples to shore up the individual *politico*'s personal position in a power struggle with potential rivals allied with the established elements. In either case, few of their actions really served to integrate the general populace into the ongoing national political system on a permanent basis. At best, such efforts represented a kind of symbolic populism that justified bringing small groups of urban lower-middle-class and upper-lower-class citizens (organized urban labor, for instance) into alliance with ambitious middle-sector politicians, usually not so much at the expense of the established elites as at the cost of advances for the unorganized urban and rural masses. At worst, these abortive moves to construct a broader power base reflect a cynical manipulation for personal political aggrandizement of unprepared persons and groups lacking enough social experience, economic skill, or political knowledge to compete effectively in the national arena.

The apparent vacillations of leaders who spoke of bringing new elements into politics may well reflect their opportunism, or a lack of any real motivation for involving the popular sectors, no matter what their rhetoric promised. Or, where a leader was sincere, failure to follow through to institutionalize more general political participation may represent a correct assessment of the difficulties involved, based on sad experience. Despite the ideological trappings in their public statements such leaders usually were quite pragmatic in practice, so when political events demonstrated the instability of the mass power base they sought to construct they abandoned it or put use of it into temporary abeyance. The hard fact is that at this stage in Latin America's development the lower classes, especially in the countryside, were insufficiently mobilized, physically or psychologically, to provide continuous, effective political support against the numerically smaller but more knowledgeable and strategically located urban ruling groups and their rural elite allies. Activating the masses in support of a personalistic political leader and his program is a very different thing from mobilizing them for continuing, institutionalized politics based upon popular initiative.

Additionally, despite the army background of many earlier popularizers, the military often acted as a barrier to their ambitions. During this period accumulated popular demands had not yet become so critical that the officer corps as an entity accepted the necessity of saddling the armed forces with a long-term moderating role in national politics. Important military elements continued to support the concept of civilian, constitutional government, or identified with the interests of the traditional elites who still dominated the decisionmaking process. Further, neither army nor civilian reformers were yet able to recruit sufficient technically trained personnel to operate a viable, nationally representative regime because they could not capture cooperation from at least a sizable minority of the skilled manpower, which at this time was allied almost entirely with the older ruling sectors. Preforce, potential popularizers recognized that members of the armed forces as such lacked the kinds of formal preparation required to administer a complex government and economy. For evidence of this fact during the 1950s, for example, they had only to consider the failures of the strong-man regimes of Generals Perón, Rojas Pinilla, and Odría, which had heaped humiliation on the military as a whole.

By the mid-1960s a new set of conditions reigned. Technology had so speeded up change that in the more developed countries the acute problems identified with the present-day national integration crisis appeared. Especially in the cities, the popular masses are aware of their potential role in national life and better able to sustain their pressures upon society for more meaningful participation in the entire governmental policy-determining process. Their struggle is abetted by the rapidly expanding disaffected portion of the established middle sector that can provide leadership. Disquiet resulting from unrequited popular needs and aspirations in a rapidly changing environment has built up steadily over the years until the cumulative effects of growth, accelerated drastically by foreign aid programs, have produced serious adjustment crises. Massive raw demands so disrupt the social and economic systems that the existing political structures are strained beyond their capacity to handle the conflicting claims.

As the character of the general population alters from predominantly rural and isolated to partly integrated and urban, with 30 percent or more of a country's inhabitants in cities and with ideas beginning to filter out to the towns and villages, shifts in the kinds, amounts, and intensity of demands on government occur. Both totally and proportionately more people leave subsistance agriculture and sharecropping to become part of the money economy in the city, or outside it as members of the rural proletariat and participants in commercial or market agriculture operations. To such persons, what happens in national politics is important, and the kinds of government programs they will condone change drastically.

In the past, the major mass-based interests—agricultural peons, small farmers, organized laborers, and the multitude of unskilled workers—were served (if at all) by government acting as a *patrón*. That is, the ruling elites considered policy or made and enforced laws less in response to the expressed needs of the common man or to the collective political pressure of a given popular interest group than out of a sense of moral responsibility or to anticipate and avoid political repercussions and violence. Consequently, much of what government provided either was symbolic—a land-reform law that was not implemented, for instance—or not so much what the masses wanted as what government leaders felt they should have. Now, as the general populace becomes more knowledgeable, this sort of government activity does not satisfy them, especially if the formal governing agencies do not exercise effective restraints over long-established and highly influential specialized interest groupings (private governments) with which the emerging masses must deal.

Inevitably, then, public authorities are called upon to exercise a greater degree of control, not only over those sectors of the populace they traditionally were accustomed to dominate but, necessarily, also over citizens and interests which previously were not considered subject to much limitation. With new expectations growing faster than the economy's ability to expand production or the willingness of established elites to share their political and social roles with the emerging masses, neither the existing power group nor the spokesmen for challenging popular interests can be satisfied. So both sets of citizens begin to question the legitimacy of civil government.

This challenge to constitutionalism comes at a time when the governmental system is particularly vulnerable, just as the communications revolution combines with vastly expanded formal education to encourage mass participation in the national life and political process, forcing government to consider popular needs. This occurs simultaneously with movement of large numbers of persons to the cities, where they can make their increasing ability to exert pressure felt most easily. Furthermore, the entire situation is exacerbated by the unintended by-products of modernization—the population explosion, breakdowns in constructive social relations, unemployment, and all the rest.

Significantly, this negative impact of development on the traditional political system has increased intolerably because of unanticipated side effects of the entire United Nations-United States foreign-aid pattern, particularly the Alliance for Progress.[3] In the case of the alliance, for one example, a program of capital investment to encourage expansion of primary production facilities was replaced by one of financial support for infrastructure and service activities which markedly speed up change and public awareness—communications, transport, education. The consequences of failure to expand basic production instruments were hidden for some little time through the practice of spending alliance funds to satisfy consumer desires, supplying such nonself-replenishing items as food, manufactured goods, some raw materials, and the like. Such policies have a double negative effect. Obviously, popular living standards and expectations are pegged at artificially high, noneconomic levels. Less obviously, but much more important from the standpoint of this study, such palliative measures allow all concerned to ignore the negative implications for the development of a viable, national decisionmaking mechanism which are inherent in the spectacle of two competing sets of rapidly expanding "nonnegotiable demands" pursuing a collision course. By supplying resources which ease temporarily the gradually growing pressures on the political system caused by mushrooming popular demands, this kind of foreign aid permits both legal and extralegal structures to continue operating

---

[3] An enlightening commentary on the alliance and its problems can be found in Jerome Levinson and Juan de Onís, *The Alliance that Lost Its Way; A Critical Report on the Alliance for Progress* (Chicago, 1970).

with uncompromising rigidity to accomplish mutually incompatible ends, until claims on the system reach unmanageable proportions. Instead of encouraging relatively peaceful, incremental involvement of spokesmen for mass interests in the operations of traditionally oriented, functional interest groups or, conversely, requiring the governmental agencies to temper their assignment of popular benefits with some regard for the limitations of the national economy, the external assistance program allows both groups to put off the painful adjustments until too late. When the moment of truth arrives, after the general citizenry has used its new knowledge and awareness to impose through the legal organs of government wholly unacceptable demands on the established informal structures, neither side has the time nor the flexibility required to allow it to evolve new attitudes of compromise to resolve the confrontation. The incompatible inconsistencies built into most Latin American countries' political processes surface, and the national integration crisis is a reality.

For all the well-intentioned desire of their architects to foster stable civil government, these disruptive consequences of foreign-aid programs may have contributed to the emergence of new-style military regimes. Over the years, officers in the armed forces saw substantial financial aid or material resources offered under assistance agreements diverted to these less than basic developmental ends, from their viewpoint subverted for venal political reasons. Given their deeply ingrained sense of national purpose, military leaders may have been tempted to assume governing responsibility in order to apply the state's resources to more permanent and practical purposes.

Somewhat similar attitudes can be attributed to a growing number of middle-sector civilians, professionally or technically trained individuals who are products of the region's expanding educational systems. Lately, many university graduates encounter difficulties in obtaining adequate employment in their specialties, and those who do find work discover that unrelenting inflation strikes hardest at fixed salary professionals. Both groups may lose faith in civil government, which they hold responsible for their precarious economic situation, especially in light of constraints upon reform imposed by the established elites who dominate the society and economy, constraints which these *técnicos* see as frustrating their ability to do all they believe necessary to help resolve their country's problems. More about this group of civilian technocrats later, for they have become junior members in a coalition with the organizers of the new-style military regimes, providing some of the technical and administrative skills which were lacking in earlier authoritarian stabilization and strong-man–type governments.

The rather sudden clogging of the on-going political system with massive demands has faced Latin American states with a difficult dilemma. On the one hand, the process of national integration must go on to include greater consideration of popular interests because technology and its consequences continue inexorably, with demonstration effect in the form of radio, films, television, and physical mobility in and out of larger cities, making all too obvious the differences between the wealthy few and the poverty stricken many. On the other hand, most Latin American civil governments have been unable to satisfy the conflicting demands facing them because traditional elites and challenging interests each seem to believe that the dislocations plaguing the political system are temporary and soon to be resolved in their particular favor.

If discontinuities in the political process are attributed accurately to temporary factors, in at least several countries the disruptive pattern should be breaking by now. Instead, observers who see recent political difficulties as due mainly to the activities of radical agitators confront an unpleasant reality. The deaths of Father Camilo Torres in Colombia, or of "Che" Guevara in Bolivia, the exile of a few extremists from Argentina or Brazil, and Fidel Castro's decision to concentrate his revolutionary energies on Cuba's internal development should have resulted in a cooling down of politics throughout the continent. On the contrary, during the late 1960s and early 1970s Latin America's political waters were boiling. Violence that once confined itself to lower-class brawls spilled over into the upper sectors of the most advanced countries, with politically inspired bombings, bank robberies, kidnappings, and murders of foreign diplomats, national government officials, businessmen, and even church prelates. In many cases it is impossible to determine whether government repression of extreme reform movements sparked this violence or whether the violence led to government retaliation, but now each fuels the other.

Those analysts who see the present political troubles as nothing more than a lag in adjustment of the political system to overly fast changes in the environment are faced with an equally hard fact. Though much of the political militancy mentioned just above can be assigned fairly to the activities of small groups of disgruntled middle- and upper-class youths, the most impressive pressures upon civil government reflect a much more broadly based and popular insistence on an opening up of the political process to allow greater representation for the newer, more popular interests which find themselves frozen out of effective participation in the political decisionmaking process.

In countries like Argentina and Brazil, and probably even Peru, during the 1950s and 1960s claims on civil government for effective political participation in public policy decisions were pressed through the ballot box and sometimes through anomic violence, with unimpressive results.[4] Clearly this failure to achieve access to the real decisionmaking process was not simply a matter of lagging adjustment in a viable constitutional system so much as a consequence of built-in disparities in the political process between the informal political structures which initiate claims and the constitutional agencies which must legalize and promulgate them. Apparently civilian constitutional government in such countries is not always strong enough to impose a common set of norms on all the competing elements in order to manage conflict in an increasingly complex environment, leading inexorably to the crisis of national integration.

Why this is so may become clearer if we review the nature and

[4] For extended consideration of the use of force in Latin America's politics, see Francisco José Moreno and Barbara Mitrani, eds., *Conflict and Violence in Latin American Politics; A Book of Readings* (New York, 1971). One of the more intriguing aspects of the region's political culture is the relative absence of mass violence in national political movements despite widespread use of force and personal violence among individuals in most countries. One insightful study on the subject is Richard S. Weinhert, "Violence in Pre-Modern Societies; Rural Colombia," *American Political Science Review*, LX, 2 (June, 1966), pp. 340–347.

operations of Latin America's political parties, voluntary associations, functional interest groups, and some other informal units making up the infrastructure that supplements the activities of formal governmental agencies.

Political Infrastructure Problems

Latin America's experience demonstrates that constitutionally bound reform governments face almost insuperable obstacles in their attempts to implement the changes required to integrate a rapidly modernizing country. Winning elections to dominate congress, to capture the presidency, and, ultimately, to take over the civil bureaucracy does not really mean full control of the decision-making function if important aspects of policy input occur elsewhere, outside the legal agencies and even apart from some of the extraconstitutional mechanisms which make up the central political structures. When a reform-bent president finally captures office—Belaúnde in Peru during the 1960s or Allende in Chile during the 1970s, for just two examples—he usually is politically astute enough to recognize that he must extend his actions beyond the legal organs of government. He tries to capture the existing functional interest associations, neutralize those he cannot dominate, and set up new ones where necessary and possible, attaching them to his political party if he has one.

To the extent that he imposes his authority over the principal power groupings in the political environment, a president can hope to rationalize their activities, to balance the competing demands of old and new, rich and poor, haves and have nots. To the extent that he fails to dominate the disparate factors in the political equation, his reform endeavors will fail. Unfortunately, in Latin America the number of contending elements is so large, their differences so marked, and their claims so insatiable, considering available resources, that a president may be unable to extend his moderating influence over them adequately within the limitations established by the constitution. And if this is the case in trying to impose some shared norms to order the actions of formally organized functional associations—labor unions, farmers' organizations, industrialists' or bankers' committees, mining syndicates, commercial societies, or business associations—it is infinitely more so in trying to reach down to informal groupings which are little more than patterns of action based on subliminal values and the activities they generate. That is what President Belaúnde discovered in Peru and what President Allende is testing in Chile at present.

In general terms, this suggests that the legal organs of government operate effectively to resolve conflict through the political decision-making process only to the extent that the informal mechanisms forming the political infrastructure work to complement their activities. It also suggests that the political infrastructures do not operate in a vacuum but as integral parts of the society around them. To the degree that Latin America's societies are fragmented, that the interests of the component groups making up the infrastructures are irreconcilable, or that the activities of major sectors of the society and economy feel exempt from the jurisdiction of the central policymaking structures, constitutional governments have neither the political influence nor the physical force required to meet the crises of change. This seems to be the case in many states throughout the region.

Regarding the general environment, we should recognize that most Latin American states do not have a pluralistic society in the North American sense. Obviously, many have a dual society, with members of marginal groups unable to share in the national money economy or participate effectively in public affairs. But such states have a splintered society as well, for at the national level social and economic forces are many, competitive, and unyielding; in governmental terms, this means that even those interests which have penetrated the bastions of national power operate in a political system where many influential sectors do not recognize the central political structures as wholly legitimate or entitled to regulate their activities. Competing groups do not subordinate themselves to a continuous and self-regulating mechanism for resolving conflict by balancing divergent interests and effecting compromise, because neither acting alone nor in combination do the formal governmental agencies or the extraconstitutional political structures provide any collective working device for "authoritatively allocating values." As Silvert has termed it, Latin America has a conflict society.

No one who has analyzed the region's problems doubts the fact that in most cases a great deal more significant change has taken place in social and economic structures than in political institutions, which seem frozen in the traditional mold. Similarly, the explosion of human and material needs has not been accompanied by any concomitant increase in interaction and dependency among the many groups involved, contacts which might bridge regional, class, or economic differences. These factors alone would strain the operations of a political system, but in many Latin American countries their negative influence is abetted by the built-in structural defects in the informal political mechanisms already mentioned.

It is difficult to absorb a large number of new elements into an ongoing political system simultaneously, but harder still if most of the previous participants are not entirely agreed upon values or the rules of the game, other than a kind of extreme laissez-faire arrangement in which every interest does much as it wishes, battling over differences whenever and wherever it pleases with little concern for anyone else. This pattern of subsystem autonomy is legitimized in the Latin American states because in addition to democratic tenets the constitutions carry over a nineteenth-century, Manchestrian "liberal" conception of political values that maximizes individual and interest-group freedom regardless of consequences for the general welfare.

In the foreign governmental systems based on the prototype constitutions from which the Latin American documents were adapted this tendency toward irresponsible particularism has been counterbalanced by the evolution of broadly based, ancillary aggregating mechanisms which tend to hold the political system together and force compromise among competing interests. Here a self-regulating party system and integrating functional interest associations, supplemented by widely shared social norms and an internally oriented, highly interdependent national economic system, permit a high degree of pluralistic latitude for the actions of the various social, economic, and political entities which make up the national community.

Because in Latin America such informal, auxiliary integrating mechanisms did not evolve, as the expectations of the awakening masses come more and more into conflict with the claims of the traditional ruling sectors the authority of a constitutional president to control the activities of the competing factions has become largely a myth. During an earlier era, when complexity of life was not so great and the range of demands not so far beyond the capacity of the economy and society to satisfy, a civilian executive might use his prestige of office or, more likely, his personal influence to act as a moderating power in major disputes. In fact, the Brazilian constitution of 1824 formally assigned this responsibility to the Emperor, and he used it. So did the presidents of Spanish American states as long as they could.

One might argue that the Latin American president's moderating function is not unlike that of the first royal Georges in eighteenth-century England, when increasing specialization in the nation's affairs produced the Tories and the Whigs as distinct political movements but before a common set of political values had developed. But important differences exist. Unlike the kings who could be above faction and party, the Latin American president almost always represents some combination of specialized interests, be they elite or popular, for the region's political movements and their leaders reflect the deep divisions fragmenting each country. Without the pressures of overfast change and with more flexible, informal political infrastructures, the British had both time and temperament to evolve into a nation. As the English political system developed, the control functions of government expanded and the particularistic activities of individuals or private entities (the East India Company, for example) were sharply curtailed. Furthermore, the two-party system grew up as an extraconstitutional, conflict-regulating device whose legitimacy most interests accepted because they found the party system responsive to their needs and reasonably neutral in their disputes, but particularly because working in conjunction with the legal government it had sufficient power to impose its decisions.

Although social and economic growth long since have called for some such change in Latin America, no analogous development of ancillary political control devices which complement the constitutional organs has occurred. Despite an Iberian tradition of strong government (that in Latin America was implemented most vigorously against individuals from the lower classes) and despite the fact that state or mixed (shared public- and private-sector control) corporations carry on many of the most important and dynamic economic functions, most civil administrations are too weak to resolve national integration problems legally. With the limited constitutional authority available to them and the dispersed political influence they yield, few presidents have been able to expand public power over the divisive activities of the more influential citizens and interest groups, traditional or challenging.

Such conditions may have been barely tolerable in years gone by, when particularistic actions did not affect life so overwhelmingly and when the masses were not participating and aware, but the world has turned. As people come into closer contact physically and intellectually, as social problems multiply, as growing economic involvement affects the well-being of more persons, the need for some sort of national integrating political mechanism becomes patent so that the activities of uncontrolled and politically immune private interests may not impinge on the rights and desires of the whole community. That such a mechanism has not yet appeared tells us much about the uncompromising rigidity of the social and political substructures out of which it would have to evolve.

We already have recognized that the time-demand factor complicates movement toward a more generally inclusive political system because the number of disparate demands injected into the social-political process in an extremely limited space of time overloads the evolutionary process. But other systems have faced this problem and solved it. If all portions of Latin America's populace who should participate in the central political system are not involved equally in the partially effective national political structure that performs the centralizing compromise function, it is because the interest groups to which they belong have been unable to shift from particularistic to more universalistic norms. As Talcott Parsons suggests, a people moving toward modernity become more interdependent; they begin to share common values and agree more easily upon methods for attaining general goals. Operationally, this leads to a pluralistic society with increasing social and economic mobilization which in time produces political mobilization; the resulting political interaction in turn leads to development of a centralizing mechanism for controlling disfunctional activities of specific groups by enforcing compromise. To date, most Latin societies have not moved very far down the road from particularism toward universality.

The most obvious reason might be that the particularistic attitudes of the ruling elites crystallized before the generalizing effects of modernization made themselves felt. Now, as earlier, few members of the traditional power groups conduct themselves as though they feel they are part of a general whole for which they should sublimate their personal interests. Not surprisingly, leaders of the challenging groups follow the established particularistic models, so representatives of both the old and the new factions act to sabotage the operations of the national, political balancing structure. But this really is only a partial explanation, more a consequence than a cause.

Basically, particularism is almost endemic in the Latin approach to life. The countries of the region share a strong tradition of corporativism that carried over from the Iberian peninsula, where medieval social and religious concepts remained influential during the colonial era. As we shall see, the tendency to operate through functional groupings transfers from social and economic activities into political operations, even into political party organization.

The extreme individualism characteristic of many Latins is the opposite side of the same coin. Just as the member of a given functional entity strives to maximize its advantages against all other interests, so does the individual who by accident or by design discovers an opportunity to improve his personal position. Even at great cost to other members of his own group, he becomes for this purpose a "majority of one." Nonetheless, taken collectively these views reinforce the group's particularistic outlook.

The effect of these deeply held particularistic attitudes upon the national political system is highly divisive. Insofar as possible, those traditional interests which have managed through long usage to legitimize their autonomy from government and the central political structures as "private governments" attempt to protect their independent status.[5] Others refuse to recognize the priority of national concerns over more immediate regional interests. Some emerging groups still are too unsophisticated politically to participate in the entire policymaking process because they do not yet understand it. They fail to provide input into decisionmaking by engaging in the political maneuvers which help delimit public policy *before* it becomes law; rather they react on the output side after implementation of governmental decisions affect them. Still others feel that the costs—material or psychological—of submitting to the central compromising mechanism may be too high, especially if effective sanctions to enforce compliance are not available. Finally, some sectors of the population who are politically mobilized and who do play a commensurate role in decisionmaking believe that they do not enjoy fair access to the real political process. This last is more a status than a material benefit problem, but it does contribute to weakening legitimacy for the central balancing function.

---

[5] I have used the term "private governments" elsewhere to describe nongovernmental, private structures of power which act to order the activities of specific economic and social interests in the absence of effective central-constitutional government controls. These structures usually exercise dual authority—internal insofar as they mobilize, organize, and police their own members and external insofar as they act to protect their members from actions of the national policymaking mechanism. Generally they are peak associations of long-established functional interest groups—large landholders societies, chambers of commerce, industrial chambers, and other entities representing what might be termed the *fuerzas económicas vivas*, but for practical purposes we might include the Roman Catholic church and the military. Because historically they have been semiautonomous, sometimes even semiofficial, the private governments have a strong tradition of independence in action that permits them to operate in isolation from the national integrating mechanism. In this sense they are fortresses of particularism. See my article, "Political Elites and Political Modernization; the Crisis of Transition," in S. M. Lipset and Aldo Solari, eds., *Elites in Latin America* (New York, 1967), esp. pp. 137ff.

None of these groupings relate wholeheartedly to the national political process, perhaps because they do not relate very effectively to each other.

Before the disparate parts of a fragmented society can be transformed from a hoard of battling semiautonomous entities into a group of cooperating subunits of an integrated, national political system, they must discover enough in common—personal contacts, shared experiences, complementarity of economic interest, a sense of nationhood—to counteract the personal and cultural differences and leaven the sometimes vicious competition for scarce resources that inevitably disrupts the decisionmaking process. They must have more to gain than they have to lose, emotionally as well as materially. Considering the speed of change, the impact with which very different peoples are brought into sudden confrontation with each other, not to mention the relative poverty of so many Latin American countries, the problem of inadequate interaction among people and minimal interdependence between interest groups scarcely comes as a surprise. This inability to relate is reinforced by personal character traits, the tendency toward mistrust, suspicion, envy, and recourse to personal violence mentioned so frequently by observers of Latin American phenomena and detailed by the region's psychologists.

Lack of interaction among the popular masses is underscored if we note that for all the multiplicity of new groupings, very few upward mobile individuals have cross-cutting organizational memberships, either in groups representing their own class or in those linking several social levels. Members of the established elites, on the other hand, do have more multiple memberships in uppersector social and economic bodies, perhaps because they have enough in common to encourage this sort of relationship within the advantaged sector. For the average lower-class person the most salient reference group is a functionally specialized unit—a labor union or farmers' organization, a small shopkeepers' association or a marketing cooperative—rather than several organizations with competing goals or even a few with multiple or overlapping ends.

This tendency in the vast majority of citizens toward functional isolation interferes with the process of extending shared values, especially because it has prevented development of one potential, informal centralizing mechanism that has worked effectively in other modernizing countries—the value-neutral national political party and the integrating political party system it produces. Latin America's political parties are creatures of their fractured environment, so in most parts of the region they are organized to impede rather than encourage interaction among individuals or mutual dependency among groups. Even the so-called mass-oriented party recruits more of its members on an associational basis than as individuals; most citizens do not join such a party but are co-opted into it when their primary reference group enters into a kind of confederal relationship with the political movement for mutual advantage of the two units. Unless it is an established private government so completely independent of the central legal-political structures that for all practical purposes it is immune from governmental intervention, every interest organization binds itself into a vassal-like relationship with one or another political party. Because few if any of the region's parties are really national, value neutral, brokerage-type mechanisms, this kind of relationship with functional associations reinforces class, regional, and other particularistic divisions rather than reducing them.

Even if those private governments which operate virtually outside the nationalizing political structures and in semiautonomy from the elected public officials could be brought more effectively under the discipline of the central policymaking system, their component members might not be much affected. The private governments are peak associations of organizations whose domestic membership is deeply ensconced in the traditional upper-class social and economic life of the country and whose foreign constituents represent relatively small, local branches of huge and highly influential international corporations domiciled in another, more developed nation.

Despite their appearance as units of corporate capitalism, the economic version of the nationally oriented organizations (which lean toward light industry, commercial enterprise, and market agriculture producing sugar, cotton, or other basic commodities for export) generally are family firms with few outside shareholders.

Here personal or family arrangements minimize the need for recourse to legal controls over internal organization or for reliance on outside sources for funding. The general public has long been accustomed to the kinds of activities such firms engage in, so little direct participation on the input side of governmental decision-making is required to protect a privileged position. The noneconomic, functionally specialized domestic groups—say the church or the army—have their own methods of defending recognized status. For their part, the international entities (often involved in mining, petroleum production, or other capital-intensive or technically complex activities) may be so rich, so strongly supported diplomatically by their home country, and play so vital a role in the host state's economy that they are nearly independent of central government control.

One indicator of the semiautonomous status of private governments and their components is the paucity of practicing *políticos* recruited from these groups. Apparently until very recently private governments did not need to place spokesmen in public office in order to protect their position. This does not mean that no members of the establishment attain political prominence. President Grau San Martin of Cuba was a prominent physician, as is President Allende of Chile; Guyana's Cheddi Jagan is a dentist and former President Belaúnde of Peru an architect, and the role of the ubiquitous lawyer in Latin America's politics is legendary. The individualistic and applied nature of such occupations, often dependent upon changes in public policy, tends to make these professionals "public men," just as those who operate from the cloistered meeting rooms of private governments or functional associations are "private men."

Albert Hirschman offers an astute variation on this theme. "The poorer sections of the country, where careers in industry and trade are not promising, often produce, for this reason, a majority of the country's successful politicians."[6] Add to his point another possibility, that able citizens from any part of the country may pursue politics or enter government as bureaucrats because they find their

[6] Albert Hirschman, *The Strategy of Economic Development* (New Haven, 1958), pp. 185–186.

path to success blocked in many important private social and economic spheres by family ties or foreign influence. This frustrating situation suggests one practical reason for potential middle-class support for any national integrating mechanism, including a military regime, that can end the isolation of the private governments. One also finds here the group from which most of the armed services' new technocratic allies are recruited.

All these factors explain why it is so difficult to evolve some sort of pluralist society with a viable compromise mechanism in Latin America's national political systems. Too high a proportion of the most influential socioeconomic structures are not formally organized, functional interest associations whose individual participants share multiple memberships in a variety of organizations. Instead, the basic structures are primary groupings based on informal relationships, kinship, personal contact, regional affiliations, or the like. Even the more structured peak associations—commercial, industrial, agricultural, and extractive units, not to mention social cliques—cannot be held fully responsible to any central control mechanism because their component parts are not easily subject to legal pressures, particularly considering the limitations found in the Manchestrian norms permeating most countries' constitutions. These conditions provide a kind of defense in depth against any civil government's attempt to break through time-hallowed practices to bring groupings whose activities can effect the daily lives of thousands of people into a single decisionmaking process for the public good.

These observations are not intended as a blanket indictment of Latin Americans for failing to place themselves under the aegis of a central conflict resolution mechanism. What is rational from the viewpoint of a statesman trying to unify his country by bringing disparate and competing interests under the control of a national political system may not be so rational to those established sectors whose members benefit from a centrifugal political power pattern or whose leaders do not trust the integrity of the center-oriented control device. One's attitude about national integration depends on his primary values, and in a traditionally fractured environment competing values are at work—regional against national, spiritual against material, and individual interest against general welfare. If no effective central political structures exist, the individual must think and act particularistically to defend his specialized interest, because nobody else can or will. Abrogating such interest in favor of a voluntary political integrating mechanism that offers neither sanctions for refusal nor rewards for consent makes little sense.

If a truly national life is to evolve, the nationalizing process must begin, but under present conditions in most Latin American countries it is hard to conceive of individuals or of groups voluntarily adjusting parochial and particularistic values to new, more generalized outlooks. Either this sort of change will flow automatically because a new set of conditions emerges to make it self-starting or some agency which is strong enough to perform the function must impose a unifying criterion.

At one time it seemed that Latin America's political parties might evolve a system that could perform the national integrating function so adequately that a majority of citizens would be convinced or perhaps forced to temper their specialized viewpoints. Experience and the hard facts of political life belie that hope.[7] We already have noted that when the earliest effects of modernization made themselves felt a number of popularizing parties developed to represent the interests of the urban middle sectors, but that they were unable to take the next giant step toward involving the urban and rural masses. This failure to broaden the membership base resulted partly because of a need to concentrate energies on servicing middle-class constituents in environments where there simply were not enough benefits to go around, but also because such parties could not recruit many individual members from the isolated and politically inert lower classes.

Since then, as development has affected more of the population,

[7] A few years ago I suggested that some such unifying mechanism as a national integrating party system had to evolve if Latin America's civil political development was to continue smoothly. Events since then show that this kind of system has not materialized. Hence the present study of another, military integrating mechanism. See my article, "Political Parties and Policy-Making in Latin America," in Joseph LaPalombara and Myron Weiner, eds., *Political Parties and Political Development* (Princeton, 1966), pp. 331–367.

another type of political movement has appeared, one that responds somewhat better to the imperatives of divided countries with multitudes of submerged citizens. This is the popular-type, mass-oriented political party that includes some individual supporters but the bulk of whose followers are recruited *en bloc* as members of functional interest groups which adhere to the party—white-collar employees' associations, laborers' unions, farmers' organizations, and so on. These popular parties often are headed by a personalistic, semicharismatic leader who elaborates what he calls an ideology but what really is little more than a doctrinaire reformist action program that speaks in universalistic terms to satisfy the yearnings of the disoriented transitional populace for a sense of cultural continuity and personal integration. Examples of these popular-type political movements are the *aprista*-style parties already mentioned, including spin-offs from the original group in several countries, and the Christian Democratic parties. Probably Cuba's *Auténticos* prior to 1952, the post-Vargas Brazilian Labor party, and Argentina's *Peronista* party could be included, among others. Although some observers describe these movements as mass parties, they are more nearly mass-oriented; they purport to represent the common people and their interests, but their formal membership is limited to relatively restricted numbers of functional, interest-group constituents and their most active membership to a very small cadre of individuals, usually middle-class professional men or intellectuals and a few functional interest-group leaders.

For a period after they became established the popular parties seemed to be pushing a number of countries toward a more democratic, representative, and integrative political system. They did activate significantly larger numbers of citizens than had the traditionally oriented parties. But both in those states where the mass-oriented parties managed to capture control of the presidency and in other countries where electoral failure and/or army veto precluded their taking power, the original thrust toward a more inclusive, integrated political system has been blunted by the devisive factors endemic in the environment.

In the beginning, the impact provided by the popular parties' ability to turn out massive crowds of previously passive citizens seemed to suggest that they could organize power to "reform the basic structures of the society, economy, and polity," as they so often say. Evidence began to accumulate, however, that the popular parties could not meet these expectations. In part the failure to follow through can be attributed to lack of sustained effort by the mass-oriented movements between elections. We all know that it is easier to incorporate blocs of members into a party than to mobilize them for continuous action, and that it is less difficult to stir up emotions of uninformed peoples during an election campaign than in the years between. But the mass parties faced serious internal organizational difficulties as well.

The coalition of very different forces which joined to form each popular party was extremely unstable. Difficulties arose from a wide variety of causes, often with several negative factors operating at the same time. Personalistic ambitions of leaders, ideological disputes, regional jealousies, class and social distinctions between urban white-collar and manual workers, differing political tactics by urban militants and apathetic country people, real conflicts of interest among such diverse agricultural people as day-wage rural-proletarians on plantations, small commercial farmers, larger market farmers, and subsistence *campesinos*—all had to be satisfied, or at least considered. In light of limited economic resources in most countries and the even more limited human resources of many party leadership groups, no formula could be derived to balance conflicting interests within the party and no way could be devised to bridge cultural, social, and economic gaps in the general population. Pressures on the parties became more acute as the citizenry became more sophisticated, particularly as the party members got to know each other and their competing interests, but machinery to ease the rising pressures did not come into being .

As these shifts occurred, the symbolic and universalistic language favoring social reform, economic opportunity, and popular government as all-embracing goods that had been mouthed by party orators in the early organizational period should have given way to more specific action programs reflecting real needs felt by every component of the movement. In practice the party could not satisfy the expectations of all members simultaneously. Inevitably, the wants of the most effective *militantes* came first, before the needs of less active members; and reforms benefiting nonmembers—the unorganized, unmotivated, uninformed masses, including Indians—got lowest priority. It became harder and harder to sustain moral indignation for reform as an abstract concept while competing sectors of the party pushed their specific claims to particular goals, especially when many popular party leaders seemed content to sell their heritage of reformist zeal for the pottage of power, social recognition, and perhaps a few hours of peace and quiet.

At the same time, many reform party chiefs began to lose their image as idealistic and self-sacrificing democrats. Leadership attitudes appropriate for an earlier period when the rank and file had no knowledge of the wide world and little experience in politics no longer served the more informed and activist portions of the membership. It was to be expected that the intellectualized, middle-class professionals who had organized most mass-oriented parties would adopt a *patrón*-like attitude toward their lower-class followers, and even that they might experience difficulty in adjusting to new situations requiring different leadership techniques. The *patrón* relationship pattern is, after all, deeply embedded in Latin culture. But it is surprising that otherwise astute politicians could carry their rigidity to extremes that undermined the potential success of the reform political movements they had labored so long to form.

Personalistic splits brewing out of irreconcilable individual ambitions probably were inevitable. So undoubtedly was the tendency to drop out that was demonstrated by certain functional groups which could not hope to attain their peculiar needs through party action because leaders representing other groups with competitive demands stood higher in party councils. Perhaps it even was fated that the popular party leadership should not be able to construct a single conciliating mechanism at the party level to balance the interests of the functional contenders within the coalition. It seems less certain that resort to extreme pressure and even violence against recalcitrant party units and their officers should have been necessary so frequently. The enforcer function of Peru's *Aprista*-party strong-arm squad, the *búfalos*, is simply a better known example of more circumspect intimidation practices elsewhere. Such actions accord with the Latin *patrón*'s pattern of thinking for his supporters and expecting blind adherence, from which it follows logically that a leader should impose his "superior understanding," by force if required. The most charitable explanation of such attitudes may be that they represent a policy of desperation brought on because the leadership could not contain the internal stresses which were disrupting the party and destroying its effectiveness.

Another cause of the popular parties' declining influence in several countries is, oddly enough, their proliferation. Personalistic ambitions, ideological and doctrinal differences, and the need of certain particularistic functional interests to attain more effective representation have caused factions to splinter off the original popular movements, or to organize independently. Such new parties usually set up their own functional subunits (labor unions, farmers groups, feminine movements, and so on) in competition with those affiliated with the original mass-oriented party, canceling out either unit's effectiveness as the sole spokesman for the interest involved and placing in question the claim of any mass-oriented party to speak for all the "people." As the historical record of the popular party movement grows longer, experience has convinced many citizens in the unorganized portions of the population, not to mention more sophisticated observers, including military officers, that in practice every such movement has to emphasize the immediate claims of its *militantes* before those of nonmembers, no matter how pressing the latters' needs. Similarly, political realities require that for regionally based parties local needs and for functionally organized parties the claims of activist particularistic associations take precedence over legitimate but unstructured national concerns.

Evidence abounds to demonstrate that most popular party leaders share the only too human trait of putting organizational strength and personal benefit ahead of abstract reform goals. In country after country where several mass-oriented movements are in competition, the "out" parties work harder to embarrass a reformist president than to support government attempts at structured change. Often allying themselves with the conservative parties, they labor in and out of the congress to freeze the legislative process or starve the executive agencies financially so that no major reform legislation is passed or implemented that could rebound to the credit of an incumbent, competitive popular party, no matter what benefits might accrue to the hungry masses. This pattern repeated itself in Cuba in the 1940s, in Peru in the 1950s and 1960s, in Venezuela and Chile during the 1960s and 1970s, to cite just a few cases.

Space permits only the barest chronical of a single country's experience with popular parties. Let Venezuela stand for them all because, with minor variations on the theme responding to local conditions, the pattern is much the same everywhere.[8] *Acción Democrática* (AD) began as a leftist, anticlerical, antimilitarist reform movement whose roots extended back to a 1945 coup executed by its future leaders in conjunction with certain reform-leaning military elements. By 1948 Ramón Gallegos, the novelist, had become President of the Republic, but his program was viewed as extremist and challenging to many established interests. Apparently the sticking points were an attempt to improve the government's share of profits from the foreign-dominated petroleum industry and an intention to arm a civilian militia to counterbalance the army. The resulting military takeover led ultimately to the dictatorship of General Pérez Jiménez.

After the military regime finally fell, a somewhat chastened and vociferously anti-Communist *Acción Democrática* came to power in 1959 under President Rómolo Betancourt, who gradually assumed a dominant personalistic influence over the party with the decline and death of Gallegos. Since then there have been at least three major splits in the movement. In 1960 Dr. Domingo Alberto Rangel, a Marxist, broke away, taking most of the youth group to form his *Movimiento Independiente Revolucionario* (MIR); during 1962 Raúl Ramos Jiménez split off a section of the non-Marxist left, partly because AD was not active enough in social reform but also because his personal political ambitions were thwarted by

[8] An essential source on Venezuela's politics is the three-volume series reporting on research sponsored jointly by the Centro de Estudios del Desarrollo of the Universidad Central de Venezuela (CENDES) and M.I.T.'s Center for International Studies, under the general theme of "the politics of change in Venezuela." See Frank Bonilla and José A. Silva Michelena, eds., *A Strategy for Research on Social Policy* (Cambridge, Mass., 1967); Frank Bonilla, *The Failure of Elites* (Cambridge, Mass., 1970); J. A. Silva Michelena, *The Illusion of Democracy in Dependent Nations* (Cambridge, Mass., 1971).

Betancourt; in 1968 a third major defection occurred when the party's former chief official, Luis Beltrán Preito Figueroa, who was very popular with the young liberal left in the movement, set up his own *Movimiento Electoral Popular* (MEP) because he was refused the AD presidential nomination.

Meanwhile, in the face of growing competition from a new popular-type movement, COPEI (the Christian Socialists), the dominant *Adeco* leadership group has sought to mend fences, restraining sharply its anticlericalism, seeking a modus vivendi with the military, trying to work out compromises with the middle class, the petroleum producers, and other organized interests. These conciliatory gestures have eased pressure from the establishment but helped drive more radical reformers out of the party. Similarly, *Acción Democrática* has been unable to devise any strategy that can satisfy its supporters in rural areas where it is strong and still capture a larger portion of urban labor, which leans more toward COPEI or the communists. In fact, the repeated splintering of the party, together with expanding influence of COPEI, lost *Acción Democrática* the 1968 presidential election, though it managed to dominate congress. Results of the presidential balloting suggest just how badly fractured is Venezuela's political system, for the Christian Socialists won with a plurality of only 29.8 percent of the votes, compared with the *Adecos*'s 28.4 percent. The other two candidates, who polled 22.7 percent and 19.3 percent, also could be classed as reformists.

This fractioning of the citizenry would be less significant if the so-called popular parties had submerged their differences after the election to work for a common good. Instead, voting with other opposition elements to control congress the *Adecos* acted as a disloyal opposition to undermine the standing of the COPEI President, Rafael Caldera. During the first eighteen months of his administration, not one piece of major legislation was enacted by congress. Near the end of 1970 a few reform bills were adopted, mainly against foreign economic interests in oil, banking, and larger industry. These laws did not represent a spirit of Christmas compromise, but a reaction to intense pressure from Venezuela's armed forces, who have recognized the need for change if the country is not to go the way of Chile. Quite likely the only reason Venezuela has not yet been detoured onto that road or toward a takeover by a new-style military regime is that a little time has been purchased with the enormous income available from petroleum production. This level of material resources is not available in other countries of Latin America, where the popular parties have been unable to bring about real restructuring of the civil political process.

In most states where they have operated, the eternal political infighting among the several mass-oriented parties, together with their internal weakness, explains the lack of impact such movements have on the political system. So does the restricted real influence formal government can have in controlling the private governments and other vested interest groups. One further change-retarding factor might be mentioned again, the traditional political parties. Despite relatively few members and a clear loss of legitimacy among unaffiliated voters, the defense posture of most such parties in protecting established interests is remarkably successful. This could be ascribed to the political effectiveness of their individual members, most of whom join on their own initiative, are better educated, more informed on issues, and frequently have cross-cutting memberships with private governments and other semi-independent interest groups. Moreover, both leaders and followers in the traditional parties are apt to be strategically located in urban areas, especially the capital; they also generally have a greater understanding of the national political process. Equally important, most traditional parties work toward more limited political ends, focusing on the policy matters which directly affect the interest of their own relatively homogeneous membership and, these days, usually working hardest to sidetrack attempts to reduce their members' privileged positions. Considering the difficulties afflicting their popular, reformist party competition, it is not surprising that the traditional parties have managed to fight their particularistic rear-guard action so well.

Quite obviously, a majority of Latin America's societies are not yet sufficiently integrated socially, economically, or politically to support political parties that cut across regional, social, and class lines. Again, it is highly doubtful that a competitive party system made up of either traditional parties or popular parties, much less a mixture of the two, will be able in the foreseeable future to supply the kind of fusion necessary to complement the formal government agencies to produce a value neutral, relatively impartial, and effective central decisionmaking structure. A few years ago, in discussing the growing need for such a device, I said "the logic of the problems facing the political structures involved in government policy formation calls for the kinds of services national integrating parties can provide. . . . Inexorably, therefore, throughout most polities in the region pressures . . . are mounting so rapidly that if a nationalizing party system does not exist, one must be invented."[9] Since then, the pressures have continued to grow, but for the reasons detailed above nationalizing party systems have not evolved. Instead, faced with repeated instances of the failure of political parties of all kinds to service the basic needs of the citizens or the government, the parties and, as a sort of unintended side effect, civil government itself have lost their legitimacy for an amazing range of persons in many states, from the Tupamaros and Maoists on the left through the disaffected middle class to nationalist traditionalists on the right. They all seek some integrating, reform-mongering mechanism. In a number of countries, therefore, another nationalizing device has been invented—the mobilizing, integrating military regime.

The Foundations of Centralization

Despite constitutional provisions calling for civilian, representative, and responsible government which have existed for a century and a half in most Latin American countries, historical precedent and a broad range of thought emphasizing political centralization help to legitimate the extralegal and even illegal system-maintenance tactics adopted by civilian *políticos* seeking to preserve the established governmental system. Such acts in turn pave the way for assumption of power by new-style military regimes, for present-day unsettled conditions resulting from overfast change and inherent structural defects in the ongoing political process convince

[9] Scott, "Political Parties and Policy-Making in Latin America," p. 367.

many citizens that extraordinary solutions are necessary. For their part, the military officers' past experience dealing with guerrilla movements suggests to them that these solutions must include popularizing and nationalizing approaches.

The widespread tendency to seek instant solutions to internal disruptions of the nation-building process through strong government action has very respectable antecedents. A tradition of centralized authority "to control the irresponsible activities of the others" not only carries over from Iberian sources but enjoys the endorsement of the Liberator himself. Even before the Wars of Independence had been won, Simón Bolívar warned of the need to establish strong and effective national government in order to counter weaknesses inherited from the colonial past. In his famous 1815 letter from Jamaica, Bolívar castigated the Spaniards not simply for failing to breed a tradition of self-government into Latin Americans but also for failing even to propogate a heritage of efficient tyranny. As a consequence, he wrote, "the (Latin) American states need the care of paternalistic governments which can cure the ulcers and wounds of despotism and war." Ten years later, after the region's freedom was assured, Bolívar demonstrated that he saw paternalistic government as highly centralized; his 1825 constitution proposed a lifetime president and other safeguards for strong national authority. Though the constitution never really was implemented, throughout Latin America's independent history it has supplied a helpful argument for a wide spectrum of political philosophers and practicing politicians—right, left, and centrist—who favor nationalizing authoritarianism.

In like view, the Roman Catholic church has supported the concept of strong central government authority as long as church and state can work together, perhaps because along with the army in many Latin American countries it is the only really national institution. Until recently the traditionally conservative role of the church inclined it to identify authority with the establishment, from whose ranks most of its hierarchy was recruited. Lately, by a strange twist of fate, the clerical radical revisionists—many of whom are foreigners or deeply influenced by foreign values—also support strong government, but now as an instrument to impose their own ideals of structural socioeconomic reform against the interests of the established orders. The Social Christian doctrines of Father Lebret and Father Vekemans, for instance, are of the University of Louvain school of religious sociological philosophers whose views were influenced by many of the same intellectual sources as Marx, though Vekemans operates under the auspices of MISEREOR, a foundation established in 1959 by the Catholic bishops of West Germany.[10] Although the core of their formulations is moralistic rather than materialistic, these priests seem to share the conclusion that real change cannot be accomplished without some form of effective government control or coercion. To some extent their views have been adopted by CELAM, the *Consejo Episcopal Latinoamericano*, or Latin American Bishops' Council.

Note that although Bishop Helder P. Câmara, who is Latin America's best known clerical reformer, has attacked his country's military government at home and abroad for certain of its activities he also has expressed an interest in "the possibility of social reform under a (military) government like that of Peru." To that end, he has proposed a continentwide meeting of technicians and military men to examine the region's social order. "I have the impression that there is an internal colonialism in Latin America, and that it is really inglorious for Latin America's armies to support slavery, to support a structure of human life that keeps millions of human beings in misery, in slavery."[11]

Much the same tendency toward centralized authoritarianism exists in the anticlerical current represented among Latin America's intellectuals by positivism. From its pre-1910 application in Mexico by President Díaz and his *científicos* and its influence on early republican Brazil, as demonstrated by the motto "Order and Progress" on the country's flag, to the present period, Compte's cold-blooded "scientific" solutions to sociopolitical problems have been implemented through dominant, central political structures manned by technocratically inclined specialists. Today, a new secular religion worshiping national development through rites of

[10] See Michael A. Quinn, "Programs and Philosophy of the Center for the Economic Social Development of Latin America," (Master's thesis, University of Illinois, 1969).

[11] *New York Times*, October 28, 1970.

socioeconomic reform, central planning, import substitution, and regional economic integration is preached by another group of technicians, CEPAL economists, with Rául Prebisch as their high priest. Apparently its most sacred sacrament is the act of expropriating *latifundia* lands, oil fields, or mining properties, especially if foreign-owned, and sharing out higher purchasing power among the popular majorities to assure a domestic market for local industrial products.[12]

If those who would bring about change back strong central political institutions, citizens favoring the status quo certainly do not oppose them, perhaps on the theory that this is the best means for the establishment to continue its control of national government. In any event, Latin America's conservative political thought always has stressed the strong state concept much more consistently than the liberal constitutional norms first adopted during the early nineteenth century might suggest. This is not the place to review the region's political philosophy, so let the title of one recent political polemic written by a moderate Columbian Conservative party leader indicate the alternatives seen under this approach—*A Strong State or a Military Dictator; Columbia's Dilemma*.[13]

Turning from intellectuals and less activist elites to practicing civilian politicians, we see that they do not always accept limited constitutional government as an absolute good, perhaps because they are not sure it is a real possibility in their country's environment but more likely because leaders of particularistic political movements find it difficult to accept the premise that in a contested election system where there are winners there also must be losers. In July, 1970, for example, after Colombian presidential candidate Belisario Betancur's defeat, one senatorial supporter claimed that in the election "representative government was defeated," and that "the army is one force that can guarantee an authentically national solution; by means of a *golpe de estado*...."[14]

---

[12] A useful statement of this approach can be found in Prebisch's *Change and Development; Latin America's Great Task. Report Submitted to the Inter-American Development Bank* (Washington, D.C., 1970).

[13] Mario Laserna, *Estado Fuerte o Caudillo; el Dilema Colombiano* (Bogotá, 1968). See also Alfonso López Michelsen, *El Estado Fuerte* (Bogotá, 1966).

[14] *Excelsior* (Mexico City), July 7, 1970.

Even a reformist poet with a long and honorable record of sacrifice in leading the battle for democracy in his fatherland can reach the sad conclusion that at a given stage of development his country cannot sustain an open, competitive political system. Soon after the unhappy near civil war that led to occupation by United States armed forces, Juan Bosch, the Dominican Republic's embittered and frustrated ex-president, proclaimed the concept of "popular dictatorship" and the need of a revolution to achieve it.[15] A few years later he tried to persuade his Dominican Revolutionary party allies that democracy is a luxury which will not work in underdeveloped areas to solve national problems. "Representative democracy has served to maintain the privileges of a minority of property and wealth, and it has not provided the stability, personal safety, health care, and education the majorities want."[16]

It would be equally dangerous to accept the notion that all members of the popular masses or of the more informed middle sectors object to strong central authority as a matter of course. For the general citizenry, which never has benefited greatly from any sort of government—democratic or authoritarian, constitutional or extralegal, civilian or military—the coming to power of a new regime means little. For the persons among them in social or economic transition, in fact, the stability provided by a military-style administration may be welcome as a surcease from "future shock," for there are limits to the amount of change the human organism can absorb. Certainly the willingness of the lower middle class and the popular majorities to support strong-man political leaders whom they identify (rightly or wrongly) as having tried to serve their interests does not indicate any rejection of effective central government, as such. The excellent electoral showing made by such persons and the movements they back after having been ousted from office demonstrate this. To cite just a few cases: Vargas of Brazil in 1950, Pérez Jiménez of Venezuela in 1968, Odría of Peru prior to the military takeover in 1968, Rojas Pinilla of Colombia in 1970, and even Perón of Argentina for over a decade.

As the experience of Germany and Italy attests, existence of a rea-

---

[15] *New York Times*, April 23, 1968.
[16] *Ibid.*, April 22, 1970.

sonably large middle class is not necessarily a bar to a strong centralizing government or even to a military-technocratic takeover. Under certain circumstances, the middle sectors may view concentration of authority and "depoliticization" of administration as the best insurance for system maintenance, a protection of their status from lower-class challenges. Their rather passive reaction may become positively supportive if the proposed popular reform is proclaimed by a demagogic leader who seems willing to wipe out the establishment in order to accomplish integration. Juan Domingo Perón was quoted during 1970 as follows: "The only revolution possible in Argentina is a violent one"; to restore social justice in the country, certain "counter-revolutionary institutions have to disappear, including the army, free enterprise, and political parties which serve the interests of monopolies." He concluded saying "If I had foreseen what was going to happen [the continuing decline of Argentina's politics and economy], I certainly would have shot the half-million or million Argentines who defended their privileges and acted against the rights of the people."[17]

More commonly, the middle class is faced with less dramatic but equally pressing reasons for accepting an extralegal, military assumption of power. Authoritarian stabilization may be welcomed as an improvement over the excesses, corruption, and inflationary pattern which accompany the administration of an ineffectual reformist president. These conditions have occurred in nearly every Latin American country where a nationalist-integrating military regime has taken power over the past several years.

If maintenance of the political status quo through a centralizing military takeover is a tactical goal for the established interests, it no longer is a prime strategic objective for the leaders of the armed forces who control the new-style military governments. Instead, they seek some way of imposing acceptance of change on the traditional ruling elites and at the same time of inculcating a feeling of greater responsibility for constructive participation into the leaders of the emerging elements, so that recurring resort to authoritarian stabilization by the military can end. Meanwhile, the military regime finds it expedient to mobilize the popular masses to provide a

[17] *Excelsior* (Mexico City), July 9, 1970.

broader power base for its attempts to include the lower classes in the national society and economy. Given the Latin penchant for dominant *patrón*-style leadership, not to mention the military's inherent hierarchical organizational pattern, it should come as no surprise that this sort of mobilization does not necessarily encourage political participation on the input side of the policymaking process for the masses, an approach not unlike that followed by Mexico's Revolutionary government for the past forty years. For that matter, under armed-forces tutelage neither are the traditional ruling elites permitted much direct participation in governmental decisionmaking.

Why then the clearly demonstrated determination of so many military officers to service the needs of hitherto underrepresented mass elements in the population? The answer to this question is found in the testimony of members of the armed forces about new kinds of field conditions they have experienced, conditions which show them the need for this rather virulent variety of paternalistic populism. A large number of lower-grade officers have participated in armed-services, "civic action" programs, which utilize military personnel and equipment for road construction, provision of potable water supplies, and the like, in the rural hinterland. Such activities are so widespread in Latin America that as early as 1963 a continentwide meeting of military representatives from participating countries was held to discuss problems and prospects for these programs. Furthermore, many military officials are veterans of campaigns against radical guerrilla bands and have seen at first hand the conditions which fuel the flames of mass discontent. Soon after taking office, for example, one of the members of Peru's ruling *junta* said, "I learned the biggest lesson of my life a few years ago when we did have a Communist guerrilla problem in southern Peru. The things the guerrillas said they stood for were the same things the people wanted. I realized for the first time that Peruvian society will have to be reshaped from top to bottom, if Castro and his friends are to be stopped. But time is terribly short now, and they have a long head start. If we fail, it is not merely Peru that will become another Cuba. It is all of Latin America."[18]

[18] *New York Times*, September 7, 1969.

Again, in 1970, a couple of years after assuming power in Panamá, Brigadier General Omar Torrijos responded to Ted Kennedy's attack on Latin American military governments by saying that "the electoral processes in Latin America have been little more than episodic events which update the Roman epoch of bread and circuses, with this difference; they have been strong on circuses and weak on bread." He continued comparing the region's so-called democracies to matchmakers who set up "a marriage among the armed forces, the oligarchy, and the evil priests," in which "the oligarchy exploits the sentiments of vanity and greed of certain military men who loan their weapons to silence the masses, while the bad priests bless this marriage to enjoy the benefits of power." General Torrijos concluded by pointing out that he had been part of all this but that when as a captain putting down a guerrilla uprising he was wounded, "my determination rose to be able one day to influence the fortunes of the armed forces, to arrange a second marriage, this time in the best interests of the fatherland."[19]

Even Bolivia's rather disordered version of a modernizing military regime produced the same mix of popularizing centrists in its series of presidents. General Ovando, who was ousted in 1970 as too moderate, spoke while in office of a need for stronger national authority to permit reform that had been sabotaged by the "pseudo-democracy of Latin America's constitutions and elections." His successor, General Juan José Torres, a non-Marxist radical reformer who during 1967 smashed "Che" Guevara's guerrilla movement in the rural backlands, sought to extend his political power base through the calling of "popular assemblies" which would ratify government intervention and seizure of private-sector properties with the aim of restructuring the society and economy. By August, 1971, General Torres had been ousted by Colonel Banzer, a self-styled conservative who called for greater concentration of power in the national government in order to implement effectively policies which would protect the rights of the popular masses.

Significantly, even in countries where national-integrating military regimes have not assumed control of government, members of the officer corps show increasing awareness of a need for popular

[19] *Excelsior* (Mexico City), July 9, 1970.

reform. One of the most popular and controversial books published in Colombia during 1970 was *Uisheda,* a novel about guerrilla warfare that heartily condemns violence. The importance of the topic is underscored not so much by the work's subject matter or wide acceptance as by the fact that its author is Brigadier General Álvaro Valencia Tovar, whose three successful field commands against guerrillas convinced him that a political crisis impends if real opportunities are not made available immediately to Colombia's masses. As commander of the country's military academy, his views are bound to influence strongly the younger officers. In neighboring Venezuela, we have seen that the military already has forced through congress limited nationalistic reforms; the country's political system can anticipate further movement toward national integration under army pressure.

New-Style Military Regimes

Growing professionalism in individual members of Latin America's officer corps and a resulting sense of collective participation in a single operational entity have produced a very different attitude toward the military's role in politics than most foreign observers expected. Rather than making armed-services personnel apolitical in the western European-North American pattern, professional training and experience have involved them in governmental affairs to the highest degree. This involvement grows partly out of a feeling of frustration at the breakdown of constitutional mechanisms and extralegal political structures under the stresses of change, partly out of the military's commitment to national development, and partly out of the kinds of skills acquired by many officers during the professionalization process.

Given the inadequacies of civilian *políticos* and the rigidities of the political systems they have manned, as well as the frequent practice of calling upon the army to provide short-term authoritarian stabilization, politization of the military probably was inevitable. If nothing else, the recurring leadership vacuum in national politics would suck the armed forces into the vortex of power, even if their near monopoly on force were not called into play by periodic rural and urban guerrilla violence. Furthermore, some military officers are not adverse to taking control for the sake of power itself. But other, more positive factors reinforce these negative motivations.

In most Latin American countries, the military sees itself as the one effective nationalizing agency in a disintegrating environment, particularly where the church has split into conservative and radical factions. With its technical approach, its organizational pattern, and the focused nature of its responsibilities, the military also sees itself as a prime agent of modernization. Because of the practical absence of possible major foreign wars, the armed services accord high priority to domestic matters, especially national integration and development, so their leaders assume as their principal internal objectives social and economic growth in an environment of orderly administrative operations with a minimum of political disruption. If they seek to expand the proportion of lower-class citizens sharing in the benefits of the national economy and taking part in the national society, it is less to mobilize such persons politically so they can participate in the give-and-take of governmental decisionmaking than to reduce the likelihood of anomic disturbance that might retard the rate of growth. At the outset of most modernizing-integrating regimes at least, the military officers are quite willing to take the responsibility of governing upon themselves.

Unlike the leaders of most other institutions in the region, Latin America's officer corps has a sense of mission, belief in its own competence, and, within reason, human and material resources enough to give its members confidence that they can complete their self-assigned development task. Most civilian politicians do not have this self-image, for their public careers usually involve a series of frustrating attempts to resolve bewildering arrays of problems and to satisfy multitudes of irreconcilable demands—regional, functional, and individual—with minimal finances and insufficient legal authority. If a constitutional president tries to meet the demands of his immediate followers he fires the indignation of competing interests; if he tries to encourage compromise and a fair distribution of available benefits among all parts of the populace, he alienates everyone, including his supporters. No civilian *politico* trying to satisfy all the citizens can focus his administration's program on a single overriding objective such as national development without courting disaster; the shift in Alliance for Progress goals mentioned above is one good example of how the realities of politics intrude on civil government's latitude of choice. Conversely, a military regime can determine precisely what it wishes to accomplish, within a single frame of reference, and impose the decision on all concerned, for it not only wields sufficient physical force to ignore most protests but it can organize and deploy its nonphysical resources more efficiently than can any disorganized potential opposition.

Considering that the armed forces generally take political control from a discredited and often disintegrating civil government, the impact of a coordinated and decisive ruling *junta* can be enormous, for its actions seem to be those of a single, self-contained entity. As long as substantial agreement on purpose exists among the commanders of the several services, military discipline and the chain of command assures a large degree of unity of intent and continuity of program. As a classic example of a "private" government, the military has a tradition of independence of action and more nearly adequate financial support than most civil government agencies. With professionalization its human resources have become superior to most governmental bureaucracies as well. Finally, most military responsibilities are limited in scope, rather clearly defined, with success or failure easily measured in physical terms without much regard for human values. Why then should not officers in the armed forces feel more capable to accomplish goals—including, by psychological "transfer," operation of a "public" government in search of national development—than their civilian *politico* counterparts? Particularly when the officer corps views most civilian leaders as inept, corruptible, and too bound by regional, class, or special interest ties to provide a truly national government.

These attitudes are enhanced by the nature of modern professional military training. As junior-grade officers, military personnel study the traditional arts of war—strategy and tactics, logistics, military engineering, mechanics and engineering to supervise servicing of sophisticated equipment, as well as close-order drill and sanitary engineering. But as field- and staff-grade officers they attend specialized training schools which provide them with the skills required to administer large-scale organizations, including governments—administrative and management techniques, personnel practices, finance, and the like. Additionally, in Latin America many advanced service institutions include in their curricula preparation in the social sciences—economics, sociology, psychology, even political science—so they graduate cadres of professionally trained officers (and in some cases selected civilian *técnicos* as well) with the very specialties in short supply for most civil governments.

Considering the overcrowding, dilapidation, and poor financing of most Latin American universities, not to mention their chronic crises of disruption, it is not surprising that the military's advanced training schools are among the best social-science facilities in the region. Equally important, educational methods are superior and teneted to produce flexible, team-work–oriented professionals. Based in part on the approach of the United States Command and General Staff College and related individual North American armed-services schools,[20] the work is often problem-oriented, stressing collective and cooperative approaches, or in seminars where lively exchange of views is encouraged. The more advanced courses recruit participants jointly from all branches of the armed forces, and some also include selected civilians. The offerings stress nationalism, national planning, and civilian as well as military aspects of national development, frequently including consideration of the need for expansion of opportunities for the rural and urban masses to assure not only civil peace but also a market for domestic production. As one officer friend who has attended such courses told me, "It is as though Raúl Prebisch had written the study plan and sent his CEPAL staff to teach the classes." Prebisch might well have, for CEPAL does offer short courses on development economics in which high-ranking officers enroll.

In another instance, I observed that the mixed officer-civilian teaching staff of one military training school went far beyond

[20] Since World War II, over 20,000 Latin American officers and NCO's have studied in training facilities in the United States and another 25,000 in the Panama Canal Zone. During fiscal 1970, some seventeen Latin American countries had officers in the United States service schools. Others have attended universities in North America and Europe on an individual basis, or studied in their own countries through short courses offered by international agencies.

CEPAL to offer a Marxist (though carefully non-Communist), ideologically socialist, and semiauthoritarian model of the development process. The material was well accepted, for while it does not reinforce democratic constitutional norms, the approach accords well with the other most influential current of thought in Latin America's intellectual heritage, authoritarian positivism, and certainly is not contrary to the military mentality. We already know that even civilian governments are shot through with elitism and reliance on planning commissions with their *patrón*-like tendency to ignore the wishes of the citizens in light of a superior wisdom. President Caldera of Venezuela recently expressed the problem succinctly when he spoke against the pattern of "military paternalism or political party paternalism. [This is the tendency] to want to impose on the public what it ought to have [instead of what it wants]."[21]

The kind of training experienced in the military's advanced schools reduces the likelihood that most officers would provide support for an old-line, individual *caudillo* but it does offer an alternative model, one that can produce a *junta*, or collectively organized military government to integrate a disrupted modernizing state, a cooperating cadre of officers skilled in administrative techniques who can work together to rule an increasingly complex economy and society. It is highly significant that in countries where such military training schools have operated for some time the armed forces attain a unity of purpose that not only shows understanding of the need for national development but also agreement on a program to attain it. Nor is it any accident that most officers commanding the new-style military regimes have shared this training experience, sometimes as students and sometimes as instructors.

When Peru's *junta* took over in October, 1968, most of the fourteen original members had participated in the offerings of the *Centro de Altos Estudios Militares* (CAEM, or Center for Advanced Military Studies), as have the military officers who replaced some of them at the ministerial or subministerial level since then. This shared CAEM experience is more important than the coincidence that in the original group eleven had undergone some sort of professional military training under United States auspices, or that the

[21] Cited by Leopoldo Zea in *Excelsior* (Mexico City), July 14, 1970.

new President, General Juan Velasco, had attended the Command and General Staff School in the Canal Zone during 1945. The continuing role of CAEM is demonstrated in the membership of the revolutionary government's Presidential Advisory Committee (*Comité de Asesoramiento de la Presidencia*, or COAP). Each of the two generals and eleven colonels making up the unit, which reviews major decree laws and coordinates all government activities, has a record of superior performance in subjects offered by the center.

The same pattern obtains in Argentina and Brazil. In both countries the local, high-level, military training institution is called the Advanced War School (*Escuela Superior de Guerra* and *Escola Superior de Guerra*), and a significantly high number of upper-grade officers and civilian officials in the armed-forces' regimes have participated in training courses. Nor is it any accident that the first President of Brazil's integrating military government in 1964 was General Castello Branco, who had been chairman of the Advanced War School's Department of Studies.[22]

Domestic military preparation of this sort is not the only way to attain managerial skills or new viewpoints. Advanced training in a foreign staff school can provide armed-services' personnel with a different conception of the military's role and responsibility in their country's life. The three leaders of the "National Guard" group that ousted Panamá's elected president in 1968 had experienced United States training a few years previously. So had several of the officers involved in Bolivia's on again-off again national reform regimes, including some members of the conservative faction under Colonel Banzer that removed President Torres during August, 1971.

The fact that the armed forces have developed a cadre of officers with administrative preparation and related specialties does not mean the military operates alone in organizing a government, for no country in the region has enough technically trained officers to ac-

---

[22] See Alfred Stepan, *Military in Politics*, for an excellent discussion of Brazil's military and its role in the country's national life. See also Frank D. McCann, "The Military and Change in Brazil," in *Culture Change in Brazil*, papers from the Midwest Association for Latin American Studies, October 30 and 31, 1969. Ball State University, Muncie, Indiana, 1970.

complish this. When social and economic erosion caused by rapid change or inept civil government impels the armed forces to act, they establish an alliance with *desarrollista* (development-oriented) civilian technocrats. These generally are young professionals who under civil government were frustrated in their upward movement within the private sector by nepotism and other ascriptive practices or in the public sector by the particularistic attitudes and humanistic norms of traditionally oriented political leaders. The quality of their educational experience and the material of their disciplinary interest—often they are engineers, economists, land reformers, lawyers, or other social manipulators—incline these professionals toward a technocratic approach, for they are specialists in the practical applications of science whose product or accomplishments are easily evaluated, if one can ignore consequences to individuals or groups of human beings. Such persons have high professional pride in their abilities which reflects formal technical training but which also endows them with an elitist and materialist viewpoint and a marked desire to manage their environment and the people in it.

For a long time, such *técnicos* were looked down on by the traditionally educated humanists whose values set the tone for the members of the establishment and by civilian leaders in politics who saw them as experts whose skills should be "on tap and not on top." To such frustrated professionals an alliance with the armed-force rulers is not difficult, for both groups share scientific and pragmatic norms, and look upon themselves as agents of modernization. For the civilian technocrats this move into power has the added attraction of permitting them to get back some of their own against the establishment.

In a very real sense, as governors military officers themselves are technocrats par excellence, with a high degree of professional pride because they are used to performing well the clearly defined functions for which they are trained. Like their civilian *técnico* counterparts they are elitists, and their sense of superiority reflects not only skills but also the tradition of military hierarchy. Many officers are formalists in religion and often puritanical in outlook, with a strong sense of moral obligation to the nation and its inhabitants but, on another level, they worship technology and apply it regardless of human consequences, giving people what they "ought to have," but only after assigning priority to the more general needs of national development. The very nature of their primary warmaking function makes officers nationalists and materialists, with little inclination to consider individual human rights or values. Unlike their civilian counterparts, the governing military *juntas* have both sufficient power and funds to be effectively pragmatic, so they can look to results rather than costs in manipulating the environment and imposing their solutions over the objections of opponents whose views or interests do not coincide.

One danger inheres in the practice of applying technical skills without adequate input of political factors to act as control devices. Evidence is accumulating in most countries under the new-style regimes that both military and civilian technocrats are so sure of their abilities that they move beyond the realm of their technical competence into fields about which they know little or nothing. Under civilian government popular reaction to failures resulting from bureaucratic ignorance, coupled with restricted legal authority, can limit excesses of this sort, even where national planning commissions are given a great deal of paper power, as in Peru under President Belaúnde or Brazil under President Goulart. Under centralized and militarized authority exercised without restraint by *técnicos*, it is less difficult to ignore the needs as well as the desires of the citizenry, because the only check is other technocrats. For the same reason, the possibility of corruption, ever present in Latin America's politics, becomes greater. Evidence of a tendency toward venality among some military officials could be adduced if space permitted, for when individuals exercise power, name government employees, decide upon large-scale government projects involving great sums of money, all without frequent, automatic legal and political checks on their operations, the possibility of falling into temptation can affect anyone, in or out of uniform.

In totaling up accounts, the very real credits amassed by each integrating-nationalizing regime—stressing the national interest, balancing the economy, curbing inflation, mobilizing the masses for a greater share in the benefits of national life—must be measured against its accumulated debits. On a material basis, these costs may include failure to implement symbolically enacted land reform in order to avoid temporary loss of agricultural production, or insistence upon adopting a particular kind of ideologically motivated restructuring of commerce or industry, limiting expansion of more efficient, larger producers. As a corollary, attempts of workers, *campesinos* or *obreros*, to improve their economic status through strikes may be smashed. On a sociopolitical basis, a series of authoritarian evils may accumulate—a permanent state of siege, censorship, or the expropriation of radio and television stations, dismissal of students and teachers from universities, making citizens "nonpersons" through cancellation of political rights, even torture. The military regimes are faced with the eternal dilemma of every real revolution. Which shall take precedence, economic development based on enforced delayed gratification of human desires or social justice that satisfies the immediate needs of long-hungry masses?

Military Regimes: Problems and Prospects

To accept the new-style military regimes' own carefully projected public image—as all-knowing, all-successful, and in complete internal agreement—would be a serious error. The experience of ruling *juntas* in country after country over the past decade suggests that the initial record of material achievement resulting from greater administrative efficiency and a reduction in political infighting (sometimes aided by nationalistic expropriation of foreign-owned properties) cannot always be sustained over time because the realities of the social and economic environment reassert themselves. Physical conditions and human attributes do not change simply because a new kind of leadership assumes political authority. Material resources remain few, unbalanced, and underdeveloped; the bulk of the citizenry remain poorly educated, ill-prepared in the skills of modern economic life, and unwilling to make the personal adjustments necessary in more intense human interaction; the basic civilian political structures remain mutually contradictory and inelastic.

The same divisive factors which weaken the integrating function of the extralegal and legal structures in the civil decisionmaking process work upon individual members of every military government. At an abstract level most armed-services officers share long-range goals for the countries they rule—economic development, national integration, and, as a poor third, social justice. But as time passes they find themselves in growing disagreement about the practical means of accomplishing these ends. Despite a facade of unity, enhanced by their virtual monopoly over force, the governing *juntas* have not been able to "authenticate" a common set of operating norms for the society, economy, and polity because their members do not share a single set of values.

This lack of agreement becomes abundantly evident if we consider some of the conflicts affecting national development policies. At first glance, the most obvious differences seem to lie between two apparently opposing approaches, each followed by several of the integrating military regimes; a review of attitudes within each country suggests, however, that internal disagreements about these development policies may be just as profound as those among the various states. Peru, Bolivia, to some extent Panamá, and more recently Ecuador, have stressed highly nationalistic, even socialistic, means of encouraging economic growth which involve expansion of public sector activities at the expense of local "oligarchs" and foreign corporations. Brazil and Argentina seek economic development mainly through encouraging external and domestic private-sector investment by limiting wild economic fluctuations and repressing political unrest. In practice, as the much longer Mexican experience demonstrates, such differences of approach may be little more than tactical, reflecting the military leadership's reading of national circumstances during a given period and subject to change as new conditions appear. Furthermore, the official attitude toward methods of promoting economic growth in a particular country is not necessarily shared by all members of the officer corps.

In every state ruled by a new-style military regime the dominant development policy has been challenged at one time or another by dissident elements in and out of the governing *junta*. Recall, for example, that as early as 1967 disputes between hardliners, demanding a more nationalistic and speedy approach to economic growth, and gradualists nearly led to open civil war between factions of the

Argentine armed forces. Since then, officers advocating austerity, strict controls over organized labor and the challenging *Peronista* movement, as well as prohibition of any return to unhampered civilian political action, increasingly have resisted those leaders trying to organize a broad-based, labor-oriented civilian political movement encouraged by greater social expenditures and a more liberal salary policy.

In oversimplified terms, the first group clusters around ex-president General Onganía, who followed an orthodox economic program that led to industrial growth and a dramatic slowdown in inflation but accompanied by wage freezes, declining purchasing power for the peso, and agricultural reverses, which led to strikes and riots throughout Argentina during 1969 and early 1970. Attempting to improve the regime's image and to ease tensions, General Alejandro Lanusse and his associates installed General Roberto Levingston as president in June, 1970. Within eight months his aggressively nationalistic economic policies, a growing relationship with certain radical *políticos*, and indications that restoration of civil government through elections would be put off indefinitely until major structural changes could be implemented, resulted in reduced foreign investments and markedly increased inflationary tendencies. These problems, together with a suspicion that he viewed himself as a potential political strong man, caused Levingston's removal from office.

Early in 1971 General Lanusse himself assumed the presidency, liberalizing the regime, lifting the ban on civilian party activities, and speaking of national elections in March, 1973. Seeking to incorporate into the political system a popular political movement that could both balance the influence of traditional parties and provide a springboard for his own presidential candidacy, General Lanusse entered into discussions with local *Peronista* party leaders. He also appointed to his cabinet several civilian ministers who expanded the government's popular welfare programs. Unfortunately for Lanusse's ambitions, these actions did not increase Argentina's national integration. Acting from his Madrid exile, Juan Domingo Perón rejected any arrangement that might reduce his personal domination over the political movement bearing his name, ousting his Argentine spokesman, Jorge Daniel Paladino, for having agreed to the proposition. On returning to Buenos Aires in November, 1972, Perón sought an anti-military election coalition of nearly all civilian political groups, including traditional middle class and orthodox left parties. Continuing agreement among these *políticos* seemed tenuous, because Perón called for "integral democracy" based on a corporate state and one dominant political movement, an unattractive prospect for non-Peronistas, civilian or military.

A somewhat similar situation exists in Brazil, where the official strategy for economic development encourages external as well as internal private-sector investment to such an extent that some outside commentators have accused the government of supporting domestic capitalists at the expense of human needs and of playing the game of foreign imperialist interests. Recently a group of younger officers have called urgently for more radical and nationalistic reforms which could weaken outside economic influence and improve the lot of the general citizenry. Not even the 1971 enforced retirement of their symbolic leader, General Alfonso Albuquerque, could stifle the clamor. As a consequence, the military leadership has begun to reorder its development priorities to support larger and more direct government benefits and services for the popular masses. Near the end of 1971, for instance, a decree law apparently based on a Peruvian model (to be discussed below) set up a profit-sharing program for private enterprises aimed at turning them gradually into mixed worker-owner cooperatives.

Peru's approach to economic development offers a mirror-image of Brazil and Argentina. Its ruling *junta* enjoys a reputation of being highly nationalistic and innovating, a regime that seeks rapid growth by replacing local and foreign private-sector interests with centrally dominated agencies. Nonetheless, after an initial burst of activity during its first few months in power involving expropriation of the International Petroleum Corporation and several coastal commercial plantations, the military government has moved slowly and indecisively toward major change, particularly as regards improvements in the material condition of the general population.

In the *altiplano* where it is most needed, land reform has been unimpressive, probably because the officers responsible hesitate to spark widespread and potentially highly disruptive socioeconomic change in this less-prepared and poorly integrated portion of the rural population before they have personnel and material resources to service the Indians' new needs. In those regions where the citizens are more a part of the national economy and society, fear of further expropriations or of new government exactions on existing private enterprise has deterred investment, leaving the economy stagnant. Attempts to revitalize it through public works programs have provided limited relief in some urban and rural areas but set off a new round of inflation. Wage controls and price freezes on food, housing, and essential services have been imposed but, inevitably, income lags behind rising costs, squeezing white- and blue-collar worker alike. Worse, meatless days and disappearance of such staples as rice accompany price fixing; so does the growth of a black market. Increasingly, therefore, strikes in mining, industry, commerce, even among schoolteachers, further disrupt the economy.

Negative popular reaction is not simply a natural response to temporary financial and material difficulties. The *junta's* more recent and highly publicized actions to restructure Peru's society and economy have produced expectations for immediate and basic improvement in every citizen's life, expectations far beyond the capacity of any government to satisfy speedily. Such popular aspirations undoubtedly have grown even farther beyond the willingness of the present military regime to satisfy in any length of time, because it wishes to invest an increasing share of national production in capital development. To this end, the government has sought to limit worker participation in decisions concerning distribution or reinvestment of profits.

By mid-1972, under the agricultural reform law some 3.125 million hectares of land had been expropriated and 2.6 million hectares distributed, mainly as cooperatives in which farm laborers can work their own land collectively. But the old order really has not changed much, for oversight of operations and decisions on priorities for use of agricultural income continues to lie mainly with the pre-expropriation agronomists or with new, state-appointed *técnicos* from off the *hacienda*. Only the 23,000 workers on the eight large, mechanized coastal sugar plantations first expropriated, representing a few hundred thousand hectares, have been allowed to elect their cooperatives' administrative councils, and this in April, 1972, after a three-year struggle. As we shall see, this concession probably represents the *junta*'s desire to work out some sort of political arrangement with the *aprista* party, which is still very influential among these plantation workers. Nonetheless, government accountants and agronomists continue to check the *haciendas*'s operations, for their sugar production represents some 7 percent of Peru's foreign exchange earnings. All the other agricultural cooperatives in the country continue to be dominated by government-appointed administrators.

Similarly, under recently decreed Laws of Industry and of Commerce affecting most fishing, mining, commercial, and industrial concerns, employees are supposed to set up "workers' communities" which share in annual profits, if any—15 percent in stock and 10 percent in cash—so they can participate in ownership and management of the firm. Legally, these communities have a voice in policy decisions, but state officials have become directors of the enterprises as representatives of the laborers. In other cases, Grace and Company's extensive sugar processing, paper, and chemical operations, for example, the government purchases majority control of the firm directly.

Almost every technique for socioeconomic structural reform means, therefore, that although the affected economic units are termed "cooperatives" or "worker communities," the spokesman for employee interests is a representative of the ruling *junta* who seems more concerned with reinvestment of profits for economic development than with distribution of income for general social welfare or for immediate material improvements in the life-style of the rank-and-file worker-owner. Some reform-minded Peruvian intellectuals see this approach as more a move toward state capitalism than to socialism. In fact, I suspect, this method of organizing change is motivated less by any conscious economic theory than by the realities of present-day Peruvian social and economic conditions, reinforced by the military's *patrón*-like attitude toward the emerging masses.

The officer corps is only too aware of what has occurred in Bolivia, a country with similar socioeconomic environment, where a nationalizing military regime proved unable to integrate the population. A series of reform leaders sought to cut back or eliminate the private sector's role in the economy without organizing effective controls over the new, mass-dominated activities. The last such leader, General Torres, legitimized his acts by seeking approval of so-called "popular assemblies," which could ratify take-overs by the workers but had no machinery to impose work discipline or a sense of responsibility to a common goal. Therefore, instead of a national development program the Bolivian "revolution" produced management collapse, production and service declines, bleeding of the enterprise's financial resources for immediate worker gratification, and a series of economically disastrous strikes in surviving privately owned mines and firms which could not satisfy the insatiable expectations of their employees. These problems combined with clashing personalistic ambitions of individual officers to so debilitate the reform government that it had no means of rallying or manipulating the organized laborers or peasants to oppose the conservative army clique's *golpe de estado* of mid-1971.

With the sobering example of neighboring Bolivia's disintegrating military reform movement fresh in their minds, most high officials in Peru's armed services seem to support massive government investment in development but at the same time to recognize a need for effective control over the heterogeneous popular elements becoming involved in the country's economic growth process. They agree far less on the specific policies which should be included in an internally consistent, rationalizing development strategy. Their lack of cohesion reflects dislocations in a rapidly changing society but also the fact that the military *junta* has had to improvise its program on a day-to-day basis.

This pressure situation resulted because Peru's officer corps was forced to take over political control from a foundering Belaúnde administration long before it felt technically competent to assume responsibility. After the fiasco of the Odría rule the military looked to CAEM (the Center for Advanced Military Studies) to provide officers trained in governing specialties in case of need to take power, but in 1968 its cadres of prepared personnel were far from complete. Therefore the incoming reform regime had neither an elaborated development approach nor enough individuals specializing professionally in such matters to prepare and implement a real program. Considering the number and quality of the country's civilian intellectual cohort, no large reserve of potential *técnico* allies was available to make up the deficiency.

Within the armed forces attitudes about the proper approach to imposed change polarize around questions of continued expropriations and economic nationalism. As the regime matures, officers who must live with reality because their primary responsibility is to plan and implement national-level economic and political programs adopt a more moderate line; others working in the field among the populace or whose ideological interpretations are not tempered by practical experience favor continuing and expanded action against large-scale domestic and especially foreign enterprise.

Their first exhilarating exposure to drastic reform initiated by the armed forces convinced many Peruvians, civilian and military, that the era of economic dependency on domestic oligarchs and foreign interests had ended. Regardless of consequences, they wish to continue a policy of government intervention and expropriation which they identify with economic development and national integration. For their part, most of the members of the ruling *junta* have discovered from sad experience that Peru's human and material resources are too weak, its capital too limited, and its economy too vulnerable under world market conditions to fund speedy development without heavy outside financial assistance. The regime's early reform measures dried up United States and Inter-American Bank loan sources and left the threat of the Hickenlooper Amendment impending, as well as frightening out private investors, just as a world glut in copper, sugar, and cotton reduced internal sources of foreign exchange needed to purchase development matériel and to service external debts. Significantly, during July, 1971, the *Club de Paris* (Peru's West German, Japanese, and other European creditors) refused to extend the repayment period of the country's outstanding and overdue debts, effectively cutting off further foreign loans from the west. Small Chinese and east European technical aid loans, and purchases of fish meal and minerals during 1972, will not solve the problem.

Under the circumstances, it hardly is surprising that the governing *junta* has moderated its stance in hopes of easing foreign pressures and attracting external and even domestic investors. During 1971 five members of the military cabinet were changed; four of them, including a very radical minister of agriculture, were replaced by officers considered less extreme. Negotiations for exploration by outside private petroleum companies were renewed, discussions for new investments by private enterprise opened, and action taken to limit disruptive strikes against externally controlled mining operations. Partly because of these moves, partly because the first impact of its nationalizing policy is fading, but also because its reforms seem less drastic when compared to those imposed in Chile to the south, the Peruvian military regime's reputation for radical nationalism is eroding rapidly.

For all their differences over economic development strategy, the armed-forces officers dominating the various Latin American modernizing regimes agree fundamentally about their approach to national political integration. They recognize a need to mobilize the popular majorities, both to capture broad-based civilian support for their reform measures and to incorporate the emerging portions of the population into national life where they can contribute to their country's growth. At the same time, most military leaders are painfully conscious of the potential threat to national integration inherent in suddenly absorbing a mass of politically inexperienced citizens who reflect the conflicts of a badly splintered and rapidly shifting environment. They are only too aware of the divisive role played historically by the traditional, elite political parties and their mass-oriented challengers when the constitutional and extraconstitutional civilian political structures were unable to reconcile differences among smaller and less-complex groups of interests, so they hesitate to restore political authority to civil governments dependent upon such auxiliary mechanisms.

For this reason, the heads of the military establishment have sought an integrating political structure that can rouse the general populace to constructive action, rationalize their contributions to society and economy but, at the same time, exercise enough control over contending factions to minimize disruptions in the development process. In most cases the ruling *juntas* seem to have selected as an organizational model Mexico's Revolutionary party (the *Partido Revolucionario Institucional,* or PRI). The PRI is widely known throughout Latin America for having handled most of Mexico's national integration problems and, equally impressive for leaders of countries with few resources but with many citizens displaying rising expectations, for having demonstrated that the best politics of scarcity may be a scarcity of politics.

Certainly it is true that even in today's more complex world relatively little individual and collective independent political activity takes place in Mexico within either the lower or the upper classes, probably because the organizational pattern of the Revolutionary party has frozen the country's political system into a premodern, apolitical mold. For Mexico of the 1930s when the party was established, as for most emerging countries of the early industrial and precommunications revolution era, spontaneous participation on the informal, political-input side of the decisionmaking process was limited, by popular isolation and ignorance and by the elites' *patrón*-like attitudes. During the twenty years of chaos following 1910, much of the authority and independence of the traditional, upper-class "private governments" had disappeared, while the newer peasant and urban labor organizations had not yet become self-sustaining, so setting up a political movement to capture and manipulate the various interests enabled the revolutionary leadership to impose its own version of national development and to minimize the disruption of confrontation among contending groups.

Because so much real power centers in the clique headed at any given time by the President of the Republic that controls the "official" party, opportunities for effective individual or group action outside the system are minimal. Although some "tame" opposition parties and dissident interest organizations go through the motions, the revolutionary party is so dominant that popular political activity originates and for all practical purposes ends with it. Organizing the party into functional sectors—agrarian, labor, and popular—with citizens co-opted into national politics through their membership in highly influential, functional interest associations whose leaders assume responsibility for disciplining their followers discourages unauthorized political action by individuals dependent upon the continued goodwill of sector leaders.

In practice, the PRI does not duplicate the aggregating function performed by the national integrating parties of Europe or North America, for it seldom plays any early role in identifying political problems or initiating compromise among conflict groups on the input side of the political process to complement the actions of formal constitutional units. Because so little independent political activity occurs, few major policy questions arise outside of government itself in Mexico; instead, most important questions to be considered originate in the executive's day-to-day operations, and the necessary adjustments or compromises required to satisfy the needs of competing interests are considered and decided by personnel in the Secretariat of the Presidency. Neither the Revolutionary party nor the Congress of the Union do much more than legitimize the decisionmaking process, though the executive's final judgment often is transmitted through the party's sector leaders to its rank-and-file members. Under these conditions, the amount of uncontrolled contention that might disrupt orderly economic growth or hamper continuing national political integration appears to be very small indeed. Or at least to observers outside of Mexico, and until very recently.

For the leaders of Latin America's new-style military regimes the Mexican model is very attractive, because it seems to combine a paternalistic centralizing political control with structuring mechanisms in the form of functional interest associations to restrict internal conflict within a limited participatory system. Over the years, members of various *juntas* may have been moved to seek similar arrangements for their own countries by seeing the difficulties besetting a reform regime whose military members could not agree on a consistent approach to economic growth, much less develop effective control devices over newly mobilized interest groups. Bolivia's problems culminated in 1971, when General Torres had no means of synchronizing working-class action by the peasant leagues, miners' unions, organized labor in general, or even the radicalized students, to defend his reform government against a take-over by military conservatives.

Certainly the principal nationalizing-integrating military groups have tried to organize broad-based, centrally dominated political structures for their own purposes, but with less than outstanding success. This inability to duplicate the Mexican pattern may result because such structures are not suited to more modernized socioeconomic environments in which formal education and the communications revolution have made larger portions of the citizenry politically aware or accustomed to individual participation in national concerns. In almost every case, traditional elitist and mass-oriented political parties with functional adjuncts have proved tenaciously unwilling to be absorbed by the military government or the controlled civilian political movements it sets up. For their part, the members of the ruling *juntas* have hesitated to provide official, armed-services–sanctioned authority to these informal movements which may be dominated by personalistic and possibly demogogic leaders who might use their power to work against the military government itself.

Brazil was the first of the new-style regimes to build on the Mexican model. The Castello Branco administration encouraged the organization of a dominant government party, the National Renovating Alliance (ARENA), and a rump opposition group, the Brazilian Democratic Movement (MDB). But the arrangement did not work quite as planned, for neither party subsumed the wide spectrum of conflicting interests found throughout the country and the leaders of political and functional groupings were not as subservient to the central military authorities as desired. Problems arose because the organizational nucleus for ARENA consisted of two existing, traditional-type elite political parties (the Democratic National Union and the Social Democratic party) while the MDB was based on more challenging elements clustering around Vargas's old Labor party, some Christian Democrats, left splinter groups from other parties, and previously unaffiliated antimilitary individuals. Since neither of these patchwork parties could act as an effective integrating mechanism among its own members, much less between them and the other party's militants, no foundation for national unity evolved. Apparently their only shared characteristic was a refusal to submit absolutely to the *junta*'s demands. By December, 1968, a group of hard-liners among the top-ranking officers forced President Arturo Costa e Silva to apply much more stringent political controls and to dissolve an otherwise docile congress for refusing to oust a member who had "insulted" the military institutions. To date since then, Brazil's leaders have concentrated their efforts on economic development and made no new attempts to construct a popular-based mechanism for effecting national integration.

Quite obviously, the military leadership in Argentina and Peru would like to co-opt some existing, mass-oriented civilian political movement to perform the national integration task, if for no other reason to permit the armed forces to retire from a difficult and often disagreeable responsibility. Unfortunately for them, in both countries the popular party best suited for this purpose is headed by a personalistic leader unsympathetic to the military regime and unacceptable to many of its members. But without this leader there can be no assurance that anyone can deliver cooperation from the functional units making up the party. Hence General Lanusse's flirting with Argentina's *peronista* party and General Velasco's dealings with the Peruvian *apristas*. For the present, in Argentina the situation is stalemated, for no arrangement can be made while Juan Domingo Perón retains the allegiance of his followers. In Peru the military is hedging its bets, for even if Victor Raúl Haya de la Torre should disappear, strong anti-APRA elements in the army might veto a coalition. Therefore, in mid-1971 a new movement, *Movilización Social*, was inaugurated "to stimulate the creation of autonomous organizations through which men and women can participate in solving Peru's social, cultural, economic, and political problems...." Though the hoard of university students and young *técnicos* recruited to help form these "multiple mechanisms of popular participation" have been told repeatedly that social mobilization is not designed to set up a pro-government party, its units together with the "workers communities" and the agricultural "cooperatives" can supply an impressive functional core for future political organization if a centrally dominated, national integrating mechanism seems desirable.

But to what end? At this stage in history a limited participatory system may not be an effective control device for contending traditional and emerging interests, or a practical mechanism for imposing national integration. The communications revolution, easy transport, expanding education, massive social interaction, and economic interdependence endow the citizens with so much knowledge and sense of their own potential that it is increasingly difficult to manipulate them. Again, even if it were possible to absorb existing, independent functional-interest associations and political movements into some nationally controlled organization, the resulting structure might freeze the various groups into relationships which soon become outdated by speedily shifting conditions.

Within the past few years, Mexico itself has discovered that the political system that served so well for so long no longer is fully effective. With transition toward modernity an ever expanding nucleus of informed persons reject restrictions on their participation in the political process; at the same time, the sector pattern set up nearly forty years ago no longer provides adequate representation for proliferating specialized activities. For one example, the PRI's agrarian sector, which once consisted of peasant leagues populated primarily by subsistence *ejiditarios,* now would have to speak also for small individual plot owners (dry and irrigated), larger collective commercial groups, rural day-wage laborers, and livestock producers, in partial competition with agronomists and other professional level specialists in the popular sector. The Revolutionary party presently is considering massive reorganization to update its now antiquated system of representation. It would be folly indeed for other countries to attempt to freeze their own highly fluid socioeconomic structures into today's mold when they know that new and uncontrolled elements will appear tomorrow.[23]

It may well be that the real solution to Latin America's integration problems is to accept the disorder of a more open system, one

---

[23] For particulars on the Mexican version of this problem, see Robert E. Scott, "Mexico: The Established Revolution," in L.W. Pye and Sidney Verba, eds., *Political Culture and Political Development* (Princeton, 1965), esp. pp. 392–395.

in which the many contending interests resolve their own conflicts, even at great human and economic cost to the community. This may be the only way for these political systems to evolve a viable and flexible decisionmaking process. In a very real sense, responsible, representative, and popular government—democracy—may be more than a moral good. In today's complex world, it may provide the only functional mechanism for producing a workable political system, no matter what the cost of attaining it. This is the dilemma of development.

Meanwhile, the national leadership in the more advanced Latin American states, military or civilian, no longer has the option of fulfilling or ignoring commitments made in the name of popular support. Until some effective national integration system is worked out, the needs and aspirations of the general populace must be considered. Just as conditions thirty years ago made it impossible for the earlier popularizing leaders to carry out their symbolic promises, so today changing conditions make it extremely difficult for either constitutional officials or military officers in new-style ruling *juntas* to break theirs, whether made in good faith or not.

Contributors

*Associates, Center for Latin American Studies
University of Illinois at Urbana-Champaign*

DOUGLAS BUTTERWORTH. Associate professor of anthropology. Born in North Bergen, New Jersey, 1930. BA, MA, Mexico City College; PhD, University of Illinois (1969). University of Illinois staff member since 1967. Specializing in Mexican society and culture. Assisted Oscar Lewis in writing *A Study of Slum Clearance: Background for "La Vida"* (New York, 1968); author of "From Royalty to Poverty; the Decline of a Rural Mexican Community," *Human Organization* (Spring, 1970), and "Migración Rural-Urbana en América Latina," *América Indígina* (1971).

ROBERT BYARS. Assistant professor of political science. Born in Freeport, New York, 1937. BA, MA, University of Arizona; PhD, University of Illinois (1969). University of Illinois staff member since 1968. Specializes in Brazilian government and politics. Author of "The Task/Affect Quotient; a Technique for Measuring Orientation of Political Leaders," *Comparative Political Studies* (April, 1972), and "The First 'Revolutionary' Government in Brazil: A Value Analysis," Occasional Paper, SUNY at Buffalo (1972).

ROGER FINDLEY. Professor of law. Born in Milwaukee, Wisconsin, 1935. BA, DePauw University; JD, University of Michigan (1960). University of Illinois staff member since 1966. Specializes in role of law in development. Author of "Influence of Taxation and Assessment Policies on Open Space" (with F. C. Latcham), in *Open Space and the Law*

(Berkeley, Cal., 1965), and "Ten Years of Land Reform in Colombia," *Wisconsin Law Review* (August, 1972).

SIDNEY J. KRONUS. Associate professor of sociology. Born in Binghamton, New York, 1937. BA, SUNY at Binghamton; MA, PhD, University of Chicago (1967). University of Illinois staff member since 1967. Specializes in Latin American race relations and housing policy. Author of "Some Neglected Aspects of Negro Class Comparisons," *Phylon* (Winter, 1970), and *The Black Middle Class* (Columbus, Ohio, 1971).

JOSEPH L. LOVE. Associate professor of history; research director, Center for Latin American Studies. Born in Austin, Texas, 1938. BA, Harvard University; MA, Stanford University; PhD, Columbia University (1967). University of Illinois staff member since 1966. Specializes in social and political history of modern Brazil. Author of *Rio Grande do Sul and Brazilian Regionalism, 1882–1930* (Stanford, Cal., 1971), and numerous articles and symposia contributions.

ROBERT E. SCOTT. Professor of political science; associate director, Center for International Comparative Studies. Born in Chicago, Illinois, 1923. BA, MA, Northwestern University; PhD, University of Wisconsin (1949). University of Illinois staff member since 1949. Specializes in political integration problems and in political elites. Author of *Mexican Government in Transition* (Urbana, 1959), and many articles and symposia contributions.

MAURICIO SOLAÚN. Assistant professor of sociology. Born in Havana, Cuba, 1935. Law degree, Universidad Villanueva (Havana); MA, Yale University; PhD, University of Chicago (1971). University of Illinois staff member since 1966. Specializes in Latin American military politics, race relations, and housing policy. Author of "El Fracaso de la Democrácia en Cuba," *Aportes* (1969); "Lo Moderno y Tradicional en Dialéctica," *Tercer Mundo* (1969); *Sinners and Heretics: The Politics of Military Intervention in Latin America* (Urbana, 1973) (with Michael Quinn).

RENE VANDENDRIES. Assistant professor of economics. Born in Herent, Belgium, 1938. BA, University of Louvain (Belgium); MA, PhD, Iowa State University (1968). University of Illinois staff member since 1968. Specializes in development economics. Author of several studies on Peruvian economics and finance, and of "Social Accounting and Its Applications in Peru," *Journal for International Education and Research in Accounting* (1970).

Index

Acción Popular, 274
Acquisition, land. *See* Land reform
Advisers, international: formerly ignored interrelationships, 10
Agrarian reform. *See* INCORA; Land reform
Agriculture: and exports, 237; statistics on, 237–238; Peruvian growth of, 279
Agustín Codazzi Geographic Institute: aerial cadastral surveys of, 182; land appraisers from, 129, 150–152; mentioned, 154
Albuquerque, Alfonso, 345
Alliance for Progress: original concept fails, 9–10; and United Nations, 13–14; objectives of, 193; unanticipated effects of, 303; mentioned, 140, 264–265, 277, 280–281, 336
Amazon Valley: rubber industry collapses in, 249
Anthropologists, 208–209
APRA (*Apristas*): enemy of military, 264; denied presidency, 275; mentioned, 273–275
Arabs: discrimination toward, 112
Argentina, 39, 343
Arrepas program. *See* INCORA
Asociación Nacional de Usuarios Campesinos, 144
Atoyac River, 212

Authoritarian personality: described, 41, 85

Baldíos: distribution methods of, 171–173, 181–183; statistics on, 171, 176–178
Barranquilla, 94
Barrios: and lower class, 110; described, 34–35
Belaúnde, Fernando: introduces changes, 275–276; mentioned, 263–264
Belo Horizonte: as typical city, 32–33; salary statistics on, 35; and politicians, 70
Betancourt, Rómolo, 323
Betancur, Belisario, 329
Biafra, 233
Bogotá: expropriation in, 145; mentioned, 100
Bolívar, Simon, 327
Bolivia: true revolution in, 13; revolutionary results in, 14; mentioned, 339, 343
Bonilla, Frank, 26, 35
Bosch, Juan, 330
Branco, Castelo, 49, 71–72, 339, 353
Brazil: literacy rate declines, 14; and popular support, 30; tradition breaks in, 30; political structure changing, 31, 49–50, 85–86; problems of, 44; and miscegenation, 56–57; and democracy, 75; and economic scarcity, 78–80; men-

tioned, 294, 343
Buenos Aires, 294

CAEM (Center for Advanced Military Studies), 348–349
Câmara, Helder P., 328
Campos Sales, Manuel, 250, 252, 254
Caribbean Sea, 92
Carnaval, 67–68, 82
Cartagena: and class conflict, 24–25; racial patterns in, 87–117
CELAM (Latin American Bishops' Council), 328
Centralization: concept of, 326–334
Chile: literacy rate declines, 14; land reform in, 18; statistics on, 20; mentioned, 39
City planners, 231–232
Class structure. See Social stratification
Colonias, 212–213, 221–222
Colombia, 18, 119, 294
Constitutionalism: challenged, 302–303
Costa e Silva, Arturo, 354
Cuba: revolutionary results in, 13, 14, 140; mentioned, 165, 294
Czechoslovakia, 8

Democratic personality: description of, 41; transcends barriers, 56; and urban factory worker, 74–75
Deodoro da Fonseca, Marshal, 254
Development. See Modernization
Dictatorship: Zé Maria on, 73
Distribution, land. See Land reform
Domestic products: statistics on, 16; trade relations disrupted, 17–18
Dominican Republic, 8

East Pakistan, 39
Economy: growth of, 2; study of, 262. See also Valorization
Ecuador, 294, 343
Elections, political: Zé Maria on, 73; and economy, 75–76; illiterate Brazilians feared, 79–80
Escola Superior de Guerra, 339
Escuela Superior de Guerra, 339
Ethnics, 56–57
European Common Market, 17

Exporters: dictate economic policy, 272–273; support military coup, 273
Exports: statistics on, 237–238; foreign involvement in, 240–241; maintain Brazilian economy, 258–259; Peruvian statistics on, 266–267
Expropriation: and land acquisition procedures, 150–152
Extinction: and land acquisition, 148–150

Factory worker. See Manpower
Favelados: accommodated by *barrios*, 34–35
Figueroa, Luis Beltrán Preito, 324
Foreign aid, 64
France, 287

Gallegos, Ramón, 323
Generation gap: in Brazil, 57
Germany, 330
Gillin, John, 52–53, 59–60
Goulart, João, 46
Great Britain, 287
Green Revolution: failure and advantages of, 17–19; mentioned, 206
Greenstein, Fred, 41, 54
Guatemala, 206, 290

Hacendado: affords adequate life, 12–13; descendants' advantages, 60
Harris, Marvin, 91
Hirschman, Albert, 316
Honduras, 290
Human nature: defined, 52–59
Hungary: foreign military conquest of, 8

Ibarra, Velasco, 289–290
Importers: manipulate prices, 242
Imports: Peruvian statistics on, 266–267
INCORA (Colombia's Agrarian Reform Institute): and *minifundios*, 125; *arrepas* program of, 126–129; methods of, 127–132; land surveys of, 128; land purchasing of, 129–130; land distribution of, 132–135; party representation in, 141; priorities of, 142; Bogotá activity of, 145; and 1974 elections, 146; misleading statistics on, 146–148; negotiates land purchase, 153–155; distributes

family farms, 155–156; and land parcelization, 156–158; and recipient selection, 158–160; land adjudication of, 163–166; title documentation of, 166–168; parcelization costs of, 168–170; and *baldíos* distribution, 171–173; inadequate surveys of, 179–182; and national policy lack, 189–191; evaluation of, 191–192; mentioned, 122–192
India, 39
Industrial revolution: result of development process, 6–7; reaches Latin America, 295; mentioned, 120
Industry: small versus large, 67; protected in Peru, 276
Inflation: index of instability, 20; Peruvian, modest, 265–266; mentioned, 36
Inkeles, Alex, 23, 28, 39–40, 46, 50
Institutions: and Brazilian politics, 31; democratic formalism of, 74–76; and social strata, 100–101; basis for overt problems, 261–262; political, tradition-bound, 309
Integration: in Brazil, 236–259; history of, 293–294; technology promotes, 305
Inter-American Development Bank: and population statistics, 16
Investment, foreign: and São Paulo, 237; statistics on, 240–241; interest rates high, 248; leads to control, 251–253; and autonomy loss, 258–259; in Peru, 281
Israel, 39
Italy, 330

Jiménez, Pérez, 323
Jiménez, Raúl Ramos, 323

Katanga, 233
Kelleman, Peter: immigrant author, 82
Kennedy, Edward, 333
Kubitschek, Juscelino, 43–44, 48–49, 71

Labor supply. *See* Manpower
Labor unions: and Zé Maria, 48; strengthen trust, 76–77
Landowners: appeal Colombian acquisition, 149–150; financial ability of, 162–163
Land reform: contradictions of, 4; failure of, 17–18; in Colombia, 119–120, 145–146, 148–149, 170–171; lacks success, 123, 141; acquisition and distribution in, 131–145; deterrent to, 142; and expropriation, 150–151; and negotiated purchase, 152–155; family farm distribution in, 155–156, 160–162; determines parcelization, 156–158; negotiated purchase in, 157; and recipient selection, 158–160; and redistribution control, 165–166; and public domain distribution, 170–171; surveying for, 179–180, 182–185; and Peruvian peasants, 279–280; unimpressive in *altiplano*, 345–346
Land tenure: questions of, 226; slows agricultural growth, 260–261; and Peruvian peasants, 271
Land titles: lack validity, 217
Lane, Robert, 23, 31–32, 40, 63
Lasswell, Harold, 42, 54, 63–64
Law enforcement: respected, 80–81
Leão, Assis José, 33
Levingston, Roberto, 344
Lewis, Oscar, 23, 68
Lima: migrants in, 200–201
Lleras Restrepo, Carlos, 141–143, 289

Manpower: skilled, scarce, 16; agricultural surplus of, 17; urban factory worker, 30–31; factory worker, 50–51; social stratification of, 64; utilization of, 120; in Peru, 193, 196; skilled, uncooperative, 301; mentioned, 36
Mass media: create pressure, 8–9
Mesas directivas: described, 224–225; aims of, 228
Mestizos: defined, 95–96
Mexico: revolution in, 13, 14; land reform in, 17; mentioned, 119, 165
Migrants: land questions of, 213–214; shantytowns attract, 219
Migration: technology sets off, 4; and agricultural failure, 13; and survival struggle, 36; and racial awareness, 113–114; in Peru, 120, 193–195, 207; Peruvian statistics on, 196–200, 270–272; positive effects of, 196–197; comparisons in, 199–201; Lima benefits of, 201–204;

Pan American Highway aids, 211; from city to suburb, 221; politics affect, 223-224; and economic growth, 270-272; increases political awareness, 302
Military regimes: responsible for stability, 290-291; leadership in, 291-293; problems and prospects of, 334-342; mentioned, 317, 334-342
Military schools: very advanced, 337
Miscegenation: prevalence of, 91-92; in all classes, 98-99, 104-111; somatic and climatic factors, 101-102; and economic success, 104-111; Cartagenian history of, 114-117; in United States, 117
MISEREOR, 328
Modernization: communication effects of, 6; changes traditional values, 7; contradictions of, 10; early stirrings of, 13-14; adaptation required for, 21; human aspects of, 23-25; political aspect of, 38-40; 318-319; factory school for, 51-52, 65-66; and racial conflict, 87-89; 97-99, 116-117; and material factors, 119-121; determinants of, 228; short-run government hinders, 233; concept of, obscured, 235; of São Paulo, 247-248; and Paulista exports, 258-259; and economic problems, 260; and Belaúnde reforms, 275-276
Monbeig, Pierre, 241
Monroe Doctrine, 294
Movimiento Independiente Revolucionario (MIR), 323

National Front coalition (*Frente Nacional*), 141, 144, 145
Nationalism: need for, 11; and Zé Maria, 43-44; gives community feeling, 294
National Planning Institute (Peru), 198, 282
National Popular Alliance (ANAPO), 144
Nigeria, 39
Nuñez, Rafael, 93

Oaxaca, Mexico, 120, 208-231
Organization of American States, 140

Paladino, Jorge Daniel, 345
Panamá, 294, 343
Pan American Highway, 211, 214-215

Parcelization. *See* Land reform
Parsons, Talcott, 312
Partido Revolucionario Institucional (PRI), 351
Pastrana, Misael Borrero, 144
Pereira, L. C. Breeser: Brazilian statistics of, 33
Pereira de Sousa, Washington Luís, 251
Perón, Juan Domingo, 331, 344-345
Peru: land reform in, 17-18; migration in, 193-207; industrial output in, 196-197; agricultural production in, 196-197; population statistics of, 199-201; urbanization in, 205-207; birth control in, 207; economic statistics on, 263; geographical description of, 267-268; upper class prevails, 275; mentioned, 119, 120, 338-339, 343
Politica dos governadores, 252
Politics: and Brazilian worker, 42-43; of *colonias*, 223-228; Latin views on, 235
Pope, Alexander, 75, 86
Population growth: statistics on, 16
Populism, paternalistic: peculiarly Latin, 290-291
Prado, Manuel, 264
PRP (Paulista Republican party): description of, 239; opposes Brazilian favorite, 254; and constitutional revision, 256; mentioned, 252
PTB (Brazilian Labor party), 49, 70-71
Punta del Este: conference of 1961, 17

Quadros, Janio, 73

Race relations: methods determining, 99-101; research on, 101-111
Racial conflict: in developing nations, 87-89; unapparent in Brazil, 56-57
Racial patterns: occurrence of, 24-25; key characteristics of, 89-92
Rangel, Domingo Alberto, 323
Ravenstein, E. G., 195
Research: methods described, 31-39
Revenues: solutions to, 243-244; statistics on, 244
Revolution: positive argument for, 14; results of, 14; reflections upon, 295-299
Riggs, Fred, 74-75

Index

Rio de Janeiro, 32
Rio Grande, 208
Rodrigues Alves, Francisco, 250
Rojas, Gustavo Pinilla, 144
Rowe, James, 74–75

Sales Oliveira, Armando de, 257
Santos, John, 81
São Paulo, 32, 236–259
Scott, James: on Malaysian bureaucrats, 52, 76
Shantytowns. *See* Squatter settlements
Sjaastad, Larry A., 195
Social stratification: in Brazil, 57; *dignidad* and *machismo* in, 68–69; requires strong leaders, 77; Zé Maria on, 78–80; racial factors in, 89–92, 97–99; extremes in, 99–101; in *colonias*, 221–223; Peru's upper class fails, 273–274; described in Peru, 276–277; elite maintains, 286; as barrier to integration, 293–294
Sorocabana Railway, 246
Soviet Union: dominant minority gratifies, 11
Spain: independence from, 92–93
Squatter settlements: organize invasion, 215; example of poorest, 216; characteristics of, 219–220; types of, 229–230; advantages of, 230; need analysis, 230–232; in Peru, 272; mentioned, 209–231

Taxation: Peruvian statistics on, 280
Tibet, 8
Tories, 310
Torres, Juan José, 333
Torrijos, Omar, 333
Tovar, Alvaro Valencia: writes *Uisheda*, 334
Tradition: *dignidad* and *machismo* in, 68–69; factory reinforces, 84–85; and Cartagenian aristocracy, 96–97; and race relations, 97; in land distribution, 162–163; independent of formal government, 287; need to modify, 194
Transportation: creates pressure, 8–9; barriers to, 16

Uisheda: popular and controversial book, 334

Unemployment: statistics on, 19; industry affects, 261; university graduates suffer, 304–305
United Nations: and Decade of Development, 13–14
United States: and racial hostility, 56, 87–88, 95, 116–117; and generation gap, 57; and working class, 60–61; and foreign aid, 64; and welfare state, 78; serves as model, 287
Universities (Latin American): described, 337
Urbanization: socioeconomic needs of, 4; overwhelms essential services, 13; fails for migrants, 18–19; and typical worker, 30–31, 35–36; Zé Maria indicts, 45; and factory worker, 51–52, 62–63, 85–86; and racial conflict, 87–89; in Cartagena, 94–95; race and class in, 97–99; comparisons of, 205–207; and haphazard growth, 208; determinants of, 228
Uruguay, 290, 294
Usufruct rights, 218

Valorization: political consequences of, 69–83; answer to oversupply, 242–244; brings changes, 246–247; fails in Amazon Valley, 249; and federal support, 249–250; and political elite, 258–259
Vargas, Getúlio, 71, 77–78, 86, 253
Velasco, Juan, 264, 339
Venezuela: land reform in, 18; political statistics on, 324; mentioned, 250, 290
Villamil, Carlos Cháux, 144, 148

Wagley, Charles, 82
Whigs, 310
Women's liberation: Zé Maria's attitudes on, 57–58

Yucatán, 294

Zé Maria: as future prototype, 24, 36–37; political views of, 28, 43–45, 49; on bureaucratic approach, 47–48; and human nature, 52–59; and religion, 56–57; on social stratification, 57–59

Both citizens and leaders in developing countries find that the importation of techniques and knowledge from their advanced neighbors is a mixed blessing. The crises of change, involving population explosion, rising expectations, competition, distribution of material benefits, and foreign relations (to name a few), seem to descend upon them all at once. These eight cross-disciplinary case studies explore modernization and urbanization problems affecting culture areas in Latin America with different levels of development — especially in Mexico, Colombia, Peru, and Brazil.

The authors worked together closely to help illuminate human and institutional predicaments in these countries and to point out institutional impediments to constructive change and evolutionary development. Based on extensive fieldwork, the articles convey the daily problems of speedy change: the confusion, uproar, and personal insecurity, as well as the political disintegration. Each study considers in depth a specific problem in a given setting, and together they demonstrate just how technology and its unintended side effects overburden the social, economic, and political structures.

The authors represent the disciplines of history, law, sociology, political science, anthropology, and economics.

ROBERT E. SCOTT is professor of political science and associate director of the Center for International Comparative Studies at the University of Illinois, Urbana. All the contributors are members of the Center for Latin American Studies at the same institution.